Vegas Pro 8 Editing Workshop

Douglas Spotted Eagle

ELSEVIER

AMSTERDAM • BOSTON • HEIDELBERG • LONDON • NEW YORK • OXFORD
PARIS • SAN DIEGO • SAN FRANCISCO • SINGAPORE • SYDNEY • TOKYO
Focal Press is an imprint of Elsevier

Acquisitions Editor: Paul Temme
Publishing Services Manager: George Morrison
Senior Project Manager: Dawnmarie Simpson
Associate Acquisitions Editor: Dennis McGonagle
Assistant Editor: Chris Simpson

Focal Press is an imprint of Elsevier
30 Corporate Drive, Suite 400, Burlington, MA 01803, USA
Linacre House, Jordan Hill, Oxford OX2 8DP, UK

Recognizing the importance of preserving what has been written, Elsevier prints its books on acid-free
paper whenever possible.

Library of Congress Cataloging-in-Publication Data

Spotted Eagle, Douglas.
  Vegas Pro 8 editing workshop / Douglas Spotted Eagle.
      p. cm.
  Includes index.

  ISBN 978-0-240-81046-1 (pbk. : alk. paper) 1. Vegas (Electronic resource) 2. Digital video—Editing.
I. Title.
  TK6680.5.S673 2008
  778.59'30285536—dc22   2008002993

British Library Cataloguing-in-Publication Data
A catalogue record for this book is available from the British Library.

ISBN: 978-0-240-81046-1

For information on all Focal Press publications
visit our website at www.books.elsevier.com

Typeset by Charon Tec Ltd (A Macmillan Company), Chennai, India
www.charontec.com

08 09 10 11   5 4 3 2 1

Printed in the United States.

To my son Joshua, for giving me the drive to complete this book.
I wish only that you could have seen it finished.

To Amanda, for showing me courage in the face of intense adversity,
and to Linda, for her constant support.

Contents

Foreword. x
Editor's Note xii
Acknowledgments. xiii
Introduction. xv

Chapter 1: Getting Started with Vegas. 1
   Installing Vegas. 1
   The Basic Tools in Vegas 3
      Track Control Pane 4
      Timeline/Track View 6
      Vegas Windows 9
      Dockable Windows 10
      Expanding the View of a Docking Window and Undocking Windows . . 10
   Monitoring 19
   Saving Templates/Layouts in Vegas. 20
   File Menu 22
   Setting Up Project Properties 25
   Edit Menu 28
   View Menu 33
   Insert Menu. 36
   Tools Menu 42
   Options Menu 61
   Cursors and Selections. 67
   Say You'll Be MINE! 69
   XP Themes in Vegas 69
   Key Features! 70
   Color My World. 72

Chapter 2: Capturing Video 73
   Getting Media from the Camera to the Hard Drive 73
   Manually Capturing DV. 73
   Advanced Capture Tools 80
   Using Batch Capture 81
   Capturing Stills with Video Capture 83
   Changes in the Future of Video Capture. 85
   Capturing/Transferring HDV 86
   Importing Media from a DVD Drive 90
   Importing Media from a Hard Disk Drive Recorder 92
   Importing AVCHD 94
   XDCAM and Sony Vegas Pro 8 Software 95
   Importing XDCAM Media into a Vegas Project 98
   Enabling the XDCAM Explorer 99
   Enabling Multichannel Audio Import 100
   Hardware Cards and Vegas Pro 8. 103

Chapter 3: Editing Tools, Transitions, Filters, and Other Basic Video Tools. 107

Importing Media to the Timeline 107
Subclips in Vegas 113
Placing Media on the Timeline. 115
   Trimmer. 116
   Previewing Trimmer Media 118
Placing Still Images or Graphics on the Timeline. 123
Editing Events on the Timeline 124
And the Envelope Please . . .? Transitional Envelopes 134
Using Keyframes in Vegas 135
Filters in Vegas 142
How Filters/Plug-ins Function. 146
Editing and Converting 154
   Aspect Ratio. 154
   Gamma. 155
   Experiment! 155
Shooting Modes 156
Output 157
Opacity Envelopes. 157
Velocity Filters. 162
Event Switches in Vegas. 164
Nesting 170
Editing the VEG Files from a Nested Timeline 172
Track Flattening. 173
AV Sync Repair 174

Chapter 4: Multicam Functions in Vegas Pro 8 177

Roll Tape! 177
Getting Media to the Timeline 178
If Timecode Is Closely Matched 179
Other Multicamera Workflows. 182
Making Multicam Selections 184
Creating Cross-fades between Active Cameras. 184
The Assembly Track 186
Editing Audio with Multicamera. 187
infinitiCAM 188
Ultimate S 3 188
DoubleTake 189

Chapter 5: Filters and Add-ons 191

Working with Plug-ins in Vegas 191
Pixelan SpiceMASTER 2 191
CreativEase 201
Boris FX. 206
Wax/DebugMode Software 207
NewBlueFX, ProDad, and VelvetMatter 212

Chapter 6: Color Correction and Manipulation **215**
  Understanding the Color-Correction Tools in Vegas 215
  Displays and Scopes 218
  Using Color Correction as FX 229
  Making Digital Video Look Filmlike 230
    Interlaced or Not? 230
    Gamma 231
    Shooting Video for the Large Screen 231
  Legal Colors 232
  Endnote 233

Chapter 7: Audio Tools in Vegas **235**
  Recording Audio in Vegas 235
  Basic Setup 236
  Recording Multiple Tracks 239
  Advanced Recording Techniques and Tools 240
  Recording with Takes 241
  How About a Flyin' Smooth Punch? 244
  Assigning Buses 245
  Using Buses for Routing Effects 247
  Audio Mixer 249
  FX Packaging 250
  FX To Go, Please? 251
  Inserting Effects without Using a Bus 252
  Using Track FX 252
  Tempo-Based FX 253
  Virtual Sound Technology 254
  Recording Multiple Tracks 256
  Synchronizing Vegas to External Devices 257
  Editing Audio in Vegas 260
  Placing Audio on the Timeline 260
  Extracting Audio from CDs 261
  Get ACIDized! 269
  Get the Mark Up 271
  Inserting Markers 272
  Rubber Audio 275
  Variable-Speed Audio in Vegas 276
  Reverse Decisions 276
  Snapping Audio Events 277
  Trimming Events on the Timeline 277
  Deleting Events from the Timeline 279
  Using Ripple Editing 279
  Grouping 280
  Working with Audio Plug-ins 280
  Automating FX in Vegas 283
  Working with Other Types of Plug-ins 285
    Noise Reduction 285
  Fingertip Mixing: Using the Mackie Control (and Other
  Control Devices in Vegas) 288

Other Controlling Devices. 291
Audiomation? 292
Training Vegas. 292
Every Breath You Take, Every Move You Make!. 293
Feeling Fat? Get Thin!. 295
Faders Flying Everywhere. 296
Mixing Audio in Vegas 296
Mixing Techniques 297
Compression 298
De-essing 302
Using Equalization 303
Using Reverb. 305
Mixing for 5.1 Surround Sound. 307
Surrounded by FX: Surround Plug-ins. 316
Mixing Surround or DVD Audio 318
I'm All Mixed . . . Down! Down-mixing in Vegas 319
Broadcast Wave Format 320
Encoding Audio to AC-3 322
Other Compressed Formats 322
How Come the Audio Cats Get All the Cool Stuff? 323

Chapter 8: Creating Titles in Vegas Pro 8. 325
The ProType Titling Tool 325
Curves Presets 335
Other Basic Tools 336
Advanced Titling Tools 338
Transferring Titles. 339
Using the Vegas Titler. 340
Title Properties 343
Adding Effects to Text. 347
Flashy Titles 350
Importing Static Graphics. 352

Chapter 9: Pan/Crop, Track Motion, and
Basic Compositing in Vegas. 353
What Is Compositing?. 353
Using the Pan/Crop Tool 353
Masking with the Pan/Crop Tool 357
But How Is This a Mask? 359
Using Track Motion in Vegas 361
The Next Dimension: 3D Track Motion Tools 369
Nesting Composites 372
Parental Guidance/Shadows and Glow 373
Ten-Bit Color and 32-Bit (Floating) Processing 374
Rotated Display Functions 377
Producing Rotated Media 378
Generated Media 380
Credit Rolls 383
Creating/Using Masks in Vegas 386

Compositing Modes in Vegas 396
   Displacement Map 399
   Height Map 402
   Bump Map 404
Using Chroma-Key Tools in Vegas 406
Creating a Garbage Matte in Vegas 409
Create a Holograph in Vegas! 412
Motion Blur 415
Supersampling 416

Chapter 10: Media Manager **419**
   by John Rofrano
Conceptual Overview 419
User Interface Layout 419
Setup and Preferences 421
Changing Options 421
Create a New Library 422
Adding Media to the Media Manager 423
Organizing Your Media with Tags 427
Seek and You Shall Find 430
Quick Text or Keyword Search 431
Advanced Search 431
Conclusion. 433

Chapter 11: Output and Export **435**
Last Steps with Vegas 435
Output Formats 435
Mastering 436
Burning to a Master CD 441
Track-at-Once CDs 442
Mastering Audio for Video 442
Using Compression in Vegas for Video 442
Using Equalizers 444
Dithering Audio in Vegas 444
Rendering Options in Vegas 445
Rendering to an AVI 446
Exporting Events to Third-Party Applications 448
EDLs and Vegas. 449
AAF Import/Export 451
Outputting Other Than AVI Files 453
Outputting an AC-3 Format File 455
Creating a VCD/SVCD. 456
Additional Rendering Options. 458
Network Rendering. 459
   Setting Up the Rendering Network (Render Farming) 460
   Rendering Clients. 461
   Monitoring the Rendering Process 463
   File Mapping 464

Additional Functions of the Network Rendering Application 465
Network Rendering Options. 466
High-Definition Video 466
4:2:2 MPEG Capability 469
New Codecs 470
Scripting 471
Using Vegas with DVD Architect 474

Chapter 12: Alternative Delivery 477
Creating High-Quality Portable Media 477
Shooting, Editing, and Delivering 477
Production 479
Editing 480
Audio for Internet Delivery 483
How Is Audio Preprocessed for the Web? 484
Delivery 486
Importing a Spreadsheet 489
Rendering for YouTube and Other UGC Sites 492
Rendering for iPod/Podcasts 492
PSP Support 493

Chapter 13: 24p HDCAM/DVCAM Workflow
for the Independent Filmmaker 495
Overview. 495
24p HDCAM Acquisition. 496
Setting Up a 24p Vegas Project 496
Additional Capture Notes 498
Remove 2-3 Pulldown from the Down-converted 60i DV Clips 499
Editing with 24p DV Video Files 499
24p Timecode 500
Create Finished Audio Tracks in a 24p Vegas Timeline 501
Create Finished Composites and Video FX, and
Export as 24p HD Uncompressed .avi Files 502
Exporting a 24p EDL 503
24p DVDs 504
Exporting the Project to DV. 504

Index. 505

What's on the DVD. 512

Foreword

Anyone still wondering when the tipping point of the HD revolution will happen is either living in a cave or simply refusing to look at the realities of modern motion picture production and the state of digital technology today. Every six months brings more and more advantages and advances, further improving and streamlining workflow and production. If you consider yourself part of the many who feel left behind, this book is a great place to get caught up and discover what is possible.

My own adventure with HD began in 2004, with my first all-HD production of a movie for television called *The Librarian* for TNT. Although I had many years of experience with digital special effects, I had never shot with digital cameras. Everything I had heard about the technology warned me that it wasn't quite ready yet. Still, I felt compelled to try. We all knew it was coming, so why not get on the band wagon early and begin to learn the new tools?

I had been told that HD never looks quite as good as film. I had been told that it was good for interiors or low-light conditions, but shooting in the sun, or any quick camera movements, would quickly reveal the limitations of the medium.

In our first week of production, our initial fears were realized. Shooting in the jungles of Mexico, the bright light breaking through the foliage caused bright white hotspots in our images, a telltale sign of video. When we asked our HD technician for help, he shrugged his shoulders and said, "That's HD."

After a few days of shooting, another HD tech arrived to help out on our second unit. Keith Collea had worked with us for years in video assist, but during the months leading up to our production, he had become a leading technician in HD cinematography. When he arrived on-set, he noticed the hotspots in our images and asked us why we didn't fix them. We said we didn't think it was possible. Keith quickly made some adjustments to our cameras and the hotspots vanished.

Alan Caso, our excellent director of photography, quickly asked Keith, "What else can you do with that camera setup?" Keith replied, "What would you like?" Alan asked, "Can you give me grain?" to which Keith responded, "How much would you like?" With a few adjustments we were suddenly giving a grainy film look to our image.

Needless to say, Keith moved over to our first unit and suddenly our limitations vanished. We learned that it wasn't the medium that had limitations, it was our knowledge of how to use the medium that needed expanding.

Whereas back in 2004 we did have to work hard to make sure our images were as good looking as film, in today's world it's much harder to get *film* to look as good as the HD images we create. Whether working with arguably the best digital camera today, Panavision's Genesis, in full 4.4.4 color space, or working in the lowest end HDV recording, world-class motion picture creation can be accomplished with greater ease and versatility than ever before.

I first met Douglas Spotted Eagle after I finished making a feature film called *Flyboys*. It was one of the first films ever to use the Genesis camera and I had fallen madly in love with the process. It created a hunger in me to learn more about what's possible in the world of HD.

It was then that I discovered the SonyV1U, prosumer camera that recorded in the HDV format. Although completely on the opposite end of the HD spectrum from the Genesis, this was an intriguing format. What was different about this camera from all other HDV cameras was the claim that it could create 24p, 1080i images. Other HDV cameras recorded in a lower resolution and then "rezzed-up" to 1080i. I was anxious to put the camera to the test.

However, once I got my hands on the camera, no one could quite figure out how to get it to actually live up to its claim. We called everyone we could think of, each of whom was sure they had the answer. Each of them was mistaken and our tests failed miserably. In my desperation to find a solution, the kind people at Sony suggested I meet Douglas Spotted Eagle. Of course, he was the only person with not only a sensible solution but a full grasp of the format.

It was Douglas who suggested I use the Sony Vegas editing software to get me to the finish line. At first glance, Vegas didn't appear to be professional editing software. I thought it was something more like an advanced consumer product. But after a few lessons from Douglas, I discovered that this was an amazingly powerful tool, deceptively simple, but with enormous depth of what you could accomplish with it.

I ended up getting his DVD series on how to use the software and was frankly shocked at what you could do. Just on my laptop alone I was able to create a completely professional edit, with credible sound mixing and color correction. It was stunning.

Since then Douglas has become the person I most rely on for the cutting edge information on what is happening in world of digital technology. With his guidance I was able to integrate HDV with high-end Genesis HD material in my new television production, seamlessly and effortlessly. His broad knowledge of the state of technocracy is tempered by his easy manner and ability to explain in simple language complex technical information that would otherwise make your head spin.

So sit back and enjoy his book. I'm sure you'll be surprised at what you'll learn. There's no one better to take you on this digital journey.

Dean Devlin
Electric Entertainment
November 2007

Editor's Note

When I agreed to take on the thankless task of technically editing this book (and believe me, I looked for a stronger word than "thankless" that was still G rated ...) I knew it would be a tedious process. Actually, it has been a great ride and I would not have missed it for the world. But make no mistake, we worked our collective butt off, and this can't be anyone's idea of a good time; you should know that great care was taken with the manuscript for this edition as well as with eradicating errors found in previous editions. And as a result, I proudly proclaim: This Book Is Error Free!

Yeah, well, we all know that's probably a lie. Christie and I, as well as additional reviewers, have worked hard to bring you the most up-to-date and error-free information possible. But on my best day I'm human and have a hard time pronouncing *Bezier* or for that matter *Favre*. So, I'm sure some errors slipped through. If you do find any mistakes in the book, please let us know via email or on the forums and we'll do our best to provide explanations, or corrections, as needed. In addition, there are bonus chapters that could not be included due to publishing constraints but are available for download from the author's web site at www.vasst.com.

You hold in your hand the bible when it comes to learning Sony Vegas Pro 8. But more than that, this book provides a solid foundation of audio and video production techniques, image compositing, and camera technology regardless of which NLE you're using. I urge you to absorb this book in small bites, and I challenge you to take the time to learn it all. Douglas is a fantastic teacher for any level of user, from novice to expert, as well as a great friend. Poring over the manuscripts for this book has already made me a better media professional, and I know it can do the same for you.

David McKnight
Sony Certified Vegas Editor
November 2007

Acknowledgments

Although my name is the one that appears on the cover of this book, this book wouldn't exist without the assistance, advice, and help of many people, most of whom have no idea that they were a part. I bear responsibility for any errors contained within, but maybe by thanking them I can distribute the blame (or maybe not).

First and foremost, Linda deserves much credit for making sure that there are always cold beverages and clean clothes, because during the writing of this book, most of which took place in hotel rooms and airplanes, I forgot the normal responsibilities of life.

Special appreciation for my partner and friend at Sundance Media Group and VASST, Mannie Frances, for answering nearly every call that came my way and keeping the phones at bay, making sure I kept on. Mannie, we did it man … who'da thunk VASST could grow so fast?

A special "Thank You" to John Rofrano for providing the chapter on Media Manager. Your contribution in this area is invaluable.

Of course, Dave Hill, Richard Kim, Dennis Adams, Brian Orr, Brad Reinke, Dave Chaimson, Bob, Steve, Andy, Leigh Herman, Bob Ott, and Curt, among so many more at Sony, too many to name, are tremendously appreciated for being patient with my constant requests for updates, answers, and readings for technical accuracy. I've also appreciated your friendships much over the years.

David and Christie McKnight technically edited and vetted the entire book, even in the midst of working on their own video projects. Thank you David and Christie!

A lot of my editing tricks are inspired by requests, suggestions, questions, and arguments from folks in the various forums I've been a part of. There are literally hundreds, if not thousands, of people who have taught me a lot or forced me to find answers to difficult questions. Thanks to you this book was inspired. Without the folks at DMN, Sony, and the DVInfo.net forums, this book never would have been. Lou, Frank, Michael, Chris, thank you for providing me a venue to meet new people and to hear the questions that I hope are answered in this book.

Of course, I can't forget to thank Windham Hill Records, who refused to finance my first music video, causing me to start editing on my own many years ago. From those days of analog, I've been forced to learn to do things that I couldn't afford to have others do. That refusal was perhaps the best thing that ever happened to me. And the video went on to be a top video later that year.

Sterling Johnson, Brian Morris, Ric Burns, Ken Burns, Jeff Spitz, Andy Dillon, James Cameron, Steven Seagal, Jerry Lonn, and Tom Bee, you've all taught me to be better behind the camera and smarter at the editing console. Thank you.

Bruce Braunstein, Paul, Louise, Bill, and Amanda, thank you for loaning your images to this book as well. Mitch, T.J., and Cheno, thanks for the help with hundreds of screenshots. You guys are great, thanks for watching my back. Jeffrey P., you da MAN! Thanks for the encouragement when writing, touring, teaching, performing get to be too much. Norman Kent, thank you for gracing this book with your beautiful pictures. You truly are the world's bestest, fastest cameraman!

Dean Devlin, Mark Franco, and crew; thanks for the support and good vibes.

To all the manufacturers that have supported Sundance Media Group, VASST, and the endeavors, thank you. There are too many to mention; most are mentioned in this book and/or found on the included DVD. I do have to mention Michael Feerer/Pixelan, Tim and Mike at Canon, Phil Shaw at Matrox, Chris Hurd, and the VASST team. Phil, Bob, Julie, and the gang at Artbeats, your support is immense! (Nearly every image in this book comes from an Artbeats library.) Thank you.

Finally, many thanks to Paul, and the team at Focal Press, for providing this opportunity to share my knowledge. We've now done several together, and it's been a great time so far!

Introduction

Interestingly enough, this book started out as a small guide to what became Vegas 2.0. The moniker of Vegas Video was dropped in the middle of the project, and the same happened with the Vegas Audio name, thereby creating a product known simply as Vegas, now known as Vegas Pro 8.

As an audio engineer, I have used Vegas as my tool of choice for a long time, thus inspiring my audio-based tutorials for Vegas. In becoming a videographer/editor to further my musical vision many years ago, Vegas Video 2.0 soon became my application of choice when I had the opportunity to see it in an alpha version in Madison, Wisconsin, back in 1999. It became the perfect meld of my two favorite passions in one application.

Therefore, I wrote this book really intending to please two different groups of users, one being the audio user, and the other being the video user. Audio users rarely think of the video user, and that's fine. Video users, however, absolutely must become familiar with the tools of the audio user, hence, the fairly intense audio for video section in this book. Moreover, this book has many tips, tricks, and techniques that I've learned over the years as an audio engineer, compressionist, and videographer/editor, some of which I felt were critical to share. Others appear merely because I felt they were of interest.

The intent of this book is to teach and inform, yet also to provide reminders to professionals who have "done it all" and "heard it all" in the course of their years of experience. Although I consider myself an experienced audio and video editor, nearly every engineer I've met has dropped some small golden nugget that I've been able to learn from. It is my hope that this book does the same for you.

The disc in this book contains video, VEG files, and test media I felt important for users to more completely grasp the concepts presented in this book. VEG files can also be found in-depth at http://www.vasst.com. These files are for your educational use. If you use them as a significant part of what you create with your video project, please give credit where it's due, if it's due. That's part of the honor system of Vegas users. Scripts can also be found in this book as well and on the VASST web site.

If this book seems too technical, I'd ask that you go back and reread the passage. I've done my best to keep descriptions and explanations as simple as possible in this book, for the purpose of getting information across, not to demonstrate my technical skills or lack thereof. Multimedia is an articulate beast; anything combining the eye and ear is bound to sorely display any errors, whether you or others see them. I hope that this book will teach you to avoid some of the pitfalls that you otherwise might step into. One of my favorite sayings is "I've screwed up more times than most people attempt to try." And I feel this is true. I've probably made every mistake that can be made in audio and video, multiple times. This book is a result of the knowledge that I've gleaned in the process of discovery.

Some of the information is necessarily technical and might be over the heads of some readers. If you sit with the book and read through a chapter once or twice, coupled with a little work in front of a computer, however, the information will make sense at some point. This book is absolutely not a white paper on any subject. It's a teaching tool for the uninitiated and a reminder/reference for the professional. A basic understanding of your camera, a computer, and a general education are all that is needed to complete the tutorials found in this book. If I've missed something or you feel I didn't reach enough depth, I can be reached at dse@vasst.com. My personal web site, outlining some of my work, can be viewed at http://www.spottedeagle.com.

Keeping my music career while expanding my video career has definitely been difficult, but pleasurable. One has benefited the other significantly. I hope this book does the same for you.

Getting Started with Vegas

Installing Vegas

Installing Vegas is no different from loading any application, but certain settings, steps, and habits can make operating Vegas more pleasant and efficient.

Before loading Vegas, make sure that any anti-virus software installed has been temporarily disabled. If a great deal of editing is to be done on this machine, it's worth considering building a separate user profile that keeps anti-virus off at all times during the capture, editing, rendering, and printing-to-tape processes. Anti-virus applications are notorious for stealing system resources and for popping up when least wanted.

Vegas may be installed either from a boxed-product DVD or from a downloaded executable file. If Vegas is being loaded from a DVD that came in a box, place the DVD into the DVD drive, close it, and follow the instructions as they appear on the computer screen. Vegas autostarts unless this feature has been disabled in the Control Panel.

Before you install Vegas 8, it will require that you update Windows XP. You'll need to load up the .NET 3.0 update, and you'll also need to install DirectX 9. Vegas 8 will not install unless these two steps are completed. Both are available from the Microsoft web site.

Complete the instructions given by Vegas's installation dialog. Vegas may be installed to any drive; it's generally best to install to the C:\ (or boot) drive, unless the application will be used on a network boot. (Special licensing is required to run Vegas on multiple machines at one time; with network rendering this will be important to observe.)

When installing Vegas Pro 8, you'll note that by default Vegas 8 will not install the Media

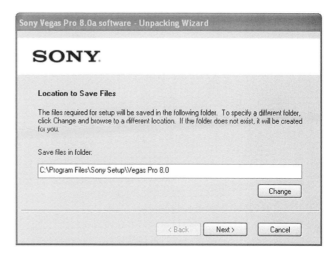

1.1   Vegas asks where it should be loaded/installed. In most cases, choose the boot drive.

Manager. You may or may not want to install this. The Media Manager is exceptionally useful for long-form projects, or for workflows that use stock media or require access to similar media throughout the project. The interface for Vegas Pro 8 is only subtly different from the interface for previous versions of Vegas, with only slight cosmetic changes. However, the Preferences dialog in Vegas Pro 8 has undergone significant changes in selectable preferences.

Register Vegas when prompted to do so; by registering, you'll be notified of product updates via email and receive other important information related to Sony Vegas Pro software.

You may register via the Internet, telephone, or another computer. Registration also gives users 60 days of free technical support and special discounts on new products.

1.2 Be sure to register Vegas so that Sony can notify you of updates and upgrades to the product and so that you gain access to the Get Media website.

1.3 Vegas displays a successful registration screen after registration is completed.

The Basic Tools in Vegas

When Vegas launches for the first time, it's a blank screen with no media in it and it makes no assumptions about how the user will be editing with Vegas.

The three primary levels at which audio, video, stills, and graphics are edited and processed are as follows:

- Event—can be viewed as an individual piece of media on a track. Many events can be on a single track.

- Track—is a single line on a project Timeline, on which all events are placed. A project can have multiple tracks.

- Project—is the culmination of all tracks that contain events. (Filters may be inserted into the Project media in addition to the above-listed Timeline options.)

These terms are used throughout this book and the Vegas owner's manual.

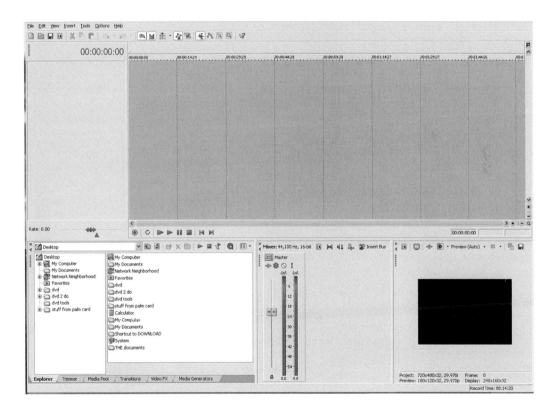

1.4   Opening the main window in Vegas for the first time.

Vegas is essentially broken up into three main workspaces:

- Track Header/Control
- Timeline/Track View
- Docked windows

Track Control Pane

The Track Control pane is where track names are listed and track-focused effects are added. Users can also define special behaviors of the individual track, such as routing to external audio cards for sound control/mixing and compositing behaviors for video. The Track Control pane is also where audio tracks and video tracks are inserted. Tracks can be inserted one of three different ways:

- Select INSERT | AUDIO TRACK or INSERT | VIDEO TRACK from the menu bar at the top of the screen.
- Use a shortcut key: Ctrl+Q (audio tracks) or Ctrl+Shift+Q (video tracks).
- Drag media from the Explorer to the blank Timeline.

The Track Control pane can be expanded or contracted, depending on the desired workspace and information space. This feature is particularly valuable on single-monitor systems in which screen space is at a premium. Hovering the cursor over the line that divides the Track Control pane and the Timeline changes the cursor to a resize icon. Clicking the left mouse button when this icon appears allows the Track Control pane to be expanded or contracted.

1.5 Tracks can be inserted from the menu, as shown here, by dragging or by using keyboard shortcuts.

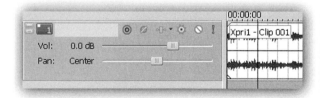 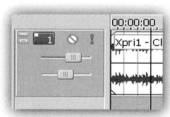

1.6 The Track Control pane can be expanded or contracted, depending on the amount of space desired for viewing either the Track pane or the Timeline.

The Track Control pane can be completely removed by using the shortcut keys Shift+F12. This step removes the control pane completely, so be aware that it's easy to forget that it's been hidden. Using the up-arrow and down-arrow keys makes it fast and easy to move above or below a selected track. The currently selected track will be a darker shade than the tracks above or below. Multiple tracks can be selected by holding the Shift key and clicking each track chosen for selection. When multiple tracks are selected, any changes made to the controls on one track affect all tracks. This feature is useful when multiple audio tracks need to be raised or lowered in volume or for panning or bus routing. When multiple video tracks require changes to opacity or changes made in compositing modes, selecting multiple tracks is a fast way to affect all tracks simultaneously. Changes made to affect parameters will not affect multiple audio or video tracks, nor will track motion assigned to one track carry over to additional tracks when multiple tracks are selected.

Each track can be given a name for reference purposes. The track name becomes the default prefix name of the media stored on the Timeline when the audio is recorded.

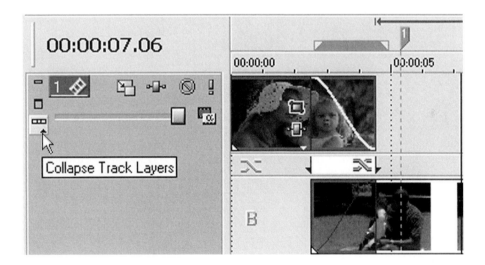

1.7   Track panes can also be expanded vertically, providing the traditional A/B roll view found in most other NLE systems. This feature uses twice the amount of screen space, which is the primary reason Vegas defaults to a collapsed track view. Expanding the view can help you become more familiar with editing in Vegas if you are coming from another NLE system. Simply right-click the track header, and choose Expand Track View from the submenu.

1.8   If a track is named before recording audio, the name on that track becomes part
of the file-naming process.

Adding a name value to a track after recording audio does not affect the filename properties of the audio. Adding a name value to a video track does not affect the name properties of the video on the named track. Adding a name value to audio ripped from a CD or imported does not change the name properties of the audio file.

▶ Tip

It's often said in the digital world that "if it ain't labeled, it don't exist." This is somewhat true in that cataloging media correctly at all levels is critical to locating and maintaining files. In today's digital world, files accumulate very quickly; be sure to get in the habit of good track, file, and project management.

The Track Control pane is also where volume, panning, and bus controls take place in an audio track, as well as track-level audio processing. Each track has an FX button on it, where either default processing or custom plug-ins can be inserted. (See Chapter 7 for more details on plug-ins.)

Timeline/Track View

The Timeline/Track View is where the majority of the work takes place. This location is where all audio and all video files are displayed, edited, and viewed during the editing process. The Timeline may be expanded or contracted both horizontally and vertically to suit the preferences of the user. This area displays all media found in the project and can be zoomed in for sample-accurate or frame-accurate edits or out for overall views of the entire project regardless of length.

In addition, the controls for starting and stopping cursor movement and playback in Vegas are found in the Timeline/Track View.

1.9 The Transport bar controls shuttling the cursor on the Timeline.

The following controls can also be controlled by these shortcuts:

- Record—Ctrl+R
- Loop—Q
- Play from start—Shift+spacebar
- Play—spacebar
- Pause—Enter
- Rewind—W
- Go to end—Ctrl+End

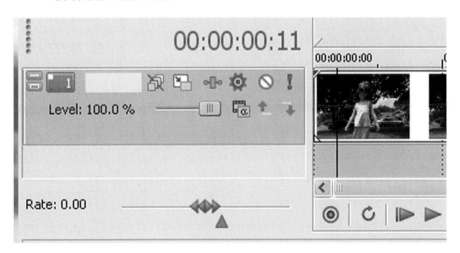

1.10 The Scrub tool can be locked at forward or reverse speeds. Double-click to restore playback to its normal rate.

These controls can also be programmed in third-party hardware, such as the Contour ShuttlePRO.

Next to the Transport bar control is a small yellow triangle used as a shuttle/scrub control. When playing media from the Timeline, this control can be slid to the right to scrub through audio/video during playback. The indicator will stay at the faster or slower speed until the yellow triangle is double-clicked. Double-clicking will restore the speed to the normal playback rate.

Scrub may also be achieved by pressing the J, K, or L key during playback. J reverses audio and incrementally increases reverse speed if the key is continually tapped or held down. K pauses playback, and L scrubs forward while incrementally increasing speed as the key is tapped or held. Speeds of up to 20× are possible within Vegas. To control the incremental speed adjustment and how fast it implements, choose OPTIONS | PREFERENCES | EDITING and select the JKL/Shuttle Speed option to suit personal preference. As a personal preference, High is the chosen setting.

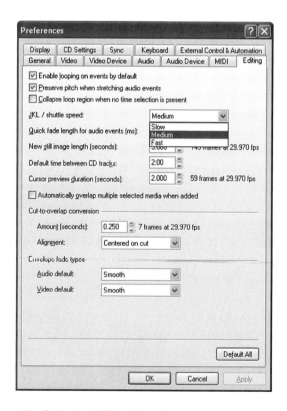

1.11   Setting the JKL/Shuttle Speed.

The Contour ShuttlePRO, Space Station AV, and Bella Keyboard all can be used for incremental shuttle control. Setting the shuttle speed to High provides the most common use of the shuttle wheels on these hardware tools.

Above the Timeline is a series of tools on a toolbar that can be customized for individual use. These tools can be removed from the top of the toolbar by selecting OPTIONS | CUSTOMIZE TOOLBAR to add/remove them from the view. The toolbar space can also be double-clicked to call up the Customize Toolbar dialog.

1.12 The main toolbar in Vegas. Buttons can be added to this toolbar depending on editing needs.

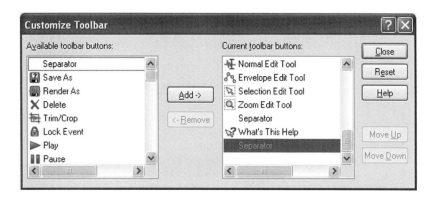

1.13 Use this dialog to add or subtract tools from the toolbar.

In the Add/Remove Tools view, select tools for display and click the Add button. Choose the tools to remove from the toolbar and click the Remove button. Audio editors might not wish to see tools related to video, just as video editors might or might not wish to see tools relating to audio. These tools are shortcuts to common editing tasks. All of these tools found on the toolbar can be accessed using keyboard shortcuts as well.

The dockable workspaces are found at the top of the screen in a default setting. Because these areas are dockable, they may be arranged to suit any specific need or desired appearance for efficient workflow. This feature greatly benefits users who have multiple monitors, as the Timeline can be stretched across multiple monitors and/or the docking windows may be stripped off and placed on any monitor. Vegas supports multiple monitors, and users will best appreciate editing with two monitors.

Vegas Windows

The three primary windows used in Vegas are the Explorer window, the FX window, and the Video Preview window. Clicking the View menu at the top of the toolbar opens several dockable windows. A checked box next to the window name means that the window is open.

Dockable Windows

The exception to this rule is that the Timing window always defaults to the top left of the Track View window. The Timing window can be docked or floated freely at any point, based on personal preference. As with all docking windows, the Time Display window can be expanded or contracted. Unlike other docking windows, however, the background or number color in the Time Display window can be changed by right-clicking the display and selecting Custom. This feature is significant in a dark studio in which the time display needs to be large and not distracting.

Expanding the View of a Docking Window and Undocking Windows

Docking windows have always been a challenge to view when several windows are accessible, but Vegas offers a great solution to the issue. Not only may docking windows be torn off and their locations saved as templates, but for the single-monitor user of Vegas, each docking window now has a button that expands the selected docking window to the full width of the docking area. Click the horizontal triangle on the upper-left corner of the docking window and watch the window expand to fill the entire docking area.

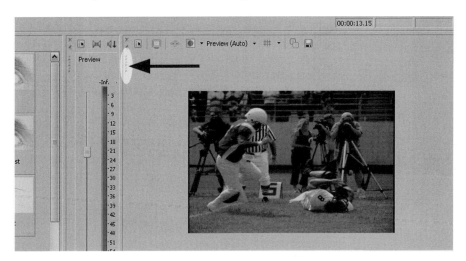

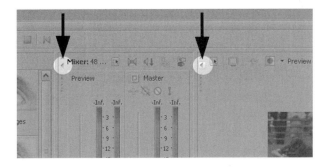

1.14 ,1.15   Clicking the Expand button found on every docking window will expand or compress the docking view.

For users of earlier versions of Vegas, tearing a docking window off has sometimes been a bit of a challenge if the small handle area of the docking window isn't accurately grasped. The most recent versions of Vegas make this much easier; with any area on the left-hand side of a docking window being grasped, the docking window may be moved. Notice that in the new version of Vegas, the docking area has small indentations to indicate the docking handle better. To move a docking window into the docking window area without having the window actually dock, hold the Ctrl key while clicking on and moving the docking window. This will allow the docking window to rest wherever it's released.

1.16 The Time Display window can be undocked and moved around the screen but cannot be removed.

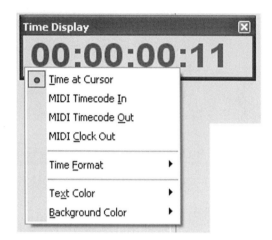

For video editors, some of these windows can be irrelevant. For audio-only studio use, many of the dockable windows might be superfluous as well, so it can be more visually efficient to hide the video-related windows. This feature is valuable to both, as it allows for custom views to be created for each individual. The following is a list of the dockable windows, their shortcuts, and a brief description:

- The Explorer window (Alt+1) provides a view of all media on the computer system and network.

1.17

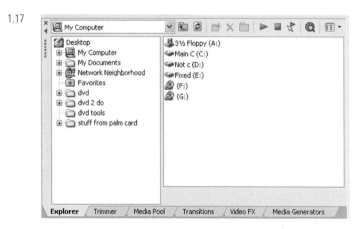

- The Trimmer window (Alt+2) allows media to be trimmed prior to placement on the Timeline.

1.18

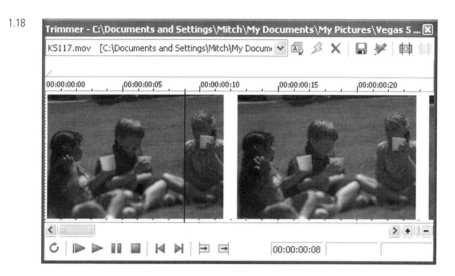

- The Mixer window (Alt+3) mixes audio, FX buses, and bus send/returns.

1.19

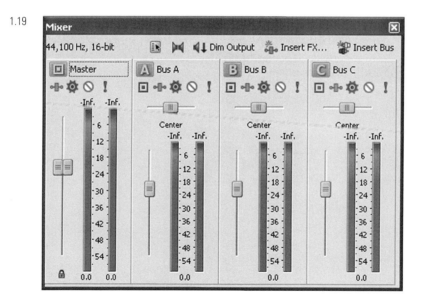

- The Edit Details window (Alt+4) displays all editing details pertaining to the current Timeline view. Re-sort, import, and view information in this window.

1.20

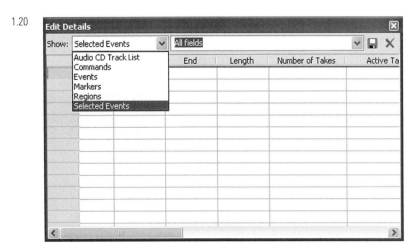

- The Project Media Pool window (Alt+5) shows all media used in the current project, length of use, and number of use and allows for filters to be applied to large numbers of events.

1.21

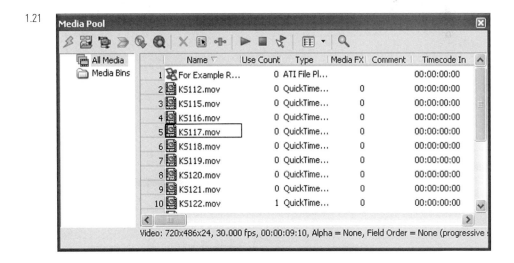

- The Video Preview window (Alt+6) provides preview of video on the Timeline.

1.22

- The Transitions window (Alt+7) displays all transitions on the system, with motion thumbnail views of how the transition will function.

1.23

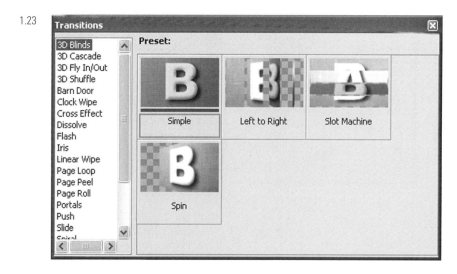

- The Video FX window (Alt+8) displays all filters on the system, with motion thumbnail views of how the filter will function.

1.24
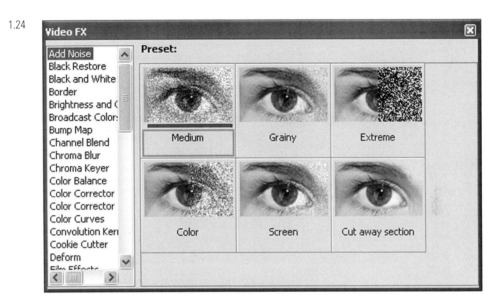

- The Media Generators window (Alt+9) generates media as simple as a title or as complex as gradient or noise generation. Test patterns are also found here.

1.25
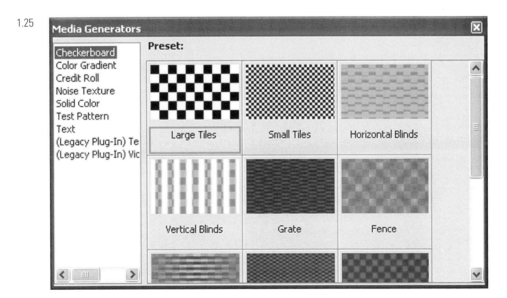

- The Plug-In Manager window (Ctrl+Alt+1) displays selected video or audio plug-ins that exist on the system, viewable by menu choice.

1.26

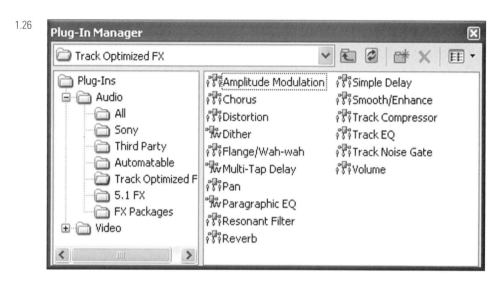

- Video displays and the Vectorscope may be opened from the Video Scopes window (Ctrl+Alt+2), providing color/luminance monitoring and matching tools.

1.27

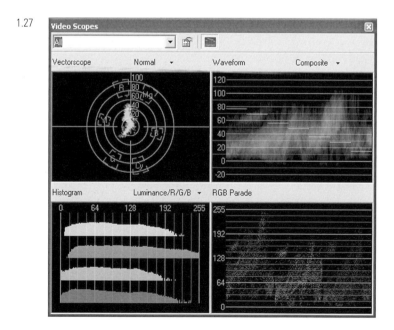

- The Surround Panner window (Ctrl+Alt+3) is used to create surround-sound keyframes and monitor the aural position of audio in a 5.1 mix. Right-clicking the Surround Panner window offers additional options.

1.28

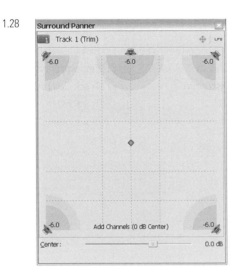 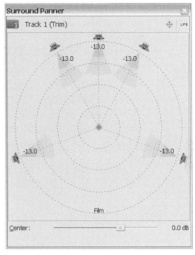

- The Media Manager (Ctrl+Alt+4) may or may not be installed. For users with media libraries, the Media Manager is a system that assists in finding media files by keyword, file type, and other media tags. See Chapter 10 on the Media Manager for more information.

- XDCAM users will want to use the XDCAM Explorer (Ctrl+Alt+5) to enable/disable views of the XDCAM Explorer. More information on the XDCAM explorer may be found in Chapter 2, Capturing Video.

- Vegas Pro 8 offers a Mixing Console (Ctrl+Alt+6), which may be docked or floated for detailed views of audio features in Vegas.

To move a dockable window, grab the vertical bar on the left side of the window you want to move and click with the mouse. Hold the mouse button down and drag the window to the desired space. Release the mouse button.

1.29 Use the docking handle to undock a tool from the docking pane. Press and hold Ctrl down while moving the window back to the docking area to prevent the window from redocking.

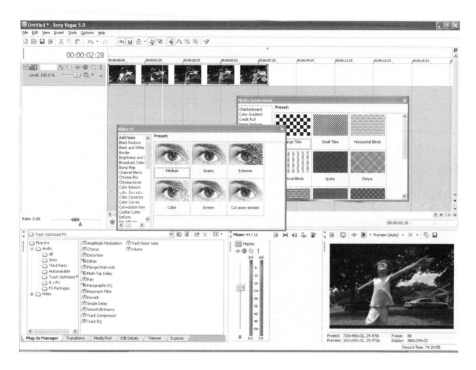

1.30   Multiple windows can be floated on the workspace. This feature is useful when working with two monitors.

Windows can be stripped from the lower section of Vegas and dropped anywhere onto the Timeline, onto another monitor, or above the main work area. If a window is dropped too close to the lower section, however, the window will attempt to dock itself. Holding the Ctrl key prevents docking and allows for precise placement of floating/dockable windows anywhere on the workspace, including secondary monitors.

If space is limited, some windows can dock on top of others. Windows can float or be left in place and then selected with the tabs at the bottom of the docking area. Dockable windows may also be expanded or reduced in size.

To place a dockable window in the lower section of Vegas, drag the dockable window to the lower part of the screen and release. The window will automatically dock and fit within the window docking area.

1.31   When multiple windows are docked in the docking area, each window has a tab for fast access.

The entire docking area can be hidden and recalled by double-clicking the horizontal bar that divides the docking area from the Timeline. This action will remove the docking windows entirely from view. To restore the docking area to view, double-click the bar again.

Monitoring

This allows you to select a second, third, or other monitor to be used to monitor full-screen video, at a high resolution or full resolution (depending on your monitor's capabilities), just like an external broadcast monitor. This is particularly useful for editing HDV without an HD/SDI monitoring system.

In Options>Preferences (or right-click the track header), you'll notice a tab labeled Preview Devices. This allows you to decide if you'll be monitoring through a DeckLink card or an OHCI/1394 card or to a secondary monitor.

Vegas will allow you to identify which monitor is your display monitor. For viewing 10801 information, you'll need to have a monitor capable of 1900 × 1280 or more if you want to see all the pixels in your image. However, if you don't have a monitor that

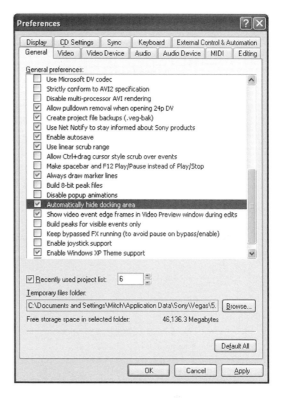

1.32a Hiding the window area makes more Timeline space visible. Audio editors will find this feature particularly useful.

meets these requirements, no fear. Vegas will display and compensate for whatever lower resolution you might have. Therefore, if you have only a 1280 × 768 monitor, Vegas will properly scale the frame to fit within that resolution space. Further, Vegas now offers a deinterlace feature on the display monitor, allowing you to view sharp, clean video on the second monitor. You can also use color management and select one of several profiles. There are calibration tools available from third parties that will allow you to calibrate your monitor for video, or your monitor may have come with a calibration disk or profile. Do the calibration, set your own properties, and save those properties as a color profile. Because Vegas can have its own color profile, you can also have a different color profile for your graphics, web, or other applications and use a specific profile just for Vegas. Be sure to leave the "Recompress edited frames" checkbox selected.

You can drag tags to selected media, or you can drag media to the relevant tag. Either method accomplishes the same result, and which method you choose is dependent only on your workflow needs.

1.32b   Notice that on the secondary monitor the video is displayed full screen. This is a great way to be able to display HDV without having an HD/SDI monitor.

Be aware that if you use a secondary display for DV, the entire screen will not be filled, simply because of the frame size being smaller than the secondary monitor will display. You wouldn't want the DV image to be scaled up, or it would be pixelated and look much like the events Vegas displays in the Preview/Draft mode.

This feature is exceptionally useful for audio editors who prefer to focus on the tracks during recording and call up plug-ins or editing tools only when desired. Video editors will also find this useful during in-depth compositing or when desiring maximum frame view for multiple tracks.

Although docking windows may be stretched or placed on a second monitor, there are users who may find themselves using the second monitor as a full-screen monitor, particularly those editing in high-definition formats.

Saving Templates/Layouts in Vegas

Vegas allows for new layouts to be created and preserved, permitting users to create their own layouts for single-, dual-, or even triple-head monitor configurations. Up to 10 different templates may be restored/saved in Vegas for each editor's profile, or perhaps for each task. Each time Vegas opens, the saved layout will open as it was saved. Moreover, a template for each type of project may be created and opened, saving time. If various users are accessing Vegas Pro 8 on the same computer, each user is capable of having his or her own personal layout template. To save a layout, create the layout appearance and save the template via the Ctrl+Alt+D and then number keystrokes. This even allows for templates to be shifted during the editing process.

To save a workspace template in Vegas:

1. Lay out the workspace the way you'd like to have it look and feel.

2. Press and hold Ctrl+Alt+D, and then press a number key that you'd like to assign the layout to.

3. Repeat up to 10 times, saving up to 10 layout templates.

4. Recall layout templates by pressing Alt+D+[number assigned to desired template].

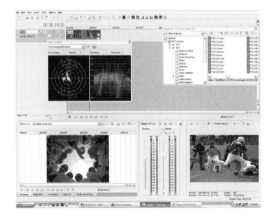

1.33, 1.34a   Vegas can save custom layouts that are recalled using Alt+D+[assigned keyboard number].

With multiple windows floating at various locations on the screen, setting up a template is always useful if Vegas should open with the same views each time. Consider having a template layout for times when audio editing is the focus instead of video editing being the focus, or for times when deep composites and track views require more screen space, or even when using a template during rough cutting and another template for finishing work.

Tip_____

Flip the docking area to the top of the computer monitor. This is great for situations in which monitors sit high on a shelf, letting the Timeline be at the bottom of the monitor, reducing eye and neck strain. This option is found in Options | Preferences | Display.

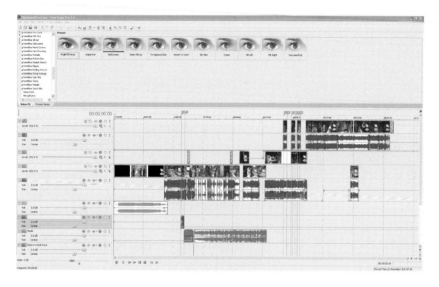

1.34b

File Menu

Several choices under the File menu are available to help create a variety of settings, some of which are duplicates of the toolbar functions.

The Open dialog opens an existing Vegas project. Open can also be accessed by right-clicking the empty Track window and selecting Open File or by pressing Ctrl+O. This step opens either a VEG file or media to go on the Timeline.

The Close dialog closes the current project. Vegas will prompt you to save, not save, or cancel. The Save dialog allows a project to be saved to a new name if it has not been named previously. The Save As dialog allows an existing project to be given a new name, which is useful for saving a number of edits that may need to be recalled at a later date.

 Tip

Saving the same project with different names allows you to save various versions or stages of a project, which lets you instantly recall various mixes and edits. This feature is valuable when a producer wishes to hear/see comparisons between project settings. Save files by time, date, or a mix of time, date, and unique name, for example, "less bass mix-04-15-03."

1.35　The File menu.

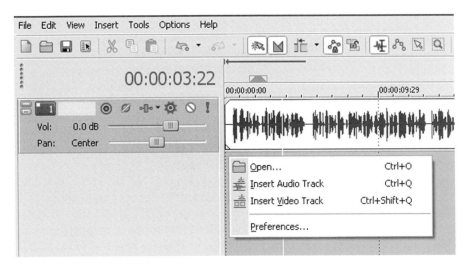

1.36   The Timeline/Project opens, and any media from the last project saved opens, unless this feature is disabled in the OPTIONS | PREFERENCES | GENERAL dialog.

The Import Media dialog allows for import of single or multiple files of any nature compatible with Vegas. Files imported are placed in the Project Media for later use. This feature is useful for setting up entire projects before editing begins.

The Capture Video dialog opens up the Vegas capture utility, allowing for the transfer of DV from a camera or DV deck to a hard drive. This dialog launches a separate application.

The Get Photo dialog communicates with a scanner that is connected to the computer, allowing images to be directly scanned into Vegas's Project Media, saving users the time it takes to open a separate photo scanning or editing application. Vegas calls on the scanning software found on the user's computer.

The Extract Audio from CD dialog is what its name implies: a means of ripping audio from an existing CD. The audio is then placed in the Project Media. This step extracts audio only from an audio CD, not a CD of WAV or MPS files. Those file types are opened via the CD/Drive selection in the Explorer window.

The Project Properties dialog is a series of choices that allows a user to create project settings related to any number of workflows. Media that is going to be edited just for the web

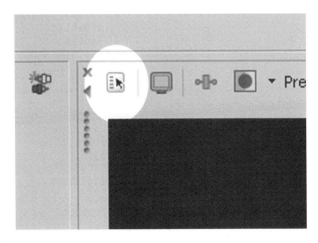

1.37   Access video properties by selecting the Video Properties button found on the Preview window toolbar.

should have project properties that relate to web-oriented video or audio. Recording studio set-ups might want to adjust properties only for audio and never see any of the video tools. The DVD with this book has projects already set up for you to use if you wish.

As with most options in Vegas, the Project Properties dialog may be opened from multiple places. Selecting FILE | PROPERTIES is one method of opening the dialog. The Project Properties button found in the Preview pane of the docking Video Preview window also opens the dialog, as does the Audio Properties button found in the Mixer dialog. Pressing Alt+Enter also opens the Project Properties dialog.

The default setting of the Project Properties is for an NTSC-DV project, which is used for projects captured from a DV camera to be edited and printed back to a DV camera or to another tape machine through a DV camera, DV-to-analog converter, or other DV device. This setting optimizes Vegas's preview and editing behaviors for the DV space. Other presets are there as well, including for PAL-DV, multimedia authoring, web-oriented editing, and MPEG-CD directed media projects. Any of these choices can be used as a starting point and then edited to suit specific needs. If you're working with HDV, be certain that the HDV templates are not confused with the HD templates. HDV uses a pixel aspect ratio of 1280 × 720 or 1440 × 1080. Choose the appropriate frame rate relevant to what was acquired with the HDV camcorder.

 Tip_____

Be sure to set the timecode readout properties (right-click the Time window) to PAL to see proper frame-rate playback.

Checking the "Start all new projects with these settings" box ensures that editors will have the same project settings each time they open Vegas for a new session. Having a series of project settings saved as templates is valuable, as it saves time and ensures correct settings in those hurried moments that are common in the studio, whether for audio or video work.

 Tip_____

Save VEG files for specific types of projects, such as a Timeline that opens with a station ID or corporate logo. Markers, chapter points, time counters, plug-ins, and other commonly used tools can be saved in a VEG file, ensuring that projects consistently open with all desired tools. This step also sets up a template that includes all consistent media. (See the DVD included with this book for VEG files.) A nested VEG file may also be used in place of a default project opening.

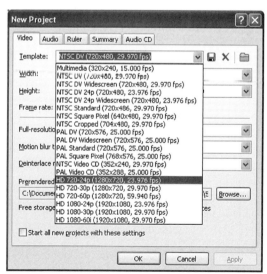

1.38   Using existing templates and creating new templates saves a lot of time when setting up an editing project.

Setting Up Project Properties

Video project types are specified in the Video tab of the Project Properties. As a general rule, it's best to use the template settings to ensure that projects flow with ease and are trouble-free. Advanced users might want to edit the settings for specific results related to third-party tools or applications.

One major consideration with Vegas is to set the Prerendered Files folder to a new default. Vegas defaults to the `C:\Program Files\Sony\ Vegas Pro 8.0\` folder. Prerendered files will rapidly fill the `C:\` drive and are generally forgotten by most users, which can easily lead to problems. Click the Browse button, locate the second hard drive dedicated to media, and create a Prerendered Files folder on that drive. Point the default prerendered files to that folder on the media drive. This process will speed up prerenders and will ensure that media moved around from computer to computer (if the drive is external) will stay with the project at all times.

Properties for an audio-only project are also set up here. Engineers wanting to work with high bitrates and sample rates will want to adjust these in Vegas. Default settings are 16 bit/44.1kHz, which are standard CD quality settings. Vegas is capable of working with 24-bit/96kHz files, although for the most part, only professional sound cards can work with these higher sampling rates.

Take note of the Master Bus Mode, which defaults to Stereo. This setting is where Vegas is adjusted to author 5.1 surround-sound files. If the applicable hardware is available to the system, anyone can now author 5.1 surround files in Vegas. (AC-3 encoding is not included in Vegas, as it's an additional purchase/plug-in package.) Vegas will output elementary linear pulse code modulation files, which are acceptable by most DVD authoring packages. Users that do not have 5.1-compatible hardware are able to select the 5.1 surround option and can output a 5.1 file. No ability to monitor/master the audio exists, however, which can potentially result in an unbalanced mix.

Up to 26 buses can be assigned in Vegas. (These correspond to the letters of the alphabet.) Buses can be used for inserting effects, such as reverbs, delays, exciters, and other

1.39 Video properties can be accessed from the FILE | PROPERTIES | VIDEO dialog or from the Properties button on the Preview window toolbar.

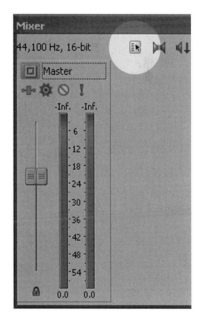

1.40 Audio project properties can be opened by clicking the Audio Properties button above the master volume controls.

audio plug-ins from Sony or other Direct X plug-in developers, such as WAVES or iZotope. Buses can also be used for submixing. Vegas offers bus-to-bus routing, discussed in Chapter 7.

Resample quality should generally be set to Best in the Project Properties Audio dialog. It defaults to Good.

This location is also where the default recording folder is specified in Vegas. Vegas sets the default audio recording to the `C:\Program Files\Sony\Vegas Pro 8\` directory. If you are recording long program material or multiple tracks, or if audio is the primary use of Vegas, it is highly recommended that this setting be set to a secondary drive. Vegas will scan the specified drive and indicate how much memory is free on the identified drive.

1.41 This dialog sets preferences for how audio-time grids are displayed on the Timeline. This is valuable, even perhaps critical, for users of ACID loops in Vegas.

Tip

Remember that it's important to have a second drive for media and that the drive controllers should be set to DMA in the Windows Control Panel.

The Project Properties Ruler dialog box allows editors to specify how the Track View/Timeline appears. Audio editors will want SMPTE time for their house standard; DV editors can set this for 29.97fps for grids defining their time space, and musicians can set this to beats or tempo.

Tip

Video editors will find the Beats grid valuable if the tempo of bed music is known. This ruler grid can mark the beat of the bed music and assist in placing edits so that they are in time with the beat of the music if the music tempo is known.

Time display formatting can also be selected by right-clicking the Time Display window and selecting the desired time format, which can be toggled between different time formats. Toggling between beat and SMPTE time won't change the timing of the audio or video; it merely allows for different grid views.

The Summary tab found in the Project Properties dialog allows users to log information about the overall project, such as engineer or copyrights. This information stays with the file in the event that the VEG is transferred to another system, user, or shared file so that the originator of the file is traceable. This data does not become part of the summary information embedded in streaming media, nor does it become part of Scott information embedded for radio play. Those summaries must be filled out separately.

The Audio CD tab in the Project Properties dialog has a form for inputting a universal product code (UPC) or media catalog number (MCN) that will be burned in the header of a Redbook-valid CD. Some compact disc players do not display this information, but the information is still embedded in the disc.

There is also an option for changing the first track number on a CD. This feature can potentially prevent a CD from playing on older or fewer-featured CD players even though the disc will be burned as a Redbook-valid CD. This option is supported only as a Disc-at-Once (DAO) burn as specified by Redbook guidelines. Track-at-Once authored CDs ignore this setting.

1.42 The Summary tab allows copyright information, engineer information, and other important information about the project to be stored. This feature is particularly important when tracking a project.

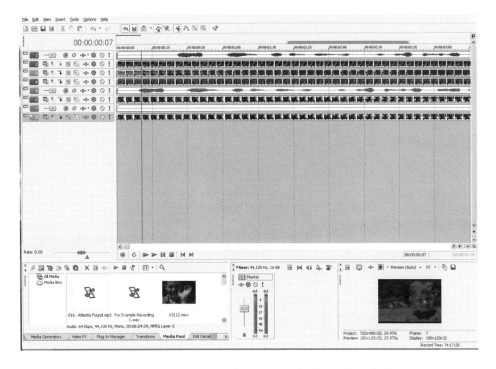

1.43 CD properties include the ability to insert a UPC code onto the disc for media cataloging.

Edit Menu

Next on the menu bar is the Edit menu. It contains several options for editing media, some of which are duplicated on the toolbar. First on the list is Undo and Redo. Vegas is unlimited in the number of times that you can undo or redo actions. After a project is saved or closed and reopened, however, the project starts with a new list of undo/redo, so a project is not forever undoable. Be sure of your choices before closing. These tools are also found on the toolbar, identified by the Undo and Redo icons.

The shortcut key combination Ctrl+Z triggers the Undo function, and Ctrl+Shift+Z triggers the Redo function.

Tip
_____

If you have a Contour ShuttlePRO or Bella keyboard, these two shortcuts are handy to have programmed as button strokes.

Next on the list are the Cut, Copy, and Paste actions. These are the same as nearly all Windows applications. Cut (Ctrl+X) removes media from the Timeline, and Copy (Ctrl+C) copies the media on the Timeline. Regardless of whether Cut or Copy is used, the media is copied to the board, so that the Paste (Ctrl+V) function can be used to place the clipboard-stored media to another location.

1.44　Undo can be accessed using the button or keyboard shortcut.

Paste Attributes is useful for both audio and video editing. It allows users to copy switches, audio pitch shifting, playback rate, undersample rate, video event effects, and pan/crop settings from one event or media clip to others. As an example, suppose that there are 10 tracks of audio, and in those tracks there are 40 events. A blur needs to be applied to half of those events randomly scattered throughout the Timeline. Rather than applying the blur to the entire track, click the event containing the correct blur settings and press Ctrl+C or go to the Copy button on the toolbar (or right-click and select Copy or use the Edit/Copy function). Then select the event to which you wish to have the same blur settings applied. From the Edit menu, choose Paste Event Attributes. This step copies the blur and any other unique information contained in the media from which the attributes were copied and pastes them onto the next chosen event(s). Video editors find this method very efficient to pan/crop several still images at once or to copy effects settings to apply to several events at once. Paste Event Attributes may be applied to multiple events of the same type at the same time, so if one event contains the desired settings, those settings can be pasted over hundreds of similar events. Imagine being able to pan/crop 500 still images at once or being able to apply a unique reverb setting to 30 instances of a particular kind of event at once. This result can also be accomplished in the Project Media via applying a Media EX to all occurrences of video or audio in the Project Media. There is no shortcut key for Paste Event Attributes.

Delete is next on the menu and is used to remove an event permanently. Select the event you wish to remove and press the Delete key or choose it from the menu.

Post Edit Ripple is the next item in the menu. Editors can choose ripple features to suit their own style of editing. Ripple editing allows you to insert or delete events on the Timeline. At the same time, ripple editing keeps events in front of and behind the deleted or inserted event in the same order and time space that the events occupied before the insertion or deletion of an event.

An example would be a long-form documentary that has been edited, containing many tracks of video information. A piece of the documentary is determined to be incorrect and must be deleted. Deleting the piece, without filling in the exact amount of time occupied by the deleted events, leaves a hole in the Timeline. Deleting the hole causes all events occurring after the deletion to slide in place, with nothing lost. The new ripple modes allow Vegas users to decide how they want those inserts/deletions and movements of events to take place. (There is a project file called ripple.veg contained in the DVD with this book.) The post-edit Ripple functions (F, Ctrl+F, Ctrl+Shift F) are also alternatives to leaving the Ripple function engaged. Ctrl+L enables/disables Ripple editing.

The Select All choice on the Edit menu allows for all media on the Timeline to be selected. This feature is invaluable for moving an entire project up or down the Timeline or for selecting an entire project to be copied and pasted into another instance of Vegas. Either selecting EDIT | SELECT ALL or pressing Ctrl+A selects or highlights all media.

The Select Event Start/Select Event End feature jumps the cursor to the beginning or end of a selected event. This feature can also be accessed by using the shortcut key [, for Select Event Start, or], for Select Event End.

From the numeric keypad, press the 7 key for Select Event Start or 9 for Select Event End. Use 4 and 6 to move or trim an event edge forward or backward in time, and use 1 or 3 to move the event forward or backward by frames. When not in Event Edge Edit mode, 4 and 6 move the event by one pixel, and 1 and 3 move it by one frame. Use 8 and 2 to move the selected event up or down vertically to the next track. Pressing 5 exits the keyboard trimming mode.

1.45 Selecting EDIT | SELECT puts the cursor where it should be with frame accuracy; however, most editors find it faster and easier to use the 10 numeric keypad shortcuts.

On a standard laptop, Num Lock needs to be enabled to use the numeric keypad. Targus manufactures a numeric keypad that is connected to the laptop via USB for the road warrior editor. This feature allows for rapid location of event edit points, which when coupled with the new ripple features, makes for efficient editing using the keyboard.

The Paste Repeat dialog allows an event or events that have been copied to the clipboard to be pasted multiple times.

To insert events at the cursor position on the Timeline and move media down the Timeline to accommodate the inserted events, copy (Ctrl+C) events to the clipboard, select the location at which events are to be pasted, and press Ctrl+B or select EDIT | PASTE REPEAT. You will be prompted to input the number of times that the event should be pasted.

Events can be precisely separated in Paste Repeat mode, allowing for many elements, including images and video clips, to be spaced a prespecified distance. Input the length of time between events into this window. The spacing/

1.46 Using the Targus keypad with a laptop makes the laptop editing more efficient.

length of time between pasted images can be determined in milliseconds, frames, seconds, minutes, hours, beats, or musical note values. Be aware of the Tempo Settings in the Project Settings, as any ACIDized files dropped on the Timeline will play back at the preset tempo, set in the Project Settings.

1.47 Use EDIT | PASTE INSERT to paste an event on the Timeline, while moving everything subsequent to the paste down the Timeline.

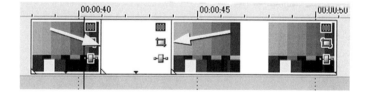

Tip

Use the Musical Note Values feature when you want a repeating instance of an instrument. For instance, a fast way of building a rhythm would be to insert a sample of a kick drum on every downbeat and third beat and a snare drum on a different track hitting every second and fourth beat. Use the Tempo dialog found in the Project Properties to set the tempo and grid for the project. ACID loops that match the tempo can also be inserted, making a fast music bed for either editors or musicians to work with. Video editors will find this method a visually and aurally compelling way to edit quickly, if bed music has not been completed but a tempo is known. This process is often called tempo-mapping and allows video editors to build rough video comps while a composer finishes a musical cue for the project.

The Trim feature is another excellent feature in Vegas. To delete all portions of the event outside the selected area, select a portion of an event by scrolling the mouse over the event(s), hold the right-click button down, and select EDIT | TRIM or press Ctrl+T.

This feature can be used on an individual event or on all events across the Timeline.

The Split tool splits a selected event or events at the point where the cursor is parked. If a selection is made on an event, only that event is split. If no selection is made, the split occurs across all events that fall under the cursor. Park the cursor at the desired point and select EDIT | SPLIT or press S. The event on the right side of the split is selected automatically, in the event that it should be deleted.

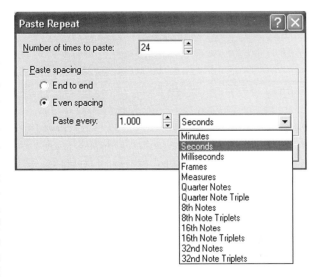

1.48 Repeating a copied image is definable in the EDIT | PASTE REPEAT dialog.

The Editing Tool dialog specifies what type of editing behavior the cursor shall have.

These same choices are found on the toolbar mentioned earlier. Pressing Ctrl+D returns the cursor to the normal Selection Edit cursor mode, which is generally the most commonly used cursor mode. None of the other cursor editing modes have shortcut keys.

1.49 The Ctrl+T edit command deletes all events not inside the selected area. Coupled with the Ripple feature, this feature is very powerful.

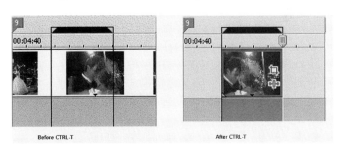

Using the Switches dialog, users that have been using Vegas in earlier revisions will find that several right-click dialogs have been augmented by shortcut keys and by selecting EDIT | SWITCHES. Mute, Lock, Loop, Invert Phase, Normalize, Aspect Ratio, Reduce Interlace Flicker, and Resample have all been made accessible through the EDIT | SWITCHES menu selection. Smart Resample, Force Resample, and Disable Resample selections are also available. Smart Resample instructs Vegas to seek media that has been time stretched, is a graphic-based event, or does not match the frame rate and the frame rate of the event is greater than 24fps. Vegas then resamples the media meeting those parameters. Force Resample instructs Vegas to resample all events regardless of their format or frame rate. Disable Resample prevents Vegas from resampling any events, regardless of whether they have been selected for resampling or not.

1.50　Although the new take being dragged
to the existing event is longer or shorter
than the event over which it is being laid,
Add as Takes trims the new media to fit
the existing media. Shuffle through takes
during playback by pressing T.

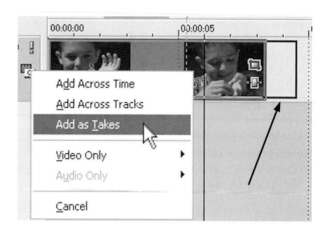

> **Tip**
>
> If you are coming to Vegas from the AVID world, you can download a free tool from the www.vasst.com site that will permit you to do overwrite edits.

Vegas's Take feature allows you to place several takes on top of one another and allows those takes to be switched to view during playback in realtime. For example, perhaps a multicamera shoot occurred, and the director or producer would like to see the scene with the different camera angles that were shot. Either multiple tracks must be used with muting on the fly or takes are used, having all of the shots living in one event and switching on the fly. This workflow is more efficient in most instances. This process is also useful when a musician wants to perfect a particular part of a song and plays the piece over and over again. Each take can be placed, and different versions can be toggled through in realtime by pressing T. Any event that has filters, effects, or other edits made to it will apply filters, effects, or edits to the take.

The Group menu allows you to create a group of clips that are temporarily locked together so that when they are moved, they can be moved together without having to select multiple events each time. To implement this feature, select a number of events and press G or select EDIT | GROUP | CREATE NEW. This option locks the selected events together, so that when one is moved, all are moved. To remove an event from the group, select the event and press U. The event can also be removed from the group by selecting EDIT | GROUP | REMOVE FROM. All grouped items can be selected at once by using Select All. This option allows for an entire group to be deleted as a whole or to have other processing applied. Grouping is a very powerful tool, and one that is worth the time to get familiar with.

> **Tip**
>
> Video editors who work with a formula-based editing situation, such as a wedding video editor, can build a template of empty events marking locations of where media should go, complete with transitions and filters. Video is then dropped onto the empty events as a take, and within minutes, a finished video is ready to print to tape. Studios doing preset-time voice-over work can find this useful as well, fitting 30- or 60-second radio spots, complete with compression, EQ, and other filtering, into an empty event to be replaced by new dialog. For recurring-format editing projects, this method is terrific for cutting repetitive actions to a minimum and keeping projects/productions consistent in appearance or sound.

One great use of the Grouping feature is to select a number of events and group them.

Now hold Ctrl while dragging the left edge of the leftmost event. Notice that all events stretch or shrink at equal values. If you need to match video or stills to a music selection, this is a fast way to accomplish this task.

View Menu

The View menu is a series of checkboxes that determine what dockable windows are available for immediate view.

Place a check mark in the box next to the name of each view to turn the view on or off.

The Mixer Preview Fader option adds another set of sliders to the menu and allows the previewing volume to be changed regardless of what level the master volume is set at. The Mixer Preview Fader option affects only media in the Trimmer and Explorer. This slider set does not affect the level of rendered files, whereas moving the master slider does affect the level of audio mixed from the Timeline.

The Show Bus Tracks option first made its appearance in Vegas 6, allowing buses to be viewed as tracks, including volume and panning automation control. This feature provides much greater control over mixed tracks that use bus mixes, while also providing a visual reference for mix controls. Buses may be automated to increase/decrease volume of an effect on the bus or to control panning. Vegas Pro 8 offers a full desk-style mixing interface, complete with automated FX, busing, monitoring, etc.

The Show Audio Envelopes option hides or shows volume control views, depending on the current view state of the control. This new feature allows volume controls on all audio tracks to be hidden at once, cleaning up the screen view substantially in the event of a large mix.

The Show Video Envelopes option has the same control over the video envelopes: composite, track fade-to-color, track keyframes, and velocity envelopes.

The Minimize All Tracks option reduces all track views to a minimum size, immediately freeing up space for users to see previews, add full-size tracks, or make a large number of tracks fit into a small area.

This option can be accessed via the ~ key. Pressing ~ again restores tracks to the previous view.

The Rebuild Audio Peaks option redraws/refreshes the wave file views on the Timeline. Vegas uses 16-bit peak samples, and on slower machines, you can speed up the system by turning off peak drawing in the OPTIONS | PREFERENCES | GENERAL dialog. This option, also accessed via the F5 key, causes all views to be redrawn.

1.51 Set the Vegas workspace to appear exactly as you would like it to appear.

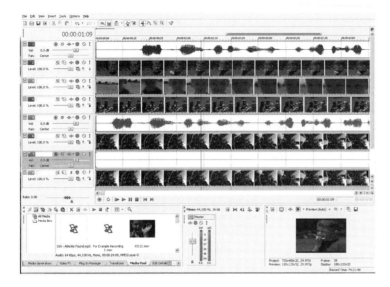

1.52 View bus behavior in Vegas, allowing full automation attributes in a mix.

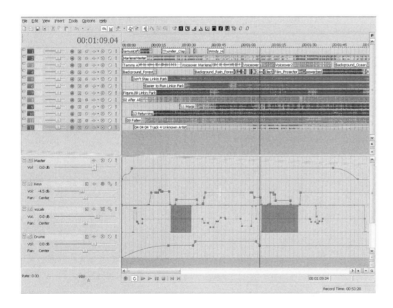

1.53 View bus behavior with the Minimize All Tracks option turned on.

Vegas stores graphic representations of wave files as .sfl files. These small files may be deleted at any time; however, if they are deleted, Vegas will redraw the graphics, creating a new .sfk file. Delete .sfk files when deleting projects.

*Tip*_____

If screen views will not be vertically zoomed in-depth, instruct Vegas to draw 8-bit file views. This option allows the process to become faster and increases responsiveness in Vegas. Change the screen draw by going to the OPTIONS | PREFERENCES | GENERAL dialog and scrolling down to "Build 8-bit peak files."

1.54   Instructing Vegas to draw 8-bit file views.

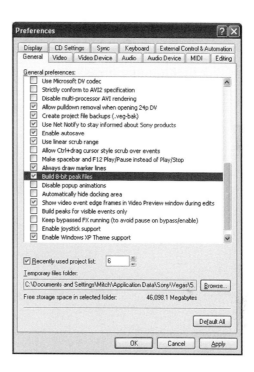

If you are struggling with your video preview edges, sometimes it's easier to see the edges if you change the background color of the Preview window from the default gray to either black or white, depending on the video you are previewing. To do this, right-click in the Preview window and select Black or White from the menu. You can also simulate device aspect ratios in this dialog. This is very handy for knowing how your image will appear on a specific display such as a television or webstream.

Additionally, the header bar of the Preview window may be double-clicked to ensure that the Preview window is showing at the project property size. This is a quick method of ensuring that you aren't working in lower resolutions than the project and that you are seeing everything at accurate resolution in the Preview window. Right-clicking and choosing "Scale Video to fit Preview Window" allows the video to scale regardless of the size of the preview window. If the display is set too small, pixelation may take place and the CPU may bog down.

Insert Menu

The Audio Envelopes option in the Insert menu has two submenus: Volume (Shift+V) and Pan (Shift+P). These place volume lines and pan lines on the Timeline on selected tracks.

 Tip _____

Select all audio tracks before using Shift+V or the menu. This option places volume controls on all audio tracks, saving time. You can select all tracks by pressing Ctrl+A.

The Video Envelopes option has three submenus: Composite Level, Fade to Color, and Velocity Envelope. Composite Level allows users to set the opacity of a track over time, by adding nodes or handles to the composite envelope and moving the envelope up or down on the Timeline at desired fade points. This feature reduces the opacity of the track, allowing video events below the affected track to become visible. Fade to Color adds an envelope to the selected track, giving control to the color to which a track will fade. The default color is black; however, any color can be selected in the OPTIONS | PREFERENCES | VIDEO dialog.

1.55 The Insert menu.

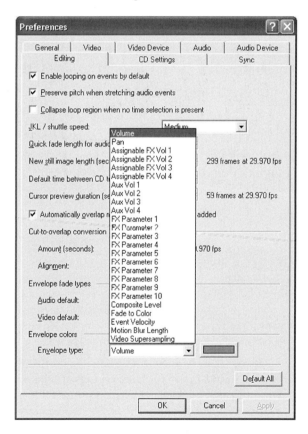

1.56 One great feature of Vegas allows users to define envelope colors.

The Velocity Envelopes option allows users to create an envelope that causes a video event to speed up or slow down. Inserting an envelope and creating handles on the envelope and then dragging the envelope either upward speeds up the event or downward slows down the event. If an envelope is dragged past the 0 percent speed point, the event reverses itself.

Tip_____

For the surreal speed effect that looks natural but slightly dreamy, slow files to 80 percent of the original speed. The event won't appear to be slow but will have a natural, dreamy slow motion applied to it. This feature is great for slowing down high-speed events.

An event that has its velocity envelope set to -100 percent will play at normal speed, but in reverse. An event that has it set to $+300$ percent will play at three times normal speed.

Tip_____

If you want speeds of greater than three times normal speed, right-click the event and select Properties. Input the additional speed in the Playback Rate window. Insert a Velocity Envelope. Files can be sped up to 12 times their normal speed by using a combination of the Velocity Envelope and the Playback Rate dialog!

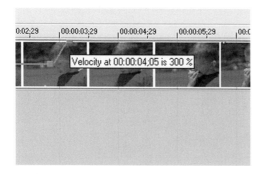

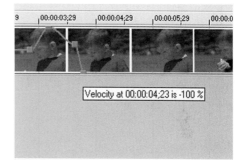

1.57 Velocity can be sped up incrementally and significantly in Vegas via the Velocity Envelope.

1.58 Velocity can also be slowed down over time. This sort of effect is extremely popular in modern editing.

Always use either the Smart Resample or the Force Resample feature with speed-altered events. The Reduce Interlace Flicker feature can be valuable with speed-altered media when flickers are seen in the previewed image.

Selecting the Audio Track option (Ctrl+Q) in the Insert menu inserts a new audio track on the Timeline beneath any audio track that is already in place. Dragging audio to a blank space in the Timeline workspace where no audio tracks currently exist creates a new audio track. Dragging an audio event to the Timeline allows an audio track to be created above or below existing audio or video events depending on where it is dropped.

Selecting the Video Track option (Ctrl+Shift+Q) in the Insert menu inserts a new video track on the empty Timeline or above existing video tracks. Dragging nonaudio events to the Timeline also accomplishes the same task by creating a new video track for the nonaudio event. Dragging a nonaudio event to the Timeline allows you to create a new video track above or below an existing audio or video track, depending on where it is dropped.

The Audio Bus option (B key) accesses the audio control or destination tracks. A hardware mixer has assignable buses, allowing the audio signal flow to be routed to a number of places before leaving the mixer. During this routing, the audio signal flow can be processed through a variety of tools, such as delays, reverbs, chorusing, flanging, or other processes. Buses can also be used as routing tools to hardware outputs. If a multichannel sound card is used, bus assignments are required to monitor the audio for multiple outputs beyond a simple stereo monitoring system. Up to 26 (based on the number of letters in the alphabet) buses can be inserted in Vegas. Buses may also be used for submixing, assigning all mixes of a group to one location for final leveling. Automated muting or muting envelopes are now available in Vegas as well.

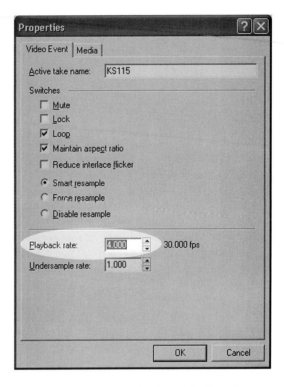

1.59 Adjust the rate of an entire clip with the Playback rate list box found in the Properties Video Event dialog.

☞**Tip**_____
Use bus assignments to route together all harmonies, all guitars, all basses, all drums, and all sound effects for submixing.

The Video Bus Track option (Ctrl+Shift+B) allows specific effects and processes to be controlled by envelope on the master video bus. Supersampling, MotionBlur, and Master Fade Out to Transparent Black are all possible with envelope control in this window.

Selecting the Empty Event option in the Insert menu inserts a blank event on the Timeline. Empty events can be used as markers for specified lengths of time in current projects or used as placeholders for takes in projects requiring a consistent edit and workflow, allowing video or audio takes to be dropped on the empty event. Empty events can have filters, effects, or other attributes assigned to them that are maintained when a new event is dropped on the empty event as a take. Empty events can also be inserted by right-clicking an audio or video track and choosing the Empty Event dialog.

Selecting the Text Media option opens the Titling dialog.

1.60 Select generated media types in this dialog.

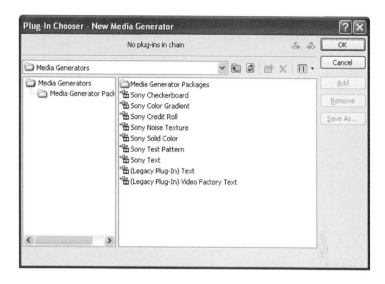

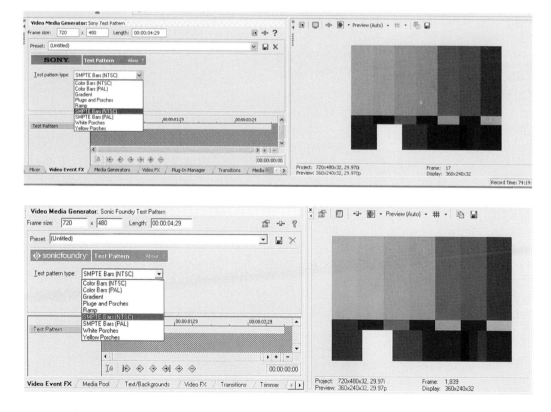

1.61, 1.62 Creating color bars is one of the functions of the Generated Media tool.

Selecting the Generated Media option in the Insert menu opens a dialog allowing users to create a variety of different forms of media appearances.

Gradients, solid colors, credit rolls, test patterns, and text can all be inserted via this dialog.

Selecting the Insert Time option in the Insert menu inserts time across the entire Timeline. If a cursor is placed in the middle of an event, that event is split and the portion of the event to the right of, or later in time than, the cursor, is moved according to the amount of time specified in the Insert Time dialog box.

1.63   Insert blank time with the Time menu option.

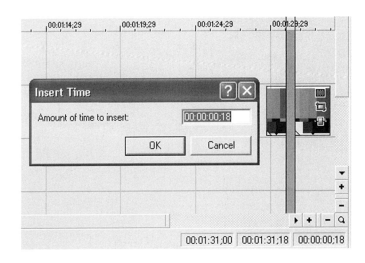

Inserting a marker is possible by selecting Marker from the Insert menu; most users, however, find that inserting a marker is more efficient by pressing M. This option drops a vertical line at whatever point in time the cursor happens to be at when M is pressed or the menu option is selected.

Regions can be defined as a space between two markers or a selection created by dragging the mouse across the Timeline. Pressing R also activates the Regions option in the Insert menu.

1.64   Regions can be created via a selection on the Timeline and pressing R.

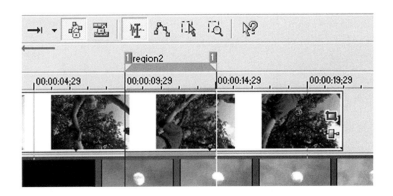

CD regions/track numbers can be assigned via the Audio CD Track Region option on the Insert menu. CD regions, however, are also assignable by pressing N when a selected event or time frame is on the Timeline. This feature is how Vegas creates track numbers for compact audio discs.

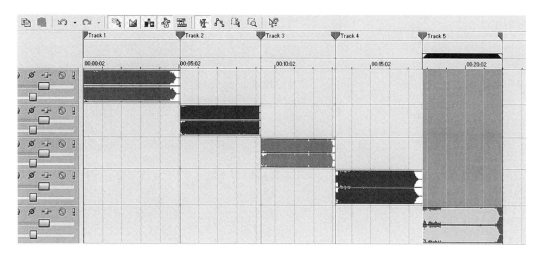

1.65   Using the regions in a CD project makes for fast track indexing.

Selecting the Audio CD Track Index option (Shift+N) allows for separations between a track number and an index in a track, similar to a chapter and subchapters in a book.

Selecting the Command option in the Insert menu creates metadata commands for streaming media. This menu selection brings up the Command Properties dialog box that gives a selection of different forms of metadata to be inserted into the Timeline for authoring of metadata-rich streaming media.

1.66   The Command tools allow for the insertion of metadata that creates a more interactive experience for streaming media or distributed disc viewers/listeners.

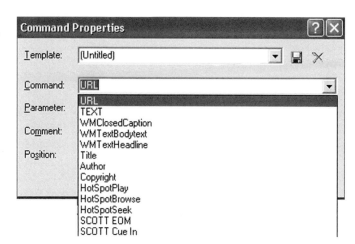

Tools Menu

The Tools menu contains tools for rapidly creating final products and quick renders of edited media and other highly useful tools. This menu is where the majority of work is done within Vegas outside of the Trimming tools and actions.

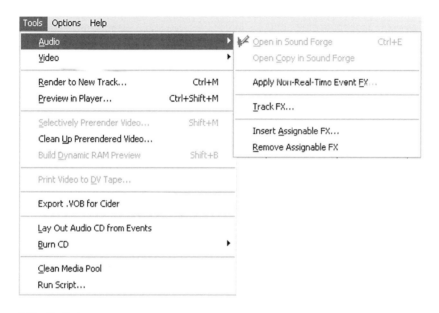

1.67   The Tools menu.

The Audio option in the Tools menu has a number of subchoices within it. These choices are also accessible via a right-click on an audio event. The first choice, Open in Sound Forge, opens the actual event—audio, video, or both—in Sound Forge, in which destructive or permanent edits can be applied to the file. Open Copy in Sound Forge opens a copy of the audio event in Sound Forge, in which a take is created that exactly replaces the original event on the Timeline. Pressing T lets users toggle back and forth between the original and the edited audio. Any audio editor can be chosen as the preferred audio editor; however, the unique relationship between Sony products makes Sound Forge a worthwhile application to have in partnership with Vegas. To set the preferred audio editor, select OPTIONS | PREFERENCES | AUDIO and browse to the .EXE of the preferred audio editor. Audio opened in any audio editing application is replaced in Vegas as a take.

 Tip
_____

> Always open audio from AVI files as a copy rather than as a destructive file. This option generates a take and does not affect the original. As a result, you can always go back to the original. It also speeds up the save process, as Vegas isn't generating a new video file for the original AVI.

The Apply Non-Real-Time Event FX option is great for slower computers or for applying processes that don't work well in realtime, such as Noise Reduction and Acoustic Mirror processes. These processes are so resource intensive that only the fastest machines can carry the load. They also take resources away from other actions taking place on the Timeline.

When using the Apply Non-Real-Time Event FX option, remember that these effects are destructively assigned to the event, allowing the processor to be free of having to deal with the load of real-time effects. Users with slower computers or with little RAM in their machines generally find this feature beneficial as well, as it frees up system resources for processing more audio, video, or mixed events. When working with non-real-time effects, you'll be prompted to provide a new name for the audio file so that the original is preserved. Vegas does not allow you to use the original filename, as the original file is currently open on the Timeline. The file with a new name is added as a take to the Timeline and can be compared against the original sound by pressing T. Users can toggle back and forth between the original and the newly affected sound during playback.

Although not readily evident, effects are broken down into various folders, including a folder called ALL. This folder allows for all Direct X plug-ins to be viewed at once. Other folders, however, show third-party effects, Sony-only effects, and FX chains, found in a folder labeled FX Packages. There is also an Automatable FX folder in which access to all FX that can be controlled with the FX automation envelopes are found. Only a limited number of Direct X FX can be automated. The folder Track Optimized contains a select group of FX, which are optimized for maximum processor performance.

Choosing the Track FX option in the Tools menu opens the effects found on the Track Control pane in Vegas. A Noise Gate, Equalizer, and Compressor are assigned by default to every audio track on the Timeline. These can be accessed via the Tools menu (TOOLS | TRACK FX) or by clicking the Track Effects button on the Track Control pane. These effects can be deleted, replaced, or augmented, depending on the user's preference.

The Insert Assignable FX option automatically inserts a new bus in the mixer section of Vegas. Selecting this option calls a list of all available plug-ins, of which as many as are needed can be chosen as a chain of effects.

1.68 Each event has an FX button on it unless the button is removed in the OPTIONS | PREFERENCES dialog.

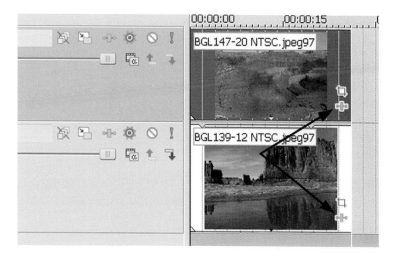

1.69 FX can be sequenced in any way desired.

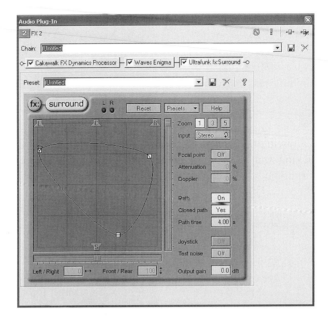

1.70 FX can be removed at any time. FX can also be A/B compared by checking and unchecking the box next to the effect name.

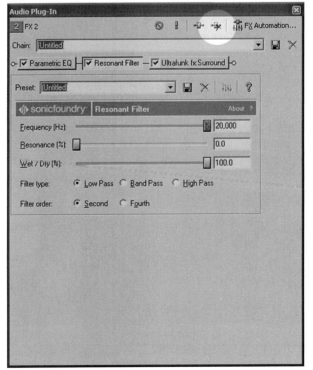

Tip

Use OPTIONS | BYPASS ALL AUDIO EFFECTS to disable all audio effects on buses, tracks, and events.

Effects in the chain can be reordered by clicking and holding an effect on the chain, dragging it to the desired priority in the chain, and dropping it. Also, right-clicking any effect and selecting the Move Left or Move Right pop-up menu option reorders effects. Effects in the chain can be removed by selecting the Remove Assignable EX option from the Tools menu or by clicking the Remove button in the upper-right corner of the EX dialog box.

Inserting video effects works exactly the same as inserting audio event effects, except that it is always nondestructive to insert a video event effect.

When the Video Effects option in the Tools menu is selected, all video effects are shown in a dialog box, allowing the user to choose multiple video effects. Effects in the chain can be reordered by clicking and holding an effect on the chain, dragging it to the desired priority in the chain, and dropping it. Also, right-clicking any effect and selecting the Move Left or Move Right pop-up menu option reorders effects.

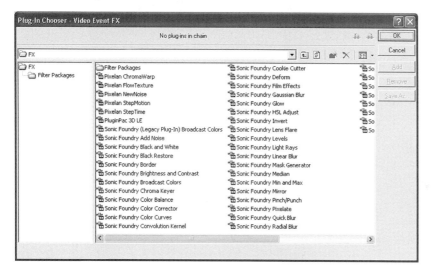

1.71   Video FX are selected the same way audio FX are. Chains of FX are stored in the Filter Packages folder.

1.72   Reordering video FX is a
        single button selection.

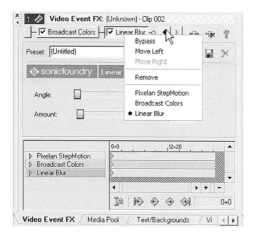

Clicking an effect on the Video FX chain and then clicking the FX Help button pops up a screen that demonstrates how the selected effect affects the video image. A short explanation of how each slider or button on the effect will behave is also included.

1.73   All aspects of Vegas have a Help Icon or button associated with them.

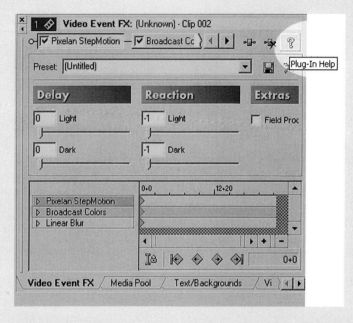

1.74   Calling up help by selecting the FX Help button opens a brief tutorial explaining how effects work.

This feature allows users to preview the event effect as a static image before it is applied to the event on the Timeline. It's also a great way to learn the attributes of each video effect.

Effects in the chain can be removed by selecting the Remove pop-up menu option or by clicking the Remove button in the upper-right corner of the FX dialog box.

The Video FX dialog can also be accessed by right-clicking the event on the Timeline or by pressing the Video FX button found on each nonaudio event.

1.75 Select the effect requiring removal or adjustment.

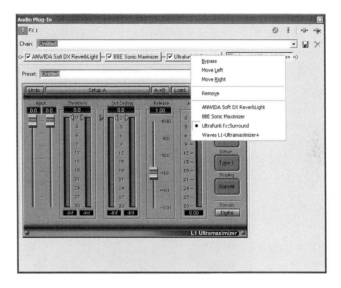

1.76 Right-clicking an event accesses a pop-up menu in which you can open the FX dialogs if the FX button has been removed from the event.

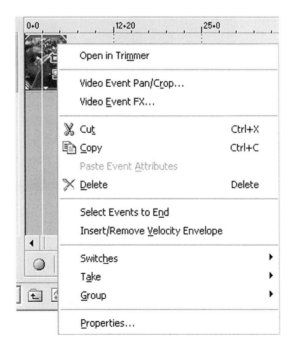

The Pan/Crop tool can be opened by selecting TOOLS | PAN/CROP. This tool is one of the most powerful and oft-used tools found in Vegas, particularly by users of still imagery. Selecting the Pan/Crop option opens a dialog on the Timeline with which the event image can be cropped to meet the screen size or forced to match the aspect ratio of the project settings or with which zooms, pans, and other movements can be applied to otherwise static images. Images facing right or left, up or down, can be reversed in view easily by right-clicking the Pan/Crop tool.

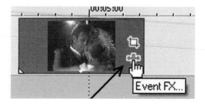

1.77 FX button found by default on all events.

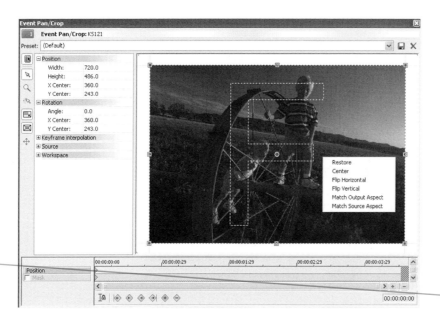

1.78 Open the Pan/Crop dialog either by right-clicking the video event or by selecting the Pan/Crop button.

Right-clicking inside the Pan/Crop tool brings up a secondary dialog. Choosing Restore restores an event image to its prepanned/cropped status. Choosing Center centers the image around the small dot or center indicator found in the middle of the Pan/Crop tool. Moving the dot to another location in a cropped image, right-clicking, and choosing the Center option moves the cropped selection to a point at which the dot will re-center itself.

Choosing the Flip Horizontal option in the Pan/Crop pop-up menu reverses the horizontal image. This option is indicated by the "F" (focus) in the middle of the event image in the Pan/Crop dialog. The "F" is backward if this choice is made.

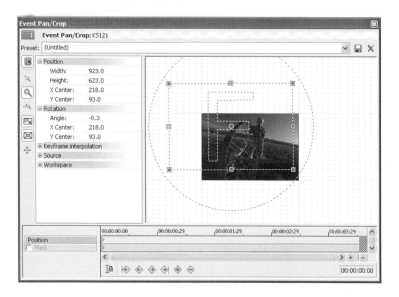

1.79   Before cropping.

1.80   After cropping.

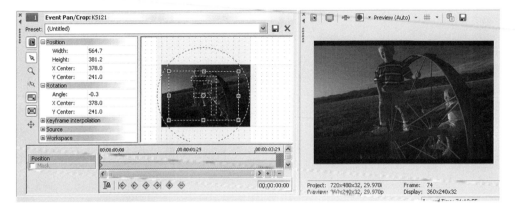

1.81   In Preview window, preview image is reversed horizontally.

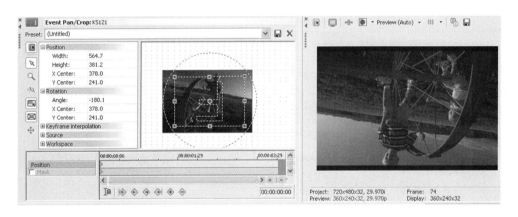

1.82   In Preview window, preview image is reversed vertically.

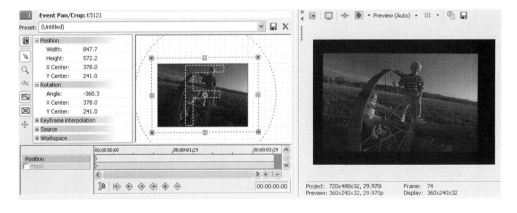

1.83   Image before matched aspect ratio is applied.

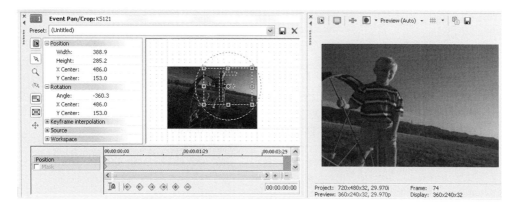

1.84   Image after match aspect ratio is applied.

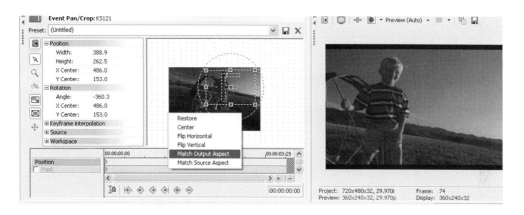

1.85   The source aspect ratio can also be applied to a pan/crop.

Choosing the Flip Vertical option turns the image upside down in the Preview window. In Vegas Pro 8, the vertical display is optimized for vertical signage.

Choosing the Match Output Aspect option assigns the aspect ratio of the project properties to the image, regardless of the original aspect ratio of the event before panning or cropping the image.

The original aspect ratio of the image in Figure 1.83 is 16:9 and does not match the project properties of this project. Choosing Match Output Aspect crops the image to match the 4:3 aspect ratio of the DV-NTSC Project Properties defined in the FILE | PROJECT PROPERTIES dialog.

Choosing the Match Source Aspect option matches the aspect ratio of the source, while maintaining any cropped status applied to the event image.

The Pan/Crop tool can be accessed by right-clicking the media or by choosing the Pan/Crop icon found on each nonaudio event on the Timeline. (See Chapter 9 for more information about the Pan/Crop tool.)

Selecting TOOLS | VIDEO | TRACK FX opens the Video FX dialog box and allows the assignment of FX to an entire track of video on the Timeline, rather than just a video event on the Timeline. This action can also be chosen on the Track Control pane of the desired track.

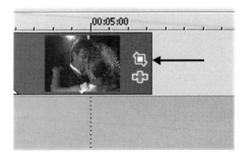

Choosing the Track Motion option in the Video Tools submenu opens the Track Motion dialog box. This dialog box allows users to create picture-in-picture imagery, motion of multiple layers of video, divided video screens, moving titles, and other motion imagery. This feature is another of Vegas's most powerful and oft-used tools for the creation of composited media, in-depth motion, and other creative motion.

1.86   The Pan/Crop button is found on all video/graphic events.

This tool is used to create the popular *Brady Bunch* screen format with multiple motion images applied to grids on a screen. A *Brady Bunch-like* VEG file is included on the DVD accompanying this book.

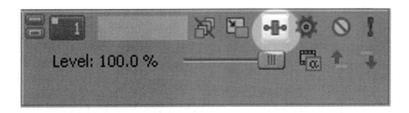

1.87   The Track FX button is found on all Track Control panes. If this button is not shown, drag the Track Control pane to the right into the Timeline. The button will become visible.

1.88   The Track Motion button is found on all video Track Control panes. If this button is not shown, drag the Track Control pane to the right into the Timeline. The button will become visible.

Tip

Try using Pan/Crop to create overlays and picture-in-picture rather than Track Motion, as the image may be cleaner. Rather than cropping inward on an image, pull the crop indicators outward so they are larger than the image.

1.89 Selecting TOOLS | VIDEO also opens the Video Tools submenu.

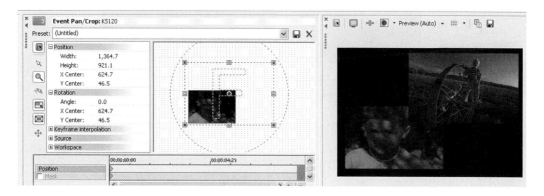

1.90 Track Motion is a fast way to split screens, build multiple video views, or move a picture-in-picture.

Two layers of video are placed in the Preview window with the Track Motion tool. By moving event images to grid points, exactly one-quarter of the screen can be filled with a video image. Shadows or glows can be applied to the event image. The Track Motion tool affects all media on the track to which it is applied. Motion can be keyframed for motion/movement. Shadows and glows can also be keyframed. (See Chapter 9 for more information on keyframing.)

Right-clicking in the Track Motion dialog opens several menus. Selecting Restore restores the Track Motion settings to a null position, removing any track motion applied, and thus restoring any event image to its original settings.

Choosing the Center option centers event imaging on the dot found in the middle of the Track Motion dialog with the same behavior as the Pan/Crop dialog. Moving the dot to the point that is desired as the center focus and then choosing the Center option moves the Track Motion box, too, so that it is centered over the dot.

Choosing the Flip Horizontal option reverses the horizontal image. This option is indicated by the "F" in the middle of the event image in the Track Motion dialog. The "F" is shown backward if this choice is made.

Choosing the Flip Vertical option turns an image upside down in the Preview window.

This option is indicated in the Track Motion window by the direction of the "F" shown in the window.

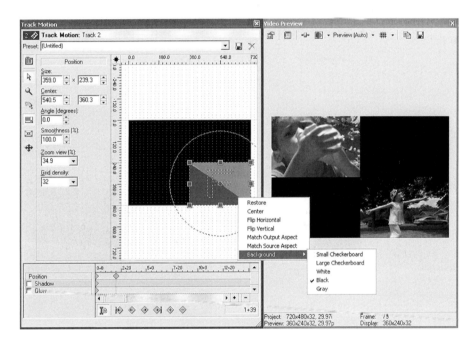

1.91   Right-clicking the Track Motion dialog opens several pop-up menus.

Choosing the Match Output Aspect option assigns the aspect ratio of the project properties to the image, regardless of the original aspect ratio of the event image.

Choosing the Match Source Aspect option matches the aspect ratio of the source while maintaining any cropped or reduced-size status applied to the event image.

Selecting TOOLS | VIDEO OUTPUT FX applies effects to the entire project. This step is the final one in the event/track/project opportunity to apply effects to the video imagery. Regardless of how many effects are placed on an event or track, applying effects at the project level causes effects to be applied over the top of existing effects. Effects can also be applied at the project level by dragging an effect to the Preview window or by clicking the Video Output FX button in the Preview window.

1.92 FX can be applied at the project level, affecting all media in the project.

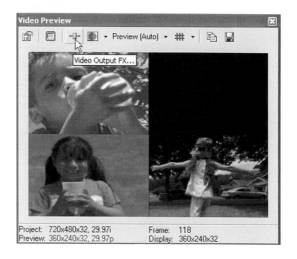

The Render to New Track option (Ctrl+M) in the Tools menu is a valuable feature in Vegas. This feature allows edited media, regardless of the number of tracks, to be rendered to a new file that is placed on a new track at the top of the Timeline. Because the media is rendered, it plays back at full frame rate, full resolution, at all times until it is filtered, is edited, or has new media placed above it. This feature is useful when large composites are made and playback is slow, yet the events are finished in the editing process and the user doesn't want to have it consistently slowing down the rest of the project. At the same time, if edits made to the composited or filtered

1.93 View streaming media or other media formats in their related players, complete with metadata.

media beneath the new track might be needed in the future, the events are still in place beneath the newly rendered track, making it accessible at all times.

The Preview in Player option in the Tools menu is a necessary tool for streaming media authors. This feature allows authors to preview selectable sections on the Timeline in a Windows Media player, a REAL Media player, or a QuickTime player complete with metadata embedded in the media stream. Files can be previewed at any speed, using templates or custom settings. In the past, authors of streaming media needed to render out entire files and, if dissatisfied with file quality, reencode the file. Sony set the pace with this tool in their 2.0 version of Vegas, and the encode quality has only gotten better with time. This feature saves enormous amounts of time and effort as encoders can see exactly how the stream will appear in a player from any place in the Timeline.

 Tip

You can bypass all video effects in the Preview window.

1.94   Prerendered video.

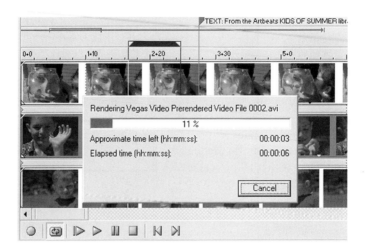

The Preview in Player tool isn't limited to streaming media. AVI, MPEG, MPS, Ogg Vorbis, and other file formats can be previewed in any of the major players complete with any applicable embedded metadata. Synchronized multimedia integration language (SMIL) embedded in REAL Media is viewable in the REAL player, along with URL flips, text information, or other call-outs.

The Selectively Prerender Video option (Shift+M) in the Tools menu is used to prerender video sections so that the user can see exactly what the rendered video will look like. When a section of video is prerendered, a new temp file is written to the hard drive/folder specified in the FILE | PROJECT PROPERTIES dialog. This drive should be the second hard drive on the system for maximum efficiency.

After a file has been prerendered, a small blue bar is displayed above the Timeline, indicating that the time section covered by the bar has a temporary prerendered file associated with it.

After an event time selection has been prerendered, moving, editing, removing, or any other edit applied to that time section invalidates the temporary file/prerender, as the temp file is no longer accurate as to what is contained in the time/event selection.

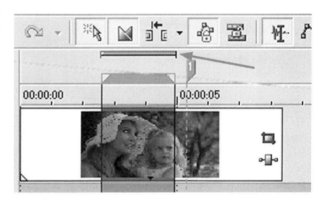

1.95   Prerendered section.

Be sure prerendered video is going to the folder you specified in Project Properties. Otherwise temp files will be written to the default `C:\Program Files\Sony\ Vegas Pro 8\`, and your boot drive will rapidly become filled with temp files that aren't readily apparent. This issue significantly affects performance in a generally undesirable manner, slowing down the entire application and system.

This tip is a great shortcut to program on a Contour ShuttlePro or other hardware device, as it is typically used fairly often.

Selecting the Clean Up Prerendered Video option presents a dialog box asking which prerendered files should be cleaned up or deleted.

The default of "Delete inactive prerendered video files" is the most often required choice, but in the event that all prerendered files should be deleted or if a section has been prerendered several times, it might be best to clean up files related to a specific time selection only. After files are cleaned up/deleted, they cannot be recalled.

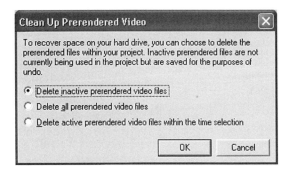

1.96   Remove unused prerenders with the Clean Up Prerendered Video dialog.

The Build Dynamic RAM Preview option (Shift+B) in the Tools menu works much the same as Selectively Prerender Video, except that it does not write a temp file to a hard drive. Instead, it uses available RAM for the temp file. This render is faster and is deleted as soon as another prerender is called on or when an event is moved or edited. The amount of RAM available for a prerender is specified in the OPTIONS | PREFERENCES | VIDEO dialog. Approximately 60 percent of RAM installed in the machine can be made available for Vegas to prerender files with. The entire RAM space cannot be used, as the operating system, applications, and services require a minimal amount. This issue is why Vegas does not show all the RAM installed in the machine as available.

1.97   Print-to-tape presents faster options for placing media on a DV tape. This option renders only the modified sections of a project, preparing them to be printed to DV or analog tape faster than completing an entire render.

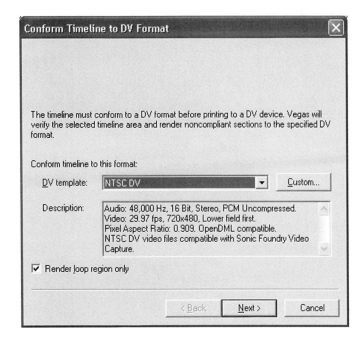

The Print Video to DV Tape option is just as it implies. This option prints the project on the Timeline to videotape without rendering the entire project as a new AVI. When Print Video to DV Tape is selected, Vegas renders all edited portions of the file to a temporary prerendered track. It can give a warning that over 80 percent of the Timeline needs to be rendered. This issue is expected in longer or more intense projects with lots of filters, edits, transitions, or color correction.

The dialog box asks for preferred black leader and tail at the end of the print-to-tape. A minimum of 3 seconds of black at the beginning and end of the print are recommended to compensate for any camera compatibility issues. It also provides an option to print an SMPTE color bar pattern and test tone at the head of the file and provides options for length of color bar and test tones. Forty seconds or more of color bar and test tone are considered standard. Check with your replicator or broadcaster for their requirements.

Selecting the Lay Out Audio CD from Events option instructs Vegas to look at audio events on the Timeline, insert index markers, and create necessary information to burn a successful audio CD. Make sure audio events are not touching on the Timeline, or Vegas will see the touching events as a single event.

Vegas autoinserts 2 seconds at the head of the audio and 2-second index spaces to create a Redbook-compliant CD master. This issue applies only to DAO.

Selecting the Burn CD option opens a submenu that lays out either audio or video CDs for burning, displaying the following options:

- Track at Once Audio CD—burns one song at a time to an audio disc.
- Disc at Once Audio CD—burns an entire project at a time, including index markers. This option is the Redbook standard.
- Video CD—burns an MPEG-1 video CD. MPEG-1 is the VCD standard.
- Multimedia CD—burns an MPEG, REAL, WMV, QuickTime, or other multimedia form of CD. MPEG-1 files are not compliant with the DVD specification and therefore won't play on a set-top player.

Both of the video formats can be burned from a template, existing file, or Timeline-based file. Files not previously rendered require rendering before burning to disc, so Vegas prompts you through the required steps.

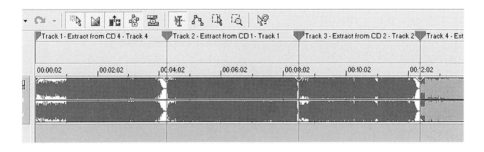

1.98   Vegas can automatically lay out a CD for burning. Using scripts can make this even faster. See the related scripts in the Tools Scripting menu.

Selecting the Clean Project Media option removes from the Project Media media references that are not active on the Timeline. This step should be done before saving a project with media. If files have been placed on the Timeline, they do not appear in the Project Media whether they were kept on the Timeline or not.

The Run Script option is a feature in Vegas that allows users to write custom macro scripts for batch processing events in nearly any **way** that a user can imagine or require. Need a script that tells Vegas to render an AVI; use the **AVI** as a master to render a QuickTime, Windows Media Video, and REAL file; beep twice; and then render an MPEG-2 file with AC-3 audio? The Run Script option can make this happen if the scripting code is written correctly. An example of a script in Vegas looks like the following listing:

```
**
* This script will remove all effects of a particular type from items
* in the project's Project Media.
*
* Revision Date: Jan. 30, 2005
**/
import System.Windows.Forms;
import Sony.Vegas;

// This is the full name of the plug-in associated with the effects
// you want to remove.
var plugInName = "Sony Timecode";

try {
    var mediaEnum = new Enumerator(Vegas.Project.MediaPool);
    while (!mediaEnum.atEnd()) {
        var media = mediaEnum.item();
        var effectsEnum = new Enumerator(media.Effects);
        while (!effectsEnum.atEnd()) {
            var effect = effectsEnum.item();
            if (plugInName == effect.PlugIn.Name) {
                media.Effects.Remove(effect);
            }
            effectsEnum.moveNext();
        }
        mediaEnum.moveNext();
    }
} catch (e) {
    MessageBox.Show(e);
}
```

Custom scripts are found on the disc included with this book.

A button can be created on the toolbar making scripts immediately accessible. To insert a button, select TOOLS | SCRIPTS and locate the script for assignment to a button. Assign the script to one of the 10 script location points.

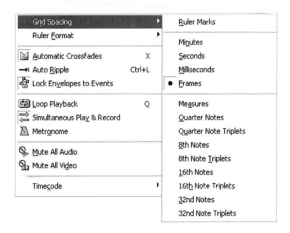

1.99, 1.100   Assign a script to a shortcut (1.99), which can be assigned to a button on the toolbar (1.100).

👉 *Tip*_____

Scripting can save hundreds if not thousands of keystrokes. Experiment with the scripting tools found on the disk in this book, and you'll quickly see how time-saving scripting tools can be.

Using the Customize toolbar dialog, assign a key shortcut to a button on the toolbar. The script is now a one-button operation. Up to 10 scripts can be loaded on the Timeline at one moment.

1.101   Loading scripts to a toolbar button makes running scripts fast and easy.

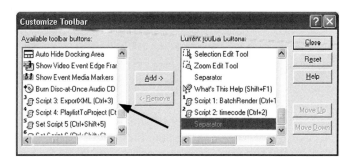

Ultimate S 3.0 is a scripting interface that may be purchased from VASST.com and VideoGuys. Ultimate S 3.0 enables as many as 200+ scripts to be accessed from the toolbar, including multicamera switching, automated lower thirds, audit tools, and other important functions. A trial version is found on the disk in the back of this book.

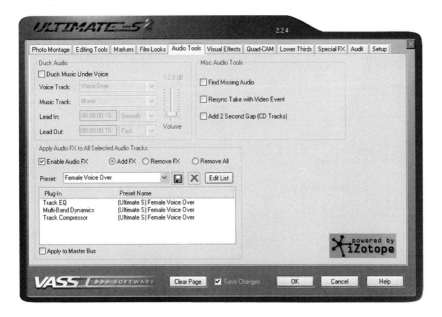

1.102   Ultimate S is a scripting tool that can enable real-time multicamera editing, create photo montages of up to 9999 images complete with motion and matched to music beats, project setup, media management, compositing tools, automated lower thirds, and much, much more. Scripting tools such as this are made for broadcast and event editors and not only will they save you time, but you'll likely find them inspirational as well.

Options Menu

This series of menus is predominantly for setting behaviors and functions of Vegas to specific needs. Many are videocentric, but others are not.

The Quantize to Frames option generally should be checked for most video editing situations; it should be unchecked if Vegas is being used as an audio-only tool. This option forces video in an event to snap to a frame boundary, preventing a trim from occurring in the middle of a frame, regardless of the grid or time settings. Pressing Alt+F8 turns the Quantize to Frames action on or off.

Selecting the Enable Snapping option causes events to line up or snap to grid markers, other events, cursor positions, or inserted markers. This feature is useful when a user wants to ensure that timing is correct in the recording studio environment, that no frames are missed in the video editing environment, and that timing is accurate in placing events on the Timeline. Snapping can be enabled via the menu or by pressing F8 to turn this feature on or off. Turning Snapping off allows media to be slid around in time if necessary. Snapping is typically left on, except in instances in which sound effects or video events should not fall on a marker, grid line, or inaccurate cursor placement.

The Snap to Grid (Ctrl+F8) and Snap to Markers (Shift+F8) choices are dependent on whether Enable Snapping (F8) is on or off. If snapping is turned on and either of these selections is enabled, events will snap to the marker or grid line to which they are dragged the closest. If no grid line or marker is present, an event will snap to the event closest to its release point when dropped or moved on the Timeline.

1.103 Notice the events snapped to frame-level grid lines.

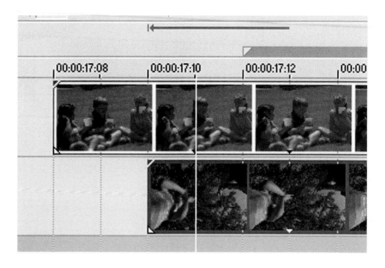

Snapping can be enabled to music tempo, video frames at selectable frame rates, or absolute times.

1.104 Assign grid spacing to personal preference or to a house standard.

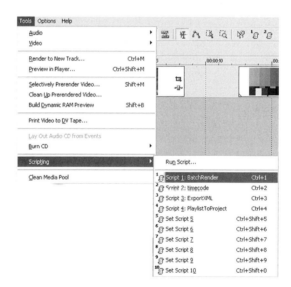

Grid Spacing options allow for a variety of gridlines to be selected, which is dependent on the user's working methods. This selection controls how tightly or closely spaced gridlines are placed on the Timeline.

Recording studios or musicians might want to use musically based timings, such as tempos and beats, to lay out a grid. Video editors might desire the grid to be frame-based at whatever frame rate they can be editing at, such as 25fps for PAL or 29.97 drop-frame for NTSC DV. Musical grids can be laid out as tightly as 32nd note triplets, whereas video grids can be laid out as tightly as single frames. Grid layouts are very important if you intend on using ACID loops in Vegas, as they'll assist in lining up audio files on the Timeline.

1.105 Set rulers for the manner in which the grid is viewed for snapping, alignment, or time selection.

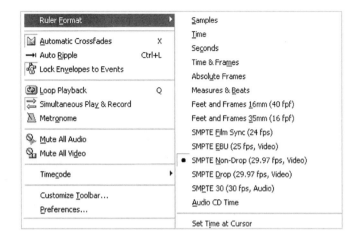

Different from the Grid Spacing options, the Ruler Format options determine how grids are laid out. If different forms of ruler formats are chosen from the selection of grid spacing, such as choosing a frame-based ruler while a beat-mapped grid is selected, the grid lines disappear from the Timeline. Vegas cannot make a distinction between incompatible ruler and grid formats, leaving it to the user to define these settings. Studios recording music to picture will probably want to use the more common beat maps but can switch back and forth between grid forms, helping calculate tempo to time for musical cues.

The Automatic Crossfades option, selectable by menu or the X key, defaults to on. When two events cross over each other, Vegas creates a cross-fade, indicated by an "X" in the middle of the space in which they are crossed.

Automatic cross-fades are generally left on. Events crossed over each other with automatic cross-fades that are turned off become hard cuts.

Auto Ripple (Ctrl+L) is a powerful feature found in Vegas. This feature allows the trimming of an event edge. Subsequent events snap into place to fill the hole left by the trim, or if the event is pulled longer, Vegas automoves all events down the Timeline for the same duration as the pulled event's time addition. If media is pasted in place and Auto Ripple is turned on, Vegas moves all subsequent events down the Timeline to accommodate the inserted event. By the same behavior, if an event is deleted, Auto Ripple slides all events forward in time to fill the space left by the deleted media, ensuring that

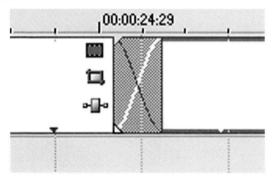

1.106 Cross-fades are indicated by the "X" between events.

whatever amount of time is added or deleted, it ripples in or out events following the changes.

This new feature also exhibits other behaviors, in that it can be track-dependent or project-dependent. Further, events can be shuffled on the Timeline, with all events moving with the shuffled events.

👉*Tip*_____

Be aware that if inserting media underneath existing events with Auto Ripple enabled, all events are shifted in time for the length of the media event insert. If video events are on the Timeline, disable Auto Ripple before inserting media. Press Ctrl+L to enable/disable Auto Ripple.

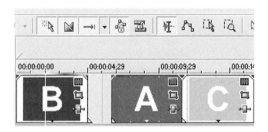

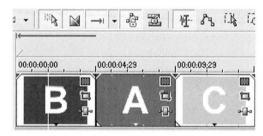

1.107   Layout of media before a ripple is executed.   1.108   Layout of media after a ripple is executed.

Notice that when "A" is moved down the Timeline with Auto Ripple turned on, "C" stays snapped to "A" and moves down the Timeline for the same duration as "A" was moved down the Timeline.

Selecting the Lock Envelopes to Event option causes volume controls, panning envelopes, bus envelopes, compositing envelopes, and velocity envelopes to move on the Timeline with their corresponding events. If 80 audio events are on the Timeline with 200 envelope changes and any one of the events is moved, if this feature is disabled the audio fades will be incorrectly timed.

The Loop tool is another one of Vegas's most-used tools and can be accessed through the menu or pressing Q. This feature allows users to draw a selection on the Marker bar and have the cursor loop over that selection over and over, while edits are being performed. Using this tool is an excellent way to tweak transitions, color correction, panning, track motion, and other edit effects and tools, while seeing the events change in realtime on either the internal or the external monitor.

👉*Tip*_____

Use the Loop tool during editing of critical spaces while watching video on the computer monitor rather than the external monitor. As Vegas loops through the selection, it draws a RAM render automatically, increasing the resolution and frame rate as it loops. Let a section loop while having a cup of coffee or on a phone call, and within a few short moments, the entire section will be playing smoothly and clearly. Be sure to have enough RAM specified in the OPTIONS | PREFERENCES | VIDEO dialog.

The Simultaneous Play & Record option, if enabled, allows audio to be recorded at the same time as audio is being monitored. This feature is critical for a recording studio. The majority of sound cards are full-duplex, which means that they allow audio to pass in both directions at the same time. Most laptop sound cards are half-duplex, not allowing audio to be bidirectional. In this case, the feature requires disabling to avoid error messages. If a laptop is used for monitoring and recording, an external sound card/device is usually required via FireWire, USB, or CardBus.

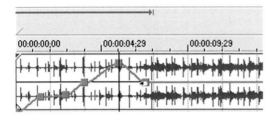

1.109   Original envelope.

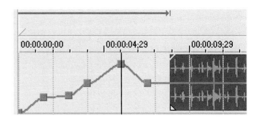

1.110   An event that is not locked to envelopes moves without affecting the position of volume/pan/FX.

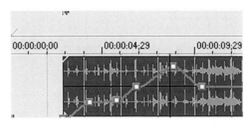

1.111   A locked envelope moves all markers; volume/pan/FX changes with it.

The Metronome feature is an audio metronome that can count time at the tempo and beat settings specified in the FILE | PROPERTIES | AUDIO dialog. This tool is handy for both musicians and video editors. The metronome is not recorded to hard disk if used during the recording process.

The Mute All Audio option is exactly as its name implies. All audio on the Timeline is muted/silenced. Deselect this feature or select a track directly to unmute the audio.

Selecting the Mute All Video option has the same effect, with the exception that it causes all video tracks on the Timeline to go dark. Individual tracks can be unmuted and viewed, or deselect this option to bring video back to the screen.

Selecting the Timecode option calls up a submenu asking what and where timecode is to be read/generated.

Timecode can be generated for MIDI devices. MIDI timecode (MTC) is read by nearly all software applications and many hardware tools. MTC is used for synchronizing software applications together or synchronizing hardware and software together.

Vegas generates MTC each time playback is started.

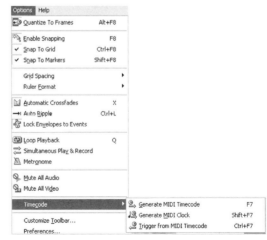

1.112   Select timecode options to fit hardware or house requirements.

Vegas also has the ability to generate a MIDI clock. The MIDI clock feature is different from MTC in that it also contains song pointer position and carries tempo information as well. Musicians will want to use this feature, as it allows Vegas to carry increasing or decreasing tempos and the slaved application or hardware will then increase or decrease in tempo according to the tempo map laid out in Vegas.

Tip

Registered users of Vegas can access Sony's web site and download the virtual MIDI router (VMR) utility at no cost or get it from the Vegas installation disk. The VMR utility allows Vegas to drive other timecode-capable applications such as ACID or trigger Sound Forge. This option is great for syncing a music bed that isn't completed in ACID to the Vegas video Timeline.

Vegas can also be started and stopped via the Triggering option from timecode. An external device that generates timecode, or that feeds a generating device that can accept SMPTE timecode and convert it to MTC, can be a master device, and Vegas can be its slave.

Vegas users can customize the toolbar to suit their specific needs and desires for Vegas's appearance. Video editors might wish to hide audio-only tools, just as audio-only studios might desire to hide the video tools found on the toolbar in Vegas. In any event, Vegas can be set up to look and feel the way any user chooses.

The OPTIONS | PREFERENCES dialog is the primary place in which the look and feel of Vegas can be set to individual preference.

1.113 Adding a custom tool to the toolbar is the same for all tools as shown in the Scripting section.

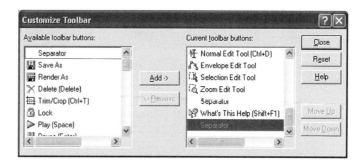

Select preferences that suit your workflow. Experiment with settings that work best for you. Each tab has several options relating to General, Video, Audio, CD, Editing, Sync, and Video Device and a tab for Audio Hardware.

Tip

Make sure that volume and pan envelopes are of greatly differing colors if the default colors are not used, so that they can be differentiated at a glance when mixing in Vegas. Applying color schemes that are similar in style, such as making all EQ gain envelopes varying colors of green, bandwidth envelopes varying colors of blue, and so on, helps in rapidly assessing a mix and determining what envelopes are performing various functions.

1.114 Set Vegas to feel the way you'd like it to feel in the Preferences dialog box.

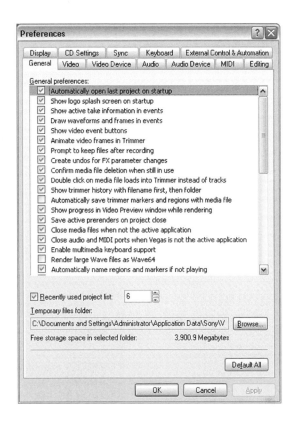

Preferences in Vegas were expanded significantly starting with version 5, including options for key mapping, human interface devices, and draggable cursors.

In the Preferences dialogs, you'll want to take note of the External control features, requiring a MIDI card, and the new scrubbable cursor features. We'll look more closely at the External Control preferences in the Mixing section of Chapter 7.

Cursors and Selections

In Vegas versions 2–4, dragging the cursor on the Timeline created a selection. For most users, this was a satisfactory workflow, whereas for others coming from various NLE workspaces, this was confusing. Since Vegas version 5, the interface has allowed the cursor and playhead to be dragged across the Timeline without creating a selection.

To enable cursor dragging on the Timeline:

1. Open the OPTIONS | PREFERENCES dialog box.

2. Check the "Allow edit cursor to be dragged" checkbox at the bottom of the General dialog box.

3. Select Apply and close the Preferences dialog box.

Tip_____

In Vegas Pro 8, not only is creating a selection easier, but also arrows and a time indicator will be displayed, showing the amount of space an event is moved, the time of a cross-fade or fade-in, and the amount of ripple action as well.

This allows the cursor to be dragged about the Timeline without creating a selection. Selections may still be created by clicking twice and dragging. One sure way to know if a selection will be created is to left-click on the cursor. If a double-ended arrow appears beneath the cursor, it's a draggable cursor or playhead. If the double-ended arrow does not appear, it's going to create a selection on the Timeline. This new function may take some getting used to, as it isn't entirely intuitive, like most of Vegas's functions are.

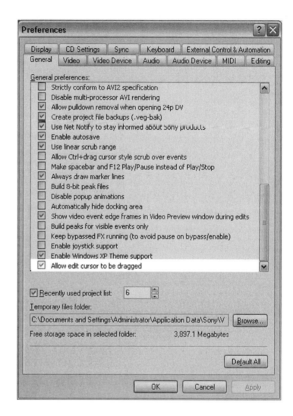

1.115 Select this checkbox if you wish to be able to drag the cursor across the Timeline without creating a selection. Leave it unchecked if you are satisfied with the method in which previous versions of Vegas have worked. It is checked by default in Vegas Pro 8.

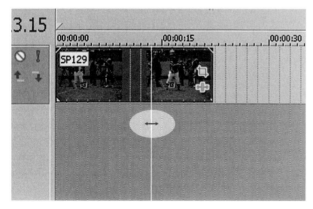

1.116 When you see this indicator, the cursor may be dragged across the Timeline without creating a selection.

Say You'll Be MINE!

One of the power tools of Vegas is to allow users as much customization as possible with the application. Layouts, appearances, key commands, and docking are just a few of the user-defined settings that may be customized by users. In the general Preferences, click on the Keyboard tab. This dialog allows you to input a series of keystrokes, and on the right side of the tab, you can choose what actions you'd like that specific series of custom keystrokes to take. This feature will be reset if Vegas is restored to factory settings; it's a good practice to archive/save these keystrokes to a thumbdrive or other location.

XP Themes in Vegas

For some users, the default colors of the Vegas Pro 8 interface aren't comfortable or inspiring. Vegas allows for themes chosen in the XP Themes dialog to determine how Vegas appears. This allows users to create their own appearances for Vegas, best suited to their editing environment.

To modify an XP theme, open the Control Panel and select Display from the options. In the Display dialog you will find a Themes tab. In this tab are dropdown menus that will allow you to select prebuilt themes for XP or view online themes that you can download. Generally, most editors prefer darker themes that are easier on the eyes in dimly lit editing rooms. A web site at http://www.themedoctor.com has a number of downloadable themes to create custom appearances for XP that will also affect how Vegas appears. You can also obtain more themes by purchasing Microsoft's Microsoft Plus add-on for Windows XP.

To have Vegas accept custom themes for Windows XP, you'll need to go to OPTIONS| PREFERENCES, and tick the checkbox for Enable Windows XP Theme Support. Without this box ticked, Vegas will use its default colors.

The icons will not change appearance with different themes applied to Vegas, only the colors, backgrounds, display, and header fonts will change in appearance. Keep in mind that changing themes will often affect how some applications may appear, so choose your themes carefully if your editing system is also used for email or other common functions. Themes may be stored/saved and recalled for specific tasks when needed. To create a theme in Windows, right-click the desktop and choose Properties, and then select the Appearance tab. Choose Advanced, and use the dropdown menu choices to select your system's appearance settings. Save a theme after creating your custom settings by clicking the Themes tab at the far left of the Display Properties dialog, naming the Theme, and choosing Save As. This will store your theme in the Documents folder unless you choose a new location in which the theme should be stored.

1.117 The Windows display properties may be accessed from the Control Panel or by right-clicking the desktop.

1.118 Save the theme, close Vegas, and restart Vegas to see the new appearance.

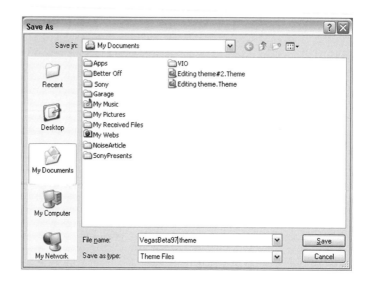

Key Features!

Vegas also provides custom keyboard mapping.

This feature allows users to create their own custom keyboard shortcuts to increase efficiency in editing.

One of the hints that you are a Vegas power user is how much you use a keyboard instead of a mouse. You'll nearly always be faster with a keyboard than a mouse, given the fewer number of hand movements. This is true with nearly any application, because both hands remain on the keyboard most of the time.

To unlock the power of Vegas Pro 8's customizable keyboard commands, open the OPTIONS | CUSTOMIZE KEYBOARD dialog.

When the dialog opens, the full list of available keyboard shortcuts is displayed as well as the key combinations assigned to them. These may be changed to fit your particular needs.

To change a shortcut or to create a new one, select the specific command by either typing keywords in the search bar or clicking on a family of commands and drilling down to the specific one.

Place the cursor in the "Shortcut keys:" box. If there is another command in the box, press the Shift, Ctrl, or Alt key and

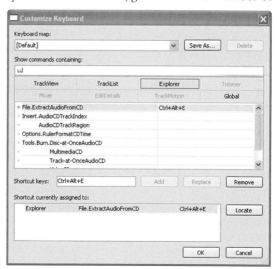

1.119a Vegas allows for customized keyboard shortcuts. In this instance, Ctrl+Alt+E have been assigned to rip music from a CD.

1.119b   In this example, Alt+G has been assigned to open the Render As dialog.

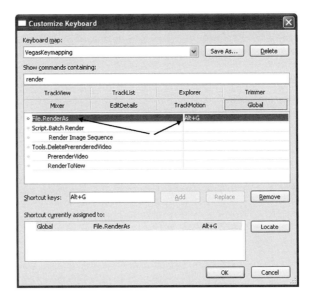

1.120   The "Shortcut currently assigned to:" box will display any shared key commands as your only warning that you are about to change an existing keyboard command.

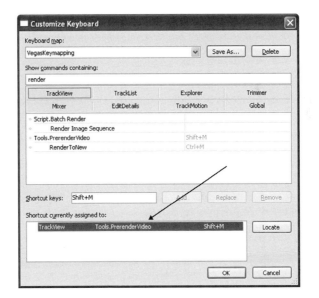

release the key. This will clear the box. Now press and hold the Shift, Ctrl, or Alt key while pressing a companion key desired for the shortcut. This will set the shortcut in the dialog box and display it alongside the command it has been assigned to run.

If a command does not appear in the available command window, then the option of assigning a keyboard shortcut is not available.

If a newly created shortcut is sharing a command with an existing shortcut, the "Shortcut currently assigned to:" box will indicate the shared command(s).

For those who operate Vegas on multiple computers, such as a desktop and laptop system, and who would like to share the key commands without having to take the time required to set up the second computer, Vegas allows a .ini file to be used to export the customized keyboard settings.

Click the Save As button in the Keyboard dialog, and an export dialog box opens. Create a name for the .ini file, and save the file to your local machine. The file is located in C:\Documents and Settings\<username>\Application Data\Sony\Vegas Pro\8.0 for XP users and C:\Users.\ <username>\AppData\Roaming\Sony\Vegas Pro\8.0 for Windows Vista users.

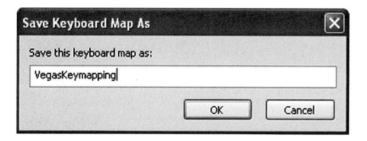

1.121   Key commands may be exported to another computer, saving time and
         matching the workflow of a desktop machine to a laptop or other computer
         on the network.

To import a customized key command set, copy the .ini file saved in the previous section to the appropriate location on the target PC. The custom key command set will be installed as part of Vegas on the second machine and will be available the next time Vegas is started.

Key commands may be returned to default settings by selecting Options and then selecting the Default All button in the OPTIONS | CUSTOMIZE KEYBOARD dialog. You can either delete any key map sets you do not want to keep, or simply choose [Default] in the Keyboard map dropdown at the top of the dialog. Keep in mind that selecting the Delete button will wipe out all customized key commands in that set, and if they have not been saved to another location, any commands you've created will be gone.

Color My World

In Display Preferences for Vegas, you'll find a dialog that allows the color of track headers, saturation of icon colors, bus or FX envelopes, and icon color tinting, further offering a custom look for your particular Vegas style. In the General Preferences dialog, check the tickbox for Windows Theme support, and any theme you create for Windows XP will then be part of the Vegas color scheme. This is the means by which you can create a dark, smoked look for Vegas should you like that sort of appearance.

Capturing Video

Getting Media from the Camera to the Hard Drive

The concept of "capture" in digital video is a nomenclature predominantly leftover from days gone by. "Capture" or "digitizing" is actually done at the camera when dealing with digital formats such as DV, HDV, XDCAM, and advanced video codec–high definition (AVCHD). Transferring media from the camcorder to the computer is really just a data transfer. Nothing is done to the media as it's being transferred from one digital storage device to another. Compression has already occurred in the camcorder/recording device stage, whereas in the old days with analog video, the camera captured uncompressed images and the capture card would compress the video into a data stream that the computer could manage.

Vegas automatically senses the frame rate, image size, and any other information that might be part of the DV stream. No special settings are required for capturing video from a FireWire-equipped camera via an OHCI card. Whether the media is PAL, NTSC, 24p, 16:9 anamorphic, or another supported format, it is captured, or transferred, from the camera with those attributes recognized.

DV, HDV, and XDCAM all use the FireWire standard for transferring video data. AVCHD and some consumer camcorders use USB2 as a transfer protocol.

Manually Capturing DV

Connect the camera to the FireWire card installed in the back of the computer. Open Vegas and select FILE | CAPTURE VIDEO, which opens the Vegas Video Capture utility. The capture utility may also be opened from the Project Media by clicking the Capture Video button.

In some systems, the camera is not autodetected. If this happens to you, go to CONTROL PANEL | SYSTEM | HARDWARE and look for the 1394 Bus Host controllers

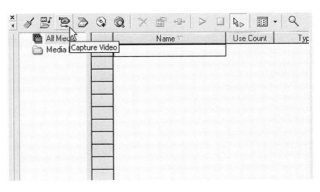

2.1   Opening the Video Capture utility.

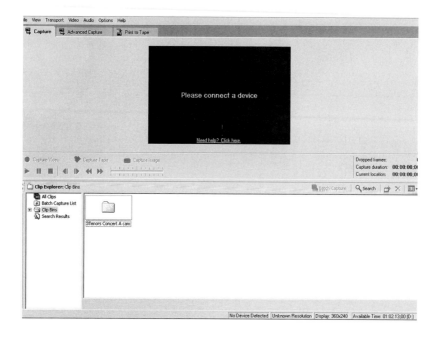

2.2   First capture window when the utility opens.

device line. Double-click the line, and the properties of the bus will open, showing the installed drivers. In some instances, a Microsoft driver and another driver, such as a TI, Lucent, or VIA driver, will be present. Right-click any driver that is not a Microsoft driver and uninstall it. Repeat for all non-Microsoft drivers.

Some 1394 cards are installed as network cards, which can cause conflicts with the camera and bus operations. If this becomes an issue, open the network adapter hardware and disable the 1394 NIC/Network card. This process should not affect other networking tasks or abilities.

When Video Capture launches, select OPTIONS | PREFERENCES. Select the Disk Management tab. The default capture location for captured files is `C:\Documents and Settings\username\My Documents\`.

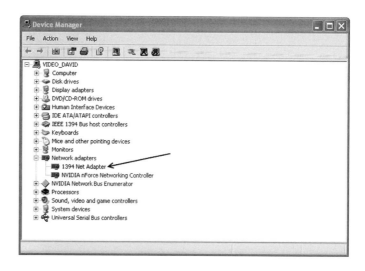

2.3   Open the HARDWARE | DEVICE MANAGER tab to adjust 1394 and Network properties.

If the camera is turned off, Video Capture will prompt you to turn it on. When the camera is turned on, Windows will automatically open screens asking what it should do with the camera.

Cancel the Windows screens, as Video Capture is already open. If you select anything else, it may override the Video Capture drivers, and then you'll need to start again by shutting down the newly launched application and recycling the camera power.

You may want to place the capture tool icon on the main Vegas toolbar if you need to regularly access Capture. This is accomplished via the Customize Toolbar function.

If a capture drive has not been specified, Video Capture will ask for a drive to be specified. Unless absolutely necessary, never capture media to the same hard drive as the operating system. Specify a hard drive and specify a disk overflow size that is at least 3 percent less than the overall drive size. This option will allow room for defragging drives and will prevent a drive from filling to total capacity, possibly rendering the drive incapable of being recovered in the event of a drive or system crash. Default overflow is 360 MB. Larger drives can require a slightly larger overflow, such as 500 MB.

Video Capture will prompt for a tape name with the Verify Tape Name dialog. This step is the first in proficient media asset management or digital asset management.

Enter the name of the tape you wish to capture. This tape name will be appended to filenames as they are captured, so be sure it's correct. You will have one more opportunity to correct this easily later on. This process is known as logging.

2.4   Windows automatically senses most DV cameras.

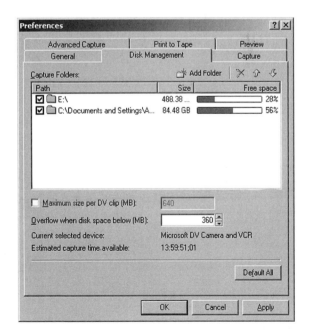

2.5   Specify capture drive. Notice that Vegas indicates capture time available based on free drive space.

Tip_____

Enter the name of the tape exactly as it's written on the tape spine in the event that you want go back and recapture the media. This process avoids errors in logging and locating tape.

The Verify Tape Name dialog also provides the following choices:

- Don't capture any clips right now.

- Start capturing all clips from the current tape position.

- Start capturing all clips from the beginning of the tape.

For the moment, select "Don't capture any clips right now" and click OK. Video Capture is now ready to capture video. Clicking the Play button or pressing the spacebar causes the camera to begin playing.

Video is not captured until you click the Capture Video button or press Ctrl+R.

2.6   Be sure to log the tapes correctly at capture to ensure quick location of clips during editing.

Video Capture can capture video from the camera/tape in several ways, including:

- Manual capture by starting and stopping (labor/time intensive)

- Capture from a specific location and detect or not detect scenes, starting and stopping with the control (user's preference, can be labor/time intensive)

- Capture entire tape with scene detection (little effort)

- Batch capture logged clips (fair amount of effort to log clips; time saving/disk space saving in end view)

Tip_____

For a rapid-start capture:

1. Connect camera to OHCI card.

2. Turn camera on.

3. Launch Video Capture.

4. Choose Capture Entire Tape.

Scene Detection is a feature in which Video Capture sees breaks in the date and time stamps created when the camera is started and stopped during the recording process. Each time the camera is stopped, Video Capture sees the change in the date and time stamp and starts a new file. So if you've started and stopped the camera 10 times while videotaping at an event and then connected the camera to the computer and opened Video Capture, Video Capture creates 10 files in the Project Media when it is activated. (Files are stored in the folder/drive specified in Disk Management. Project Media creates a pointer to that file; files are not actually stored in Project Media.)

☞ Tip_____

When using DV tape, be certain that the timecode isn't broken on the tape. Broken timecode often happens when reusing old videotape or when cameras aren't allowed to run for a moment following shooting. This problem also occurs when tape is viewed in the field and allowed to play past the end of timecode. Avoid this problem by:

1. Always recording blank time completely over previously used videotape by recording with the lens cap on for the length of the tape;

2. Allowing 5–10 seconds of tape to roll by when recording in the field, if you know you will be reviewing tape in the field;

3. Using Last Scene Preview, on many camcorders available today.

Video Capture is capable of batch capturing an entire tape while left unattended. Click the Capture Entire Tape button. Video Capture will rewind the tape to its beginning/top and then start to capture the tape to the folders/drives specified in the Disk Management preferences. If the specified hard drive does not have enough space to store an entire tape, be certain to specify more than one drive. Video Capture will automatically roll files over to the next specified drive.

Begin capturing tape by either pressing Ctrl+R or clicking the Capture button in the capture tool. Video Capture will start capturing from the moment you click the button. If the camera or tape deck is OHCI/1394 standard, the device will start playing and transferring media from the tape to the hard drive. Clicking the Capture Entire Tape button instructs Video Capture to rewind to the beginning of the tape and start recording. Video Capture will autodetect scenes in the tape and create new files for each scene. (Enable Scene Detection is enabled by default in the OPTIONS | PREFERENCES | CAPTURE dialog.)

☞ Tip_____

Hard drives formatted as FAT 32 drives do not allow files larger than 4GB, or about 18 minutes in tape time. Video Capture will automatically find the best point at which to divide files in the event of FAT 32 drives. NTFS drives have a file size limitation of 4TB, which is roughly 330 hours of DV.

In the analog tape world, such as a VHS or Betacam SP, a digital video converter (DVC) is required to convert analog to DV. Several converters are available on the market today, from the very high-end Convergent Design SD to the Canopus ADVC 1394 card. YUV input, composite input, and S-Video input are all common input features, making it fairly simple to find a converter that meets your specifications.

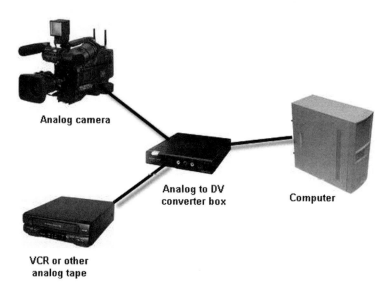

Analog camera

**Analog to DV
converter box**

Computer

**VCR or other
analog tape**

2.7　An analog camera or video deck, such as a VHS or BetaSP machine, uses composite
S-Video or component video output to a DVC, which converts the analog video to digital
video so that the computer can see the video signal as data.

If an analog machine is used with a converter or analog card, the machine must be turned on and Play enabled before capturing video. Scene detection does not take place with analog tape machines passed through a converter. Machine control is not possible with analog machines, with the exception of some high-end converters that read DV control signals and translate them to RS-422 control signals, to which some analog decks will respond. DV control can be disabled in the OPTIONS | PREFERENCES | GENERAL dialog. Typically, leaving DV control enabled does not affect a DV capture but can create some confusion if shifting between DV and non-DV sources.

In the Video Capture OPTIONS | PREFERENCES | CAPTURE tab, set the minimum clip length to 5 or

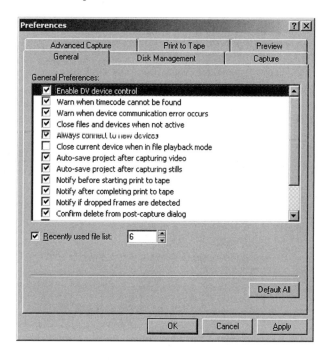

2.8　Disable the DV control when working with non-DV decks or analog
capture cards.

10 seconds. This instructs Video Capture to ignore the OOPS!-type of files, in which a camera was inadvertently started and stopped, leaving small video clips on the tape. Of course, if working with animations or other projects that require short shots, you might wish to leave this set unchecked, which is the default setting.

Animation-type capture is also possible by selecting a maximum capture length of only one or two frames. Experiment with clay models or action figures to get the hang of editing this type of captured media.

When Video Capture has captured the entire tape or when you have manually captured all clips desired from the tape, Video Capture will prompt you to save the capture session. This feature is useful if there is any possibility that you will be going back to the tape to recapture at some future point.

Lost video, accidentally deleted video, and failed hard drives are all reasons to recapture tape, so it is generally good practice to save the capture session.

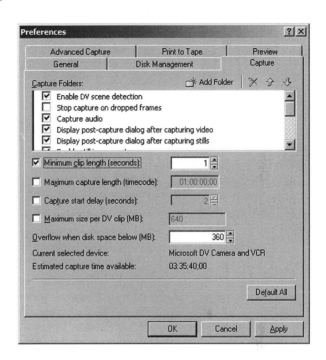

2.9   Setting the minimum clip length.

2.10   The postcapture dialog provides information about clip length, dropped frames (if any), location of media storage, and frame and data rate and checkboxes to place media in the Vegas Project Media. Unchecking the "Show after every video capture session" option will prevent this dialog from popping up after each capture.

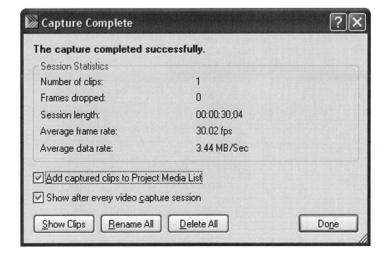

2.11 Store the capture session if any likelihood exists that the same tape will need to be recaptured later or if the session needs to be shared on a network.

After capturing video and closing the Video Capture application, the captured media will appear in the Project Media.

Video Capture has other tools available for logging and capturing in Vegas. Click the Advanced Capture tab. This tab opens a different view of Video Capture. Comments, ratings, length of clip, and in/out information can all be logged and added in this view. Use this feature to keep track of media and how it appears for rapid editing decisions later in the editing process. These comments appear in the Project Media and can assist in making editing choices.

Advanced Capture Tools

The Advanced Capture tab has dialogs that allow for more advanced file management.

Open the Advanced Capture tab at the upper left of the capture utility. Detailed capture logging tools are located on the right side of the capture screen.

2.12 Advanced Capture tools offer efficient capture logging and automated capture tools, saving tremendous time in the editing/ capturing process, in addition to saving disk space.

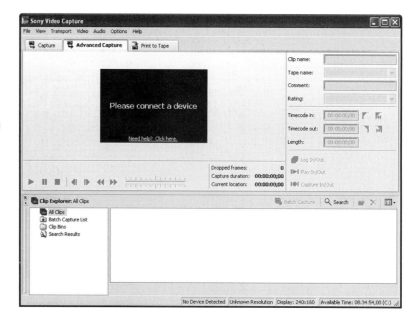

Using Batch Capture

Batch Capture functions only with OHCI devices. To use the Batch Capture tools in Video Capture, click the Advanced Capture tab. Begin playing tape via the control seen on screen. To mark the point on the tape where you want capture to begin, click the Mark In button.

To mark the place on the tape where capture should end, click the Mark Out button. Video Capture will note the in/out times in the windows next to the Mark In/Out icons and will show the clip length in the Clip Length field.

The Mark In/Mark Out dialogs contain two buttons for returning the tape to the in or out point. Selecting the Cue to In (Shift+I) or Cue to Out (Shift+O) buttons will cause the tape deck or camera (T/C) to autolocate to the selected in or out points indicated in the In/Out dialog boxes.

To log the clip, click the Log In/Out button under the Length field. Video Capture creates a note based on the tape deck or camera in/out markers and displays the clip in the current bin in the right pane of the Clip Explorer. Change in/out markers as many times as necessary to mark the clip correctly. The clip is not logged until you click the Log In/Out button. Only the displayed times in the T/C in and T/C out fields are used to mark the clip for batching later on.

Mark as many clips as necessary. Multiple tapes may be logged at once. Be sure that tape names are changed in the logging dialog so that Video Capture knows when to prompt for a new tape to be put in the deck.

As clips are marked for batch capture, an icon of the capture will appear in the list view/bin window.

These icons have a red dot in the center, indicating that they are marked for capture. When all clips are logged, click the Batch Capture button found above the list view/bin window. Clips can be automatically marked for batch capture by selecting the OPTIONS | ADVANCED CAPTURE checkbox.

In this same dialog box, clips can be commented on and rated. Comments assigned to an individual clip can be viewed in the Project Media after the clip is identified

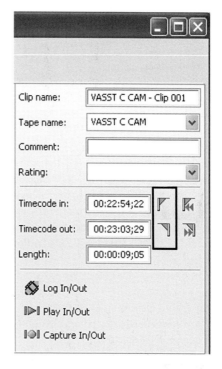

2.13 Use the Mark In (|) and Mark Out (O) buttons to mark timecode points for a batch capture of selective clips

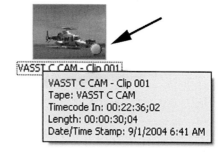

2.14 The red dot on the clip indicates that a clip is marked for batch capture.

in Vegas. The new Project Media search tool allows Vegas to search for keywords based on these comments, so while this feature is convenient, it's fairly indispensable for long-form work in which rapid searches for specific clips are needed. It's also good media management, even if it takes a bit of time to do.

Video can be graded on the quality of shot, helping to assign the priority clips for later identification and location.

The Capture and Advanced Capture dialogs provide the ability to create and use Clip Bins. Each master tape or B roll might have its own bin, and clips can be sorted in any fashion that makes sense to the project editor or producer. Remember how Radar O'Reilly stored the maps to the minefields on *M*A*S*H* under "B" for "BOOM"? Each person has their own method of sorting and storing files. Media bins accommodate this. Right-click the Clip Bins folder, select Create New Bin, and name the bin with the filename information that relates to the part that the clips will play in the project. If the "Add Clips to Media Bin" checkbox is selected in the postcapture dialog, clips are autoadded to the Project Media bins in Vegas, and bins from Video Capture may be dragged to the Project Media in Vegas as well.

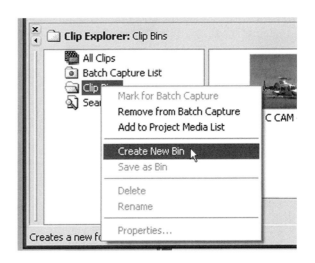

2.15   Right-click the Media bin to create a new bin to aid in locating, managing, and logging media.

2.16   When video is lost, moved to a different folder, or corrupted, but is associated with an event on the Timeline, the event will provide a placeholder on the Timeline that can be replaced with a take or recaptured from the DV tape.

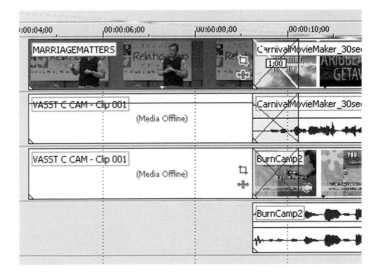

Bins from the Video Capture utility can be imported to the Media Pool in Vegas by creating the bin in Vegas before capturing media.

In the NLE world, if a clip is on the hard drive, it is considered to be online. If the clip disappears from the hard drive but is part of a project, it is considered to be offline, and Vegas shows the file as offline in the Project Media, shown as grayed out or missing media with the text "Offline Media" in the lower-left corner of the Project Media. Vegas provides the opportunity to recapture offline media by right-clicking the offline media and selecting "Recapture Offline DV Media."

Recapturing media from the Project Media launches the Video Capture application automatically, and you will be prompted to place the correct tape in the deck/camera if you have not already done so.

This is a point at which careful logging/labeling is invaluable. Video Capture will seek out the timecode related to the clip that is marked for recapture and start the capture process with no assistance. The recaptured media will need to be directed to a folder on one of the drives.

2.17 To recapture DV media with Video Capture, right-click in the Project Media in Vegas and select "Recapture All Offline Media."

Capturing Stills with Video Capture

The Video Capture tool allows stills to be captured and cataloged during the capture process. To capture stills, click the Capture Still button. Still images by default are stored as JPEG files unless otherwise specified in the OPTIONS | PREFERENCES | CAPTURE dialog. In this same dialog, Video Capture can be instructed to deinterlace video images and to apply the correct aspect ratio to still images. If the "Saved Captured Stills as JPEG" box is left unchecked, images are stored as uncompressed bitmaps.

Stills captured to the clipboard can be opened in any photo editor for color correction, image correction, resizing, or other manipulation.

Many video cameras have the ability to capture stills as well.

Still images are generally captured to videotape and can be narrated during the still capture on the video camera. Video Capture treats these still images as video because the tape is moving and the still image generation is created by the video camera. Default still-image length on most DV cameras is five seconds. If Scene Detection is enabled, Video Capture creates a new file for each still photo taken with the camera.

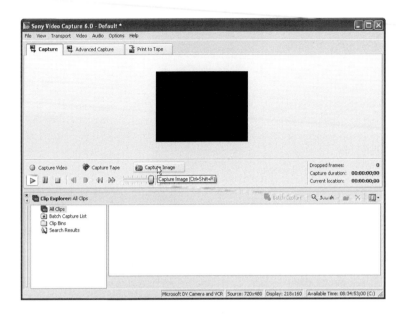

2.18   Still images can be captured directly with Video Capture.

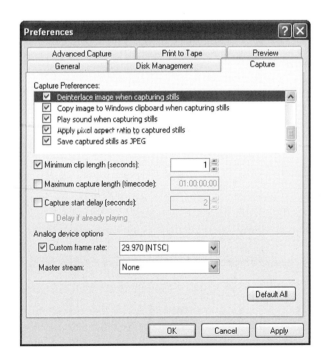

2.19   Specify preferences for managing still images in Video Capture
        and for viewing formats.

Changes in the Future of Video Capture

In the very near future, most DV cameras in the consumer and semiprofessional markets not only will sport IEEE 1394 and S-Video connectors but also will have USB mini connectors (Type B) as well. This option will occur because of increased manufacturer support of USB2 as a data transfer protocol.

All DV cameras currently have a FireWire/IEEE 1394 connector on them. Sony cameras label this output as an iLink connection. Having both USB2 (Type B) connectors and 1394 connectors means that cameras will be able to connect to any type of computer, regardless of hardware configuration. Both formats operate reasonably the same.

Another major change coming in digital video is the advent of portable, battery-powered hard drives that will be built directly into cameras. As drive speeds and sizes increase, these drives or similar storage mechanisms will be stored in the cameras themselves.

Never use USB2 when FireWire is present. Vegas Capture doesn't do very well with USB2 camera dialogs. USB2 uses more system resources than does iLink/IEEE 1394.

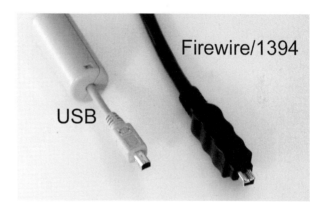

2.20   USB Type B connector and FireWire/1394 four-pin connector. HDV and DV cameras often have both types of connectors.

2.21   The ADS 3.5 drive kit has a self-powered housing with a six-pin FireWire connection.

2.22 The four-pin FireWire output from the DV camera plugs directly into the FireWire input on the drive kit. Video captured directly to the drive kit will not require capture, as it is already in digital format on the drive, and merely needs to be plugged into the computer/electric system.

2.23 The nNovia A2D can not only capture from a DV camera, but also capture video and audio directly from an analog camera, converting it to DV on the fly, removing the process of capture.

Capturing/Transferring HDV

HDV uses a different capture application than the standard DV capture application. Batch capture tools are not available in the HDV capture application. To access the HDV capture application, go to File/Capture Video. The Capture Video dialog box will open.

Choose "HDV or SDI" in this dialog. This will open the HDV capture utility. Notice that this application has far fewer options than the DV capture application.

In the Capture dialog, choose Preferences in the upper-lefthand corner. This will allow the choice of 1394 connection or AJA SDI (serial digital interface) connection (if an AJA SDI card

2.24   Capture choice dialog box.

is present). For HDV, choose the IEEE 1394 MPEG2/TS device. If the HDV camera/deck is connected, Vegas will display the status of the deck in the Capture Preview window.

One of the most common errors when capturing HDV in Vegas is that the camcorder is not set
up for HDV capture. If the HDV capture utility is opened and configured, and the dialog reports
that the camcorder/deck is not available, yet all connections are made, the camcorder/deck is
turned to VCR mode, and a tape is inserted in the deck, it's quite likely the camcorder/deck is in
DV down-convert mode instead of HDV mode. Open the camcorder/deck menu in VCR mode
and be certain the camcorder indicates it is outputting HDV. Most of the HDV devices will specify output resolution in the display window.

2.25

Note that in this dialog, the device is stopped and is ready for control via the Vegas capture
application.

The device may now be controlled via the capture utility. Start/stop, Rewind, Fast-forward, Capture are all enabled, so that the camcorder/deck does not require any local control.

Prior to transfer of the HDV stream to a hard drive, it's important to specify the location to which the video stream will be stored on the computer. In the Preferences dialog, select Disk Management and Add Folder. Browse to a folder on the system in which the HDV media is to be stored. Alternatively, this dialog may be accessed by selecting the GB Free button found next to the Preferences option.

2.26

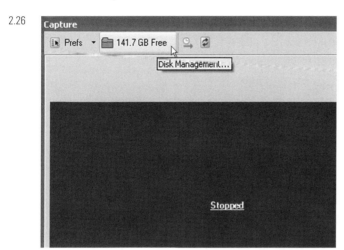

It is highly recommended that the storage location not be the C: drive location. As mentioned previously, it's best to store video (and audio) on a drive separate from the OS and application drive.

2.27

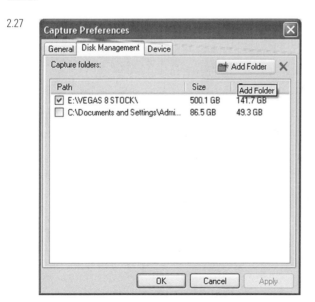

In this dialog, specify where the HDV video stream is to be stored. If a folder has not been previously created, a folder may be created anywhere on the system by selecting the Make New Folder option.

2.28

Create a new folder on the system, in which the HDV stream will be stored. It is recommended that the OS/Application drive not be used to store video content. Once a capture folder has been established, the transfer process may proceed.

Capturing either an entire tape or user-defined start points are the two capture options available for HDV. If the Capture Tape option is selected, Vegas will instruct the HDV device to rewind to the start of the tape and begin capture from that point. If the Capture button is selected, capture will begin from wherever the tape may be at that moment in time.

Tape may be shuttled forward/backward via the shuttle option in the capture tool; this tool is slightly latent, so be prepared for the tape mechanism to be slightly slow in responding to input from this slider. Alternatively, the JKL shuttle keyboard shortcuts may be used to shuttle tape forward/backward.

Capture may be directed to start at a specific frame by selecting the Go to Frame option on the Capture toolbar.

If you have clicked away from the capture application, sometimes the HDV device will lose connection with the capture application. If this occurs, select the Reconnect to Current Device option on the toolbar.

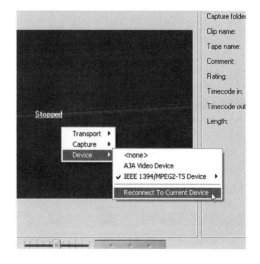

2.29

The capture device is started via the Capture button and may be stopped by either selecting the Stop button or simply hitting the spacebar. Vegas will then open a dialog asking users to keep the current capture session as a file or not.

It's not necessary to save this capture session information; the Project Media feature in Vegas keeps tabs on this same information, making it very easy to recapture media. It should be noted, however, that frame-accurate recapturing of HDV is not always possible; all efforts to keep media available via archive are a very good practice.

Vegas will offer an opportunity to save a capture session. Generally this is not necessary, as batch capture/recapture of HDV is not frame-accurate.

Sometimes, various HDV devices might not be seen immediately. You may need to cycle the device on/off/on for Vegas's video capture application to see it correctly.

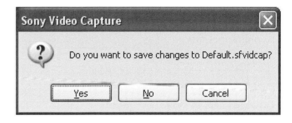

2.30a

1. In the Control Panel, choose System, click the Hardware tab, and click Device Manager.

2. Click on the AVC devices, where you'll see a connected device.

3. Right-click and choose Update Driver. You want to search manually for the new driver.

4. Browse to Sound, Video, Game Controllers; you want the SONY folder.

5. In the Sony folder, specify the DVHS driver.

6. Reboot the camera or HDV deck.

The other option in the setup of the HDV/SDI capture utility is to choose where you'll store files. When you select this option, a dialog will open up providing additional Preference choices.

On the General tab, there are four choices. If the computer being used to capture HDV is a slower machine (3.0 GHz or slower), it's a good idea to disable all but the last choice in the dialog. This will task the machine with less processing horsepower, even though these preferences may not seem to be significant.

Importing Media from a DVD Drive

Camcorders that record to DVD are very common, and Vegas is capable of importing most types of DVD-based recording formats.

Browse to File/Import DVD Camcorder Disc. The disc may be in the camcorder or in the computer DVD device; it's a simple matter to point to either device. Any disc to be imported to Vegas does need

2.30b   DVD camcorders allow you to shoot video directly onto recordable DVD media and can be useful when little or no editing is required.

to be finalized prior to import. Vegas will import the video and stereo or 5.1 surround information.

Be sure to uninstall the Sony Handycam USB driver from your Add/Remove Programs prior to attempting to import media via the Vegas import tools. The Sony Handycam driver may prevent Vegas from recognizing the DVD camcorder.

If the disc to be imported contains 5.1 surround audio, set up a 5.1 surround Vegas project prior to import. Vegas will then properly import the six channels of audio to corresponding surround tracks. The 5.1 audio imported to a stereo project (Vegas default) will be down-mixed to a two-channel mix.

2.30c

2.31

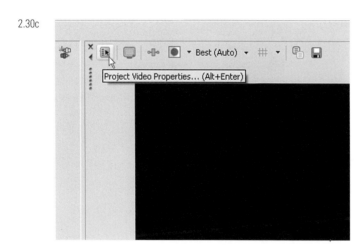

Project properties are accessed via File/Project Properties or by selecting the Project Video Properties button found in the upper-left corner of the Preview window.

Once the import begins, Vegas will ask for a location where the video should be stored. This is a transfer of the data contained on the DVD to a hard drive location. It is not practical to attempt to edit footage directly from the DVD.

This dialog determines where DVD content will be stored once it has been transferred. It is highly recommended that a location separate from the operating system/application drive be chosen.

Once the media is imported, it is then added to the Project Media window in Vegas. From here, you may drag the media files directly to the Timeline or open them in the Vegas Trimmer prior to adding to the Timeline. Files may also be previewed in this window by pressing Play or selecting the Auto-Preview option.

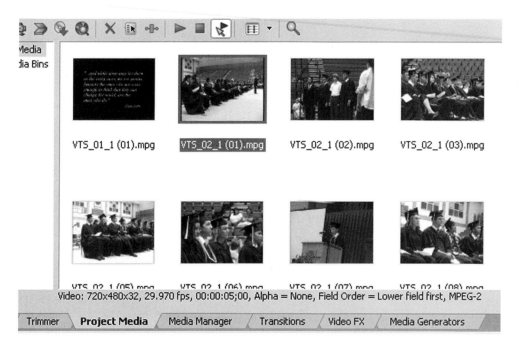

2.32

The Project Media window displays all media used in the project.

Importing Media from a Hard Disk Drive Recorder

Hard disk drive (HDD) recorders such as the Sony DR60 are very popular, as they reduce the importance of tape as a recording medium and allow for fast transfer of files, saving tremendous amounts of capture time. A 60-minute tape requires 60 minutes of transfer time (realtime), whereas 60 minutes of recorded media on a HDD unit takes approximately 15 minutes. It's not difficult to see the benefits of a tapeless workflow.

Connect the HDD unit to the computer via 1394 and turn on the power to the HDD unit. The computer should recognize the HDD unit as a drive. In Vegas, browse to FILE | IMPORT | HARD DISK RECORDING UNIT.

Vegas will ask where you'd like to transfer files from the HDD unit. Specify a location.

This dialog determines where HDD content will be stored once it has been transferred. It is highly recommended that a location separate from the operating system/application drive be chosen. Once the files are transferred, they are found in the Project Media window. Files may also be accessed via the Vegas Trimmer.

It is possible to edit files directly from some HDD recorder devices; generally this is not the most efficient means of editing. HDD units generally do not have the fastest data transfer rates, and this limits the speed at which edit previews will take place. Transfer media to the editing

2.33

2.34

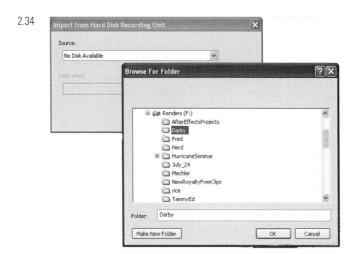

computer hard drives for best results. Additionally, this ensures that the HDD unit may be cleared and used for other recording.

Be sure to set the HDD unit to record AVI Type 2 files for best results when working with DV. Although Vegas may import other formats, this is the best DV format for Vegas to work with. HDV file format should be .m2t.

When transferring media from an HDD device to a FAT32 drive, Vegas will import/copy the files exactly as they are found on the HDD device. When importing to an NTFS drive (recommended), Vegas will create a single AVI Type 2 file from any smaller AVI files created as a long file. Similarly, Vegas will generate a single .m2t/HDV file from smaller files created as a result of the FAT32 limitations found on HDD recording units.

Vegas uses the Index (idx) file on your HDD device to ensure that transferred files are not retransferred.

Importing AVCHD

Advanced video codec–high definition is a fairly new format in the video industry, and Vegas Pro 8 is capable of importing AVCHD content. This highly compressed format has several codecs that various manufacturers may use; at the time of this writing, Vegas Pro 8 imports AVCHD from all Sony camcorders, all Canon camcorders, and most Panasonic camcorders.

AVCHD media may be recorded on an HDD unit, DVD-based camcorder, or some form of static memory such as the Sony Memory Stick, Compact Flash, or SDHC. Although possible, it is recommended users should never attempt to edit video directly from the card. The editing experience will be much better from a hard drive due to the highly compressed format's CPU requirements and transfer ratio.

2.35   Sony CX7 camcorder.

Depending on the camcorder, users may or may not have to use an import application. In the case of Sony and Canon camcorders, the camcorder may be connected directly to the computer via USB, or the card may be inserted into a card reader, and then viewed through the Vegas Explorer. Select the files individually or as a group in the Vegas Explorer, and drag and drop them to a location where you'd like the files to be stored. The dragged/dropped files will not appear in the Project Media window, however. Once these files are added to the Vegas Timeline, these files will appear in the Project Media window.

Be sure to set Vegas to the file properties closest to the output of the AVCHD camcorder. Most AVCHD camcorders are 1440 × 1080, which means that the HDV 1440 × 1080 project preset should be selected.

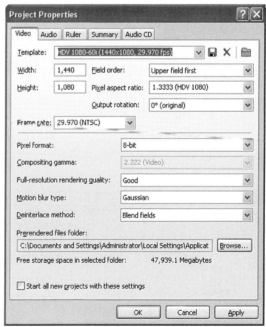

2.36

This is the template to be used for most AVCHD camcorders. PAL users should select the 50i template. AVCHD is extremely compressed. This means the CPU is going to be working quite hard to decode the video information and display it in the Preview window.

Only the very fastest, most optimized computer systems will be able to preview AVCHD at full frame rates. As computers grow faster and applications are better optimized to deal with AVCHD, preview speeds will improve. In the meantime, there are tools such as VASST GearShift that may be used to convert the AVCHD files to a more efficient file format such as HDV or Cineform codecs.

2.37   GearShift from VASST.

XDCAM and Sony Vegas Pro 8 Software

Sony Vegas Pro editing software offers in-depth XDCAM support, along with an XDCAM browser that displays and sorts with XDCAM SD, XDCAM HD, and XDCAM EX formats.

The workflows for XDCAM are varied, but will be similar to the following:

Use the Import XDCAM Disc button in the XDCAM Explorer to import clips. Proxies, full-resolution clips, or both sets of clips together may be imported. Once imported, the clips appear as thumbnails in the XDCAM Explorer. Edit your project using the proxy files.

2.38a

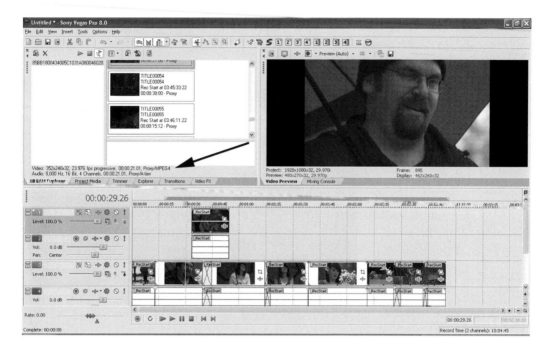

2.38b

This is an XDCAM Proxy Timeline. Proxy media may be shifted once the project is complete.

Using the Conform XDCAM Media in Current Project button in the XDCAM Explorer, conform the edited project to full resolution. Sony Vegas 7d software will conform the full-length file, regardless of edited length on the Timeline. Vegas Pro 8 will conform the full-resolution files to the trimmed length of the proxies, thus saving storage space and potentially reducing the conform time.

2.39a

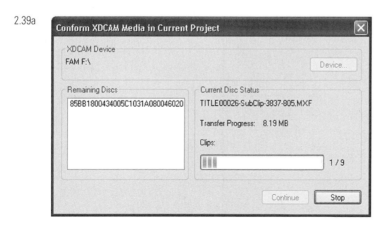

2.39b

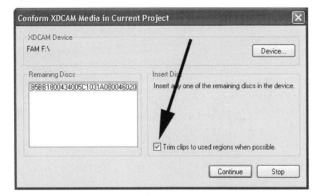

2.39c

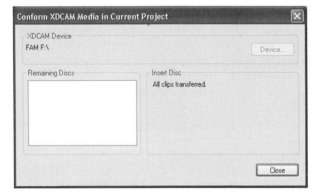

Conforming the Timeline will replace all Proxies with full-resolution XDCAM files.

2.40

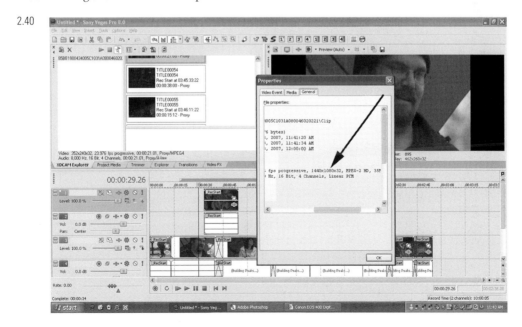

Output your project by clicking the Export Video to Sony XDCAM Disc button in the XDCAM Explorer. Confirm the hardware settings and choose a file path for your rendered project. This file can be automatically deleted after the export is complete.

Once the file is conformed, it may be output to an XDCAM device. Be sure to use the XDCAM templates to ensure compatibility.

2.41

Importing XDCAM Media into a Vegas Project

Before connecting the XDCAM hardware to perform FAM operations, install the ProDisc PC Utility software driver and PDZ1 software on the editing PC. The driver is not part of the standard Vegas installation and can be obtained from www.sony.com/xdcam.

Once the driver is properly installed, the XDCAM camera or deck needs to be switched to i.LINK File Access Mode and connected to the computer via iLink.

All XDCAM hardware can be configured for FAM operations by changing the i.LINK Mode setting in the operational menu from AV/C (the default setting) to FAM.

- On XDCAM decks, you will be forced to reboot the XDCAM device after changing the i.LINK Mode setting. On XDCAM camcorders, you need to power the deck off and back on for the mode change to take effect, but this can be done at your convenience.

- Connect the i.LINK cable after switching the i.LINK Mode. When XDCAM devices are set to File Access Mode and connected to a computer, "PC REMOTE" is displayed on the LCD/Viewfinder, the hardware controls (with the exception of the Eject button) are disabled, and there are no linear VTR, output, display, or menu functions available to the operator.

A few things to remember when working with XDCAM hardware:

- To terminate File Access Mode safely—for   2.42 example, if you need front panel or menu control—use the Safely Remove Hardware button on the Windows taskbar, browse to the XDCAM device, and remove it from the system. The camera/deck will now function normally.

- To reenable File Access Mode, cycle power on the XDCAM device or disconnect and then reconnect the i.LINK cable.

- Until a disc is inserted, the FAM-enabled XDCAM device will not be assigned a drive letter or path and will not appear in the Windows Computer Explorer.

This is the directory that will open when the XDCAM disc is registered/mounted.

If Windows preferences are not set to display new Explorer windows when a drive is detected, wait a few seconds and then click on the My Computer icon to verify that the XDCAM device is properly mapped and available.

Enabling the XDCAM Explorer

Vegas is unique in that it provides a built-in XDCAM browser and workspace, the XDCAM Disc Explorer. Because this tab is not needed for all Vegas workflows, it may be disabled/enabled in the application preferences to conserve processing power, memory, and screen space. The first time Vegas Pro 8 is launched, this option is disabled.

Enable the XDCAM Explorer by navigating to the General tab of the Preferences window and checking the "Enable XDCAM Explorer" box found at the bottom of the Preferences options.

2.43a

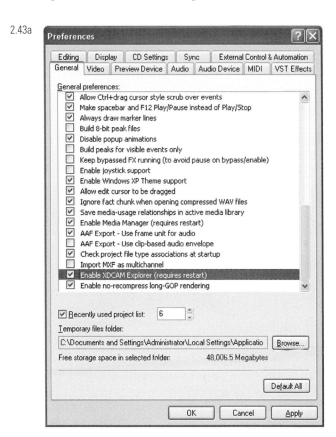

The Preferences dialog is found in the Options Menu or by right-clicking in any unused area on the Timeline.

Click the Apply button after making your selection. You will be prompted to restart the application. When you return, you'll see the XDCAM tab in the docked windows area.

2.43b

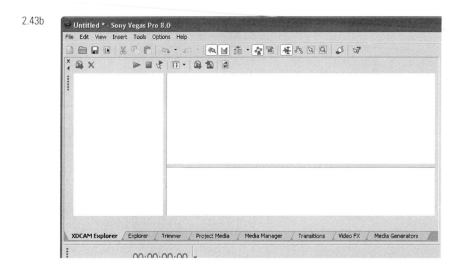

This is the XDCAM Explorer. You'll next need to import files to populate the Explorer.

Enabling Multichannel Audio Import

Once Vegas is set to import XDCAM clips, you'll need to instruct the application how to handle MXF files with multichannel audio. Audio from MXF files can be imported in stereo or as up to eight individual channels. If you select Import MXF as Multichannel in the General tab of the Preferences dialog, all the individual audio channels will be automatically available when the clip is placed on the Timeline.

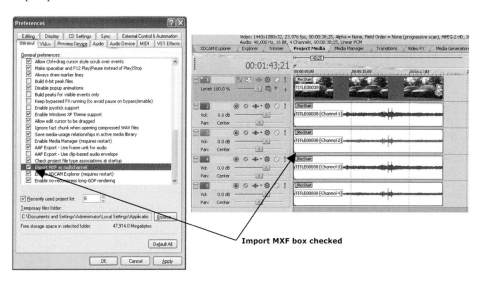

2.44a   Enable multichannel audio in the Vegas Preferences.

If you leave this selection unchecked, the audio will be brought in as stereo and will enable one stereo track when the clip is placed on the Timeline. If audio is imported in this manner, the additional channels may still be accessed and assigned to their own tracks at a later point (after locking and conforming the video, for example) by right-clicking on an audio event and selecting Channels in the context menu.

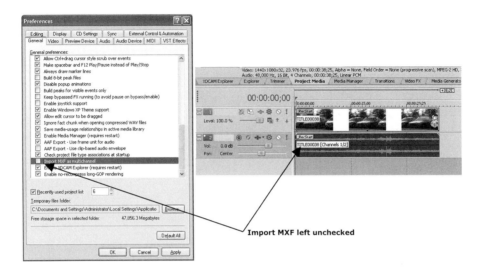

2.44b   Importing XDCAM discs.

With the XDCAM deck, camcorder, or drive unit connected and set to i.LINK FAM, click on the Import XDCAM Disc button to open the Device dialog. This will enable browsing of the XDCAM device.

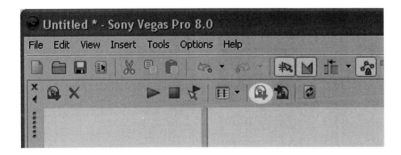

2.44c   Import XDCAM Disc.

Currently there are no XDCAM devices online, so the upper panel shows us a "Device Not Set" message. Click the Device button to browse to the XDCAM hardware. This will open a dialog box that you'll use to select either FAM or FTP import and then browse to the appropriate device.

Check the box next to File Access Mode and click the Browse button. This opens a browser window.

You should see the XDCAM device followed by the drive letter it has been assigned. In this case the deck appears as the F: drive. If the disc has a name, the name will also appear. Highlight the XDCAM device and click OK. Be sure to select the Root Directory or uppermost level of the XDCAM device and not any of the folders contained inside. This will return to the Device Settings dialog box, which should now display the drive location of the XDCAM hardware. Select OK.

This will return you to the Import XDCAM Disc dialog. The XDCAM device is now online and can set the resolution required for capture as well as the location in which to store your imported material.

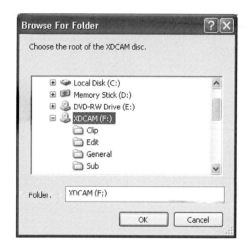

2.45

You can choose to import Proxy resolution files, full-resolution files, or both. As noted previously, deselecting both options will result in only the XML being imported for each clip.

Select or change the Capture Folder by clicking Browse in the center panel. In the lower panel, the option of assigning a unique name to the disc is available. For this example, name the disc "Vegas 1080."

Disc names are used within the system in much the same way Reel and Tape names are used when performing tape-based capture. For example, when transferring material during the Conform process, you will be asked to have "Vegas 1080" and any other discs used for the project ready.

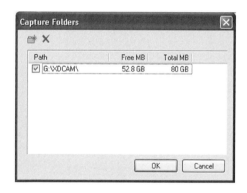

2.46

Checking the "Overwrite Any Existing Disc Name if Present" box will rename the disc using whatever information is entered in the field above. This name will live with the disc until it is changed again by the operator. The name lives within the Vegas system and on the Professional Media disc.

Click OK to begin transferring files. A progress window will appear as clips and associated XML files are being transferred to the system.

Once the transfer is complete, the disc (identified by either the name you applied or the disc's UMID) appears in the disc list in the left panel of the XDCAM Explorer, and the clips are displayed in the right panel. Clips may now be edited on the Vegas Timeline.

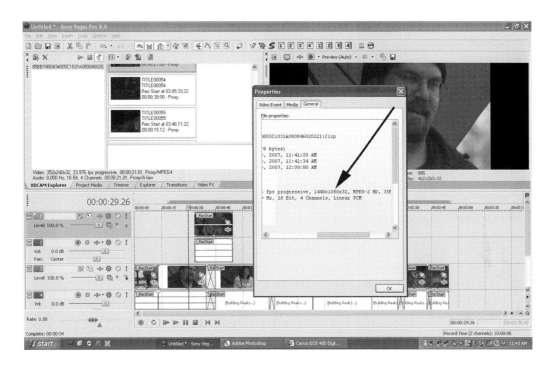

2.47   The Vegas XDCAM Explorer, fully populated with various XML, proxy, and full-resolution XDCAM files.

Hardware Cards and Vegas Pro 8

Vegas Pro 8 also offers support for AJA XenaLH and LHe hardware cards. These cards offer 10-bit ingest/output via component input connections to camcorders that offer component output. Using these cards requires a fast computer and large RAID and will use the Sony YUV codec instead of using the MPEG2 codec from HDV and XDCAM camcorders or the DV codec output from DV camcorders.

Some users feel that access to the 10-bit codec does offer a better image. It's true that chroma smoothing is managed differently via the analog input/output mode of the camcorders and the digitizing of the footage using the YUV codec, but the image source is still whatever the image source is. In other words, don't expect HDCAM-like output from an HDV camcorder simply because the footage is captured via a 10-bit card and analog output.

Be certain the latest AJA Xena Windows Win32 bit driver is installed.

One benefit of these systems, however, is in live studio work, in which the camera head is used and no recording system other than direct capture is part of the workflow. In this case, the camera is used to acquire the image, and the live video stream is output from the camera as a 4:2:2 uncompressed image and digitized by the AJA card as a 4:2:2, 10-bit stream straight to the computer hard drive. In this environment, the image quality is limited only by the glass and sensors in the camera. Extremely high quality footage is possible, as the compression stage in the camera is bypassed.

The AJA Xena is a great choice for 10-bit, uncompressed capture in Sony Vegas Pro 8 software. Capture via this card is accomplished using the same capture tool as used for HDV. Only the capture device needs to be changed. In the Preferences dialog, select the AJA Video Device. This will prepare the AJA card for capture, and the Details dialog will open, displaying information about the device.

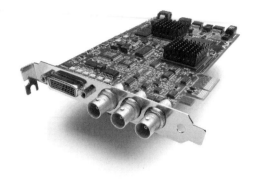

2.48

It's best to select the Conform Output to the Following Format option. This means that no matter what is on the Timeline, output will be configured to match your preview monitor. There are two options: Always and Only When the Project Does Not Match Any Available Format. "Always" means that regardless of project settings, output to monitor will conform to the preview monitor settings. An example of using this option might be if you've got PAL footage but are previewing on an NTSC monitor. Otherwise, choose the Only When the Project Does Not Match Any Available Format option. This will instruct Vegas to conform output when the project settings don't match standard formats.

Other options in the Preferences include setting Progressive Segmented frames and Timecode. Use the PsF option if the project properties are for a progressive format, such as 24p, 25p, and 30p formats. The Timecode offset is used in the event that the captures are not frame-accurate. Use the slider to offset as compensation adjustment.

The Audio format option allows for multichannel format if your playback device supports multichannel output. Otherwise, leave this set to two channels.

The 10-bit option is for capturing 10-bit files. If this option is used, be sure to set the Project Properties to 32-bit floating point. If the 10-bit option is not selected, then video will be captured with 8-bit accuracy. Bear in mind that using this option will require a large RAID array and RAID controller for capture without dropped frames.

Blackmagic Design/BMD DeckLink cards have been supported in Sony Vegas 6/7, but are not fully supported in Vegas Pro 8 at the time of this writing. Blackmagic Design has announced beta driver support for Vegas 8. Release Candidate drivers should be available soon.

In the Disk Management tabs of both capture utilities, the only option available is to select a specific disk that you'd like to capture media to. The primary consideration here is to be certain that you're never capturing to your system disk. This is particularly important with HDV or SDI capture, as dropped frames would be a virtual certainty if media is captured to the system drive. For adequate SDI capture, you'll need a RAID 0 configuration. The RAID could be either SATA or SCSI, although SCSI is generally preferable, and a minimum of four drives, although a RAID of eight drives (10k speed) or more is a good idea. Blackmagic Design suggests you could possibly squeak by with only six 10k drives, but they don't recommend it. Hardware controllers for the SATA RAID are highly recommended, although there may be a software RAID controller available that will provide the necessary throughput. SDI and HD require a fairly significant amount of bandwidth, and so the drive array will need to be up to speed. One significant benefit of working with uncompressed media is that it actually requires less processor power than DV or transport streams require, as there is no compression taking place. The challenge in working

with uncompressed files lies with throughput, not with processor speed. If you visit the www.
blackmagic-design.com web site, you'll find a speed test utility that will let you know if your
system is ready for processing uncompressed SD and uncompressed HD files. For SD file transfer and storage, 30 MB per second is a safe benchmark data rate.

You'll need approximately 180GB of storage per hour of SD video. HD (without audio) is
approximately 170MB per second, or roughly 600 GB per hour of uncompressed HD storage.
1280 × 720p files require slightly less bandwidth and storage than 1920 × 1080 files, asking for an average of around 170 MB per second. When working with uncompressed files on a
marginal system, consider 24p as your frame rate, as this can significantly reduce throughput
requirements, dropping the required data rate to just under 150 MB per second. As you can see
from these data rate requirements, you'll not be able to get into uncompressed SD or HD very
inexpensively. Check the Blackmagic Design web site for additional details on supported and
recommended motherboards, processors, and RAM configurations. Finally, on the Device tab,
you'll specify the default for capture, whether it's a DeckLink card or an HDV device captured
via 1394.

When an HDV device is selected, the connected device will display, such as you see in this illustration showing the Sony HVR Z1U camcorder.

2.49

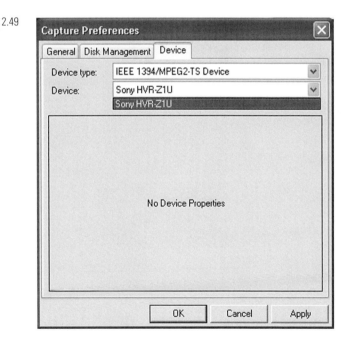

If you plan on using one of the Blackmagic Design cards, you'll need the following:

- A fast RAID
- RAID controller card/system

You will also need to speed test the system prior to capturing/ingesting video.

You can download the system speed test software from the Blackmagic Design web site.

The Blackmagic Design and AJA hardware cards supported in Vegas provide users with some options that previously weren't very easy to work into the Vegas workflow. Most importantly, rather than working with DV, users can work with 4:2:2 uncompressed footage on the Timeline in Sony Vegas. Previously, to import uncompressed to the Vegas Timeline required capturing with a third-party application, importing to Vegas, rendering to the desired codec, and then outputting via the third-party application. With the Xena and DeckLink cards, you can import analog media or SDI media as uncompressed media. This means a deeper, richer picture, fewer artifacts, better color-correction processing, and a higher-quality output, depending on the originating camera or format.

Another benefit, especially for footage destined for broadcast, is that the signal can be transferred via SDI, or serial digital interface. Coupled with a device like the Convergent Design SD Connect or HDV Connect, users can import uncompressed video directly from a BetaSP or HDCAM system and output back to that same device via SDI.

If you aren't using BetaSP, SX, or HDCAM in your workflow and are primarily working with DV or HDV, you likely will find an SDI card to be unnecessary. If your only output format is MPEG-2 for DVD, SDI is of even lesser importance to most editors.

SDI requires a completely different setup on the equipment side compared to DV. For instance, most professional monitors don't come with SDI input and output, so you'll likely need to purchase an SDI plug-in card for the monitor. Additionally, you'll need a BetaSP, SX, or HDCAM deck that has SDI input. Any switchers you might use also require SDI input and output. SDI-capable equipment isn't inexpensive and is really necessary for only a few areas of the video industry. Just being aware that Vegas can grow with you as your video skills and client base grows is a good thing.

Editing Tools, Transitions, Filters, and Other Basic Video Tools

Importing Media to the Timeline

Aside from capturing media, many methods can be used to bring media into Vegas. Vegas is format agnostic and resolution independent, meaning that nearly any form of media recognized by the Microsoft Windows operating system can be imported to the Vegas Timeline as an event.

Vegas has an Explorer that by default opens in the lower-left corner of the dockable tool space. This Explorer can be dismissed from view and recalled at any time by pressing Alt+1. The Explorer is a dockable tool that can be sent to a second monitor to preserve space on the Timeline.

Open and view the Explorer. Any form of media that can be imported is shown in the Explorer. Media files, such as GIF, TGA, JPEG, BMP, PNG, TIFF, MOV, AVI, WMV, and MPG, are all media file formats that can be opened in Vegas.

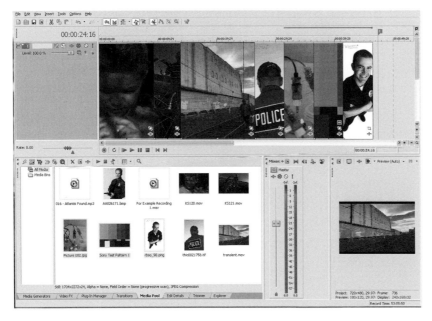

3.1 In this picture of the Media Pool, different media formats are placed as events on the Vegas Timeline.

Tip

If QuickTime files are to be viewed and edited within Vegas, the QuickTime full install is required. Visit www.quicktime. com and download the current player. When installing, three choices are presented: Full Install (recommended), Custom Install, and Minimal Install. Choose full installation so that Vegas is able to access authoring tools for the QuickTime MQV file type. Without this installation, Vegas won't be able to access or edit QuickTime files or TIFF files.

All media formats may be placed on the same track, which means that an AVI file might be next to a JPEG file, which in turn might be next to a QuickTime file, which might be next to a WMV file, and so on. About the only Windows-recognized media format that cannot be opened inside of Vegas is the REAL (rm.ram) file format, as this format is protected by Real's protection algorithms.

To place media on the Timeline, drag the media from the Explorer to the Timeline, where the media becomes an event. If a track is not present, Vegas automatically creates one for the media that has been dragged and dropped. Double-clicking a file in the Explorer window automatically adds the file to the Timeline as an event and creates a track for the file if a video track isn't already present.

To insert a new video track manually, right-click the track control pane and select INSERT I VIDEO TRACK or press Ctrl+Shift+Q.

Media can also be opened in the Trimmer window. For those familiar with other NLE systems, the

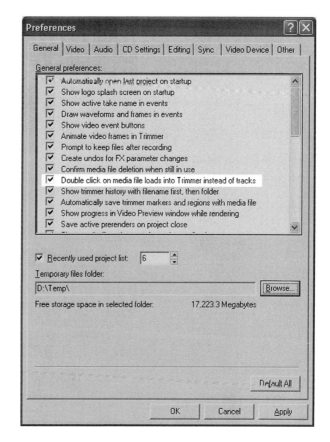

3.2 Selecting preferences for loading media in Trimmer.

Trimmer window is much like a source window in which media can be previewed and trimmed to the desired length/information before being placed on the Timeline. To accomplish this task, right-click the media and select Open in Trimmer. Vegas can be set to open files directly in Trimmer, by going to the OPTIONS I PREFERENCES I GENERAL dialog and checking the "Double-click on media file loads into Trimmer instead of tracks" checkbox.

Media can also be dragged directly into the Media Pool, which is where Vegas stores location information for all media used in a project. Media can be stored in the Media Pool regardless of whether the media is found on the Timeline or not. Any event or piece of media placed on the Timeline, however, is automatically added to the Media Pool.

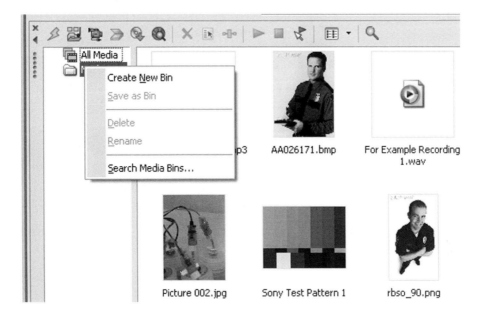

3.3   Creating and naming the media bins.

Vegas has media management features in the Media Pool. The use of media bins allows users to preset where media will be pointed to and how media is located. A master project bin resides in the Media Pool, to which all media is pointed by default. This master bin is labeled "All Media Folder." Beneath it is a folder labeled "Media Bins." Right-clicking the Media Bins folder opens a menu/dialog that allows for new bins to be created and named.

Be aware that Vegas does not copy media and place it in bins. There is neither point nor value in having two copies of the same piece of media on the hard drive simply to fill bins as some NLEs demand. On the contrary, Vegas points to a file from within the bin. While the media is always accessed from the bin, it truly resides wherever it was stored in the acquisition of the media. Bins are simply a means of collecting the storage points of all media and putting those indexes in one place.

Bins can be dragged from project to project in Vegas or stored as project bins so that they'll always be found within the preferences of Vegas. Bins can be created for audio, video, graphics, and anything else you like, with subbins for every bin format. This way, you'll always know where media is stored.

Bins can be dragged from one open instance of Vegas to another open instance of Vegas.

Media can also be imported from other projects by selecting FILE | OPEN, choosing the VEG file from which media is to be imported, and checking the "Merge media from Vegas project files into current project" checkbox, as shown in Figure 3.5. Media is then automatically added to the Media Pool in the same folders from which the imported Media Pool came. If the imported project has no bins specified in its Media Pool, Vegas will add media to the All Media Folder, where it can be dragged to specific bins within Media Pool for consistent file management.

Use bins to sort media by the name of the tape that the media is captured from, or create a bin for bed music, a bin for various takes, or a bin for JPEGs, BMPs, or PNGs. Good project management starts with locating and knowing where all media is stored at all times. This process also assists in clearing out a project when it is finished.

3.4   Bins separating various media types for efficient file location.

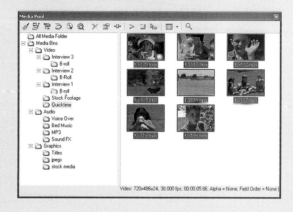

The Media Pool has several additional options for file import. Audio from CDs can be extracted directly from the Media Pool toolbar. These options include the following:

- Sweep Media Pool—removes all media from Media Pool that is not in use on the Timeline of current project.

- Import Media—imports media from other VEG files/Vegas projects to the Media Pool.

- Capture Video—opens the Video Capture application to transfer video from a camera to Media Pool.

- Import Photo—opens a scanner or camera attached to a computer for importing photos to the Media Pool.

- Extract Audio—extracts, or rips, audio from a CD to the Media Pool.

- Get Media from the Web—provides a direct link to Sony's partners, some of whom provide free media for your use.

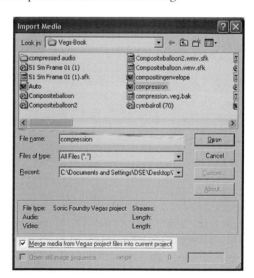

3.5   Importing media from other Vegas projects, which are either open or closed.

Tip_____

When copying media bins from one project to another, the media itself is NOT copied. Be aware of this so you don't lose any media thinking you have duplicates due to a copy/paste of the media bin.

3.6   Import buttons from the Media Pool.

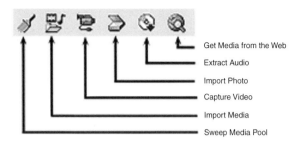

Get Media from the Web

Extract Audio

Import Photo

Capture Video

Import Media

Sweep Media Pool

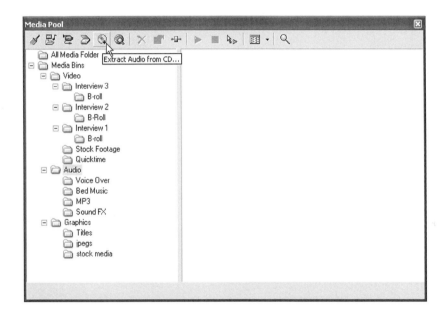

3.7   Choosing this button autoextracts audio from a CD inserted in the CD/DVD player.

Imported media is placed in the All Media Files folder in the Media Pool and, once imported, can be dragged and dropped into a specific bin. Vegas supports import to the currently selected bin; bins contain only links or pointers to existing media.

Bins are also searchable, which makes cataloging files very valuable. Comments inserted in the Batch Capture/Advanced Capture dialog can be searched/located in

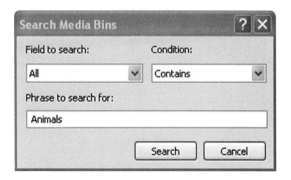

3.8   Search media bins to find elusive files that might not have been properly named or cataloged.

the bin search operation. Located media can be dragged and dropped into any bin in the Media Pool.

The Media Pool toolbar contains other useful tools for managing the Media Pool contents, including the following:

- Remove Media—removes media from the Media Pool or bins but does not delete media from the storage drive.

- Media Properties—opens a dialog indicating the type of media, storage location, length, size, and other properties of the media file.

- Media FX—allows FX to be placed on media before it's placed on the Timeline. This option is very useful for single, long-length files that need the same format, such as of color correction or special FX, but will be trimmed in the editing process. Select the file to be affected, then press the Media FX button, select the desired FX, and adjust accordingly. This process does not alter the original file.

- Start Preview—plays/previews selected media file in the Preview window.

- Stop Preview—stops playback of selected media in the Preview window.

- Auto-Preview—when pressed, any time a media file is selected, it will be displayed in the Preview window automatically. This process is exceptionally useful when quickly going through media, saving time.

- Views—determines how media is shown in the Media Pool, whether as icons, detailed information, or a list.

- Search Media Bins—uses keywords or attributes to locate media whether captured or imported and does not work over nonmapped network drives.

Vegas and its media management features are helpful, powerful, and useful. Take the time to use them correctly, and projects will be much easier to manage.

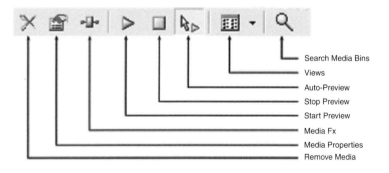

3.9 File management viewing attributes in the Media Pool.

Editors coming from other NLE applications often ask about having subclips or selections appear in the media bins. Vegas does not have this as a destructive function unless subclips are rendered to new files. Subclips may be created either in the Trimmer or on the Timeline, yet this does not discard remaining media from the original file. Rendering straight cuts to a new file is faster than realtime, because nothing is actually done to the clip. However, some people won't want to render subclips. For those, here is a workaround.

Open a clip in Trimmer. Make regional selections and name the regions. After selecting/naming all regions on a clip in Trimmer, right-click in the open area of the Trimmer and press S or select Save Markers/Regions, which will embed the markers/regions in the file.

In the Explorer window, enable the Regions view as shown here. Notice that the regions created in the Trimmer tool are now visible in the Regions view of the Explorer. These regions will not show things such as effects or envelopes, but are a means of quickly locating selected regions especially if the regions have been named with a recognizable name and then sorted by name.

3.10   Enabling the
        Region view.

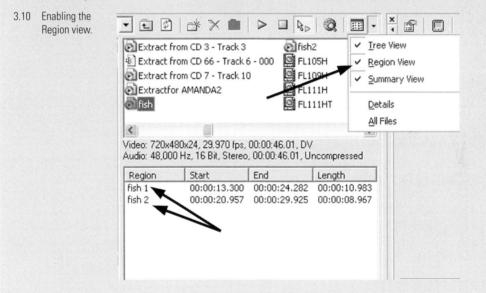

Subclips in Vegas

Vegas has the ability to use subclips. What is a subclip? Well, in Vegas they might be better known as "subevents" as they are reference files to a certain area in a larger event, often called "clips" in other DAW and NLE applications. Subclips may be created in a couple of different ways.

First, a file can be opened in the Vegas Trimmer, a selection made, and the subclip button pushed. A dialog opens, asking you to name the subclip. This does not affect the original event or clip in any way. In this dialog, you can also decide if you want the subclip to play in reverse from the original clip.

Second, an event loaded on the Timeline might be edited on the Timeline for length, selecting different in and out points. Right-click the file on the Timeline and choose Create Subclip from the menu that appears. This will deposit the subclip in the Media Pool. The subclip may be renamed in the Media Pool.

Subclips in Vegas may behave differently compared to subclips in other applications. Creating a subclip is not destructive to the original file. If you used Regions in older versions of Vegas, subclips are effectively the same thing with greater access to the media. Subclips show up in the Media Pool as well, whereas Regions show only in Regions view.

If you are capturing analog tape and planning on editing it, the subclip feature is very useful. This will allow you to load your entire .avi file into the Trimmer tool, select the sections you want to keep, and create subclips with them. If they are named sequentially (default) in the dialog boxes, they can be used almost like a story-

3.11 Subclips are useful to identify sections to be reused or to discard unused media. Subclips may be copied from project to project using media bins found in the Media Pool.

board and dragged to the Timeline as one group by selecting all subclips in the Media Pool. Performing a "Save As" and choosing to copy all Media Pool will then save the subclips, and the originating .avi file may be deleted from the hard drive, leaving only the parts you wish to use in the overall project.

> To copy subclips from one project to another, you will not be able to copy or paste them. You must create a new bin in the Media Pool, load the subclip into the new bin, and move the bin from one project to the new project.

If for some reason you need to locate other scenes in the media that the subclip originated from, or you need to change the in or out points of the subclip, right-click the subclip in the Media Pool and choose Open in Trimmer. While in Trimmer, press the Select Parent Media button in the upper-right corner of the Trimmer, and the parent media will open with the subclip area indicated by the selection tool. In or out points may be shifted, and the subclip may be re-created with a new name or using the original name.

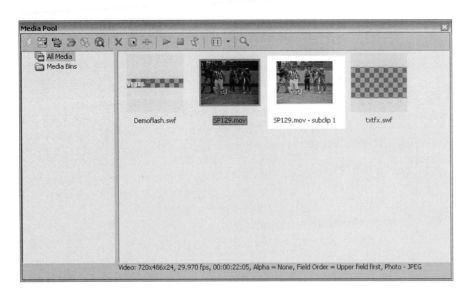

3.12a   This is how subclips will appear in the Media Pool.

Subclips are clips of media and, therefore, may not be dragged out on the Timeline in a standard Timeline editing function, as for all intents and purposes, the clip has been "cut" from the original media. If you need to extend the in or out point of an event that's been inserted as a subclip, you'll need to open the subclip in the trimmer and change it's in or out points and then reinsert it into the Timeline. Subclips may be added as takes, and therefore can be dropped onto slugs or empty events marking a time space. To open a subclip in the Trimmer, simply right-click and select "Open in Trimmer."

Use FILE | SAVE AS and check the "Copy and trim media" box found in the Save As dialog box, to save subclipped media and delete any media that is not part of the finished project. This is great for saving space on the system hard drive. Be sure to sweep the Media Pool for unused media before saving.

Placing Media on the Timeline

The Media Pool is a great place to start building a project and makes for a much more efficient workflow. Getting media to the Timeline from the Media Pool is well organized and easily traceable. The Media Pool is not the only way to work within Vegas, however.

Media can be dragged to the Timeline directly from the Explorer within Vegas or from the Windows Explorer. Notice that the Explorer window also has an Auto Preview button on the Explorer toolbar, just as the Media Pool does. Leaving this checked allows rapid preview of various media formats shown in the Preview window. A search can be done in the Windows-Find feature (START | FIND or START | SEARCH in Microsoft Windows XP) and dragged directly to the Vegas Timeline.

Trimmer

The Trimmer tool in Vegas is similar to the Source window in most NLE applications. In this window, media may be trimmed, marked, regionalized, subclipped, or added to the Timeline, among other uses. Previous versions of Vegas locked the Trimmer to the Preview window, whereas Vegas Pro 8 does not.

What do you do when you've got a lengthy video file but need only small sections contained within that file? Open the file in the Trimmer.

My method of working with the Trimmer is to start with OPTIONS | PREFERENCES, and in the General tab, set the preference to open files from the Explorer in the Trimmer when double-clicked. Alternatively, files may be right-clicked in the Explorer window and the "Open file in Trimmer" option chosen.

When the file opens in the Trimmer window, several options are available.

The most common use of the Trimmer is to locate the desired in/out point of a file and either mark those points or add the media between the I/O points to the Timeline.

If you create a selection in the Trimmer and:

- Select the A key, media within the selection will be added to the Timeline from the cursor.

- Select Shift+A, media in the selection will be added up to the cursor.

- Select the Subclip button (upper right), a subclip will be created. (The subclip is not a true subclip wherein a copy of the selected media is made, only the in/out points are

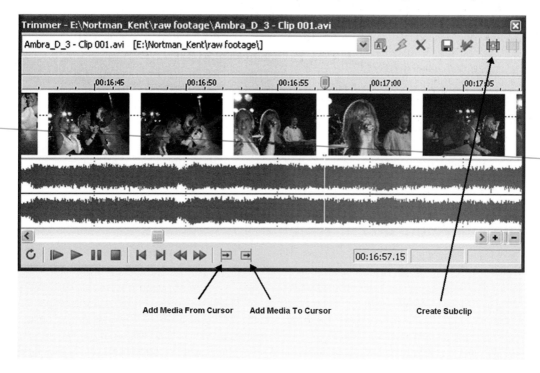

Add Media From Cursor   Add Media To Cursor   Create Subclip

3.12b

recorded. Treat subclips like regions; if you delete the original file, the subclip is deleted as well.) Subclips may be opened in the Trimmer window, and by selecting the Open Parent Media button in the upper right, the original file from which the subclip came will be opened, highlighting the subclip region.

In the lower-right corner are three timecode windows. These three windows indicate:

- File timecode start
- File timecode end
- Length of selection area within the file (if any)

3.12c

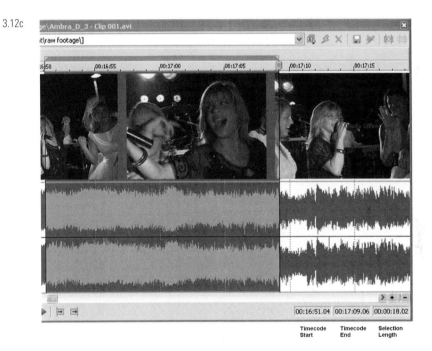

Selecting media in the Trimmer window and selecting the R key on the keyboard will create a namable region. Marked regions may be saved within the file itself. In the OPTIONS | PREF ERENCES | GENERAL dialog, there is a checkbox for saving markers and regions with a file. This is valuable, as regions can instantly be recalled either on the project Timeline or within the Trimmer tool. If, for example, a long file from a multicam project has some B roll in it to be inserted at a later point, you'd want to regionalize the section. The regionalized section will display on the Timeline with small green lines embedded in the file, referencing the region.

Markers may also be added in the Trimmer. I'm a big fan of markers; I use them like "sticky notes" in projects so that other editors can see comments. Placing the cursor at any point in time in the Trimmer or on the Timeline, select the M key. This drops an orange marker on the event or Timeline. If the event is marked in the Trimmer window, the marker lines will be embedded in the file, similar to region markers.

3.12d   A named region.

Region markers and time markers are different, as region markers indicate an in/out point, whereas time markers merely mark a moment in time. A marker may indicate an in point, an out point, or merely a reference point.

If a specific selection length is required, create a selection of any length and double-click Selection Length in the Trimmer window. The length will highlight, and a specific time may be typed in using either the Num pad or keyboard numbers. Using the same method, a start point and/or end point may be manually input to generate a selected area in the Trimmer.

Previewing Trimmer Media

By default, media in the Trimmer will mimic the Timeline; spacebar will play, JKL functions identically, and the Trimmer frames will be displayed in the Preview window. However, Vegas Pro 8 adds a new Trimmer behavior: the ability to turn off Preview in the Preview window.

Right-click inside the Trimmer window (with a media file loaded in the Trimmer), and in the menu that opens, select "Show Video in Preview Window." If it is left unchecked, files will play in the Trimmer window, mimicking a Source window in other NLE systems.

This is beneficial when video shown in the Preview window should remain visible, yet video in the Trimmer does not have identified in/out points, or for any other reason that you'd like to see a frame in the Trimmer while viewing moving or static video in the Preview window.

The Trimmer in Vegas does not buffer frames; the Timeline does. This means that playback from the Trimmer may stutter depending on available system resources, file type, or resolution.

You can open files from the Timeline in the Trimmer via one of two ways. First, you can right-click the file and select Open in Trimmer. Second, you can set the general preferences to automatically open a file in the Trimmer by double-clicking the file.

Consider using the Windows Explorer rather than the Vegas Explorer to locate and identify files. Media may be dragged directly to the Vegas Timeline from any window containing files, including the Windows Search application. Moreover, the Windows Explorer provides thumbnail images for video and still image files, making it more efficient to locate and place media on the Timeline. The Windows Explorer may be kept open and on top of the Vegas workspace.

Notice that the file takes a moment to build an audio preview. This graphic represents the audio. This process can be sped up by checking "Build 8-bit peak files" in the OPTIONS | PREFERENCES | GENERAL dialog.

 Tip

The graphic drawing reference files are stored in Vegas (and all other Sony products) as SFK files. These files may be deleted at any time. If a file that does not have a linked SFK file is loaded, Vegas will redraw the file and save it as a new SFK file.

After the file is drawn in the Trimmer, select the portions of the media that are to be used. Place the cursor at the point at which the video clip should begin and press I for in point. Place the cursor at the point at which the video clip should end and press O for out point. This process automatically creates a time selection in the Trimmer. Media can now be scrubbed over or the Play (spacebar) button can be clicked in the Trimmer.

An alternative to pressing the I and O keys to select the in/out points is to draw the selection directly in the Trimmer. Place the cursor where the in point should be and draw by holding down the cursor and dragging the cursor to the out point. You can also work in reverse by placing the cursor where the out point is desired and dragging the cursor to where the in point should be. Notice that as the cursor is dragged the video plays in the Preview window. Dragging the cursor with the left-click button held down behaves like a scrubbing tool in the Trimmer window.

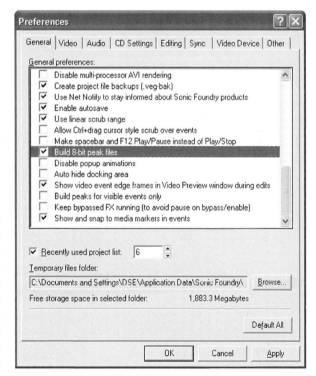

3.13 Reducing the size of screen peak draws will speed up screen draws in Vegas.

After a time selection is defined in the Trimmer, a few choices can be made as to how the media can be handled. Media can be placed directly on the Timeline by pressing A for Add, it can be dragged directly from the Trimmer to the Timeline, or a region can be created. If using the Add feature, place the cursor on the Timeline where the added media should be placed. After the media is added to the Timeline, it becomes an event.

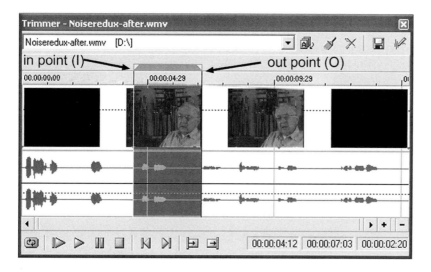

3.14 Time selection created in the Trimmer by pressing I and O for in/out points.

If no time selection is defined as a drawn area, as an in/out point, or as a region, media can be selected from the start point to where the cursor is parked. By pressing A, media in the Trimmer is added from the start to the moment at which the cursor is set. Alternatively, pressing Shift+A adds media up to the cursor to the end of the file.

When placing events on the Timeline, keep a fast, visual reference to them by using the scribble strip on the Track Control pane. This feature also helps others quickly know what you are intending with the track. For example, a master track might be named as such, whereas a picture-in-picture track might be named "PIP track." Good track management is critical, especially in the digital realm where filenames on a hard drive can be extremely varied.

3.15

Regions are great, as a defined region will stay with the media even after Vegas is closed. To define a region, press R, and Vegas will open a field in which the region name can be defined. Multiple regions can be defined, and region in/out points may overlap. When new media is loaded into the Trimmer and replaces the media-containing regions, the defined regions will stay with the media file and will be shown any time a file is loaded into the Trimmer. (By default, this option is turned on in the OPTIONS | PREFERENCES | GENERAL dialog. It can be unchecked if for some reason this feature is not desired.)

Markers and regions are exceptionally important for many editors, especially those that are creating keyframes by the frame or in very tight visual spaces. Vegas has the ability to see markers or regions inserted in the Trimmer on the Timeline for greater consistency in editing. If a region is created in the Trimmer and several markers are placed at desired points inside that region, these markers (and regions) are visible in events on the Timeline. Markers and regions cannot be edited on the Timeline if added in the Trimmer. Events can be reopened in the Trimmer, however, and edited there if necessary.

3.16 Buttons found in the Trimmer tool act as shortcuts for the A or Shift+A commands.

3.17 Regions may overlap and may also be named. No limit exists on the number of regions that can be created in the Trimmer.

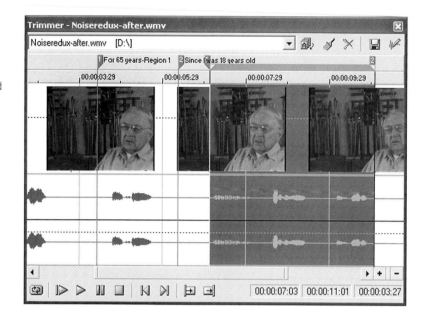

3.18 Markers/regions inserted in Trimmer appear in events on the Timeline.

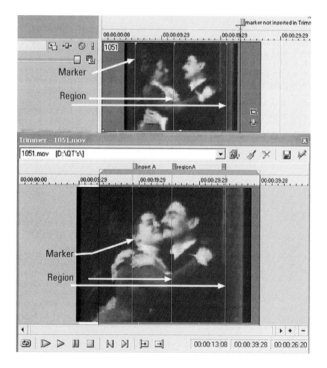

3.19 To clear markers/ regions on events, open the event in the Trimmer, right-click the Marker bar, select Markers/ Regions, and select Delete All or Delete All in Selection.

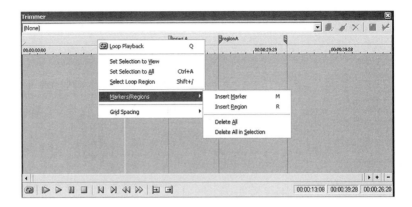

Placing Still Images or Graphics on the Timeline

Photos play a large role in creating video, regardless of the format. Vegas is capable of reading nearly every photo or image format that the Windows environment will allow. Some formats, however, are more optimal than others. Whether scanning via the Vegas Get Photo option, which uses your scanner utilities, or scanning outside of Vegas, the process is essentially the same.

Scan photos at a resolution of not higher than 300 dots per inch (dpi). Because video has a resolution of 72dpi, extremely high resolutions not only are extra effort, they can also cause your image to look poor if the resolution is set too high. If no pan or crop will be done with the photo, a resolution of 72dpi is sufficient. Generally, a resolution of 150dpi is recommended. This resolution is a comfortable size for Vegas to manage quickly and yet provides the ability to pan or crop the image without fear of pixelation. If the Pan/Crop tool will be used to zoom in very tightly on the image, a higher resolution of 300dpi may be called for.

 Tip _____

Double-click a gap in the Timeline. In the Trimmer, mark an in point, but don't worry about an out point. Now select the A key on your keyboard. This will add the clip to the gap, filling the gap exactly. Should you need to move the in point of the event, simply slip edit that point (Alt-drag left or right).

Earlier in this book, we looked at pixels in the computer world as being square and pixels in the DV world as being rectangular. This issue affects stills and graphics that will be inserted into the Vegas Timeline, as Vegas treats graphics and stills as DV when they are square-pixel images from the digital still camera, image editing application, or other source.

With most DV editors, still images and graphics must be created with the correct aspect ratio in mind when planning on dropping the stills or graphics into the DV Timeline. Vegas isn't quite as rigid when it comes to this issue, as the Pan/Crop tool allows the correct aspect to be maintained. When working with stills in an image editor, however, the correct size (NTSC) for a still image is 655×480. This size compensates for the square pixel being stretched in the nonsquare pixel world of DV. The math to derive this pixel aspect ratio (p.a.r.) is as follows:

$720 \times .909$ (p.a.r. of DV) $= 654.48$.

For those who like to round down, 654 works equally well. The correct aspect for PAL images is 704×576.

One experiment that demonstrates square versus nonsquare pixels is creating an image in your favorite image editor, such as Adobe PhotoShop or Paint Shop Pro, that is nothing but a circle at a project size of 720×480. Then drop the image straight into Vegas and don't use the Pan/Crop tool. Create the same image at 655×480, place that image in Vegas, and notice the difference. Users of other NLE systems might be familiar with saving files at sizes of 720×534/NTSC. For example,

$534 \times .909 = 485.4$.

This format works equally well, and either format is usable.

Tip
_____

For best results, save still images, graphics, or titles created outside of Vegas at 655×480/150 dpi (NTSC) or 704×576/150 dpi (PAL). If you plan on zooming deeply into a photograph, consider doubling the resolution, or creating images at 1310×960.

Files should be saved as portable network graphics (PNG) files for optimum use in Vegas. Vegas reads JPEG, BMP, GIF, TGA, and most other formats, including the Adobe PSD file format, as well as the TIFF format. The Adobe PhotoShop files, however, will not be broken down into individual layers; they will be shown as one layer. If an alpha channel is present, Vegas will recognize the alpha channel, and those areas will be transparent. TIFF files can be used in Vegas only if QuickTime is installed on the host system (www.quicktime.com). Because Vegas uses QuickTime to read the TIFF file format, TIFF files will slow down the rendering process somewhat. TIFF files also show problematic symptoms in automatically displaying alpha channels. PNG files are a lossless format, so the image is not compressed when saved in the image editing application.

Files may be scanned in at their normal aspect or size and then cropped within Vegas at any time to match aspect ratio, regardless of the original aspect ratio of the photo. This feature is a major time-saver. Sony has created a script (see Chapter 11 for more information on scripts) that will match aspect ratio on all images on the Timeline.

In Chapter 9, the pan/cropping section demonstrates how to match aspect ratio of images when they are not of the correct aspect to fill the screen.

Editing Events on the Timeline

Each piece of media placed on the Timeline becomes an event. Events are then edited to form the final production. Events may be on single or multiple tracks.

Events containing video may be edited using any number of methods. One issue that exists with some NLE systems, however, is that a frame might be split. Vegas gets around this issue for videographers by offering a Quantize to Frames option, ensuring that frames are not split and forcing edits to occur on frame boundaries. When working with video, Quantize to Frames should nearly always be enabled by selecting OPTIONS | QUANTIZE TO FRAMES or pressing Alt+F8. When working with audio only, this feature may, and generally should be, disabled.

The first editing behavior is to edit on the Timeline by extending/reducing the length of an event on the Timeline. This type of editing is called trim-editing.

When a trim-edit occurs with the Ripple tool enabled, media subsequent to the edited event will slide to the left to fill the hole left by the shortened event or slide to the right to make room for the lengthened event. Trim-edits can be done with only a numeric keypad. Selecting keys on the keypad moves the cursor to the beginning or end of an event, and the keypad can be used to edit an event by frames or pixels.

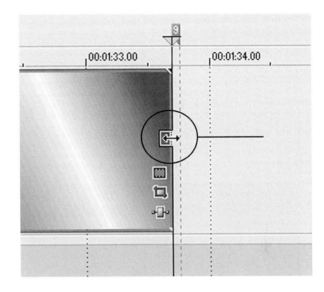

3.20 When the cursor is placed at the head or tail of an event, the cursor changes to a trim-editing cursor. This allows the event to be dragged out or dragged in, thereby lengthening or reducing the event.

Table 3.1   Keyboard Shortcuts Used in Trim-Editing

Shortcut	Description
Press 7 or 9	Moves the cursor to the next event edge, either backward or forward.
Press 1	Trims the event edge to the left by one frame.
Press 3	Trims the event edge to the right by one frame.
Press 4	Trims the event by one pixel to the left.
Press 6	Trims the event by one pixel to the right.
Press 5	Exits the numeric keypad trimming mode.
Press 0	Creates a region/loop around the cursor. The length of the region is specified in OPTIONS | PREFERENCES | EDITING.

Pressing and holding Ctrl+Alt while the cursor is placed between two events will lengthen one event while the other event is shortened, depending on whether the cursor is dragged to the right or left. This feature allows both events to continue to occupy their current total length, while editing the point at which one event ends and the other event begins.

Slip-editing is another basic editing format that allows an event to remain a static length while changing the in/out points of the event. You can slip-edit by holding the Alt key down while moving the mouse inside an event. During slip-edits, the Preview screen shows the first frame and the last frame of an event based on the slip-edit point.

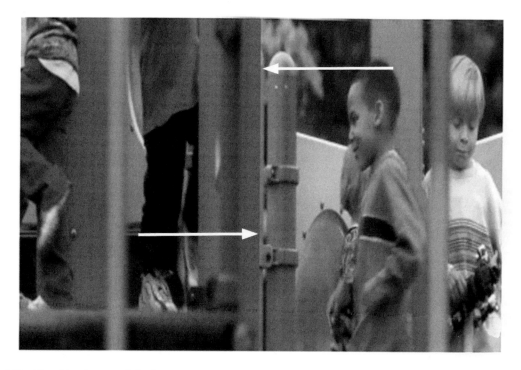

3.21   Slip-editing shows a split Preview screen, displaying the in/out points of a slip-edited event.

The second edit function is to perform a transition. The most basic transition is the cross-fade, otherwise known as a dissolve in the rest of the video world. A cross-fade occurs when two events overlap, and one blends into the other as one event fades out and the subsequent event fades in. By default, Vegas cross-fades events together any time they are overlapped. Automatic cross-fades can be turned off at any time using the Automatic Crossfades button found on the Timeline or by pressing X.

Place two events butted against each other on the Timeline. Now drag the front of the second event partially over the end of the first event. An "X" appears in the space in which the two events overlap.

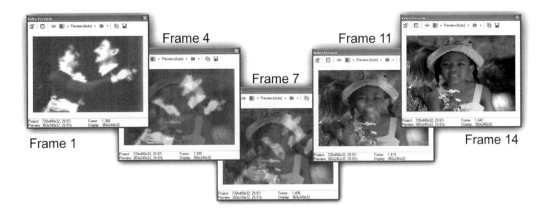

Frame 4

Frame 11

Frame 7

Frame 1

Frame 14

3.22   An example of a cross-fade.

3.23   Cross-fade is indicated by an
        "X" between the two events.

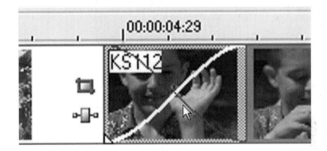

Now play the Timeline by pressing the spacebar or clicking the Play button found on the control bar of the Timeline. The two events will fade from one to the other in equal time. If a faster cross-fade is desired, drag the second event farther away from the first event, or trim either the end of the first event or the beginning of the second event directly on the Timeline. This process is accomplished by placing the cursor in the middle edge of either of the events on

3.24

the Timeline and clicking and dragging in either direction. This process shortens either the outgoing or the incoming event and causes the cross-fade to be shorter in duration.

The shape of the cross-fade can also be controlled. Right-clicking a cross-fade brings up a Crossfade menu, which has several choices regarding the way the cross-fade should occur.

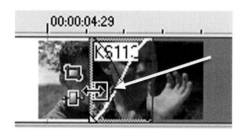

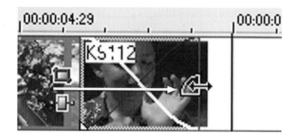

3.25 Grabbing and dragging the end of the first event is shown by a small boxlike icon indicating that the end of the outgoing event is being dragged.

3.26 Grabbing and dragging the beginning of the incoming event is demonstrated by a small quarter-circle-shaped icon. This feature helps eliminate confusion as to which event is being edited.

☞ Tip _____

Create a time selection over a cross-fade, beginning slightly before the cross-fade and ending slightly after the cross-fade. Then press Q, which instructs Vegas to play continuously and loop over the cross-faded area. While playing over the area, all edits and adjustments are seen in realtime in the Preview window as Vegas plays.

After right-clicking the cross-fade, choose the Fade Type menu. A series of cross-fade attributes opens. Choosing one causes this menu to close. Surprisingly, the attributes of a cross-fade have a great impact on how some visual events mix.

Cross-fade behaviors can also be applied to the head or tail of an event. Positioning the cursor at the top of the beginning or end of an event will

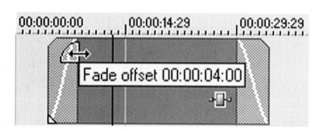

3.27 Fading in from black is a common editing necessity.

change the cursor to the quarter circle form. The head or tail of the event can then be dragged inward to create a fade. This process creates a fade in or out from black.

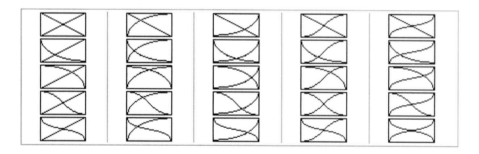

3.28 Vegas offers many cross-fade styles.

The default fade-in color can be changed by selecting OPTIONS | PREFERENCES | VIDEO and clicking the default colors.

3.29 Track fade colors can be customized to create a specific background color.

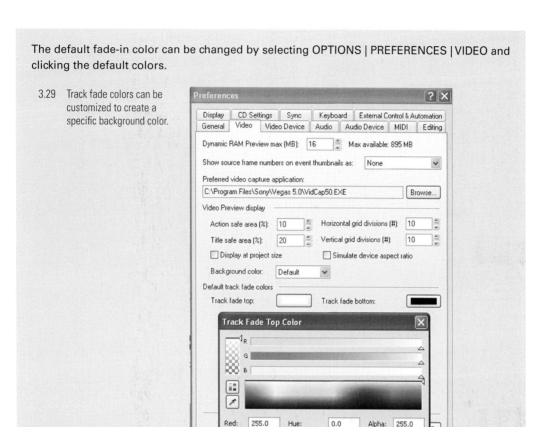

Many of the popular music and children's television shows use colorful backgrounds. Using a customized background is one means of achieving this without having to insert a graphic or generated media event.

A cross-fade is a form of a transition. Vegas has hundreds of built-in transition possibilities, and several thousand more transitions can be installed from third-party vendors, such as Pixelan, Boris, and DebugMode.

To change the transition from the default cross-fade to another transition, select the Transitions tab in the lower-left corner of the dockable windows area to open the Transitions window. If you can't see a tab, press Alt+7, and the Transitions window is displayed. This window is dockable and may be placed anywhere on the screen that is convenient. To change a transition from any style back to a cross-fade, right-click the transition and select TRANSITION | CHANGE TO CROSSFADE or press the / key on the numeric keypad. Other transition choices are also available if you right-click the Transition menu.

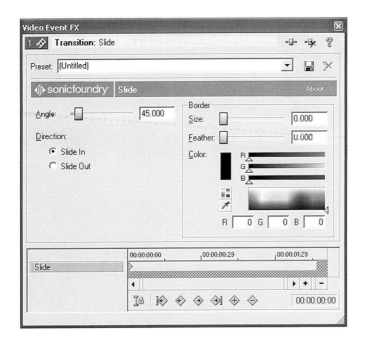

3.30 Slide transition replacing cross-fade and looped for real-time preview.

3.31 All transitions have dialog boxes to edit transition attributes. The Transition dialog box can be called at any time by right-clicking a transition and choosing the Transition Properties menu.

To preview transitions, click the different transition styles and pass the cursor over the choices. Each transition preset becomes active as the cursor moves over it. When you find a desired transition effect, click and drag the transition over the top of the "X" that defines the cross-fade point. The transition dialog window will open, allowing for you to fine-tune the transition, adjusting colors, edges, softness, speed, and other parameters that vary with the different transitions.

Transition properties can be placed on fades as well. This feature is great for bringing in or sending out video for the beginning or end of a presentation.

When you create a fade-in or -out on a video event and then drag a transitional element to the fade, the fade creates a transition from transparent black.

When the Transition Properties dialog opens, at the bottom of every dialog is a keyframe Timeline. This Timeline allows for unique and defined behaviors of a transition in time by adjusting keyframes and the sliders around them. (See "Using Keyframes in Vegas" for more information on how to use keyframes.) Feathering of edges, rates of transition, and color of borders all can be controlled with the available attributes of the specific transitions.

Right-clicking a cross-fade or transition opens a dialog that allows for more transition choices. Vegas will also keep the last five types of transitions in memory so that when you right-click, the last five transitions used are found for rapid access.

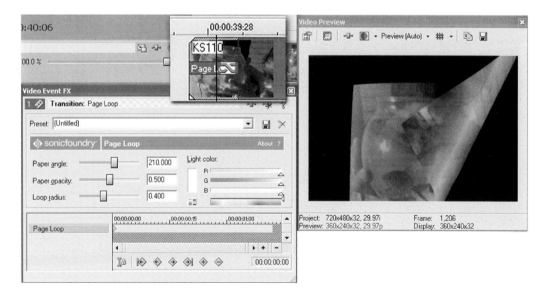

3.32   Transitional element applied to the fade-in of an event. Notice how the transition files out of black, which is the default track fade color.

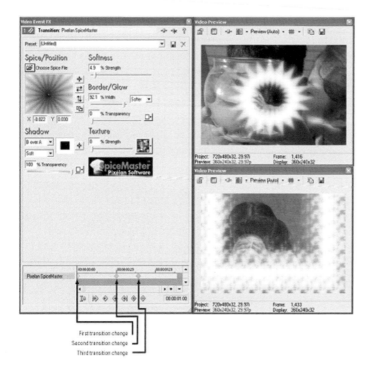

First transition change
Second transition change
Third transition change

3.33   Selecting other transition types with shortcut keys or by selecting in the menu.

Edited sequences can be quickly put together in Vegas using Cuts Only, in which events are butted against each other. Position the cursor at the point at which two events are butted up and press one of the following shortcut keys related to an automatic transition.

```
Press / to cross-fade events.
Press * to create a dissolve.
Press - to create a linear wipe.
```

The two events are pulled together to create a cross-fade, dissolve, or linear wipe.

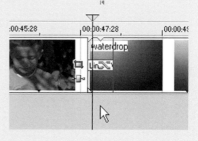

3.34

3.35

One unique feature in Vegas is that when an event is slid out of the area in which a transition occurs, Vegas will remember where the transitional element took place and recall all features of the transition. Whether the original event is placed back in the area in which the transition occurred or a new event is placed there, Vegas will still hold the transition location and information. This issue results from transitions living within events.

Users of older versions of Vegas will find new transitions in the Transition Selection menu, including Portals, Page Rolls, Page Loops, and more.

For experienced NLE users, Vegas's method of displaying cross-fades and transitions is definitely unorthodox. Vegas can display the traditional A/B roll as well, should this be the desired

3.36   Expand Track Layers button

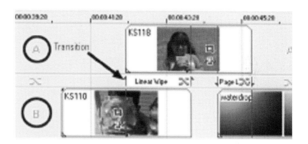

3.37   Vegas displays A/B roll views, although A/B roll views take up twice the amount of screen space as a single-track view.

3.38   Transition types may be selected by right-clicking any transition, and the last used transitions will be displayed and may be chosen in this submenu.

look in the workspace. Click the Expand Track Layers button found on each Video track to show the standard A/B roll.

The concept behind hiding the A/B roll view and showing transitions as cross-fades stems from Vegas's origin as an audio editing tool, in which cross-fades for audio are always viewed as single tracks. Further, it makes more sense in a real-estate-challenged environment, such as a computer screen, to bring as many elements together as possible.

And the Envelope Please …? Transitional Envelopes

Of course, we've seen how Vegas can easily drop in a transition and preview it on the fly to an external monitor, but there are other features and functions hidden in the transition process.

Cross-fade or overlap two events to create a transition as described above. Drop a transition on the overlap. Any transition except the Dissolve will work for this. Now right-click the transition area, and select INSERT/REMOVE ENVELOPE | TRANSITION ENVELOPE from the

submenu. This will insert an envelope in the transition area that is similar to a velocity envelope. By double-clicking on the envelope, envelope points or handles may be inserted.

These points will allow the control of the transitional behavior over time. For instance, maybe the transition needs to reverse itself or perhaps only pause in midtransition. Illustration 3.40 shows a transition reversing and pausing itself.

Transitional envelopes are great for building creative and unique transitions, but the feature may also be used for powerful compositing techniques. By using lengthy transitions coupled with transitional envelopes, entire composites and virtual transitions may be created with only three or four video events. To do this, you'll need to reduce the opacity of the tracks containing the transitional envelopes and layer them over another video event on a lower track. This technique can yield beautiful results when combined with complementary media.

3.39   Right-click the transition for this submenu to appear.

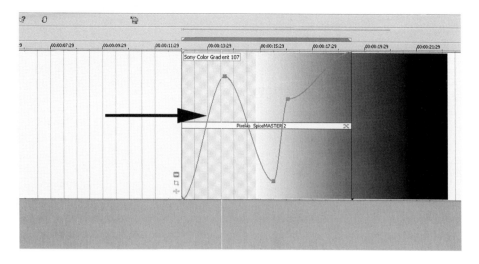

3.40 Where the envelope is pulled down, the transition will reverse. The flattened line indicates that the transition is paused and will hold in that position.

Using Keyframes in Vegas

Vegas has always had a unique method of keyframing. Keyframes are often misunderstood and are sometimes difficult for newcomers to the world of video editing.

Keyframes are nothing more than indicators in time, defined by how an event should behave at a specific moment and an instruction sent to a process at a specific moment during that time. They animate sequences of images or control effect parameters over time.

We live our lives by keyframes. All of us have specific moments in time when we do certain things, such as going to bed, eating a meal, traveling to work, or making a phone call. Appointment books are nothing more than analog keyframes.

In the video editing world, animation world, and audio editing world, keyframes are used to instruct an event to color correct, change speed, delay, move onscreen, pan, change volume, and much more at specific points in time. The tools that define these instructions are keyframes. Keyframe windows are nothing more than standard clocks, but instead of being round, they are linear.

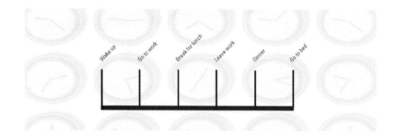

3.41 An average daily keyframe.

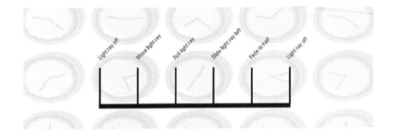

3.42   Keyframes instruct an event regarding how to behave over time.

Vegas departs from most applications in regard to keyframes in that Vegas is event-, track-, or project-based, and separate events can have their own sets of processing and keyframing within those processes, independent of the Timeline. What this means is that an event can be moved on the Timeline, and the keyframes will stay with it!

Imagine doing a 52-minute project for television, and, after the entire editing process is complete, a three-frame error is found in the first 2 minutes of the program. In most applications, if an event is moved even three frames, the entire project will be affected. With Vegas, this is simply not so. In fact, the entire series of events that exists in the hypothetical three frames can be moved to the end of the Timeline, with keyframes and processing intact.

3.43   The selected event length is displayed in the lower-right side of the Timeline.

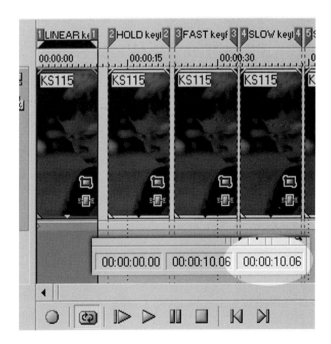

Notice that the length of the event illustrated is 10 seconds and six frames. Double-click the event, and, in the lower-right corner of the editing Timeline, Vegas displays the length of the event selection. You can also right-click the event and look at its properties, where the media length is displayed.

3.44 Event properties are seen when the event is right-clicked and Properties is selected.

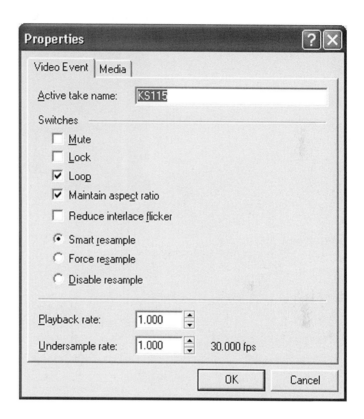

Insert the DVD found in this book and browse to the \veg\ folder. Locate and open the VEG file titled Keyframes. The Timeline will open with the video file shown in the example.

Now, click the Event FX icon found on the event. (If you don't see the icon, go to the OPTIONS | PREFERENCES | GENERAL dialog and check "Show Video Event Buttons.")

This process opens the Video FX plug-in folder. In this example and DVD project, the Wave plug-in has been selected.

Note the first keyframe in the keyframe Timeline, which is indicated by a small diamond.

Now click the 5-second indicator on the Timeline in the Keyframe Timeline window and select the Horizontal Only preset in the Preset dialog box. Notice that a new keyframe or diamond appears on the keyframe Timeline. This diamond indicates that over time the slider will begin to move, causing the event image to change gradually over time, getting more and more wavy until at the 5-second point, it reaches the full effect as dictated by the slider position.

3.45 The Event FX button is found on every event by default. This feature can be turned off in the OPTIONS | PREFERENCES | GENERAL dialog.

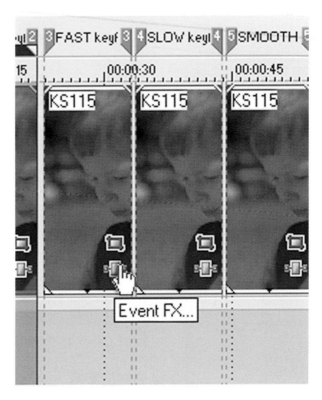

3.46 The first keyframe may be moved anywhere on the keyframe Timeline. Attributes of the first keyframe are shown regardless of the position of the first keyframe, as it is the first indicator of time-based event/track/project behavior.

What if you don't want the event to become more wavy over time but instead want the effect to come in only at a determined time? Click and hold the first keyframe and slide it to the right. Now right-click the keyframe and select one of the keyframe behaviors. Attributes that can be assigned to keyframes comprise Hold, Linear, Fast, Slow, and Smooth.

Hold instructs the keyframe to freeze the settings for the FX in place until a new keyframe is shown, at which point the process jumps to the new settings. Linear creates a gradual change with no curve in the manner in which the sliders move. Fast causes the instructed behavior to slope in quickly and then gradually slow to meet the setting dictated by the slider. Slow does just the opposite; it slowly slopes toward the settings for the second keyframe and speeds up as it reaches its indicated position. Smooth provides temporal and spatial behavior, appearing to start slowly, speed up, and slow down again in time as the controls reach their keyframed positions. All of these attributes are demonstrated on the DVD.

3.47   Keyframe velocities/attributes can be changed by right-clicking a keyframe.

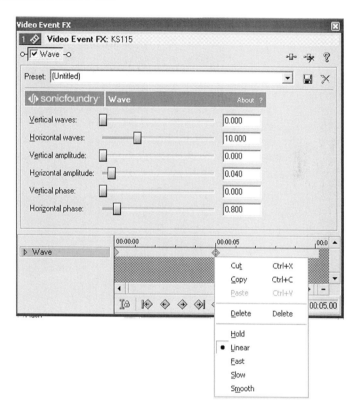

Vegas is efficient in how it syncs the locations of keyframes to a cursor position. This feature can save hours of time trying to place keyframes correctly.

Move to Region 6 on the editing Timeline of the Keyframes project. Place the cursor anywhere on the editing Timeline inside the event contained in Region 6. Notice that inside the keyframe Timeline, the cursor will move in sync to wherever the cursor is located on the editing Timeline. Now move the horizontal amplitude slider. Notice that Vegas automatically inserts a keyframe at that moment in time.

Now double-click the time indicator inside the plug-in.

Be aware that with the automation features in Vegas, keyframes may be automatically created when looping video and adjusting filter attributes. This is a great feature, if you intend for this to happen. However, if multiple keyframes start appearing and they're not desired, be certain to disarm automation in the video track. You'll have to relaunch the plug-in. You can also disable the sync to cursor in the plug-in dialog.

Enter a new time of 00:00:06:10, which will move the cursor inside the keyframe Timeline and will move the cursor to the same position on the editing Timeline. Now slide the vertical amplitude slider all the way to the right. Notice how the preview of the event image changes to match the setting, while at the same time Vegas inserts a new keyframe at the position of 00:00:06:10. Either move the cursor tool with arrow keys or mouse or double-click the time indicator inside the keyframe tool or the main editing window time indicator to place the cursor with frame accuracy for keyframing effects or other processing.

Nearly everything in Vegas is keyframable. Pan/Crop settings can be keyframed, as can Track Motion behaviors. Track Motion will show up on the Timeline of the main editing window. Region 7 of the Keyframes project contains Track Motion keyframes. Notice that they are displayed on the edit Timeline. Track Motion can dramatically affect how events are shown, and, to prevent confusion about oddly sized events on a track, these are displayed prominently.

Keyframes are unlimited as to their application. They can be applied to as many FX as necessary to make an event meet the desired appearance. Some effects seen on television today contain hundreds of keyframes in 1 to 2 seconds of video.

3.48   Double-click the time indicator inside the plug-in to place the cursor at the exact time.

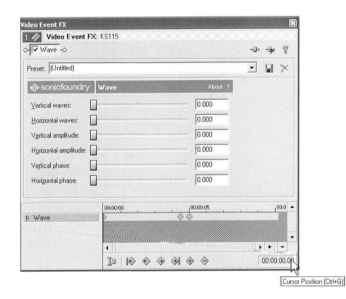

3.49   Track Motion keyframes can be viewed directly on the Timeline by double-clicking a track keyframe and expanding the Track Motion Keyframes view.

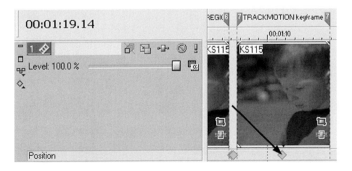

Keyframes can be copied and pasted inside the keyframe Timeline. Move the cursor to the Region 9 event on the editing Timeline. Click the Edit Generated Media button in the upper-right corner of the event.

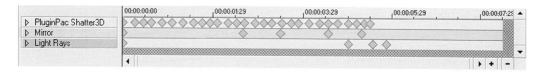

3.50   This event keyframes page contains 28 keyframes in less than 3 seconds of video. Multiple keyframes allow for powerful uses of FX.

The Edit Generated Media dialog will open, and five keyframes will show on the keyframe Timeline. While holding the left mouse button down, draw around the five keyframes. When all keyframes are selected, they'll have a white diamond in the middle of each keyframe and will become white in color. Copy the keyframes by either right-clicking and selecting Copy or pressing Ctrl+C. Move the cursor inside the keyframe Timeline to 00:00:01:15 by either clicking the cursor to position or double-clicking the keyframe time display. Now paste the keyframes by right-clicking and selecting Paste or by pressing Ctrl+V. Repeat the action again at 00:00:03:00. All five keyframes are now repeated three times. Play the media. Notice how it loops the keyframe attributes. These keyframes can also be copied and pasted into another keyframe Timeline of a similar nature.

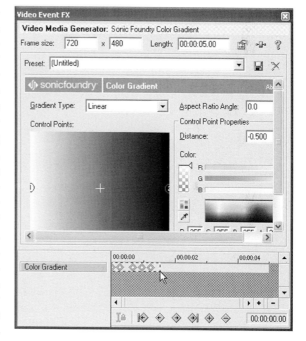

3.51   Keyframes can be copied and pasted within their own keyframe Timeline or pasted as event attributes to another event.

To complete the explanation of Vegas's keyframing attributes and their incredible power, go to the editing Timeline of the Keyframes project. Click and hold Region 1, Linear Keyframe setting. Slide it to the end of the project, past Region 8 Multiple Keyframes-FX. Place the cursor at the front of Region 1 and play. Notice that the keyframes stayed with the event. Therefore, events can be copied and pasted, slid on the Timeline, or moved to completely different tracks. If a keyframed event is copied in one instance of Vegas, it can be pasted into another instance of Vegas with keyframes intact. This feature is unique in the NLE world. Keyframes placed on events stay with the events. Keyframes placed on a track will stay with the track.

Tracks, however, may not be moved horizontally in time; they may be moved only vertically in priority. Keyframes may also be applied at the project setting. Any video plug-in that shows up in Vegas is keyframable. Audio plug-ins are automatable, which is similar to keyframing, yet are managed and viewed differently. (Vegas uses keyframes to control the surround-sound movement, which is discussed in Chapter 7.)

Learning to understand and manage keyframes is perhaps the most important and valuable lesson to be learned and understood in the video editing world, whether working with Vegas or other NLE systems. Various NLEs have unique keyframing attributes, but regardless of the system, all NLEs use keyframes in one form or another.

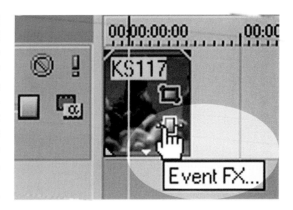

3.52 Click the Event Video FX button found on each event by default. It is seen on every visual event, regardless of whether it's a still photo, graphic, or video event.

Filters in Vegas

Vegas is jam-packed with filters to enhance, correct, and design graphic and video events, either bringing substandard images to an acceptable level or allowing editors the expression of artistic freedom.

Filters, also known as plug-ins,

3.53 Dragging FX or clicking an FX button on the Track Control pane has the same effect.

are found in the Plug-Ins folder and are accessible from many points in Vegas. Opening the VIEW | PLUGINS menu will show the effects found in Vegas. Vegas comes with more than 40 plug-ins, ranging from color-correction tools to swirls, waves, and pixelate filters.

Although all filters/plug-ins have presets, learning the settings and behaviors of the plug-ins makes for very creative and powerful image processing in Vegas.

As with nearly all other aspects of Vegas, plug-ins can be inserted at the event, track, or project level. Plug-ins can be dragged and dropped or selected from menus selected at the event, track, or project levels.

Plug-ins dropped on

- An event affect only that specific event on the Timeline
- A track affect all events on the track that are affected by the plug-in's attributes
- Project/video output level affect every track, event, and final output in the project
- Media in the Media Pool will affect all events relative to that media in the Media Pool

To add plug-ins to an event, click the FX button on the event. These buttons are visible by default, but if for some reason they are not shown, the OPTIONS | PREFERENCES | GENERAL dialog has a checkbox for "Show Video Event Buttons" that should be checked. If having the buttons visible is not desired, uncheck this box. Events can also be right-clicked and Video Event Effects chosen from the menu.

FX can also be dragged directly onto events from the FX menus. To view all FX at one time, press Alt+8 or select VIEW | VIDEO FX to open the FX selection box.

To have a thumbnail preview of some FX properties, keep the FX window open and in the dockable windows section or drag it onto a second monitor. It also makes for a great space from which to drag and drop FX.

Dragging FX to a Track Control pane places FX on an entire track. Each track also has an FX button on it. Any FX dragged to the Track Control pane will result in all events having FX applied to them. The only way to control FX on individual events is to use keyframes.

FX can be applied at the project-level by dragging FX to the Preview window or by clicking the Video Output FX button on the toolbar in the Preview window. All video, graphics, and still events on every track will be processed at the project or output level.

The primary use for FX at the project or output level is for plug-ins along the lines of the

- Timecode plug-in
- NTSC/broadcast clamp
- Black restore

Any FX, however, can be placed on the project.

As many FX as necessary can be applied to events, tracks, or the project. FX are arranged in the order in which they are applied; this order is easily changed by either dragging one plug-in to its place on the plug-in bar or by clicking the "Shift plug-in left/shift plug-in right" button found on the FX Chooser plug-in bar.

3.54   Inserting FX at the project level.

3.55   The timecode plug-in places a timecode burn on the project window.

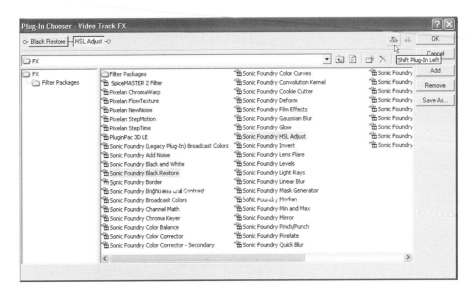

3.56   Arranging the order of plug-ins can be done via button press or by dragging plug-ins to the desired priority.

You can save chains of FX in Vegas. Many times, a project requires repetitive use of the same series of FX. Creating presets and inserting FX in sequence can be time-consuming. For example, a project might have poorly shot video and requires color correction, brightness adjustment, and broadcast color clamp. Rather than inserting these FX time after time, the series of FX, complete with presets, can be recalled after it is saved as a chain. This process saves tremendous time, especially in an editing house where a set flow of work exists.

Each editor can create his or her own chains to suit his or her own workflow.

To save the chain of plug-ins as a preset:

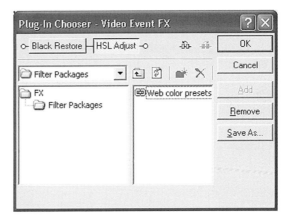

3.57   Find preset chains in the FX packages folder, which are shown each time FX are to be applied to events, tracks, or projects.

1.   Select the plug-ins and arrange their priority.

2.   Click the Save-As button. The Chain dialog is displayed.

3.   Name the chain/preset.

4.   Press Enter to accept the changes you've made to save the preset.

The chain preset is now displayed in the plug-in chooser and is available from the Filter Packages view. (The same process applies to audio presets.)

Vegas has a tremendously powerful feature that allows video output to be viewed at both pre- and postprocess settings. Oftentimes, editors find themselves wanting to see original video next to the processed video. This option has not been possible in the past without complex hardware. Now it is possible with Vegas's split-screen preview.

The Split Screen View Selection Tool button is shown on the Preview Window toolbar.

Selecting this button in the Preview window makes Vegas automatically split the preview screen, which shows affected media on one half and original video on the other half. However, Vegas allows users to define the areas where preview or original video is viewed by drawing a square or rectangle over the screen. Drawing the shape on the preview screen creates a hole where original video is seen.

3.58   Split Screen View Selection Tool button.

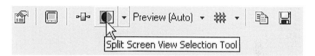

3.59, 3.60   The area to view the original versus processed video is user-defined.

The split preview of processed and original video is also viewable on an external monitor, which makes color correction in Vegas advanced compared to even exceptionally high-end NLE systems. The capability to compare processed video to original video on an external monitor without rendering a file provides editors with a newfound speed, workflow, and freedom from concerns about accuracy in the editing workflow. This feature coupled with RAM renders allows editors to immediately see full-motion/full-frame-rate accurate views of edited media, limited only by RAM and processor speed.

The split-screen Preview window can be used to show contents of the clipboard during the preview of a Timeline section. Position the cursor on the Timeline and click the Copy Snapshot button in the Video Preview window to copy a frame as a still image to the clipboard. Move the cursor to another point on the Timeline.

On the Split Screen View Selection Tool button, click the dropdown menu arrow and select Clipboard. The contents of the clipboard are displayed in the Preview window or external monitor. The area in which the clipboard contents are displayed is defined by the area drawn with the cursor inside the Preview window area. If the entire clipboard clip is to be shown, redraw the cursor over the entire Preview window area. The underlying clip indicating the location of the cursor is no longer shown. Turn off the split-screen preview or redraw the viewing area to view underlying events. Double-clicking the Preview window returns the Preview window to its default state.

How Filters/Plug-ins Function

Whereas far too many plug-ins are available in Vegas to describe the attributes of each, some common plug-ins are of great benefit to understand. Each plug-in has a series of presets but experimenting with the settings increases the power of the plug-in tremendously. A number of third-party filters are available, some of which are described in the following list:

- Add Noise—adds grain or noise at various levels.

3.61

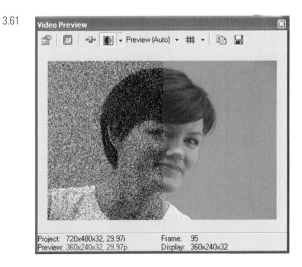

- Chromakey—removes colors from an image and replaces with other information, similar to the weatherperson on the television news.

3.62

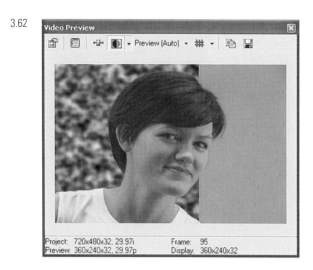

- Convolution Kernel—embosses, finds lines, or creates a motion photographic image from video.

3.63

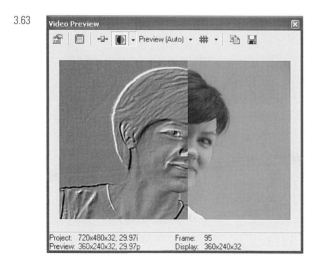

- Lens Flares—hides anomalies, makes still images look more like video, and gives flair to wide-video shots.

3.64

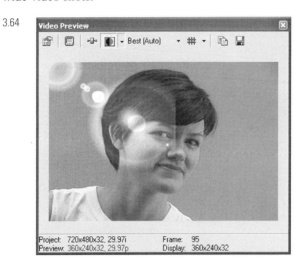

- Mirror—creates mirrored images of any portion of the screen. When used correctly with generated media, the plug-in can emulate a kaleidoscope.

3.65

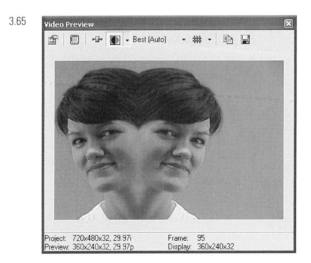

- Pixelan's ChromaWarp—provides infinite artistic choices for the beginning and experienced editor.

3.66
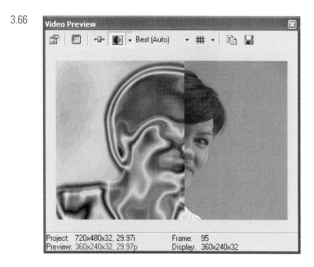

- DebugMode's 3D Pak—adds some wonderful 3D elements to the Vegas editing toolbox.

3.67

Some of these plug-ins are free, and demo versions are included on the disk in this book.

Vegas has a feature that is often overlooked yet should not be. Vegas has the ability to build a RAM preview of the final appearance of an event so that it can be seen full motion/full frame rate. The RAM preview is important to be able to see, particularly in situations in which keyframes are inserted in tight time spaces. Slower processors or FX-heavy, multiple events can tax the processor so much that some keyframes simply can't be drawn due to lack of processor power. Using a RAM render causes these sections to be drawn without creating a temporary file on a hard drive.

To initiate a RAM render, make a selection on the Timeline. Pressing Shift+B instructs Vegas to begin rendering the time selection to RAM. The amount of RAM installed in the computer determines the length of time that RAM can render. This is why as much RAM as possible is best in most editing systems. By default, Vegas allocates 16MB of RAM to the RAM preview. Opening the OPTIONS | PREFERENCES | VIDEO dialog gives users the ability to adjust the amount of RAM to be used for RAM preview renders. Vegas subtracts 128MB of RAM from all available RAM for preview purposes. Even if only 128MB are available, Vegas makes allowances for up to 16MB of RAM. However, any available RAM in excess of 128MB can be used for RAM renders. (One hundred percent of RAM may not be used, as the operating system and Vegas require 128MB of RAM space to operate properly.)

When a project contains a large number of still images (i.e., JPEGs, PNGs, etc), keep the Dynamic RAM setting in the OPTIONS | PREFERENCES | VIDEO tab set to approximately 75 percent of total system RAM. When working in projects that don't have large numbers of graphic images, keep the Dynamic RAM value to 512MB or lower.

Although RAM renders benefit external previews, previews on external monitors may not be full frame rate in slower machines. If full resolution/full frame rate are required for an external preview, a standard prerender may be required on edited/recompressed media. Pressing Shift+M opens the prerender dialog.

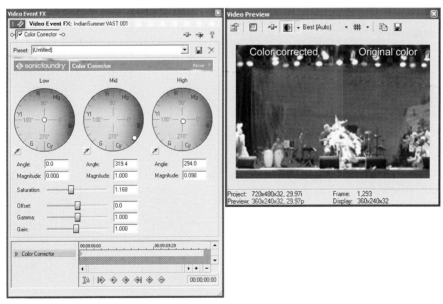

3.68   Color correction can be viewed in realtime on an external or internal monitor.

One of the more in-demand, necessary, and powerful plug-ins added is the Color Corrector tool. This palette-based tool offers extremely fast color correction, and, when combined with the Split-Pane Preview window, it's simple to view changes in color on either an external monitor or a gamma-corrected computer monitor.

The Color Corrector plug-in can be dragged and dropped on an event, track, or entire project. It can be used to simulate color effects as well, such as those seen in the movies *Payback* and *Traffic*.

Double-clicking the dot in the color-correction palette resets the palette to zero. Most controls in Vegas act in this manner; double-clicking directly on a control resets that control to its default or null value.

Colors can be sampled using the Eyedropper tool found in the low/mid/highlight palettes to assist in selecting the color curve.

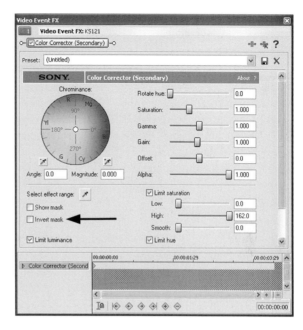

3.69 The Secondary Color Corrector in Vegas, adding an Invert Mask option.

The Secondary Color Corrector makes replacing colors easy and intuitive. This filter allows the *"Pleasantville"* look to be created quickly and easily. See Chapter 6—Color Correction and Manipulation—for detailed information on how to use this small but powerful tool, Secondary Color Correction. Briefly, it allows for a color or series of colors to be replaced or used as masks through which other media can show. Start by selecting a color to be replaced. Shut off external monitor preview while selecting colors. A single color or gradient of color can be selected. Best results are obtained by working with a single color and using more than one instance of the Secondary Color Corrector.

☛ Tip

Any time video has a final destination where it might be viewed on a television monitor of any kind, it is strongly advised that a good-quality television or broadcast monitor be used to preview video; otherwise it is far too easy to have incorrect colors, borders, or margins. If video will be seen only on a computer monitor as streaming media or intranet media, an external monitor is unnecessary.

One of the most sought-after looks in DV production is the ability to have video appear more filmlike. Although shooting and production are a huge part of this process, there are some steps that can be taken to make video more filmlike.

Making video look more like film has been a goal of videographers since desktop video was a concept. Video simply cannot look exactly like film, due in part to the perfection of video and the conversion process, the compression process, and the interpretation of imagery. Film, shot on celluloid, is an analog format that has its own warts but warts that have defined how our eyes see images. Someone once said, "Video is what the eye sees, film is what the imagination sees." Kodak's Tom Wallis commented, "Film feels organic to audiences, and that's why they associate a film look with fantasy and video with reality." There is a great amount of truth to this, hence the desire to make video look more like film.

Many companies offer "cure-all" plug-ins to make video more filmlike, but in the opinion of all but the most amateur, these plugs merely make video look like video treated to look like film. Compared to the real deal, it's pretty clear what is what. Some of the more expensive tools, such as Magic Bullet from Red Giant, can do an excellent job with video shot like film, but Vegas can approximate most of that same look without the plug-in tools.

First off, to make video more filmlike in appearance, the video must be shot like film would be shot. Great lighting, shadows, and depth of field are critical. DV cameras allow for too much depth of field in most cases, so videographers who are aware of this also are aware of the many workarounds to get a good shot with tight foreground focus and weak background focus. For instance, using a Neutral Density filter and opening the iris to full helps. Blurred backgrounds quickly indicate a sense of "unreality" and go a long way to getting video to look more filmlike. Shooting through pantyhose behind the lens or shooting through a Tiffen Black Mist filter can help soften the look too. Opening the iris and reducing the amount of light that can pass the filter will call for more and better lighting, too. With cams like Sony's PD150/170, you can easily underexpose and then correct in post if you know what you are doing. Be cautious of this workflow with cameras that are noisy in low light. Take careful notes, as voice notes on the tape or have an assistant write down the settings. Starting each roll with a gradient or shot colorbars will help define colors under conditions when it comes time to correct in post.

Next on the list is cadence. NTSC video is shot at 29.97fps, and PAL video is shot at 25.00fps. Film cameras shoot at 24.00 frames per second. The 24 frame "stutter" gets DV closer to film pretty quickly. Many great filmmakers who find themselves having to work with digital video shoot with PAL cameras, as it's not a big thing at all to match 25 frames to 24 frames per second. In fact, if you plan on making a feature that looks like it was shot on film, acquiring a PAL camera should be a consideration. Panasonic offers the DVX100, a DV cam that shoots at 24fps. Some folks don't care for the video quality, whereas they love the cadence of 24fps. Some folks just aren't interested in learning another camera or another format. Another difference is the interlaced format of NTSC video and film being progressive scan. But what if you don't have a PAL or 24fps camera?

This is where Vegas and its format-agnostic, resolution-independent feature set comes in. Vegas is indeed optimized for capture, editing, and output of DV files, yet it does offer other alternatives, too, thereby removing the limitations so many applications impose on the editing process.

Vegas is capable of working with 24p natively, performing what's known as 3:2 pulldown during playback. This is referred to as "inverse telecine." Telecine is the process of converting 24 fps to 29.97 fps. Therefore, pulling the frames back out is known as inverse telecine or IVTC. For a simple explanation about pulldown, go here:

Vegas will easily convert 29.97 fps footage (commonly referred to as 60i) to 24p, which is actually 24.976 fps. This creates the cadence of film, where during the process essentially 6 frames or 12 half-frames per second are removed from the stream. Another way of expressing the difference between 24p and 60i or 50i is: NTSC is 59.94 fields (60i) per second, PAL is 50 (50i) fields per second. Film is 24 full frames per second. NTSC and PAL have the look of reality because of the smooth motion rendition. Part of the film look is the much slower 24 fps acquisition rate. To simulate this with video, you must throw away or blend fields to create 24, 29.97, or 25 frames per second instead of twice as many fields per second. The interpolation of the removed frames is pretty critical to making this all look right. Also important to consider is working with 24p titles, transitions, and generated media to keep the image accurate. To my knowledge, Vegas is currently the only application working with native 24p transitions, titles, FX, and generated media. Nevertheless, here's a workflow to edit your 60i or 50i (PAL) as 24p media without losing quality.

3.70   Letterboxing goes a long way to helping video look more filmlike. These images are before and after filmlike processing as described here.

Editing and Converting

First, edit your media on the Timeline as individual events and cuts-only. Do not do any transitions, titles, or FX at this time. You might want to leave heads and tails on the rendered events for future transitions or edit requirements. Render these individual clips out by double-clicking the event to select the event as its own region. These events will be rendered out to a compressed or uncompressed 24p format. Save the .veg file. Some users might have issues with the render to DV instead of uncompressed, but the Vegas codec holds up just great, and most users will have no issue with the quality of image going from DV to DV. Once all the events have been edited, render them individually by creating a template containing the following settings:

1. Set the Project Properties/Deinterlace mode to Blend Fields (default).

2. Choose FILE | RENDER AS.

3. Name the file, choose .avi as the file format, and select NTSC or PAL DV (inserting 2:3 Pulldown).

4. If you wish to render Uncompressed, select the Custom button. In the General tab, select rendering quality of Best. Select the Video tab, in the Video Format dropdown box, and select "Uncompressed."

5. Render this event to a folder where it can be located later. Render all events as 24p (NTSC-DV or Uncompressed).

After all events have been edited, open the saved .veg file if you've closed it down, and set the Project Properties to 24p (NTSC or PAL). If you've rendered to Uncompressed, replace the events in the Media Pool with the 24p uncompressed files you created earlier. Do the same if you've rendered to 24p DV. As soon as all the events in the Media Pool have been replaced, notice that any uncompressed events are letterboxed. (DV compressed files won't have this issue.) This is due to uncompressed media being a square-pixel aspect ratio and DV media being nonsquare pixels. To correct this, right-click the first event on the Timeline and select Properties. In the Properties dialog, select the Media tab.

Aspect Ratio

If you've rendered uncompressed media, select the Pixel Aspect Ratio dropdown in the Media tab and choose .909 as the aspect ratio. The first event's image will no longer be letterboxed in the Preview window.

Uncompressed or DV, right-click the first event again and choose SWITCHES | DISABLE RESAMPLE. This will prevent the project from trying to reinsert the missing frames for playback.

Copy the first event, then right-click the second event and choose Select Events to End. Right-click again and select Paste Event Attributes. This will cause all events to have the resample disabled and correct pixel aspect ratio. Now you can begin editing.

One of the first things viewers associate with the film look is letterboxing or 16:9 screen. So, using Pan/Crop on the first event, choose the 16:9 crop preset from the Pan/Crop dropdown menu. If you choose this option, you'll need to apply this to all events on the Timeline, so once again copy the first event, select events to end, and choose Paste Attributes. This will apply the letterbox to all events on the Timeline. Depending on the framing of the shots, you might need to adjust individual events for composition.

Tip_____

If you're working with HDV, the pixel aspect ratio of the graphic in PhotoShop or other graphic editor should be 1.333, not .909, which DV requires.

Apply transitions as necessary. Apply titles and any other overlays. These will be generated at 24fps and progressive scanned as determined by the project properties.

Color correction can be applied at the track level to create a similar look for all events. However, if individual events were shot under different lighting circumstances, it might be advisable to put all similar events on single tracks or save color-correction presets per shot location so that color correction may be quickly applied to groups of shots.

Gamma

Another difference in film from video is gamma, or an adjustment between input and output, and how the eye perceives the difference between film and video. Although Vegas doesn't have a specific plug-in for gamma compensation, it does have Color Curves, which essentially accomplish the same goals. Drop the Color Curves filter on the Preview window to apply it to the entire project.

Experiment!

After applying these basics, the next steps are entirely experimental and subject to personal preferences and will vary depending on the desired final output appearance. However, adding an HSL filter to saturate the colors, adding a touch of Glow, will go a long way to getting a great filmlike look. For the demo file, I used the Zenoté Glow set to 1/4 Tiffen, plus the Zenoté Film Grain set to 35mm plug-ins. Sony has a good Glow filter as well; I find I like the Zenoté a little better as it's slightly smoother, and the Film Grain is a little quicker to use; but the Sony Film Grain can be tweaked to look

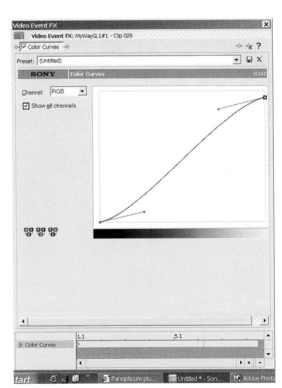

3.71 Notice this curve and how it compensates for differences in gamma. View this on an external monitor and be very surprised at how powerful this underestimated tool is.

similar to the presets of the Zenoté plug. Adding Motion Blur to pans or transitory elements can also make a difference in a shot. Consider using SuperSampling on Motion Blur shots. Don't forget that Pixelan has some excellent film-look plug-ins for Vegas as well. Their Spicefilters are some of the coolest plugs available for Vegas.

From this point it's entirely your desire, degree of experimentation, and quality of original video that will determine the final output. The demo video was shot entirely with existing light, backlit, and generally poorly composed, but the quality of color shift and filmlike imagery is clear to see regardless of its original quality. Had it been lit correctly and shot with an eye for filmlike composition, it would be even more effortless to create a filmlike appearance. It can't be stressed enough that the lighting, shooting technique, and composition make all the difference in the world. Don't expect to shoot with a palmcorder and no tripod with a digital zoom and expect to have imagery that looks like it was shot with an Arriflex. It's not only a pipe dream, it's impossible. Even the most expensive, top-end plug-ins can't work these sorts of miracles, but Vegas surely comes close to being a miracle worker with bad footage and can make really good footage look fantastic.

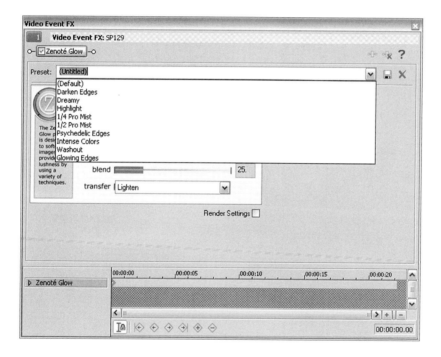

3.72   The Zenoté plug-ins go a long way toward creating a filmlike appearance.

Shooting Modes

When shooting with most any DV camera, shoot in interlaced mode rather than in frame or "film mode" as some of the cameras call it. Otherwise you are throwing away pixels that otherwise add to the quality of the original image. Some cameras actually cut the frame rate to 15 fps when shooting in a Progressive mode. Other cams simply shift pixels to create a film look.

It's generally better to do deinterlacing at the NLE rather than throw away data that can otherwise improve the picture. Spend some time studying lighting, contrast, and camera angles. Experiment with ND filters and lighting, and not only will you find that your image improves substantially, but you'll become a better shooter and editor for it. Hollywood rarely uses a zooming lens, but rather uses a prime lens (a fixed focal length) and a dolly or jib to move into or out of a shot. Try shooting without using a zoom. You'll find a better look, and a more disciplined shooting style will help you plan shots better.

Output

In case it's not immediately obvious, to print this to tape requires a camera or deck capable of receiving a 24p stream. If you already have a camera, most of this tutorial is of no value, so we'll set that aside. This technique is most valuable for printing to DVD and competing with some of the bigger fish in the market when it comes to film look. I showed a video that was created with these techniques at a small film festival in Milwaukee, Wisconsin, in September of 2004. A reasonably well-known director asked me what kind of film I'd shot it on. He was shocked when I told him it was shot on a pair of DV cameras. The video won first place in the children's category. It was shown from DVD. Render the project out using the Vegas 24p NTSC or PAL template. You can render it as a DVD Architect NTSC/PAL video stream if you intend on rendering an AC-3 file for the audio or render it as a 24p NTSC/PAL file in which the audio will be packaged with the video stream.

 *Tip*_____

Be sure to check out the ReelPak products by David Jimerson, as they mimic many popular film looks and are very fast to render.

These small tips should help you to create a look that approaches that of film fairly easily. It is indeed a process in terms of the steps required; at the same time it provides a great alternative means to a 24p camera and, more importantly, as the 24p formats and technologies develop, it allows owners of typical DV cams to have the 24p look without buying a new cam. The greatest advantage of this workflow is that up to 25 percent more media can be stored off onto a DVD when the media is 24p. To preview this media on an external monitor, you'll need to insert the pulldown, but Vegas can also do that on the fly. (See Chapter 10 for more information.) Playback might be a little slower due to the inserted frames in realtime, but it's still capable of being viewed on an external monitor for color correction and other filter tweaking. (The output frame rate must be at 29.97fps/NTSC or 25.00fps/PAL to be viewed on an external monitor.)

Opacity Envelopes

Each video track in Vegas has an opacity control, although no shortcut key is available. Opacity is the level at which an event is visible. At 0 percent opacity, an event is completely transparent, and at 100 percent opacity, the event is completely visible with zero transparency, which is the opposite of how PhotoShop and Ulead control opacity.

The opacity of a track can be altered in one of two methods. The first method is in the Track Control window, in which level/opacity for the entire track can be set. This is not controllable over time but rather sets the level or opacity for every event on the track.

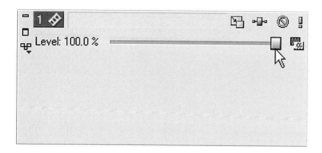

3.73   Track Control pane-level adjustment.

✍ Tip

Be sure your opacity levels are always at 100 percent. If you have a track that seems to be rendering too slow, this is sometimes an indicator that the opacity slider has been moved.

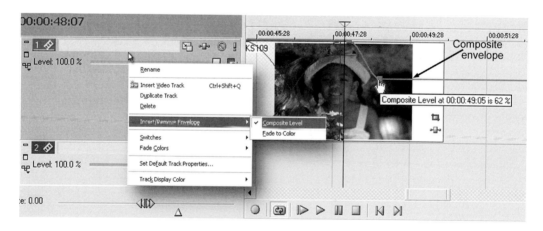

3.74   Adjusting opacity over time. No limit exists as to how many handles/nodes can be placed on the track Timeline.

The second method is to set an opacity envelope in the track, which is done by right-clicking the Track Control pane and selecting Insert/Remove Envelope and then selecting Composite Level from the submenu that will open. This process will insert a blue line (default color) at the top of the video track. Double-clicking this blue line inserts handles or nodes. These handles/nodes allow the compositing envelope to be pulled down and adjusted for opacity level at any point on the video track. To delete a node, right-click it and select Delete.

The following are the envelope modes you have to choose from:

- Linear—straight line fades with no velocity or curve to the actions.

3.75

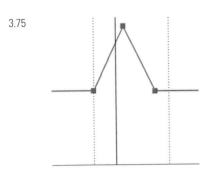

- Smooth—smooth fade ramps slightly into the event before ramping back down.

3.76a

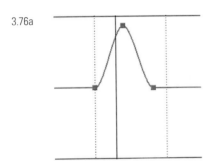

- Fast—fast fade quickly raises or quickly lowers settings.

3.76b

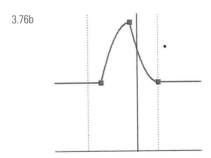

- Slow—slow fade gradually moves in or out.

3.77

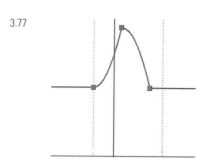

- Sharp—sharp fade moves quickly to the peak movement.

3.78

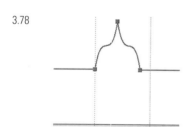

- Hold—hold position has no subtle movement at all and is fairly harsh and obvious.

3.79

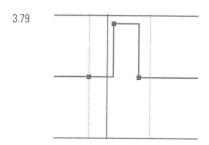

Using the opacity envelope or envelopes, an event can be faded to another event on a different track or to a transparent black.

Open the project called Compositing Envelope.veg, which is on the tutorial DVD. Two video tracks are on the Timeline. Track 1 already has a compositing envelope on it. On the control pane for track 2, right-click and select Insert/Remove Envelope, and then select Composite Level. A blue line, similar to the line found on track 1, will appear. Double-click at the first marker on this line to insert handles/nodes. Pull the handle down to 50 and notice how the gradient found on track 3 becomes visible.

By using compositing envelopes, you can create beautiful fades over multiple layers of video. Compositing envelopes also allow for rapid transition from one event to another with overlay or multiple images. With compositing envelopes in place, as many tracks as the imagination might create can be visible.

If multiple cameras are used on the same shoot, the opacity envelope is an indispensable tool. Place video from multiple cameras on different tracks on the Timeline, lining up their sync with the audio on each track, so that all video tracks are lined up with sync. Delete the audio tracks that are unused, keeping only the audio master track.

For this example, we'll assume three tracks of video and one track of audio are being used. On video tracks 1 and 2, insert compositing envelopes. Leave video track 3 without any adjustment at this time. Play the video until you'd like a fade or cut to occur and drop a marker at that point, pressing M. Stop playback and double-click the compositing envelope at the top of video track 1 to insert a handle. Double-click again slightly after the first handle. Now pull the opacity envelope all the way down to the bottom of video track 1. Now the events in video track 2 are visible. Play the Timeline again, until another fade or cut is desired. Drop another marker and repeat the actions performed above at the new edit point. Now video track 3 is visible. Again play the video until a new fade or cut should occur. Now events from track 2 or track 1 can be brought in by double-clicking the bottom of either video track on the compositing envelope, inserting two points, and pulling the compositing envelope up. In this manner, an entire show can be roughed out quickly.

After all fades and cuts have been made using the opacity envelope, each time a track has been removed from view with the opacity envelope, you can place the cursor on the event, making sure the event is selected. Press S to split the event. Repeat the split at the point in the event just before it fades in again. Now the middle portions of the event can be deleted.

 Open the `compositingenvelopes#2.veg` project from the DVD. (This project also includes the use of the Pan/Crop tools, discussed earlier in this chapter.) This project demonstrates the use of the same video track, panned and cropped, to create the false image of a three-camera shoot from one camera.

The compositing envelope is used to create the original edit points. In this project, you'll need to split out the unused video. Removing the unused portions of the event is not necessary, merely helpful in viewing the overall project.

For more information on multicam editing, view Chapter 4—Multicam Functions in Vegas Pro 8.

Compositing envelopes may be automated, including Mutes, just as Volume, Pan, and other envelopes may be automated. If you own a Mackie Universal Control, you'll be able to use the faders as compositing controls for video, thus giving you an automated video switching system as well as an audio mixer.

Velocity Filters

Velocity filtering allows for media to speed up, slow down, reverse, or freeze-frame, all without cutting clips of media into individual pieces as previously required in most applications. Velocity filtering, or envelopes, as they are known in Vegas, can be applied to any number of clips. The speed at which the envelope interacts with the media may also be controlled via keyframes. Every effect, envelope, or filter can be keyframe-controlled in Vegas, with a variety of shapes for the envelope properties.

Open the `velocitytraining.veg` file found on the DVD.

Notice that on the Timeline a green (default color) line is in the middle of the event. This line demonstrates how the velocity envelope is adjusted. The second event on the Timeline is for you to adjust your own velocity envelope.

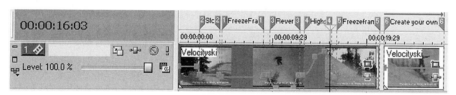

3.80 Velocity envelope inserted, with regions expressing each change in velocity. Handles have various envelope settings on them.

Start by previewing the first clip. Notice how it slows down during the first moments of the event, slowly climbs back to regular speed, and then freezes frame at the end? [You might need to perform a RAM render (Shift+B) if the processor cannot draw the video at normal speed.]

In the second half of the event, the video actually reverses to give an instant replay type of feel. Again, the event freezes frame at the end, allowing time for a blur, added title, special effect, or just a simple dissolve to the subject shot. This option is especially effective with video of high motion, such as sports, chases, or fight scenes. Notice how during the freeze-frame, the Pan/Crop tool is used to create an artificial camera zoom. Another great space to use the velocity envelope is when you have a series of camera zooms that maybe weren't as smooth as they could have been. The envelope can slow down the jerkiness of a poor zoom or speed up a zoom that was too slow. A velocity envelope applied to speed up a fast zoom makes it faster, more frantic, and draws immediate attention to the subject on the screen.

To insert a velocity envelope into a media clip, right-click the clip and select Insert/Remove Velocity Envelope. A green line will appear. The line will be set by default to normal speed, or 100 percent. Double-click the Timeline, and a node or handle will appear. Move down the Timeline a few seconds and double-click again, inserting a second handle. These handles are similar to keyframes, allowing the setting of velocity or speed on the individual event. To delete a node, right-click it and select Delete.

Now, move the handle up or down to set the desired speed. If the desired percentage of speed change can't be precisely achieved by moving the handle up and down, right-click the handle. The dialog box shows the fade choices and speed settings. Select Set T and type in the desired setting. Slow the envelope down just as the zoom reaches its end and make sure the handle on the keyframe is set to Smooth if the media is being sped up or slowed down over a short number of frames. By setting the envelope handle to Smooth, the media won't appear to jerk or jump from slow to fast or from fast to slow.

As the event is sped up or slowed down, artifacts may occur. Avoid this problem by right-clicking the clip, selecting Properties, and checking the Resample box. This process causes the render to slow down somewhat, yet carefully resamples the video to assure smooth picture and motion in almost every instance.

In Vegas, a feature for resampling is available, which allows for smart, forced, or disabled resampling, as shown in Figure 3.81. If Smart Resample is enabled, which is the

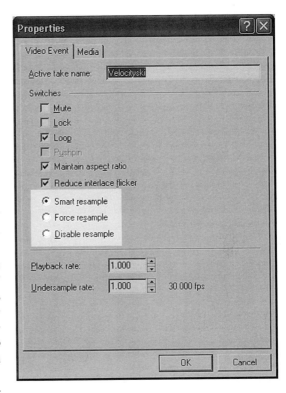

3.81 Resampling features found in Vegas provide for smooth slow motion and velocity events.

default option, Vegas determines whether the event requires resampling. Force Resample is similar to the resampling found in older versions of Vegas, in which Vegas is instructed to resample the event whether it requires it or not. Disable Resample turns resampling off.

Velocity envelopes have been used in nearly every form of special effect there is and can be used for titles, movement control, color keying, and other forms of effects. One favorite is to use an envelope during a title shot, slowing or freezing the subject matter, panning/cropping the media as though the camera zoomed in on the subject, and dropping the opacity of the media so that the title can punch through. This method is exceptionally effective when coupled with a mask and moving media behind the text. Velocity envelopes can be applied to all moving media, including GIF files.

 Tip

Here's a tip for using velocity envelopes on long files: use the Split tool (S key) to split the clip before the actual change/handle of the velocity envelope. Otherwise, the envelope affects the entire file and slows down the render process if the rate is accidentally set to any level but 100 percent, when only a small portion of the event needs to be affected and perhaps resampled.

3.82 Right-clicking on an event calls up the Switches dialog.

Open in Trimmer

Video Event Pan/Crop...
Video Event FX...

Cut   Ctrl+X
Copy   Ctrl+C
Paste Event Attributes
Delete   Delete

Select Events to End
Insert/Remove Velocity Envelope

Switches
Take
Group

Properties...

Mute
Lock
Pushpin
✓ Loop

✓ Maintain Aspect Ratio
Reduce Interlace Flicker

● Smart Resample
Force Resample
Disable Resample

Event Switches in Vegas

Right-clicking any event in Vegas calls up a Switches dialog. These switches dictate how selected events are treated. Events can be muted, locked, looped, video events maintained to aspect ratio, interlace flicker reduced, and audio events normalized. As mentioned previously, Smart Resample, Force Resample, and Disable Resample are also options in the Switches dialog.

Muting a selected audio event or video event prevents the event from being heard or seen on the Timeline. Muted events are dark on the Timeline, demonstrating the muted status.

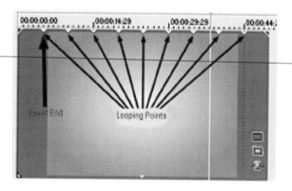

3.83 Looping events is helpful for extending titles and generated media.

Locking an event prevents it from being moved or edited. Locking events is good practice when a section is complete in a long-form video. Locking events causes those events to be grayed out, indicating that they are locked.

Looping events causes events to repeat if they are dragged past their actual end. This option allows events to be extended on the Timeline.

If FX have been applied to an event that is being looped, the FX hold at the last keyframe. This option can be a valuable artistic editing tool with titles, generated media, and backgrounds. If a loop is applied to a generated media event, keyframes loop with the generated media length.

Normalizing an audio event is typically for bringing audio to its maximum volume, based on the highest peak found in the audio. When normalizing is used, Vegas looks for the loudest point of the audio and adjusts the entire file to the loudest possible level without dipping. The maximum level for normalization can also be set manually, if necessary.

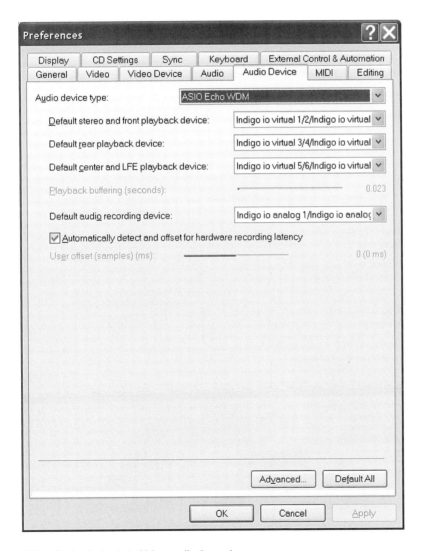

3.84a   Setting the level at which normalization peaks.

Aspect ratio lock can be applied to an event as well. This option prevents Vegas from stretching the aspect of the event's contents should it not match the project settings.

Sometimes graphics or stills that are converted to video do not display well on an interlaced monitor, depending on the colors and resolution. Reducing interlace flicker generally repairs this condition. Without applying "Reduce interlace flicker," graphics and stills often show fringing on video edges or crawling lines on the screen.

When editing long-form video and some short-form videos, it's helpful to be able to lock various events together in a group. By doing this, Cut, Copy/Paste, and Delete can be executed simultaneously, and multiple events can be moved simultaneously. It's also an efficient means of tracking sectionalized video.

To create a group:

1.   Select all events to be included in a group.

2.   Press G or right-click any event.

3.   Select GROUP | CREATE NEW in the submenu that opens.

No limit exists as to how many groups may be created; however, no two groups may share the same event. Groups may be shifted, copied and pasted, or deleted together. After a group is created, right-click any event in the group to select all events in the group. Select GROUP | SELECT ALL from the submenu.

Audio and video files are grouped by default when placed on the Timeline. To remove audio or video from a group or to separate them, select the event to be removed from the group and press U to ungroup that event. The event will be removed from the group. To remove all events from a group, right-click any event in the group and select Clear.

Grouping can be temporarily ignored by clicking the Ignore Event Grouping button on the toolbar. This option instructs Vegas to ignore the groups temporarily, while allowing events to be moved. After this button is released/selected again, however, the group is restored with all event members.

Groups or individual events can be locked on the Timeline to prevent them from being moved.

3.84b

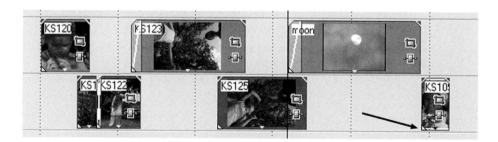

3.85   Six events are grouped. Notice the dark color at the top and bottom of the events. The seventh event is not grouped. Notice the white at the top and bottom, which indicates that this event is not part of the group.

3.86a   Two open windows of Vegas. The first instance, or copy-to instance, doesn't need the Explorer, Trimmer, or other tools open. The second instance, or copy-from Timeline, is where media location, sequencing, markers, and other finishing aids are created.

The Shuffle feature, which is part of the new Ripple Editing toolset, is also a powerful and efficient means of creating a storyboard and rough cut on a single Vegas Timeline. At Sundance Media Group, we commonly use one instance to rough cut, one instance to edit/finish, and a third instance rendering in the background. There are still three Ripple modes, but the difference in the way the Ripple works is just perfect, especially for long-form editing.

My personal workflow is to place all my media on the Timeline with slugs to indicate text or other overlays. Then, I play back the Timeline. Once I locate an undesirable area, I'll highlight that area as though a region were being created. With Ripple enabled in All Tracks, Markers, and Regions, I'll then simply press Ctrl+X (which is mapped to a button on my Shuttle Pro), and this deletes all media in the selected area. Ripple then automatically pulls all events that are downstream so that the next events butt up against the edit point just created by the deleted media/split point. This is a terrific means of working with HDV and rough-cutting either long-form .m2t files or CineForm files and cutting them down to size. From here, it's an easy matter to export as an EDL, AAF, or finish edit inside of Sony Vegas.

Another workflow is to leave Ripple off and simply make the cuts, leaving holes like you see in Illustration 3.86b. These holes can easily be cleared by using a scripting tool like Ultimate S 3.0, or you can double-click in the holes to create a region, enable Ripple, and delete the hole. Ripple will fill the hole with the media that has slid down.

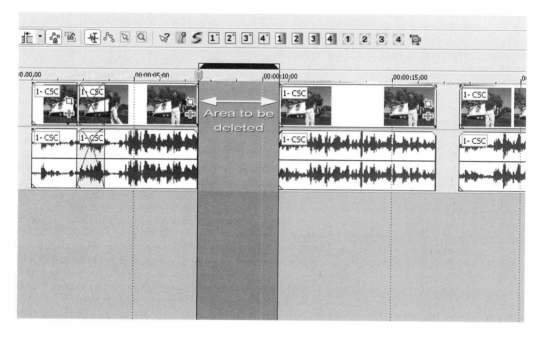

3.86b   With Ripple turned off, holes are left in the Timeline where the deleted media once was. Use Ultimate S 3.0 to clean these up quickly.

If you intend on doing a lot of this style of cutting, you'll want to use a script, as a script can literally ripple hundreds of files in one shot, whereas otherwise you'd have to find every single hole and delete and ripple each hole manually.

In a facility that uses multiple editing stations, one editor creates the rough cuts and saves them as a rough-cut VEG file. A second editor grabs the VEG file without ever copying media and does the color correction and finish work on the project. With a network, this workflow is exceptionally fast, particularly in a small company setting. Additionally, with nested VEG files, it's very easy to create various segments to be placed in a package. The editor of a stem may continue working on his or her assigned segment while others work on their segments, while at the same time, the producer or director might be assembling the package. Simply drop the segment VEG file on the Timeline as though it were a video file. This will slow the computer system.

Some NLE systems use a layout concept called storyboarding, which uses thumbnails that can be dragged into a specific order and placed on the Timeline for fine editing. Vegas does not have this feature. The following two methods, however, can be used by those desiring to edit with a storyboard workflow.

AVI clips in the Windows Explorer (not the Vegas Explorer) show thumbnails if the thumbnail view is enabled. Clips can be shuffled from position to position in the Explorer, creating a sort of storyboard that works for most general purposes.

A more powerful and useful method of storyboarding is to have two instances of Vegas open at one time. The first instance is the active editing workspace, and the second instance is used for creating a storyboard/rough cut that is then copied and pasted into the first instance. What makes this option the more powerful storyboarding tool is that comments, markers, regions, and trims, in addition to storyboarding capabilities, are retained in the second instance. With either a single or a dual monitor setup, this is a fast and powerful way to storyboard and edit.

Create a rough cut in the second instance, copy the Timeline by selecting a region (press Ctrl+A) or the entire Timeline (press Ctrl+C) and then paste into the first instance (press Ctrl+V). Be certain to have "Automatically save markers and regions" enabled in the OPTIONS | PREFERENCES | GENERAL dialog. Otherwise, markers and regions created in the copy-from instance will not be carried over into the copy-to instance.

3.87 Notice that clips are not in numeric order; rather they have been shuffled to create a storyboard.

Nesting

Nesting projects is similar to having subprojects in other NLE systems. This feature allows users to take individual project files (VEG files) and drop them on a single Timeline. Why would you want to do this? It may be that you've got several scenes that you've built in various instances of Vegas. In earlier versions, you needed to render each segment as a file and then compile the file in a master Timeline. Or, you'd have elaborate copy/paste schemes and risk losing any Track motion or other Track-based behaviors. With Vegas, you simply grab a VEG file from the Explorer window and drag it to the Timeline. Vegas then renders a small file very quickly, and that acts as a reference file. This saves the hassle of multiple renders. Further, it avoids rendering a file twice, once as a scene and again as a scene in a longer, completed project. If you've decided to modify a segment of the production, when you modify the VEG file in its own application, the master Timeline, which contains several VEG files, is automatically updated. Another use for this feature is that you might have several people working on various pieces of a project. As each of them updates his or her portion of the project, the master Timeline is also updated. You can even color correct or match images in the master project!

To import a nested VEG is very simple. Open a new project in Vegas. In the Explorer window, locate VEG files from your project. You may find it helpful to name projects with project names and chapter numbers, but you'll likely find your own naming conventions once you start working with this feature.

3.88   All the media on this Timeline, except the audio and chapter headers, is a VEG file. This is an assembled Timeline of chapters and scenes.

Drag the VEG files from the Explorer window to the Timeline. Regardless of how many tracks of video and audio are included in the selected VEG file, it will show on the new Timeline as a single piece of media, much like an AVI, QuickTime, or other file format. Before you can actually play the file back cleanly, the application will render a temporary file that carries the extension of .sfap0, and this file will be rendered to the location that you've specified in the Project Properties dialog. It's a good idea to render these temp files to a location other than the default C: drive. Rendering the file to the temp format will not take Vegas very long, depending on the contents of the VEG file being placed on the Timeline.

If you have Auto-preview enabled, large uncompressed VEG files or files containing substantial numbers of tracks may appear to freeze when the VEG file is selected. Remember that the Explorer window is not buffered, and so you'll want to just leave Vegas alone when it appears to lock up. Eventually, it will play the file, but you may cause the application to lock up if you get impatient and start pressing buttons.

Vegas provides an option in OPTIONS | PREFERENCES, General pane, that allows users to "Ignore fact chunk" with nested VEG files. This is enabled by default. If you experience difficulty with audio files in nested projects, open the Preferences dialog, be sure this box is checked, and restart Vegas. You'll want to delete the related .sfap0 file(s) as well, requiring Vegas to rerender the .sfap0 file(s).

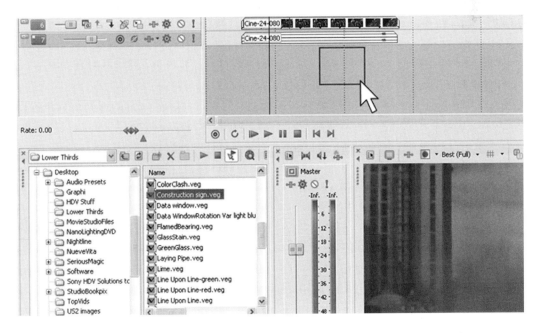

3.89   Drag VEG files from the Vegas Explorer to the Timeline; Vegas will treat them as though they were video files.

Select another VEG file and repeat the process of dragging it to the Timeline.

Now that you've got two VEG files on the Timeline, drag them together to create a cross-fade just as you would with two video or audio files. Notice that the media behaves exactly as it would if it were a single video file. Add color correction, special FX, or any other filter to the audio or video of the nested VEG file.

A good workflow in Vegas for long-form projects is to:

1. Create intros, outtros, and any chapter headers separately as individual VEG files.

2. Create any stock or reusable lower-thirds or overlays as separate VEG files.

3. Edit each chapter as a separate VEG file, potentially without any titling or text. This can help ensure consistency from chapter to chapter and also allows a single process filter to be applied to any text you might want to process, such as using the Broadcast filter on all text events.

4. Place all relevant VEG files on the Timeline, creating transitions from chapter headers, intros, or outtros on a master, nested Timeline.

One of the benefits of this workflow is also that all audio can be processed identically, helping to achieve a balanced, consistent audio output in Vegas. You can also drop your incident music in the chapter points, allowing it to fade from the chapter header into the file if you'd like to do so. Regardless, this is my personal workflow for most long-form projects in Vegas, as it allows me to have complete flexibility at all times.

Editing the VEG Files from a Nested Timeline

Files on a nested Timeline might require editing in place. For example, you might be working with stock lower-thirds that you've created for various projects in Vegas Pro, or perhaps you're using the lower-thirds tool found in Ultimate S. This is very easy to do in Vegas.

Right-click the VEG file to be edited and choose Edit Source Project from the submenu that appears. This will open a new instance of Sony Vegas. When the new instance of Vegas opens, you'll edit the necessary areas and close the second instance of Vegas. When you close the second instance, Vegas will ask if you want to save the modified VEG file. Choose Yes from the options, and finish closing Vegas. The nested version of the VEG will be autoupdated.

One caveat to be aware of is that if you're using a file that you've designated as a "stock" file, such as a lower-third, teaser, or overlay, when you edit

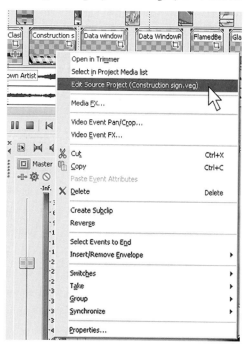

3.90 Right-click a VEG file on the Vegas Timeline to open a new instance of Vegas so that you can edit the VEG file.

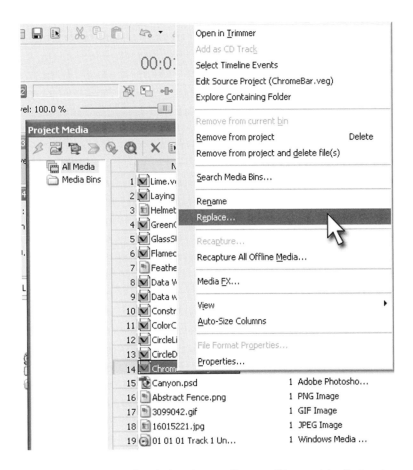

3.91   You can also choose Save As from the second instance of Vegas and then Replace the
        VEG file in the Project Media window.

the original VEG, the original file is modified. One workaround for this is to do a Save As when you have finished editing the lower-third. Give the file a new name and continue. This will NOT update the VEG from the nested project. However, you can then go to the Project Media window and locate the original VEG file. Right-click the VEG file you'd like to replace with the newly named version of the same VEG, and choose Replace from the submenu that appears. This will keep the old version of the VEG in its current location and allow you to browse for the new version to be used in its place.

Track Flattening

Yet another use of this feature is to "flatten" intense composites or bring deep composites in as part of a bigger project without having to render out the composite. Personally, this is one of my favorite features. In our shop we've used a few lower-thirds that needed to be rendered out in the past. Now, you may just drop any lower-third directly on the Timeline. Try this out by downloading some of the VEG files from the vasst.com site or by grabbing one of the lower-third VEG files found on the DVD in the back of this book. Drop them on top of existing projects. Import them one of three ways:

1.   Choose FILE | IMPORT | MEDIA, and browse for the desired VEG file.

2.   Drag a file from the Explorer window.

3.   Double-click the file in the Explorer window.

Notice them in the Project Media window (which was called Media Pool in previous versions). You'll see a thumbnail of your VEG file complete with any alpha channel that might exist.

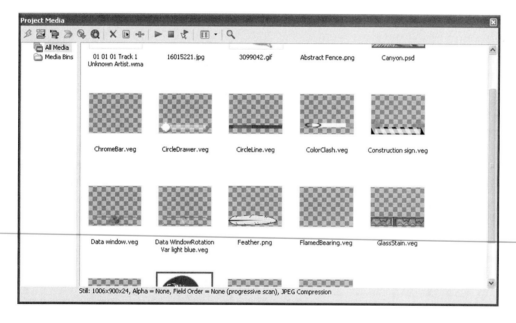

3.92   These are all VEG files that have transparency or alpha channels. Notice that the Project Media folder displays the alpha channel when appropriate.

AV Sync Repair

Ever had video and audio drop out of sync? In previous versions of Sony Vegas, users needed to use the Trimmer or a scripting tool such as Ultimate S to resync audio or video that had lost its mate. Sony Vegas Pro offers a resync option to help users get frame-accurate audio to video (or video to audio).

What a great tool this is, in my opinion. Vegas will provide a display any time audio and video have become out of sync. You can resync either by slipping the audio back into place automatically or by telling the audio to be in sync from a particular point in the event or clip. Simply right-click and choose Synchronize.

Audio or video that has lost its synchronization is indicated by a red box in the event that will show how far out of sync the events are. If you don't see this, you'll need to choose VIEW | ACTIVE TAKE (Ctrl+Shift+I).

Right-click the audio or video. Choose Synchronize, and you'll be presented with two choices. Generally you'll want to choose By Slipping, as this will slip the audio into place based on where the audio is. However, if you've looped or slip-edited the video file, you may want to select By Moving.

Choosing By Moving will move the right-clicked event to be synced with the other event related to the right-clicked event. Choosing By Slipping will slide the corresponding event to be synced with the right-clicked event. Files that have been slip-edited to the point that they're looping the end of the event to near the in point of the event may be synced better by choosing By Moving.

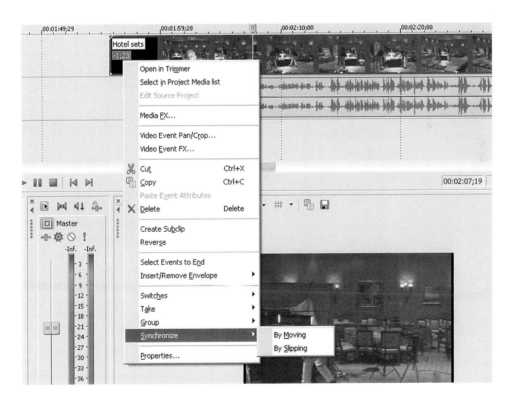

3.93 Right-click out-of-sync audio files to synchronize them with video.

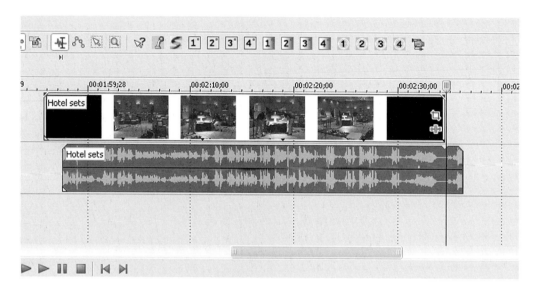

3.94   Here, the audio has been resynced by slipping. Notice that the audio is in sync but the end of the audio file extends beyond the video and is looped.

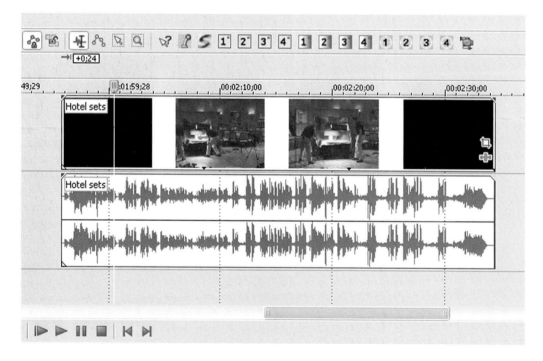

3.95   In this image, the audio has been resynced by moving rather than slipping. Notice that the audio is in line with the video clip.

Multicam Functions in Vegas Pro 8

The concept of Multicam is simple yet powerful. Up till now we've talked about editing with media from different sources, typically one video track or "camera" with various additional flavors of cutaways and composites. With Vegas Pro 8 and Multicam, you now have the ability to switch multiple camera angles in realtime, with the added bonus that, because this is nondestructive, nonlinear editing, you have the opportunity to go back and make changes and adjustments to your "shooting script" in a matter of seconds without any loss of quality.

Earlier versions of Sony Vegas haven't offered multiple-camera editing functionality as part of the stock feature set, yet users have had access to third-party plug-in tools for Vegas since Vegas 4 and live camera switching since Vegas 6. However, Vegas Pro 8 now offers users a Multicam feature that works very similar in workflow to those third-party tools.

Roll Tape!

Efficient use of the Multicam tools begins at preproduction. Plan on setting camcorders to as close a timecode point as possible or, if using camcorders that offer timecode matching such as the Sony HVR V1U, sync up the timecode from a master camera. While it's not hypercritical that the cams be synced, it is exceptionally helpful when it comes time to sync multiple cameras to the same point in time if the timecode is identical on all the camcorders

Another option is to use a slateboard/clapper after all camcorders have been put into Record mode; this places a spike/transient in the audio stream that can be easily identified as a sync point. It's also a good idea to place a slate or other indicator at the end of a take.

Some shooters manage by having synchronized clocks kept near each camera, captured at the start/stop of each tape, thus providing a visual reference. In any event, take steps to start cameras as close in time as possible, with timecode that is as close as possible.

Set the time/date at the same time in all cameras. The closer this is, the easier the timecode can be matched in post.

Don't start or stop camcorders if possible during the shoot. This will generate long files, but helps tremendously when syncing content in post. Again, this is not critical, but is most helpful. Each time any one camera is stopped and restarted, the tape from that camera has to be synced. If shooting a multicamera live event with several tapes per camera, a little preproduction planning can make for a smoother experience in the edit suite.

Getting Media to the Timeline

Media should be captured or transferred to a local hard drive prior to beginning a Multicam edit. I'd recommend naming each tape clearly, with a comprehensible yet simple name. The tape name will become part of the Multicam window, so you may want simple names related to the operators or positions, such as "Cam-1," "Steve-O_Cam," or "Wide-angle."

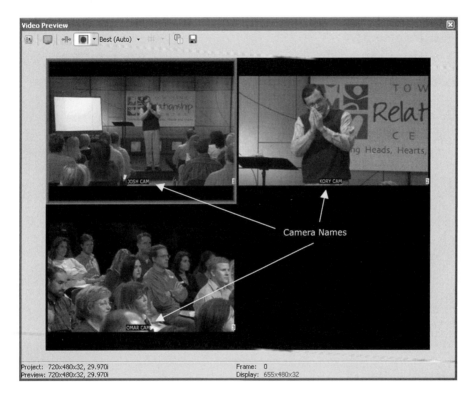

4.1   Whatever name you give your files will appear in the Multicam window. Keep 'em short and clear for best results.

 Tip _____

My recommended workflow: Create a unique folder for each tape. Give the folder the same name as the label on the tape. Give the files to be captured a name relevant to the folder, yet short and easily understood during the Multicam. This will help with media management and viewing Multicam windows. Right-click Multicam files in the Explorer and add them to the Project Media (formerly known as the Media Pool).

If you're familiar with "Takes" in Vegas, using the Multicam tools will make sense from the st art. If you're not, it will make sense as we go along. There are multiple workflows to choose from for multicam editing; we'll examine them here.

If Timecode Is Closely Matched

In the Vegas Explorer, right-click Multicam files and choose Add to Project Media list.

Browse to the Project Media tab and select all media to be included in the multicamera shoot. From Tools, scroll down to Multicam, and choose Lay Out Tracks Using Media Timecode. Vegas will add media to the Timeline based on embedded timecode with a pair of tracks (audio and video) for each camera point. Vegas will attempt to sync the media as closely as possible. You may need to slip/slide media to ensure perfect sync. Media is most easily moved via a 10-key keypad using the 1 or 3 key on a selected event.

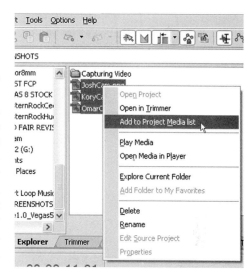

4.2

Tip

Be certain Quantize to Frames is enabled prior to layout of tracks using media timecode.

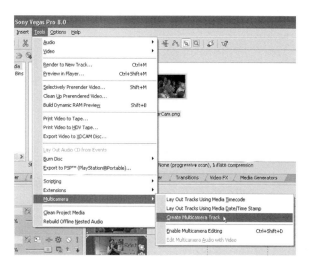

4.3

Once the tracks are laid out and synced, it's time to create the multicamera track. Select all the media in the project (Ctrl+A). In TOOLS | MULTICAMERA CHOICES, choose Create Multicamera Track.

This will take all of the synced tracks and create one track containing all of the various camera angles. They will appear as one track, but will actually contain as many Takes as there are camera positions. Right-click the media, select Takes, and you'll see all the camera files in this dialog.

Right-click the media to see camera positions in the Takes dialog.

Once the single track containing all the elements of the Multicam project is set up, it's time to create the Multicam view so that all cameras may be viewed at once. This is where the beef of the Multicam view comes into play. Use the shortcut Ctrl+Shift+D or go to

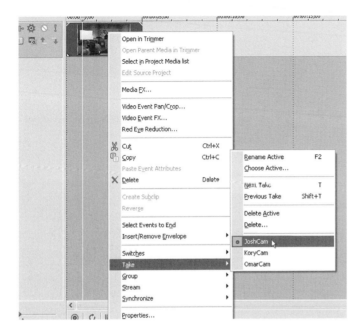

4.4

4.5   Notice the blank area in this preview? This is because there is no video information in this block of time, so Vegas keeps the window blank.

TOOLS | MULTICAM | ENABLE MULTICAMERA EDITING. This will create a preview of all cameras as individual windows in the Vegas Preview window. If the project is using four cameras, then there will be four preview panes.

If there is a blank area in the Timeline, Vegas will create a blank space until the video begins. As an example, suppose there are four cameras, three that start with the general action and the fourth put in record mode halfway through the presentation. Vegas will leave this area blank, and unless this view is specifically selected during multicamera edits, Vegas will ignore this window until the video information begins.

Although it's obvious which camera is active in the Preview window, it should be mentioned that the active camera is indicated by the blue square (default color) that surrounds the active camera.

 *Tip*_____

Active camera color indicator choices may be set in the OPTIONS | PREFERENCES | VIDEO tab. Additionally, if you'd prefer to see only the camera number, and not the file name, this, too, may be enabled/disabled in the Preferences window.

Blue border around active window

4.6   The blue highlight around the camera preview indicates it is the active/selected camera.

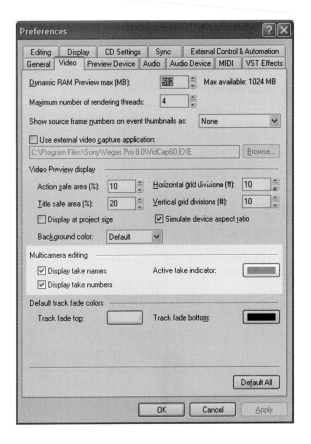

4.7

Other Multicamera Workflows

What if the cameras weren't timed at all? Or perhaps there is simply no timecode? Perhaps you're working with stock media from various sources and want to cut it into place along with multicamera shots/angles?

Have no fear, timecode isn't necessary.

Build the Timeline the way you normally might work, synchronizing cameras the way you'd normally build a Timeline, a pair of new tracks for each audio/video file or a new track for each video file. You can also use stills or other media types on a track if you wish.

4.8

After aligning all tracks/audio, select all the media using the Selection Edit tool, Shift-clicking media, or using the Ctrl+A shortcut. In TOOLS | MULTICAMERA CHOICES, choose Create Multicamera Track. This will create a single track, filled with Takes, just as outlined previously. As before, enable Multicamera Editing using Ctrl+Shift+D or the TOOLS | MULTICAMERA | ENABLE MULTICAMERA EDITING choice.

Tip_____

If you're planning on cutting to a master audio track such as a music bed or dialog track, leave this track out of the selection prior to creating the Multicamera editing view. Otherwise, the master audio track will become an audio take.

Making Multicam Selections

Previewing multicamera screens in realtime is nice, but what really counts is being able to select cameras in realtime. The Sony manual refers to this as selecting "active Takes," but in this section, I'll refer to "active camera." Vegas Pro 8 offers a couple of methods for performing active camera selections.

The most intuitive method of selecting a camera or take is simply to click in the Preview window on the camera that should be active at any point in time. Don't worry if you don't select the exact frame on which the camera should switch, this can be dealt with later. Selecting cameras may be done during real-time playback, but if there are a lot of cameras, it may be best to go through section by section, as any more than four cameras may cause Preview to slow down too much. If this does happen, be sure that the Preview window is set to Preview/Auto, or even Draft/Auto.

 *Tip*_____

Preview performance depends on CPU speed and availability of system resources. If Preview on an external monitor is preferred, start with preview settings of Preview/Auto for any format other than DV. For DV, Preview/Full should generally be appropriate.

During playback, when a camera preview is selected, it creates a "split" in the master camera track. This causes the selected Take to come to the top of the track, although visually, nothing will change on the track. Playback may be stopped at any time, rewound, and played. During playback, the active camera will shift from Take to Take/Camera to Camera, as designated during the selection process. In this manner, camera takes may be previewed prior to generating an assembly track.

Another method of selecting active camera tracks is to use the number keys found at the top of the keyboard (not the Num pad/10-key). Each camera preview window is assigned a number regardless of filename that may be displayed. These number assignments are tied to the number keys found at the top of the keyboard, and keyboard numbers may be used instead of clicking the preview window to select the active camera.

Creating Cross-fades between Active Cameras

In the previous methods of selecting active cameras, the cuts are all hard cuts/butt cuts. Many times users prefer putting cross-fades between cuts. Vegas Pro 8 provides options for creating cross-fades between cuts. Before creating cross-fades, you'll first want to set the preferred length for cross-fades.

Open the OPTIONS | PREFERENCES dialog and choose the Editing tab. In this tab, there is an option labeled "Cut-to-overlap conversion." This parameter determines the length of the cross-fade to be inserted.

Preferences

General | Video | Preview Device | Audio | Audio Device | MIDI | VST Effects
Editing | Display | CD Settings | Sync | External Control & Automation

☑ Enable looping on events by default
☑ Preserve pitch when stretching audio events
☐ Collapse loop region when no time selection is present
☐ Cut, copy, and delete grouped events

JKL / shuttle speed: Medium

Quick fade length for audio events (ms):   10

New still image length (seconds):   5.000   150 frames at 29.970 fps

Default time between CD tracks: 2:00

Cursor preview duration (seconds):   2.000   60 frames at 29.970 fps

☐ Automatically overlap multiple selected media when added

Cut-to-overlap conversion

    Amount (seconds):   1.000   30 frames at 29.970 fps

    Alignment: Centered on cut

Interpolation and envelopes

    Audio default type: Smooth

    Video default type: Smooth

    Default Track Motion smoothness: 0.0

    Default Pan/Crop smoothness: 0.0

Default All

OK   Cancel   Apply

4.9

Whereas this setting is entirely a personal preference, my preferred length is .250, or seven frames. One sure mark of amateur video editing is long cross-fades. Get into the scene and get out of the last one. Long cross-fades have their place, but they're more of a rarity than many editors realize.

Regardless, set the length at something other than the default 1 second/29 frames unless this is the desired length for all camera cross-fades. Cross-fade lengths may be changed on an individual basis later if necessary, or a tool like Ultimate S may be used to change all cross-fade lengths at a later point as well.

Creating a cross-fade instead of a hard cut is simple. Holding the Ctrl key while clicking an active camera in the Preview window or pressing a keyboard number will generate a cross-fade.

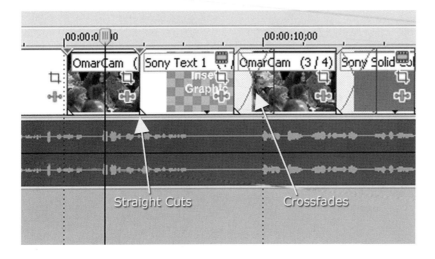

4.10

The Assembly Track

Once all the active cameras have been chosen, an assembly, or master track, is created. This will take all of the selected cameras and restore them to full screen preview, with either butt cuts or cross-fades, depending on how the Timeline has been edited. Building the assembly track is as simple as disabling Multicamera Editing in the TOOLS | MULTICAMERA | MULTICAMERA EDITING selection, or Ctrl+Shift+D as a shortcut. The camera cuts are still visible, but not the active windows any longer.

4.11

If the cuts aren't exactly as they should be, there are several options for making changes. If the cuts are far off from where they should be, it is probably most prudent to reopen the Multicamera Editing function, and reedit those areas. Ctrl+Shift+D will open the Multicamera Editing Preview.

If the cuts are only off by a few frames, it might be more efficient to perform a rolling edit on those points. Rolling edits are discussed elsewhere in this book, but for a refresher, place the cursor at the edit point/cut point, hold the Ctrl+Alt keys, and click/drag the cursor to the right or left. The Preview window will display the out point of the event on the left, and the in point of the event to the right, displayed as a split screen in the Preview window.

Another option for switching out a shot without reopening the Multicam dialog is to right-click the event to be switched out, and in the Takes menu, select the preferred or alternate take.

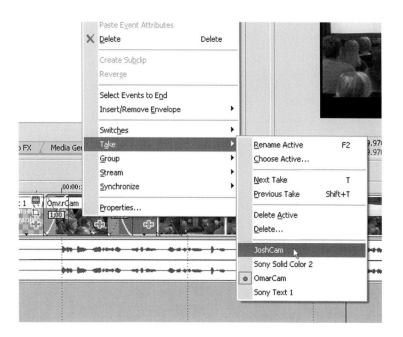

4.12

Editing Audio with Multicamera

Although most multicamera productions use a master audio track, it may be that audio from specific cameras should be edited along with the video. For example, camera 1 contains audio from one interviewee, and camera 2 is recording audio from a second interviewee. Perhaps both cameras are receiving an audio feed from the interviewer. When cutting from one camera to another, the audio should follow the cut so that the audio is properly represented from shot to shot. In any event, it's very simple to set up Vegas Pro 8 to edit audio along with the video. In TOOLS | MULTICAM options, select Edit Multicamera Audio with Video.

In addition to the Vegas Multicamera tools, there are third-party tools for editing multicam in Sony Vegas Pro 8 (and earlier versions of Vegas). Some of them are paid tools, and others are free.

One of the benefits of the third-party multicamera tools is that the camera tracks are always visible and may be easily sooled for color-correction comparison or accessed in the Project Media to apply master color correction, level filter, or other FX to the entire file. Additionally, third-party tools make it easier to work with incomplete tracks, or if graphic files from PowerPoint or other sequential files are to be used, many users seem to prefer the multicamera tools found outside of Vegas Pro 8.

infinitiCAM

infinitiCAM from VASST is a very popular multicam tool, allowing for an infinite number of cameras to be set up. It comes with setups for 50 cameras.

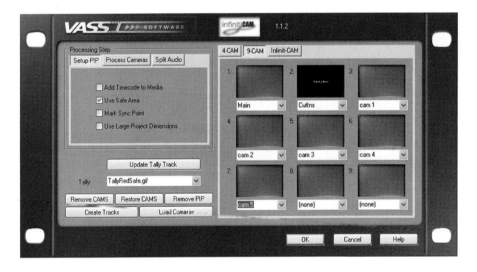

4.13   infinitiCAM provides the Vegas editor with an unlimited number of cameras.

Camera tracks may be added at any time using infinitiCAM. Tracks may be reassembled without any difficulty and easily edited without having to disassemble the master track. Users may choose instant setups of four or nine cameras. Selecting camera audio or master file audio is also a one-step process.

Ultimate S 3

Ultimate S 3 is a plug-in for Sony Vegas that allows for up to four cameras, in addition to over 300 other functions such as compositing, photo montage control, and project audits.

Ultimate S 3.0 can instantly set up a four-camera project complete with track names, tally indicators, and four-way previewing for live switching between cameras. US3.0 also offers very fast synchronization of cameras, via marker tools, although lining up audio cues is typically as fast and as clean as using markers.

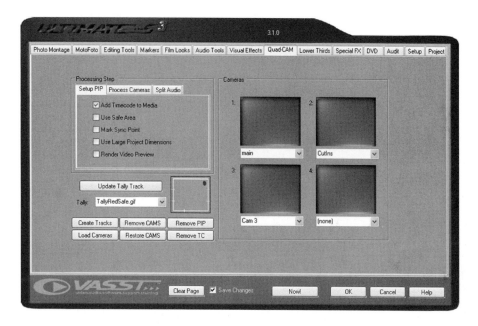

4.14   Ultimate S 3.0 allows for real-time switching of camera tracks and instant assembly/disassembly of mastered camera tracks.

DoubleTake

This is a freeware application (found on the disc in the back of this book) that allows for two-camera editing. For many event videographers, this is all that is needed for cuts or dissolves between cameras.

Place both camera tracks on the Timeline in Vegas. Using audio or visual cues, synchronize the two cameras. Run the DoubleTake plug-in tool, and use the Process One button to run the picture-in-picture (PIP) step. Set up the markers indicating camera switch points. Following the camera selection process (which simply uses the Marker tool, or M key), run the plug-in again. The PIP will be removed, and all selected camera switches will be in place. DoubleTake acts much like an A/B roll in a typical post room.

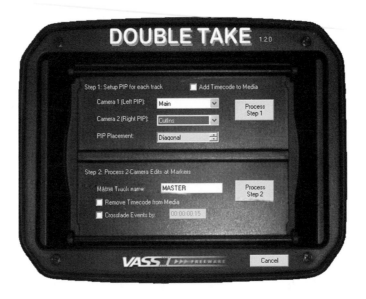

4.15   DoubleTake is a freeware multicamera switching tool for Sony Vegas.

There are other third-party tools available for multicam functionality in the Vegas application. Although the third-party tools have been required in the past for efficient multicamera work-flows within Vegas, many users still prefer these third-party multicamera tools over what is now included in Vegas, simply because of the ease in stepping back, and the speed and flexibility offered to the Vegas Pro 8 user. In time, the built-in Multicam features of Vegas will mature, but for now the general consensus is that the third-party multicam tools mentioned here offer a more robust feature set.

Filters and Add-ons

Working with Plug-ins in Vegas

Several third-party manufacturers have stepped up to Vegas and have written plug-ins for the product. The tools that come with Vegas provide a wide variety of additional expressions and emotions for editors in Vegas; however, these plug-ins give editors far more arrows for their bows, as well as a feel that the standard Vegas plug-ins don't provide. Pixelan Software, Boris FX, Red Giant, RM Tools, Panopticum, NewBlue, ProDad, VASST, and DebugMode have released powerful new tools for Vegas, and demos of some of these products are found on the DVD in the back of this book.

Pixelan SpiceMASTER 2

Pixelan, long famous for their plug-ins for Avid, Adobe, Pinnacle, Media 100, Ulead, and other fine editing products, created the SpiceMASTER plug-in several years ago. Often mistakenly thought to be just a transition tool, this plug-in provides tremendous power to users. This tool has 500 BMPs alone that can be used as backgrounds, foregrounds, masks, and more. Combine this feature with other tools, and all of a sudden, there are millions of possibilities.

5.1 Spice explosion with Bump Map applied over Generated Media makes a very realistic solar flare.

Installing SpiceMASTER takes only a few minutes. Five hundred Spices provide the backbone of how images are manipulated, and the Spices are automatically installed to a folder that you can find quickly and easily. When working with Vegas and DV, load only the DV/720 × 480 Spices (for NTSC) and 720 × 576 (for PAL), as the other sizes will be of little use in Vegas. (If other applications are used, loading other Spice sizes might be of benefit.)

After installing the SpiceMASTER application, open Vegas and insert a video track, placing two events on a track with a cross-fade.

In the Transitions tab, select the Pixelan SpiceMASTER 2 plug-in. Drag it to the transition between the two events, or right-click the cross-fade and choose Pixelan SpiceMASTER 2, and a dialog box opens. This dialog can be confusing to first-time users. The dialog box instructs users to disable the Sync Cursor button in the Vegas keyframe Timeline.

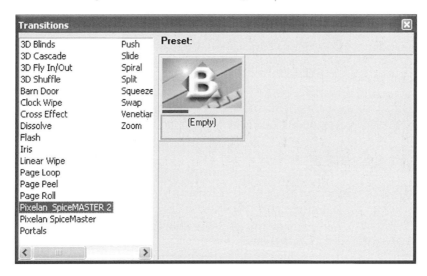

5.2   Locate SpiceMASTER 2 in the Transitions tab.

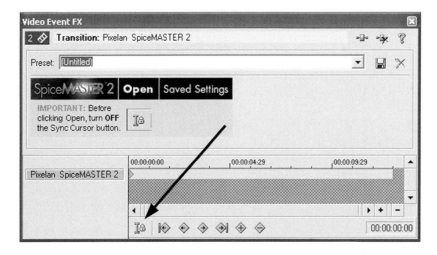

5.3   Disable the Sync Cursor button in the Vegas keyframe Timeline.

The Sync Cursor button must be disabled to use some of the more powerful features of SpiceMASTER. SpiceMASTER 2 has its own keyframe Timeline that allows for a level of control that the Vegas keyframe Timeline cannot allow on its own.

The first window that opens shows the keyframing area, Preview window, Choose Spice File button, and controls for how the Spices behave and appear.

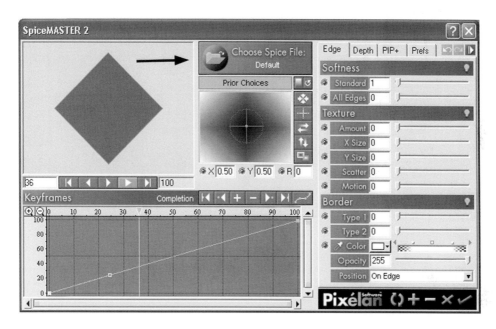

5.4   Main SpiceMASTER 2 window with the keyframing area to the lower left, the Preview window in the upper left, and the control panel to the right.

The Keyframe window is where the velocity or attack/release of the Spices is controlled. The keyframer controls every aspect of how a Spice behaves, based on user input. SpiceMASTER has added a Bezier curve control that allows the user to smooth or ramp keyframes. The keyframer allows images to be brought in and out with a Spice, to be frozen, and even to be reversed. The line in the keyframer is a linear indicator of how the Spice will flow from start to finish. In the case of a transition, the keyframe controls the outgoing event, with Spice behavior on the left and the incoming event controlled on the right. Where the Spice falls in the center and how it behaves is entirely up to the user, who can slide the curve to satisfaction. A line from 0 on the left to 100 percent on the right and without a curve represents a traditional, straight transition. A line shaped like the line shown in Figure 5.5 creates a slow outgoing transition with a slight hold in the middle of the transition and a rapid curve to the new event at the end. With the two events on the Timeline and a SpiceMASTER 2 transition inserted, click the Choose Spice File button, which opens the menu of Spices from which you can choose. Spices are animated in the Library, demonstrating how the motion of the effect will appear in the transition. Select a Spice. The effect is shown in outline in SpiceMASTER's Preview widow.

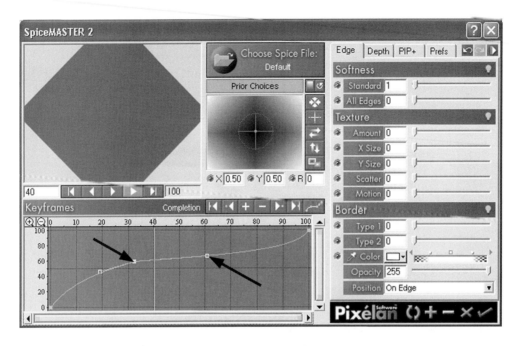

5.5   Notice the keyframes holding a curve, controlling how the Spice flows between two events.

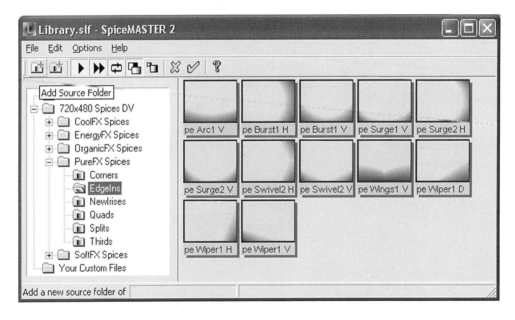

5.6   Spices are animated and will display their action in the Chooser window.

Just below the preview image is a Transport bar. This bar has a Play button that can be used to play the built-in preview or to show how the keyframe points are controlling the effect. This option saves time by allowing users to see how a Spice transition will flow in realtime. At the same time as adjustments are being made to the keyframes in the keyframing tool, the Vegas Preview window can also be active, showing in realtime what adjustments are being made to the transition and Spice behavior.

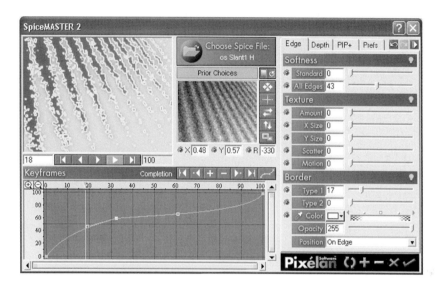

5.7   A selected Spice displayed in the Preview window.

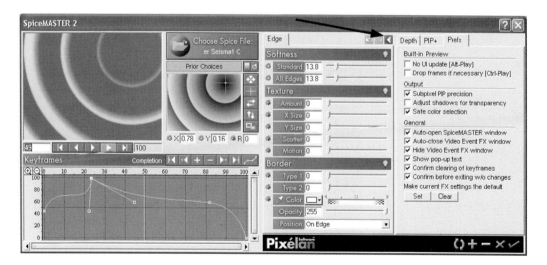

5.8   Click the Dual Pane button to see all controls in the SpiceMASTER 2 interface.

The keyframer takes a bit of adjustment for Vegas users familiar only with Vegas's keyframing techniques. The concept of keyframing in SpiceMASTER, however, is exactly the same as Vegas, minus the sync cursor capability. Users will find the keyframer in SpiceMASTER more capable and very fast to use. The cursor bar in the keyframer allows scrubbing in the keyframe window to see exact points in the behavior of the Spice Timeline.

5.9 Above the keyframe tool is a cursor that can be scrubbed across the keyframer, allowing for frame-by-frame adjustment of keyframes.

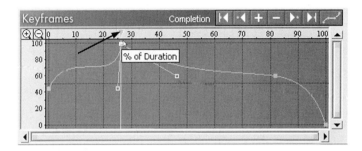

Using the mouse or cursor, grab the top of the cursor bar in the keyframer and scrub across the Timeline. Notice how in both the Vegas Preview window and the SpiceMASTER Preview window, changes are seen as the cursor bar rolls over time. This ability allows keyframe points to be set to exact moments in time. Stop the cursor in the keyframer where a desired change should be made. Adjust for softness, adjust for color or transparency, or just adjust the curve. A new keyframe is inserted. When the new keyframe is inserted, observe the small Bezier curve indicator that appears to the right and left of the keyframe. This small line is what controls the Bezier curve properties of the keyframe. Raising the line upward causes the keyframe to adjust the image rapidly, whereas lowering the curve slows down the keyframe's adjustments to the image, depending on whether the event is the incoming or outgoing event.

5.10 Changing the Bezier points in a file, coupled with the use of a Climactic Spice, gives a sense of foreboding in this image overlay. Using a standard overlay without a Spice would be too sharp or clear and would not have the "mysterious" nature of this image.

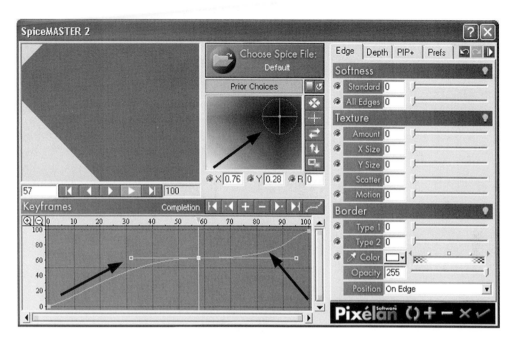

5.11   Bezier curves control the velocity and depth of the incoming event's transparency, coupled with the moving position of the transition. Transition appears slowly in the upper-right corner, moving to the center, with a rapid slide to fully opaque in the last frames of the transition. These Bezier curves function in a manner similar to that of the Bezier masking tools found in Vegas's Pan/Crop function.

5.12   Image appearing from the upper-right corner as displayed in the previous example.

Nearly every aspect of the SpiceMASTER interface has a built-in preset that can be mixed with other presets to give deep functionality and a unique transition between events. Using a softness preset coupled with a texture preset presents more than 1000 possibilities alone, and all five of the control panes contain dozens of presets in addition to any random manual adjustments you might wish to make. To reach the presets, select the Light Bulb icon found on each control pane.

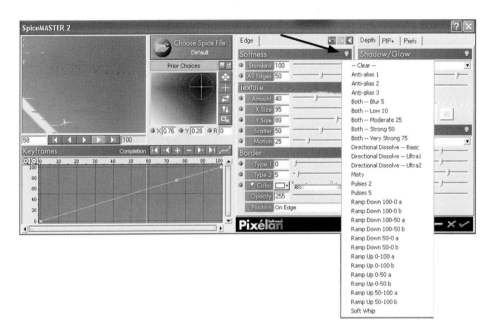

5.13   Each control pane contains a series of presets for users starting out. Personal presets can also be saved.

The true magic behind how Spices function is the ability to make Spices more organic and rich in motion and depth, in addition to allowing editors more creative inspiration. SpiceMASTER and accompanying Spices are not simply transitions. The Spices can be used as filters or as associates to filters in Vegas that create extremely deep and creative images and effects over text, still photos, video, or generated media. Combined with bump or height mapping, the compositing tools found in Vegas take on even greater power and opportunity for creative flow.

Inserting a Spice as an effect or filter is as simple as dragging the SpiceMASTER effect from the Video FX tab and dropping it on an upper event. (You'll need two tracks; otherwise, the Spice will be flowing over the default solid color background.) This process is useful as a means of showing an event via a created mask, for creating a virtual transition, or for moving a Spice over an event as if it were an event on a separate track. The angle, opacity, softness, and so much more can be controlled in the SpiceMASTER tool, but possibilities are virtually without limit. Colors can be applied to borders with one color on the outside border and a second color on the inside border, with varying opacities for each border setting. Keyframes can be applied to change the opacity or color of the borders, or simple presets can be applied.

5.14   Same transition as in Figure 5.12, with a texture and softness preset applied.

Spices can be added to an unlimited number of tracks. One creative opportunity is to place three or more tracks of video on the Timeline, with different Spices flowing over each track. Shift different Spices around to find what best displays all tracks as a deep composite. Spices make incredible masks that can be inverted, softened, position-shifted, and more.

5.15   Combining a Spice with a Cookie Cutter Mask and a Spherize filter creates the appearance of a super fish-eye lens coming out of a foglike mist.

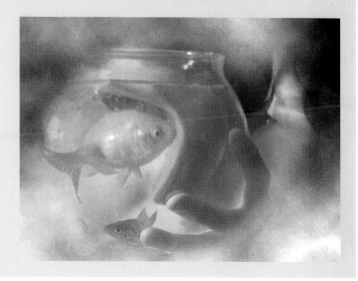

Spices can also be used directly on masks, creating beautiful flowing titles or other masked information. Using multiple Spices on multiple masks and events allows for even greater creativity. In the next example, the image flows from one Spice to another without one Spice interfering with the flow of another. One Spice is applied to the mask/letters, while a second Spice is applied to the generated events, acting as a child to the parent. The background event also contains a Spice masking a still of camera lenses in a very subtle background motion.

Extremely soft, subtle transitions or filter flows can be created, in fact, far too many to list in this book. The tips and tricks presented here were intended to whet your appetite.

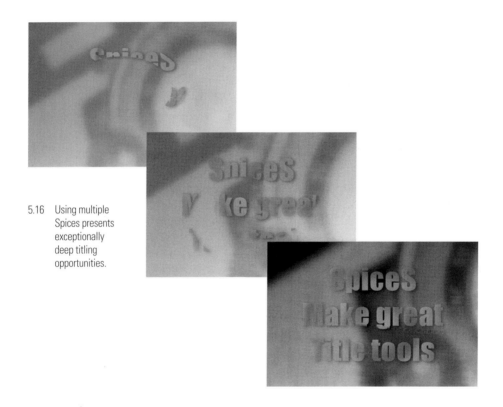

5.16 Using multiple Spices presents exceptionally deep titling opportunities.

Tip

The SpiceMASTER 2 projects in the previous examples can be found on the disc in the back of this book, in `spices.veg`.

CreativEase

CreativEase, also from Pixelan, opens many, many doors in Vegas. Five primary filter tools are available: Color Effects Pack, Blur Effects Pack, Depth Effects Pack, Grain Effects Pack, and Time Effects Pack. If there were one set of plug-ins that I think all Vegas users should own, this is the one.

The ChromaWarp plug-in is a color-shifting plug-in that displaces pixels over time or over color space. Psychedelics, inversions of colors, additive or subtractive tints, or even complex color correction can be performed with the ChromaWarp plug-in.

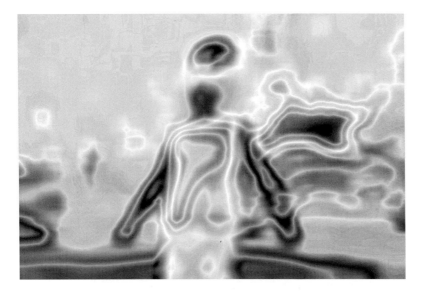

5.17   ChromaWarp can be used to create a psychedelic among many other user-adjustable
         settings. This plug-in can be used to quickly simulate an infrared heat signature, a
         negative film image, or other color-based effects.

The FlowTexture plug-in uses Spices from SpiceMASTER or other graphic files to create textures with displacement mapping. Extremely complex textures, bump maps, displacement maps, and rippling effects can be created with this effect. Coupled with other effects, the possibilities are essentially endless. This plug-in is great for flowing over titles, creating motion backgrounds, or creating unique visual images. The next example provides the appearance of a Monet-style painting over video using the Moderate Displacement preset and some minor adjustment using the Seep 1 Spice.

The NewNoise plug-in is used for creating film noise, color streaks, random color patterns, and grain effects among other effects that are noise or granular based. The streaking on the screen in Figure 5.19 is just one of the many presets in the NewNoise plug-in.

5.18   A stippling-style painting is simple to achieve with the FlowTexture plug-in.

5.19   Streaks preview in realtime with the NewNoise plug-in. Reduced opacity and a slight blur create the illusion of high-speed motion while an event is playing at normal speed.

5.20 Properties of the SpiceFILTERS are adjustable and have tremendous options. All filters have several presets in addition to adjustable parameters.

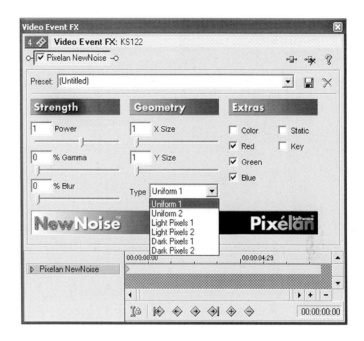

The StepMotion plug-in is similar to an audio time delay or reverb, creating visual echoes of the event. Dark or light pixels can be selected for delay, either via preset or manually adjusted parameters. No wedding videographer should be without this filter; when applied to a bride with a flowing wedding dress, the filter creates a beautiful effect of dream-like motion. Applied to motion graphics such as the echo rings found on the DVD in this book, to the sweep hand of a clock, or to another motion over the top of reasonably still backgrounds, the filter creates a stunning effect. Try using this filter on bullets or other fast-moving images on a screen to give a new look to an old image. Images can be frozen in time, ghosted, and echoed.

The StepTime plug-in can also provide ghosting, but more importantly, low frame rates can be simulated, in addition to strobing, stop action, and more. Using keyframes, various strobe and stop motion effects can be blended or keyed to other clips, music beats, or other effects. By using the key parameter and a strobe, events underlying the event with a strobe on it can be revealed, creating a timed alpha revealing any underlying events without needing to composite them together. This feature is powerful for titles or for creating a dream sequence in which two different images are required to set up the feeling of alternating perspectives. One powerful effect is to take the same image on two tracks, reverse the lower track, and apply a strobe with a key. At the midpoint, the two images come together and then fly apart again. This same technique can be used to create a stunning effect by copying a track and desaturating the lower track so it is black and white, while the strobe on the event above is in color. This process creates a strobe between the black-and-white event and the color event.

CreativEase opens many doors to creativity, color enhancement/correction, and special effects. Have fun with the demo version on the DVD!

5.21   The StepMotion plug-in acts like a video version of an audio delay. Added to high motion, it
provides amazing effects.

5.22   Using a key and a strobe, events can be composited without using a parent/child, with opacity
creating a unique good-against-evil effect. To add some softness to one or the other, add a
StepMotion filter to one or the other event in the adjust, or overlay, mode.

5.23 Blend the strobe with a black-and-white image beneath to create color strobing over a monochrome image. The SpiceFILTERS are powerful, effective, and inexpensive.

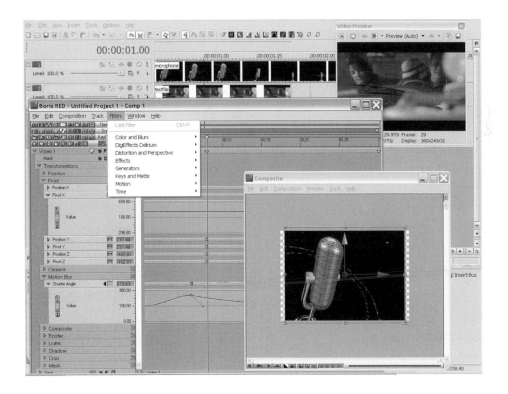

5.24 Boris RED Vegas.

Boris FX

Boris FX makes a series of compositing, titling, and special effects tools for a wide variety of NLEs, in addition to providing a standalone product. Boris FX has released Boris RED and Boris Graffiti for Vegas. Graffiti LE is bundled with Vegas, giving users an upgrade path to the full version of Graffiti or RED. Figure 5.24 shows the Boris RED interface working within Vegas. Boris RED is both a Vegas transition and a filter, with a surface generator (or what Boris terms a *synthetic importer*) in the works. Boris FX is very aware of the workflow that Vegas offers users and molds its development around this. Within Vegas, users can both apply a Boris effect to the Timeline and preview it in the same manner they are accustomed to with other Vegas filters. After the effect is applied, users can launch the Boris user interface from the native Vegas FX Property page, create their effect, and upon closing, automatically import the Boris effect into the Vegas Timeline.

From this point, whenever the Vegas cursor is scrubbed across the Boris effect in the Vegas Timeline, users can view the Boris frames natively in the Vegas Preview window. *Instant Boris FX* by Chris Vadnais is an outstanding resource for those wanting to learn the Boris interface inside Sony Vegas.

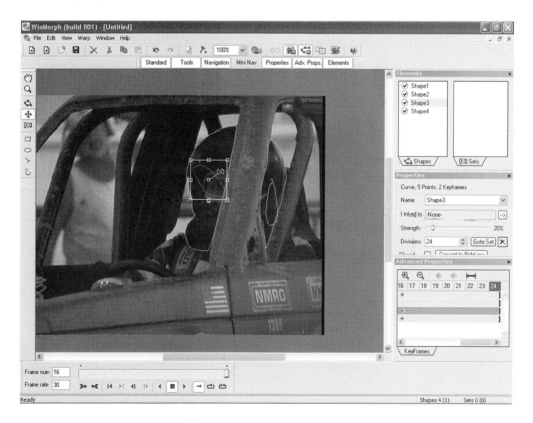

5.25   Drawing morph and warp characteristics can be done with built-in shapes or freehand drawings in the WinMorph workspace.

Wax/DebugMode Software

The DebugMode products that work under Vegas are the result of the work of Satish Kumar, a software programmer who also enjoys Vegas. These plug-ins bring new capabilities to Vegas not otherwise possible with $x-y-z$ plane adjustment to create multidimensional imagery.

The PluginPac filters offer useful attributes in that shapes can be rapidly shifted in three dimensions and moved on various $x-y-z$ planes and aspect ratios. Three PluginPac filters are available: PixelStretch, Shatter3D, and 3D LE.

PixelStretch allows pixels at a defined space to be shifted, stretched, and pulled into unbelievable shapes. Laser beams can be created from letters, faces can be distorted, and, when combined with other plug-ins, amazing images can be quickly created. Like the Pixelan plug-in tools, the PluginPac tools can unleash incredible creativity.

As its name implies, the Shatter3D plug-in creates the image of shattered glass or other fragile material. The number and size of the shards or shattered pieces are controlled by the parameters of the plug-in.

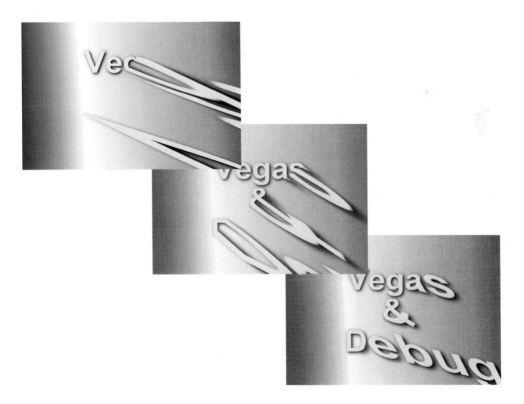

5.26   PixelStretch stretches a defined area of pixels, keyframable over time.

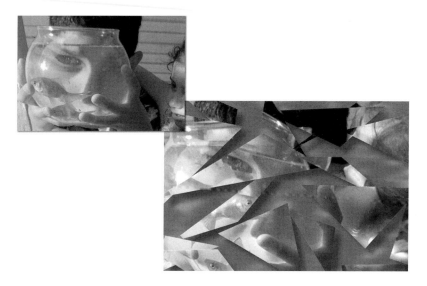

5.27   Shattered images can be very complex with the Shatter3D plug-in.

5.28   The Shatter3D plug-in controls.
        Although Vegas has terrific 3D tools,
        some users might find the DebugMode
        tools more controllable and intuitive.

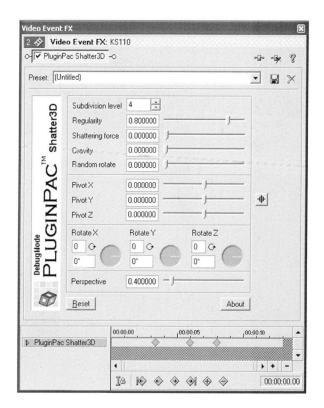

Tip
_____

The images from the PluginPac examples can be found in the debugfiles.veg files on the disc in the back of this book.

The parameters of the Shatter3D plug-in allow images to be simple or deep, with keyframe ability over time. Shattering images can be reversed in the middle of an event, allowing an image to be shattered and restored during an event. The plug-in has controls to simulate the amount of force with which the image is struck, the angles of the shards as they fly across the screen, the angle at which the shards are viewed, the rotation of the shards, and the perspective/depth of focus.

The 3D LE plug-in is fantastic for creating 3D images that fold together and move apart with varying angles and depths and for creating trapezoids and multiplane angles. These can be combined with shadow and glow from the Track Motion tool and used as transitions or event flybys. This tool is also great for creating the ubiquitous *Star Wars* titling effect.

Tip
_____

More tutorials and information on the Pixelan and DebugMode plug-ins are available at www.pixelan.com and www. DebugMode.com. The tutorials for WinMorph on the disc in this book are courtesy of Satish.

5.29   A 3D transition flies in to lock to one side of the screen before closing like a door.

5.30   Trapezoidal screens created with the 3D LE PluginPac are fast and simple to do.

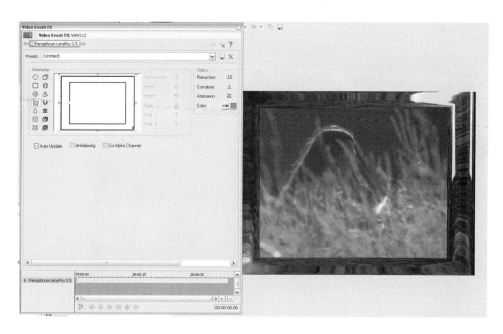

5.31   The Panopticum LensPro plug-in offers wonderful effects. It's a slow rendering plug-in; be sure to check the Auto Update box. Frames and lens effects are beautiful and well worth the wait. No other plug-in currently offers these effects. Visit http://www.panopticum.com for more information on the Engraver and the LensPro plug-ins for Vegas.

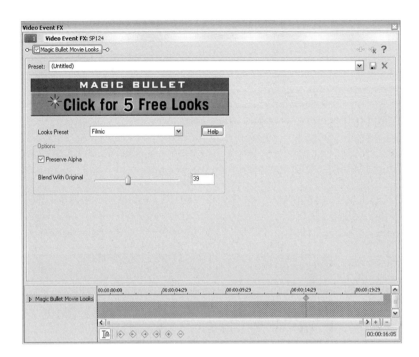

5.32   The Magic Bullet plug-in installs with Vegas and is a great tool, albeit a slow renderer. Similar looks may be achieved with Zenoté plug-ins. Magic Bullet's Film Looks plug for Vegas does not allow any control over the parameters of the plug-in.

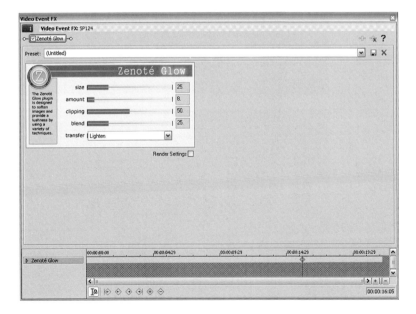

5.33   The Zenoté plug-in suite is fantastic for getting a good film look, cleaning up noisy DV files, or adding blur or jitter to an image. The Zenoté plug-ins are not heavy on the processor and allow for very fast real-time previews and render relatively quickly. Visit http://www.zenote.com for more information on these fine plug-in tools for Vegas.

NewBlueFX, ProDad, and VelvetMatter

NewBlue, ProDad, and VelvetMatter are newcomers to the Vegas plug-in world, beginning with Vegas versions 6 and 7. All three offer powerful features for the Vegas user. These manufacturers have developed not only FX filters for Vegas, but also transitional plug-in tools, adding to the dozens of transitions found in the Vegas application (these plug-in tools also work in Vegas Movie Studio and Movie Studio Platinum). NewBlue tools offer Air Brush, Colorize, Dream Glow, Duochrome, Line Drawing, Metallic, and Pastel Sketch, to name just a few.

ProDad's Heroglyph is a titling tool that may be added to the titling tools installed with Vegas. ProDad also develops Adorage, which generates more than 10,000 effects in Vegas, including particle generators and light rays.

VelvetMatter develops the Radiance plug-in for Sony Vegas, and it's one of my most favorite plug-in tools. Although it's quite different, it creates effects similar to those generated by Trapcode's famous "Shine." Glints, Starbursts, Rays, DeFocus, and Fill Light are all part of the package.

5.34   Image before VelvetMatter Radiance.

5.35   Image after applying VelvetMatter
Radiance.

5.36   The VelvetMatter Radiance GUI.

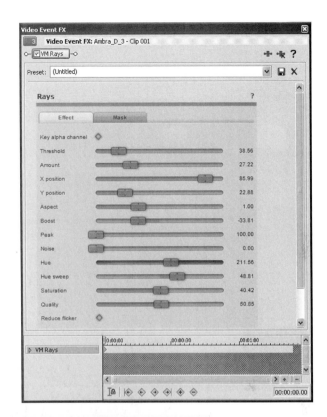

5.37   Version 2.0 NewBlueFX plug-ins.

5.38   The NewBlueFX GUI.

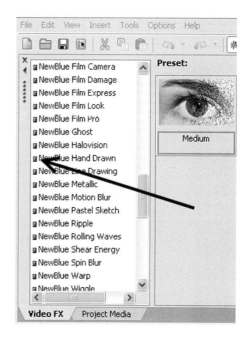

5.39   A blue square here indicates 8-bit image processing.

It's important to note that at the time of this writing, very few of the third-party FX plug-ins for Sony Vegas are 32-bit capable and will render the image as an 8-bit image regardless of the project settings. In the FX and Transition windows found in Sony Vegas Pro 8, any FX or transitions that are not floating-point-capable will be indicated with a small blue square next to the transition or FX.

This small square indicates the FX is not 32-bit floating point capable, and any media to which this filter is applied will be managed in the 8-bit space.

VASST develops script-based plug-ins for Sony Vegas, as well as Direct X-based plug-in tools for Sony Vegas. The VASST Ultimate S 3.0 plug-in tool is one of the most popular plug-in tools available for Sony Vegas, providing tools such as Photo Montage, MotoFoto, project auditing, compositing tools, multicamera tools, film looks, and many other features (nearly 300 in all). Edge Detective, also from VASST, creates cartoon-like footage, line drawings, and other edge-based FX. There is a demo of Edge Detective on the DVD included with this book.

Color Correction and Manipulation

Understanding the Color-Correction Tools in Vegas

Vegas has many color-correction tools capable of repairing even the most difficult footage with greatly improved result. A color-correction toolset, a secondary color-correction toolset, levels, waveform monitor (WFM), vectorscope, parade scope, histogram view, and optimized hue, saturation, and luminosity (HSL), color curves, broadcast filter, and more make Vegas one of the more powerful color-correction-capable NLEs available today. (See Figures 6.1, 6.2, 6.3, and 6.4 and Color Plate 6.1).

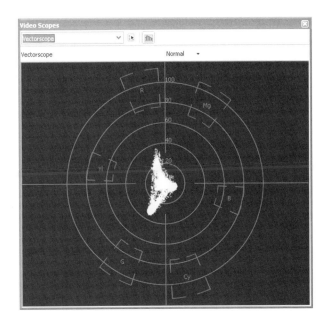

6.1   Vectorscope.

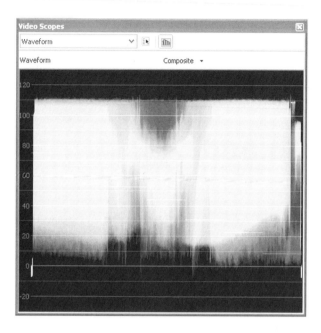

6.2   Waveform monitor.

Tools that can be used for color correction include:

- Black Restore
- Brightness and Contrast
- Broadcast Colors
- HSL plug-in
- Levels
- Color Curves plug-in
- Color Balance
- Color Corrector
- Color Corrector—Secondary
- Gradient Mapping
- Pixelan ChromaWarp (third party)

The color-correction tools found in Vegas provide the ability to set apart colors or a range of colors and to command isolated colors to suit emotional, artistic, accurate, or whimsical expressions. Also, tools are available to maintain color shift from event to event in Vegas, which assists in matching shots from two different cameras or from DV to other video sources. Finally, Vegas provides tools that can limit or force colors to remain legal or become broadcast legal in Vegas.

These scopes and monitors are all tools to help identify color values and luminance values and to assist in color matching. Just having them doesn't correct color; they are for reference. Although we'll briefly discuss how to use them, this chapter is not intended to teach you how to read them and gain an in-depth understanding of how they work. This chapter, however, provides a basic overview of how these monitoring and display tools function within Vegas and the editing world.

Broken down to the most simplistic form, a waveform monitor is for reading luminance, or brightness, and most other tools are for reading chrominance, or color. Keep this information in mind while working with the tools. In the majority of color-correction use, both the WFM and the vectorscope are open at the same time, which is why menu choices for both are in the Video Scopes menu.

 Tip _____

Before starting any color correction processes, be sure you've got exposure set correctly. My method is to convert the image to grayscale using the B/W filter, and then use Levels to adjust the exposure. Once the exposure is correct, you'll want to remove the B/W filter. The black/bottom values should be setting right at 7.5 IRE on the scope.

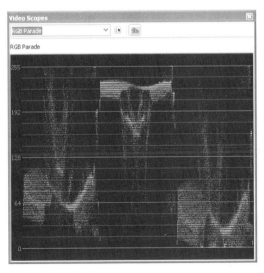

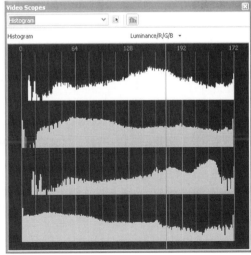

6.3   RGB parade display.   6.4   Histogram.

Displays and Scopes

The Histogram tool is one of the most valuable tools in Vegas. A histogram gives a good indication of color balances overall, as shown in Figure 6.5.

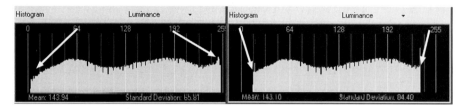

6.5　The histogram on the left contains illegal colors; however, the histogram on the right is legal, using the Broadcast Colors filter.

A histogram also provides a very fast way to view illegal colors. Illegal colors are usually created by inserting text, adding color-altering filters, or using improper color correction. Although the Broadcast Filter may be used to bring colors into legal status, it's better to find and identify exactly why images are out of legal, saving render time and preventing the Broadcast Filter from washing out the contrasts of the image.

The parade display in Vegas shows which colors are within individual limits and also demonstrates the level of the total video output, as shown in Color Plate 6.2. This important tool can help you discover color distortion at output. A standard parade display shows level information on RGB, instead of showing the total level of the modulated video output.

Illegal colors are colors that are not compliant with NTSC standards. Illegal colors overmodulate the broadcast signal, causing distortion of video and audio. No one will put you in jail for using illegal colors, but the strain on the eyes and ears, in most instances, will drive viewers crazy. If you've ever seen a low-budget car-lot advertisement on television with buzzing audio and distortion on the announcer's sibilants, chances are great that the commercial contains illegal colors, most likely the whites used in titles. (Distortion is actually across the entire audio signal but seems more apparent with an overmodulated color signal.)

Color value in the NTSC world is measured in IRE. Color value in the RGB world is measured in RGB component values. For example, in the IRE world, extreme black is 7.5 IRE. Extreme black in the IRE world, however, is really just a very dark gray, measuring at 16.5 in the RGB world. Extreme white in the IRE world is 100 IRE. Again, this is really just very bright gray, measuring at 234 in the RGB world. RGB extreme black is 0, whereas extreme white is 255. Any color value in the RGB world that goes below 16 or above 234 is illegal by NTSC broadcast standards. Any color value in the IRE scale that goes below 7.5 IRE or above 100 IRE is also illegal.

Legal colors are related to NTSC broadcasting. Because most video equipment in the NTSC realm is calibrated or manufactured to the same specification, however, practicing legal color on DVDs, videotapes, and hard drives is a good practice. The Internet currently has no color limits. Many MPEG-2 files delivered on DVD are also presented with "super black," or black values extending to 0 RGB.

6.6   The video event with illegal colors.

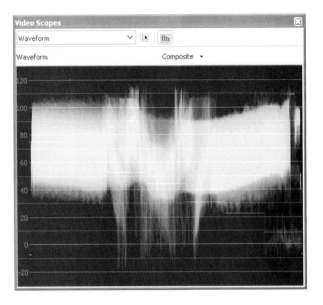

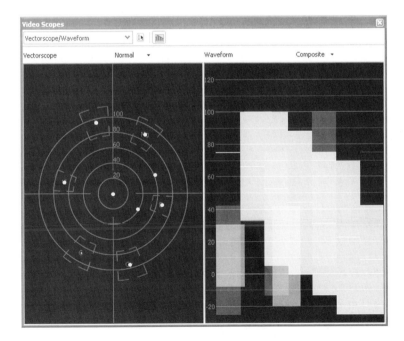

6.7   Standard SMPTE colorbars, inserted as generated media in Vegas Pro 8. The white dots represent positions of the individual colors found in SMPTE colorbars (WFM in Composite mode, with indicators enlarged for illustration).

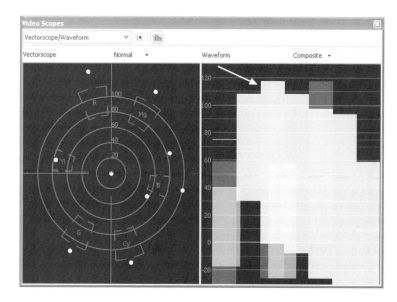

6.8　Colorbars with saturation in the Color Corrector tool at 1.500 (all other settings reset to null).

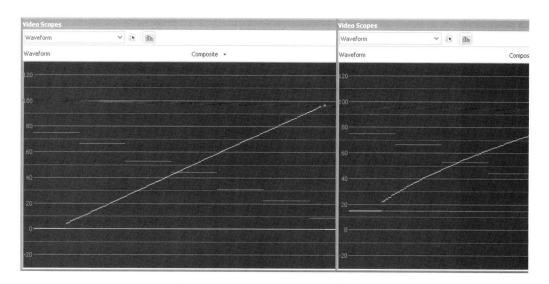

6.9　Ramp with gamma at 1.500. Notice that the curve of the waveform display has changed significantly in the right image (all other settings reset to null). The ramp is used to demonstrate gamma, as colorbars aren't a good choice to express gamma.

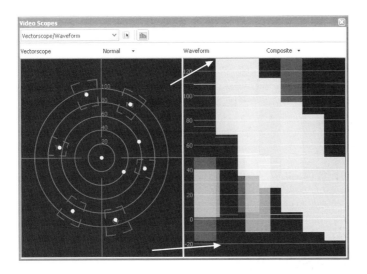

6.10 Colorbars with gain at 1.500. Notice that the WFM breadth and height have expanded significantly (all other settings reset to null).

The parade display can be updated by enabling the "Update scopes while playing" button. Leaving this enabled will take a hit on your CPU. (If your playback seems to be choppy, it might be a good idea to open the scopes and check that the Update Scopes option is not enabled.) Place the cursor over the highest part of a color display in the parade scope to display the RGB value of that color point. The Vegas scopes always operate in the 601 color space; be aware of this when color-correcting for HD, which uses the 709 color space.

Figure 6.6 demonstrates the waveform view of the same video event, which is showing illegal colors. This instance shows how the waveform monitor can demonstrate illegal or clipping colors.

Figure 6.7 shows the same event with the Broadcast Colors clamp set to Lenient. This tool brings the colors to a legal status, but the blue channel is still clipped.

Working from an SMPTE colorbar pattern, examine how various changes affect the display of the WFM/vectorscope. (The waveform monitor displays IRE in percentages, not IRE levels. Use the Broadcast Colors clamp/plug-in if a 7.5 IRE pedestal is required.)

The images shown in Figures 6.7 through 6.11 are in `colorbars-scopes.veg` on the DVD in this book.

These figures demonstrate how the sliders in the Primary Color Corrector tool affect the display of images and how they appear in the WFM/vectorscope. Knowing how each of these controls works is key to using the tools correctly and to achieving the desired image quality.

Pedestal, also called setup or lift, is a baseline for indicating black. Without knowing exactly where black exists in relationship to other colors, it's difficult to process colors accurately. Each video display (histogram, WFM, vectorscope, parade) has a Settings button in the upper center. Select options from Settings to determine a Studio RGB setup (RGB-16 for black, 7.5 IRE for black, or none).

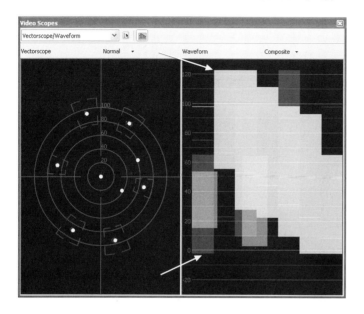

6.11   Colorbars with offset at 50.0. Notice the positioning of the colorbars (all other settings reset to null).

6.12   Color Corrector tool found in Vegas.

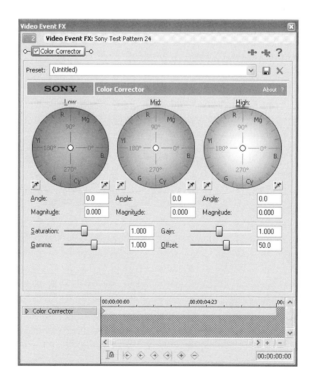

6.13 The Secondary Color Corrector tool found in Vegas Pro 8. Note the Invert Mask feature.

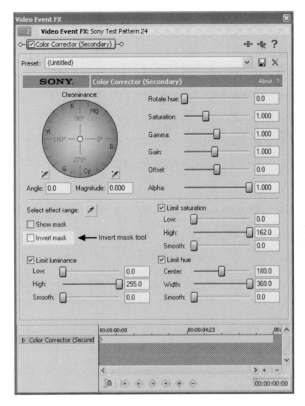

These new tools allow concise and accurate color selection in Vegas to be isolated and managed. Each of the color wheels is controllable with a mouse or a joystick, making it easier to fine-tune each color. The color wheels match the position of colors on the WFM.

The Primary Color Corrector tool works much like an equalizer in an audio system. The three wheels control lows (blacks), mids (largest range of color information), and highs (whites). Thinking in this mode may help some editors work with the colors more comprehensively.

Shadows and contrasts fall into the category of black. Facial colors, clothing, paints, and predominantly everything focused on in a frame, all fall into the midrange color category. Whites are the sparkle and the high end of various hues of color, providing detail in most instances. Dulling the high end, as in audio, generally results in less clarity of a picture image. Sometimes illegal colors, however, function much like distortion and need to be reduced to bring colors to a more reasonable and appreciable level. Depending on how the image was captured/acquired and with what, resolution levels might not allow colors to be intensified without seriously degrading the image.

All plug-ins in Vegas are dockable with scroll bars. This feature means that the workspace is less cluttered, yet all controls are accessible from within the docking space (see Color Plate 6.3). This process makes color correction more efficient when working on a single screen, such as a laptop, as all correction parameters are accessible without having the screen covered with the correction tools.

6.14 Color wheel and vectorscope color distribution is the same.

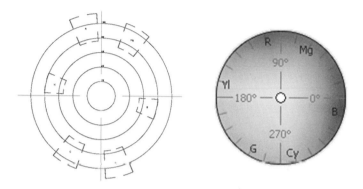

6.15 The Define Effect Range is enabled by using the Eyedropper tool to select the color range to be affected.

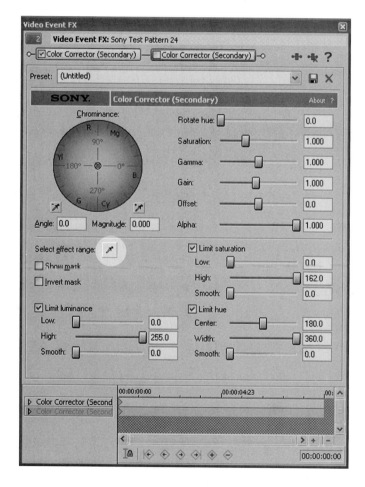

It should also be understood that when working with most of the color-correction tools, manipulating images in the midrange will usually have some impact on the blacks/lows, the whites/highs, or both.

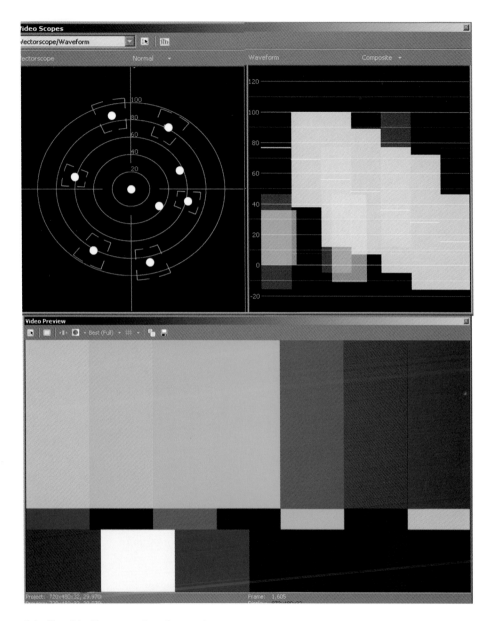

Color Plate 6.1   Vectorscope/waveform monitor.

Color Plate 6.2   In this screenshot, the blues are clipping in the image, even though the eye doesn't see extreme
                   blues. This result occurs because a blue gradient is being overlaid. The gradient is only five
                   percent opaque, yet that is enough to clip the blue channel.

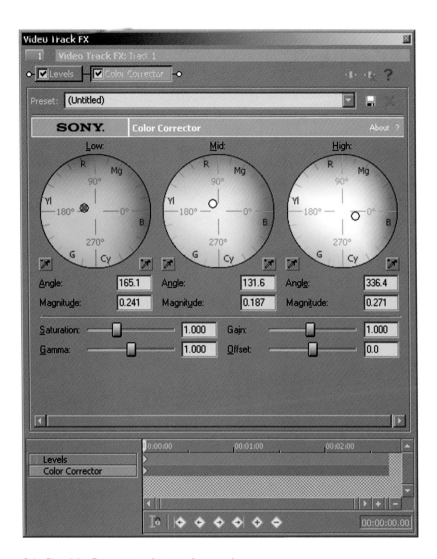

Color Plate 6.3   Easy-access color correction controls.

Color Plate 6.4   The original shot.

Color Plate 6.5   The image on the left is dull and uninteresting. The image on the
right has depth and more interesting detail.

Color Plate 6.6   Video event on scope.

Color Plate 6.7   Still image event on scope before color correction.

Color Plate 6.8   Still image event on scope after color correction.

Color Plate 6.9   This image is dull, lifeless, and lacks contrast.

Color Plate 6.10   Using the brightness/contrast filter, the image now has contrast and color, but appears cold, harsh, and unfriendly.

Color Plate 6.11   The left half of the image is improved, or corrected. The right side is the original image. The Split-Screen Preview tool is invaluable for comparing events while editing.

Color Plate 6.12   The original image coloring is on the left, and the corrected image is on the right.

Color Plate 6.13   The original image. Overblown whites have destroyed any hope of detail in the main
                    subject.

Color Plate 6.14   The image after correction. Rather than trying to restore detail that doesn't exist, bring up the
                    surrounding colors to make the image less objectionable, more realistic, and potentially usable
                    in the absence of more acceptable footage.

Color Plate 6.15   The top is the original image, and the bottom is the gradient-covered image. Notice the subjects in the bottom image are clearer, and the colors are more balanced.

Color Plate 6.16   Gradient applied to the image using the Gradient Map plug-in.

Color Plate 6.17   Which contains more detail – the warmer images on the right, or the cooler images on the left? The images are exactly the same. The image on the left has the Sony Gradient plug-in with the Warm preset, and the image on the right has the Sony Gradient plug-in with the Cooler preset.

Color Plate 6.18   The original and the color-enhanced image with the Secondary Color Corrector tool.

Color Plate 6.19   The left half is the processed image, and the right half is the original image. The Secondary
                    Color Corrector tool removed all color except for the red in the trees.

Color Plate 6.20   The processed image is on the right, and the original image is on the left.

Color Plate 6.21   The right side is deinterlaced using duplicate tracks.

Color Plate 6.22   Gamma reduced, saturation increased.

Color Plate 6.23   Settings for the Saturation Adjust filter remove all saturation except for lower-mid levels and leave the clothing in color while everything else is desaturated.

Color Plate 6.24   By blowing out or overextending the gain and luminance of an image, a look of infrared or night goggles can be created.

We'll use the color image in Color Plate 6.4 as a color-correction starting point. This image is flat and dull. In reality, however, we know that the rocks of Moab, Utah, should be red and vibrant, and the sky should be deep blue, with white clouds. A brightness/contrast filter could be applied to the image to bring up the brightness; however, that process would then brighten the shadow and landscape areas as well, causing detail to disappear. The overall image would appear washed out and soft in appearance. Using the Secondary Color Corrector, colors can be selectively adjusted.

Open the `rocks.veg` file found on the DVD in this book.

Four views of the same event are provided in the rocks.veg file found on the DVD. Version 1 has no color correction whatsoever. Version 2 has red added to create a richer and deeper color. Version 3 has the red added in version 2, and the sky has been brought to a deeper color for greater depth. Finally, version 4 has green added to the trees to set them more in the foreground of the shot. In Color Plate 6.5, the left half of the screen is the original shot, and the right half is the color-corrected shot.

Let's look at how this was done.

Apply a secondary color corrector by selecting the Event FX button on the event, which opens up the Secondary Color Corrector dialog. First, select the color intended to be isolated and to be enhanced or edited. Use the Eyedropper tool found in the Secondary Color Corrector tool to select the rocks and define the effect range.

After the color range is selected, move the color wheel target around in the color wheel. This step causes colors in the Preview window to change with the rotation, demonstrating how the targeted color space is affected. Open the scopes view (Ctrl+Alt+2) and look at how the image shows up in the vectorscope.

With the orange of the rocks selected as the target color, move the target dot to an angle of 118.5 and a magnitude of .480. You can either key the numbers in the dialog box or drag the target dot to that quadrant/location. Adjust the Saturation slider to 1.00. The rocks take on a reddish/orange hue. Adjust the saturation to the point that it is satisfying to your eye. These numbers are relative to a computer monitor and not previewed on an external NTSC monitor.

After the color of the rocks is brought to a point at which you are satisfied, click the Event FX button on the same event and insert another Secondary Color Corrector tool by clicking the tool and the Add button.

Use the Eyedropper tool again to select the blue in the sky. Now set the angle to 324.5 and the magnitude to .382. Adjust saturation to 1.00. Adjust the Limit Saturation/Low setting to 20.0 and the Limit Saturation/Smooth setting to 50.0. Finish the correction on the blue/sky area by adjusting the Offset setting to 6.5. Now the rocks and the sky should be a pleasing color and depth. Again, keep in mind that various monitors display the images differently, so check this image on an external monitor or adjust to your eye and satisfaction.

Notice that after the red and blue have been corrected, the trees in the foreground are darker and inconsistent in color with the rest of the image. Another Secondary Color Corrector tool is needed, so click the Event FX again, select the Secondary Color Corrector tool, and click Add to insert it. Using the Eyedropper tool, select the green trees and bushes in the foreground. Set the angle to 211.0 and the magnitude to .485. Set the Saturation level to 1.070. In the Limit Luminance, set the High level to 76.0. Notice how the color of the green pops out to match the color levels of the rocks and sky.

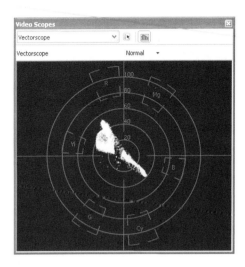

6.16 Original color in vectorscope.

6.17 Color display for corrected version. Notice the extended blue, red, and yellow/green display.

On the Timeline is a still frame event that must be color-matched as closely as possible to the video event preceding it. This process is difficult to do because of differences in resolution, location, and time of day. A reasonable compromise, however, can be made between the two images, making a transition between the two less objectionable. Secondary Color Corrector tools and Color Curves tools are used to bring the two events closer together in color value. The vectorscope is used to match the colors more closely together in terms of relevance. The rocks and sky are the two common subjects in the two events, so we'll use those to make our corrections and changes (see Color Plate 6.6).

Finding a middle ground for the two images, particularly when the original video image is washed out (see Color Plate 6.7) and has been corrected to bring out more color, means that the still image event must be washed out and colors reduced to match the video event. Using the vectorscope, we can see a footprint of the two images. Because little can be done realistically to bring the video image up any further in resolution quality and color depth, the still image event must be corrected and brought to resemble the footprint displayed by the video event.

The Primary and Secondary Color Corrector tools are exceptionally powerful. However, don't forget the other correction tools. Color Balance, Color Curves, HSL, and Saturation Adjust are all tools that are equally powerful. Color Plate 6.8 has a Secondary Color Corrector tool, Gaussian Blur, Color Curves, and Saturation Adjust on the image to bring it as close as possible to the video event transitioning into it. Select the Event FX button on the still image event to see how the image is brought to corrected color values.

 Open `wedding.veg` from the DVD found in this book.

In this wedding scene, we can see how the opening shot is lacking contrast, depth, and personality (see Color Plate 6.9). It's also fairly dark, which would make most of us reach for the brightness/contrast tool.

Using the Primary Color Corrector tool, highlights and color can be brought out while maintaining warmth and personality. In this example, the face tones, the green in the trees, and the red in the bunting can be brought out, which will make for a warm and interesting image (see Color Plate 6.10).

When matching two events on a Timeline, one technique is to do a screen capture of one of the two events, preferably the correctly colored event. Move the cursor to the second event so you can see it in the Preview window. Select SPLIT SCREEN | CLIPBOARD and draw a rectangle around the area of the second event on the Timeline. The screenshot will be shown next to the second event, making it easier to color-match/correct the second event to the first event.

6.18 Use the Select Adjustment Color Eyedropper to select colors to be restored/repaired.

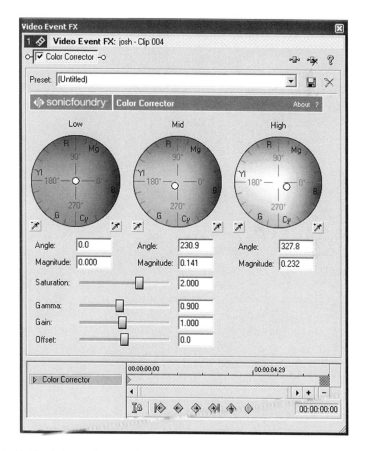

On this same event, several individual Secondary Color Corrector tools can be used to bring out the same features while maintaining the mountain shadow in the background. This particular image has many approaches, depending on whether you are matching other imagery to the shot. In this case, many images needed the same level of color correction, so the Primary Color Corrector was applied to a single video track, affecting all events.

Another way the Primary Color Corrector tool is used is to sample low, mid, and high light colors. Sometimes, this process is all that is needed to correct a color.

Select the Event FX in the first event on the wedding.veg Timeline and insert a Color Corrector tool. Using the Eyedropper tool, choose Complementary Color from the Highlight tool and sample the color of the shirt collar from the man in the Preview window. Notice how this sets the neutral white for the entire shot. Using the Midrange Color Selector, use the Select Complementary Color eyedropper to sample the green in the evergreen bush. Sample a brighter portion of the green for best results. The color will immediately pop and balance the overall image. Because the colors are still not as saturated as they should be, increase saturation to a value of 2.00 and decrease gamma to a value of .900. These settings create a warm and pleasant color space without washing out the resolution of the shot (see Color Plate 6.11).

As you can see, the Primary Color Corrector tool is useful and powerful, with the ability to repair or improve errors or difficult shot situations. For example, white-balancing a camera is often overlooked or, in many cases, not possible with lower-quality DV cameras. Consequently, images might be too blue or green from fluorescent or mercury vapor lighting, yellow from tungsten lighting, or washed out from too much light.

Open colorfix.veg from the DVD found in this book.

Color Plate 6.12 shows how tools in Vegas can compensate for a forgotten white balance in a classroom containing fluorescent lighting. Skin tones, neutral whites, and color depth are all regained by using this tool.

To understand how this process works, insert a Color Corrector tool on the first event on the colorfix.veg file. Using the Select Complementary Color Eyedropper in the high tones, draw a square on one of the ceiling tiles on the upper part of the image in the Preview screen. The angle/magnitude settings should automatically set to approximately 130/.584. Using the Select Complementary Color Eyedropper on the High color wheel, select the ceiling where it's slightly darker. A sample can also be taken from the lightest portion of skin. The angle/magnitude settings should automatically be approximately 130/.450. The skin tones immediately become warm, the surrounding colors are no longer blue from the lack of white balance, and the image is much deeper and more interesting to look at. This same method works equally well with footage shot under tungsten lights that is overly yellow in color. The Primary Color Corrector tool is powerful and may be turned to for quick color repair on almost any image.

Some images simply cannot be brought to a correctable state, however. Sometimes, poor-quality shots must be used. In this case, adding noise, saturation, and generally unacceptable color management helps rather than trying to hide poor color balances in the image (see Color Plates 6.13 and 6.14).

Another use of the Color Corrector tool is to apply a color gradient over an image. In buildings with large walls or obstacles, it is sometimes difficult to get a good balance with lighting if it's a live shot or a run-and-gun. Using a gradient over the image creates a balance and offers unlimited possibilities (see Color Plate 6.15). Used like a Neutral Density filter on a camera, gradients can be used to restore or enhance images.

When working with the Color Corrector filter/tool, remember this order of use:

1. Select the brightest point of an image with the High Complementary tool.

2. Select skin tones or midrange colors with the Mid Complementary tool.

3. Select the darkest point of an image with the Low Complementary tool.

By doing so, color balancing is almost automatic, white-balancing a shot that was incorrect is virtually hassle-free, and a great starting point is established for correcting colors.

This element can be built with any kind of image—simply create a gradient, such as the one in the `gradient.veg` file.

In Color Plate 6.16, notice how the warmer look of the original image seems to be flat on the left side, while the bluer image created by the gradient on the right side appears to have more depth.

In addition to using a gradient to correct a color space, gradients can be used to enhance an image overall. Warm images generally seem flatter, shallower than cooler, more contrasted images. Our eyes tend to believe that warmer colors have less detail.

Sony has a Gradient Filter plug-in that provides exceptionally fast and simple changes to the emotion of an image (see Color Plate 6.17).

Using Color Correction as FX

Color-correction tools can also be used for artistic expression, creating certain moods and emotions that cannot be obtained with lighting or camera lens filters in a low- to mid-budget project or, in some cases, cannot be obtained in the real world at all.

Inserting or replacing colors that aren't part of the original shot is fast and easy with Vegas. Using the Secondary Color Corrector tool, colors can be selectively replaced, graded, or enhanced.

In Color Plate 6.18, the original black-and-white photo is given a sense of warmth from the Secondary Color Corrector tool. A similar effect is possible with a Sepia filter or by layering a sepia-generated color on a track above and reducing the opacity. When you use the Secondary Color Corrector tool, however, you can insert keyframes, changing the transparency and chroma value of the overlaid color.

Color Plate 6.19 shows how colors may be desaturated using the Secondary Color Corrector tool. This particular image has the "Desaturate all but red" preset selected. We'll see how this same effect can be managed with another tool later in this chapter.

Color Plate 6.20 demonstrates a shot taken with a low-end camera, which did not allow compensation for a bright sky. Using the Secondary Color Corrector tool, the sky was brought to a richer and more vibrant color. Without using a glass filter on the camera lens, this shot would have been difficult for even the most high-end camera.

As an example, the movie *Pleasantville*, along with various commercials on television, has made the all-black-and-white-except-one-color look very popular. This type of work is nearly impossible to create with only a camera without doing lots of preproduction work. In Vegas, it's a few steps to create this look cleanly and quickly.

You can use a Saturation Adjust filter in Vegas to single out a color quickly, while desaturating all remaining colors. Color Plate 6.23 demonstrates the Saturation Adjust filter, applied to remove the color of the rocks and surrounding color. Only the climber's clothing is in color. The Saturation Adjust filter works much like an audio equalizer, allowing colors to be selectively reduced or enhanced to create an artistically pleasing image. Of course, the Saturation Adjust filter may be applied to any image to bring down oversaturated colors, pop up undersaturated colors, or bring an overall balance to images on the screen (see Color Plate 6.24).

 Tip

When using the Secondary Color Corrector tool in Vegas, use caution, as overextended colors can quickly become illegal, washed out, or destructive to detail in an image. Color correction is meant to be a corrective tool, not a fix-all for poor camera skills or poorly shot footage.

Inversion Layer

Using the Secondary Color Correction tool, Vegas users have been able to create easily the *"Pleasantville"* look that is so very popular, particularly with wedding videographers and editors. Vegas 6 and later versions make this even easier by adding an Invert Mask to the Secondary Color Corrector, making this effect possible without using a copy of the same event as a mask.

Open the Secondary Color Correction tool and apply it to an event, selecting the color you wish to remain, or pass through. Now simply slide the Saturation control completely to the left, or to none, and select the Invert Mask tick box. Notice that the image is now black and white and desaturated, but the color you selected is allowed to pass through.

The new Invert Mask option makes for very easy creation of the *"Pleasantville"* look. This is particularly effective in wedding videos, used to pass only red found in bouquets or perhaps the white found in the bride's dress. Multiple color passes may be used as well, allowing for two or more colors to pass.

The wedding examples are just salvageable but can't really be brought to full life, as the video camera was not white-balanced, the backlight was brighter than the foreground, and the entire scene was shot in the shadow of a building. Sometimes footage can only be saved, not enhanced. Plan shooting schedules accordingly and remember that footage shot well saves a tremendous amount of time in the postproduction process.

Making Digital Video Look Filmlike

Notice that this section heading says "filmlike" and not "like film." Video cannot look just like film. It's a different medium. It can be made softer, with adjusted gamma, grain, and color saturation, but it still will not look the same as 16 or 35 mm film. I'll preface this section by saying that if you are interested in shooting only media that looks like it was shot on film, shoot on film. If you are interested in exploring how to make DV more palatable to the eye, read on.

Making DV look more filmlike requires starting at the lens and shooting aspects of the production. Using nothing but prime lenses, using dolly shots rather than lens zooms, and shooting with lighting intended for film are all part of the process. Shooting through filters, such as the Tiffen Black Mist series filters, helps warm the image as well. Practice shooting in a progressive scan or frame-based mode rather than shooting interlaced images, and, if the camera is capable of multiple frame rates, shoot at 24p, shoot with a PAL 25 frames per second (fps) camera, or learn how to operate the camera properly in progressive scan mode. In progressive scan mode, the camera must be handled different from when shooting in interlaced modes. Pans can easily become mush and blur in the hands of the inexperienced. Handheld shots become a wash of colors in those same hands. Managing the camera correctly is half the battle in getting a good filmlike appearance from the digital information.

Interlaced or Not?

One of the first exercises in the process of making DV look filmlike is to deinterlace. We discussed interlacing in Chapter 3, but to revisit, interlacing is the process in which lines, known as fields, are drawn for every frame of video. NTSC DV has a frame rate of 30 or 29.97 fps. PAL DV has a frame rate of 25 fps. This information means that NTSC DV has 30 half-frames of lower fields/lines and 30 half-frames of upper fields/lines. PAL has 25 half-frames of upper fields/lines and 25 half-frames of lower fields/lines. These lines generally should be removed or blended to gain the smooth look of film. Video shot in progressive scan mode does not have these temporally offset fields. Be certain that when editing progressive scan footage in Vegas the project properties are set for Progressive Scan. If the setting is not correct, Vegas might insert the fields in transitions or other generated media.

Removing interlacing can be done within the project itself, by setting Vegas to the project settings of progressive scan versus interlaced. Several ways to accomplish a properly deinterlaced image are available. The first and fastest way is to set the project properties to Progressive Scan. To do so, open the FILE | PROPERTIES | ADVANCED dialog, and in the Deinterlace menu, select Blend Fields. This method is fast and easy and ensures continuity.

Another way, or "look," is to blend fields manually. This process creates a slightly softer image and may be preferable to your eye. When manually deinterlacing, create a new project. Set the Project Properties to Progressive Scan, and insert a new video track (Ctrl+Shift+Q). Place events on the Timeline. To deinterlace for a filmlike appearance, duplicate the video track. Select an event on the top track, right-click, and then select PROPERTIES | FIELD ORDER | UPPER FIELD FIRST. Using the Track Opacity/Level slider on track 1, set opacity to 50 percent. On track 2, be certain that events are lower-field first. This process deinterlaces the footage by drawing all parts of the frame, rather than drawing only half the frame (see Color Plate 6.21).

There is no "wrong" way to achieve deinterlaced footage with Vegas to obtain a filmlike appearance, but using a deinterlacer such as Mike Crash's Deinterlacer often provides a better result than mixing tracks or using the Vegas default tools.

Gamma

Another big difference between DV and film is the gamma curve. In Vegas, the gamma can be reduced using a color-correction tool (see Color Plate 6.22). Increasing saturation is also good practice for obtaining a more filmlike look.

Shooting Video for the Large Screen

You need to know a few things about shooting for a filmlike appearance. First, if the video will ever be transferred to film, do not shoot with filters such as the Black Mist 2 from Tiffen. Shoot clean and with clarity. The same goes for using film-look plug-ins, such as grain. All of the digitally created film look is created in the transfer from DV to film. You need to understand going in that DV-to-film transfers are exceptionally expensive. An average 90-minute project will cost a minimum of $30,000 to transfer from DV to film; http://www.dvfilm.com has lots of information on how to make this happen if this is your end goal. If video will be shown on a large screen, digitally projected, test the footage before sending out the entire project as an uncompressed file. Projection can create problems, such as pixelation or overblown colors, so the entire project should be checked over before public viewing. Rendering uncompressed footage, which is generally advisable for large-screen projections, can take a long time, particularly when motion blurs and supersampling are applied. Be sure to have everything checked out before starting this process to avoid long periods wasted because of haste in the postproduction process.

Legal Colors

Video that will be broadcast or displayed on NTSC display equipment must be brought within legal color guidelines to avoid clipped colors and clipped/distorted audio and to avoid embarrassment as a professional. The best means of handling illegal colors is to have color correction, titles, still images, and filtering monitored so that the video isn't allowed to become illegal in the first place. Fulfilling this requirement, however, sometimes can be a challenge. Vegas provides a Broadcast Colors clamp that ensures that colors are legal. Although Vegas 2.0/3.0 had the Broadcast Colors clamp as well, later versions of Vegas bring a number of parameters to this tool that were unavailable in the early versions. The Broadcast Colors plug-in can be considered as similar to a limiter in the audio world. The new tools can be considered more of a video compressor as they allow some elasticity as to how Vegas manages illegal colors.

These options give editors many choices in working with color values. With technology changing rapidly in the broadcast industry, these limitations are less stringent, although the standards will most likely persevere for many years to come.

Rather than dropping the Broadcast Colors filter on an entire project, which would absolutely ensure that the project is legal, consider inserting the plug-in on events that are demonstrably beyond legal colors. Use the histogram or waveform monitor to display and indicate luminance issues. Inserting the Broadcast Colors filter on troublesome events rather than on an entire project will speed render times. More importantly, adding the filter to individual events will not clip or affect color values that may border on the edge of legal and then have a potentially negative impact on the overall picture if much of the project is at near-illegal levels.

6.19 The Broadcast Colors tool has a broad palette of options.

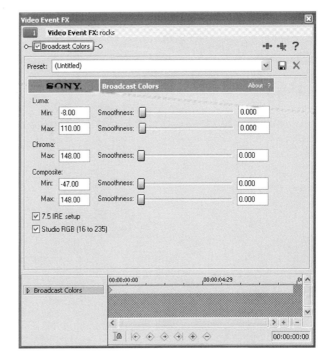

The Broadcast Colors plug-in presets bring colors to within 7.5–100 IRE levels or 16–234 RGB levels. Luma and chroma (light and color), however, are adjustable separately, as is the composite blending smoothness of luma/chroma.

> Even though the Internet does not have color limitations, inserting a Broadcast Color, Black Restore, or Levels filters on events can indeed benefit video streams over the web. Encoding is an art form, have no doubt. The fewer color variations in a stream, the better the stream. Redundant frames are the key to good streams. The Levels plug-in can limit colors. This process would not be useful if the HSL and Restore Black filters were used to crush blacks and reduce color saturation. Be aware, however, that the Broadcast Colors plug-in will not ever add anything to colors but only ensure that colors are within legal ranges.

Endnote

For more in-depth reading on WFM/vectorscopes, pick up *Color Correction for Digital Video* by Steve Hullfish and Jaime Fowler.

Audio Tools in Vegas

Recording Audio in Vegas

Vegas was one of the early multitrack editors available for the PC before the advent of Vegas Video 2.0. Having set the standard for audio on the PC with Sound Forge several years previously, a multitrack tool was a logical step, and like Forge, it became a standard for the Windows environment.

Vegas can be used for a basic voice-over-only setup or as the heart of a full-blown multitrack studio setup for recording live bands, film scoring, television production work, or other professional audio requisite.

For those doing audio for video, it's often thought that video is more difficult to edit than audio. Perhaps so, but audio has the greater importance of the two media forms. Those who would argue the point might want to take any movie, turn the sound off, and see how enjoyable the film is. Even in the days of silent film, a musical score accompanied the film, and most theaters had a piano or organ player who performed the score along with the silent film. In current times, audio and video artists and engineers are crossing formerly strongly drawn lines in the authoring of various forms of media.

Vegas manages media at three levels:

- Event
- Track
- Project

Events contain graphic, video, text, or audio information. Events can be individually edited and have effects added, processed, and controlled. Events live on tracks.

Tracks contain multiple events. Tracks can control, process, and add effects to all events on the individual track.

Projects contain a single track or multiple tracks. All events contained in all tracks can be controlled, processed, and finished. (Effects may be added in the Project Media as well; however, this is not a Timeline management of media/filters.)

Basic Setup

To record audio from a microphone plugged into the computer, a microphone and soundcard are needed. Plug the microphone into the soundcard's microphone input and open Vegas. The Timeline/workspace will open with no audio or video control panes. An audio control track will need to be inserted, which is done by pressing Ctrl+Q or by selecting INSERT | AUDIO TRACK. Click the Record button on the control pane of the new track. Vegas displays a dialog box asking for the location to which audio files are to be recorded.

7.1 Clicking the Record button will call up a dialog asking for the destination of audio.

👉 *Tip*
_____

Recording to a second hard drive is highly recommended for purposes of keeping audio files off the system drive. This process allows input/output to run more efficiently and helps ensure flawless recording.

Audio is now ready to be recorded. Click the Record button on the transport control to begin recording. Click the Stop button on the transport control to stop recording. You won't believe how many people will not think of that! This is all there is to recording basic audio in Vegas. From here, much, much more can be done.

When the Record button is armed (clicked), an icon that looks like two speakers is located in the Track Control pane next to the Record button. If a multichannel card is installed on the system, a number will appear instead of the dual speaker icon.

Clicking the speaker or number icon allows audio input to be converted from stereo to mono or a unique input channel to be selected on the multichannel device. If voice or a single instrument is all that needs to be recorded, it's good practice to use a mono input, as it saves disk space.

The Input Monitor option also appears in the same menu as the stereo/mono inputs. Vegas allows inputs to be monitored with effects/processing as it's recording. For musicians, this upgrade is fantastic, as a reverb can now be monitored with compression added during the performance. The reverb/compression/other processing is not recorded to the track—it is there only to assist the vocalist in getting the best performance possible, without using additional external hardware. This upgrade gives Vegas the ability to be a multitrack recording system with no additional hardware whatsoever. The ability to monitor inputs with processing is entirely dependent on processing speed and system ability. FX Automation envelopes are bypassed during monitored recording.

7.2 Click the Record button on the transport control to begin recording.

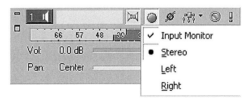

7.3 Audio may be recorded in stereo or mono and may be live-monitored in Vegas.

7.4

7.5

Checking the Input Monitor box enables processing to be heard through the output speci-fied in the output/bus assignment dialog. To assign outputs other than the default soundcard outputs, select OPTIONS | PREFERENCES | AUDIO and specify input/output settings. If only a two-channel soundcard/Blaster-type card is present, nothing more can be set, as there is nothing for audio to be assigned to.

If a multichannel soundcard is available, such as an Echo Audio Layla, M-Audio Delta, or other similar card, up to 26 input/outputs can be specified. Multichannel cards are required for mixing 4.1, 5.1, or 7.1 surround sound.

7.6   Echo Audio Layla.

To use multichannel audio cards, select OPTIONS | PREFERENCES | AUDIO and choose Windows-Classic Wave Driver or ASIO Driver in the Audio Device Type list box; otherwise, multichannel cards will not be properly accessed.

7.7   Setting preferences for a multichannel
       soundcard.

In general, multichannel soundcards do not have microphone preamplifiers (preamps) in them; however, a few models do come with them. In the event that your multichannel card does not have a preamp built in, you will need one to drive channel inputs properly. If you don't have one, audio will be very noisy and not very loud. Separate preamps are typically better; however, many of the built-in preamps, such as the M-Audio Quattro and PreSonus FIREstation, are excellent and, for the investment, a terrific value.

Additionally, Vegas is capable of working with multiple soundcards. Consult your soundcard manual for information on configuring more than one soundcard.

7.8   M-Audio Quattro.

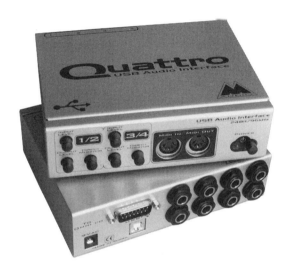

7.9   PreSonus FIREstation.

The volume control found in the Track Control pane is for playback volume only. Adjusting this during the recording process does not affect the recording process at all. Output from the soundcard, soundcard mixer, preamp, or other external input device determines the level of incoming audio.

To adjust the volume of incoming audio when not using a soundcard mixer, select START | PROGRAMS | ACCESSORIES | MULTIMEDIA | VOLUME CONTROL. Select OPTIONS | PROPERTIES and click the button to adjust the volume for recording. In the Record Control window that is displayed, recording input volume can be increased/reduced.

Recording audio in the digital realm can be tricky, particularly if one is familiar with analog techniques and practices. In the analog realm, it's acceptable to hit 0 dB and sometimes go slightly past 0 dB. Tape has a saturation level that digital does not enjoy. Record audio in the digital realm with peaks hitting at around −3 dBFS and averages at around −15 dBFS. Because of the low-noise/no-noise digital signal-to-noise ratio, it is also easier to expand audio levels later in the editing/recording process. Bear in mind that digital 0 and analog 0 are −20 dB apart based on the Advanced Television Standards Committee (ATSC) standards (www.atsc.org). When using analog meters to view digital information, be sure that tones are used to match up analog meters to digital output. When working with audio for video broadcast, the analog broadcast standard is +4 dB into a source impedance of 600 ohms. Traditionally house reference meters are set to 0VU based on the +4 dB level. A good maximum level to target is −3 dB for maximum levels at input.

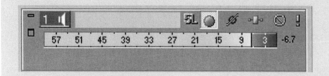

7.10   Levels peaking at approximately −6 dB. The instrument is an acoustic guitar with no compression and is prone to unexpected peaks. Therefore, levels are marginally lower than they might otherwise be.

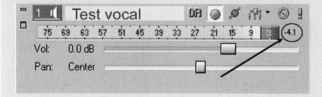

7.11   Level set correctly for the loudest point in recording.

Recording Multiple Tracks

Multitracking is what Vegas is all about. The ability to monitor tracks while recording is critical. Vegas provides this ability with most low-end soundcards and with nearly any multichannel card.

  Recording and monitoring tracks is fairly fast and self-evident. Start by inserting a second audio track (Shift+Q) and assigning its inputs as you did for the original mono track. If the second audio track is to be mono, set it up this way now. Track 1 will play back through whatever soundcard is assigned. Track 2 will play back through the default assigned soundcard as well. Depending on the soundcard, this process can demonstrate latency during the recording process. This process is also one in which a professional soundcard is invaluable. Professional soundcards use ASIO drivers, which dramatically reduce latency in the hardware/software relationship.

In a computer audio system, latency means any delay or wait time that increases real or perceived response time beyond the response time desired. More specifically, latency is the time between when sound is input to Vegas, processed, and returned to headphones or speakers. A contributor to computer latency includes mismatches in data speed between the CPU and input/output devices and slow buffers. Drivers and buffers can be set in Vegas to reduce latency. Small buffers reduce latency but increase the risk of dropouts. Larger buffers lessen the likelihood of dropouts but increase latency.

Vegas has the ability to access ASIO drivers used by most professional soundcards. Latency can be reduced to as little as 5 milliseconds, which is virtually indiscernible to the human ear. This idea means that although the CPU is processing the incoming, outgoing, and affected audio information, the ear will hear audio playback in correct time.

Clicking the Record button (Ctrl+R) on the Transport bar starts the recording process, while at the same time audio is playing back through the soundcard.

Advanced Recording Techniques and Tools

Vegas has many advanced tools for recording audio. Vegas has a metronome for monitoring a click track during recording sessions. (This feature requires that Vegas's properties be set for beats and tempos.) Although this feature doesn't affect playback or recording speed from the Timeline, it does affect the tempo at which the metronome is heard. Metronomes are useful for video editors as well, as they can help set a cadence for video to be edited at.

👍 *Tip*

Ask the scorist for the video for a tempo map, and Vegas can be mapped out accordingly, so that when the score is complete, the audio is dropped into place if tempo-based editing is the goal. The metronome will speed up and slow down according to the tempo map created in the production stages.

Tempos cannot be adjusted over time, as they are fixed in the setting specified in the AUDIO | OPTIONS dialog. Although Vegas can't change tempos without an ACID loop acting as the driving click track, true tempo maps may be created in Vegas by using an ACID loop as a click track, shifting tempo over time.

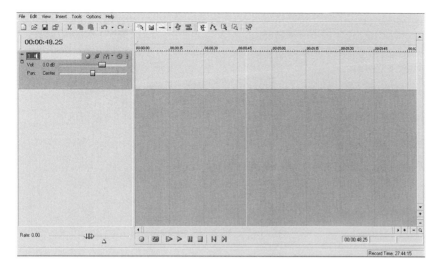

7.12   Setting a tempo grid in Vegas.

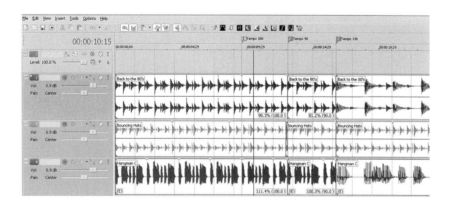

7.13   Completed tempo grid.

Recording with Takes

Rarely is a performance perfect every time; consequently, Vegas allows for takes to be recorded, just like in the movies when you hear "take 1, take 2." In Vegas, takes can be recorded in a number of different ways, as the number of takes is limited only by hard drive space.

Setting up a loop over the area where multiple performances are wanted instructs Vegas to continually loop over the area. If the area that requires multiple takes is a single event, double-click the event, which will set up the loop. Press Q or click the Loop button on the Transport bar.

Click the Record button on the Transport bar, and Vegas begins recording. To stop recording, press the spacebar or click the Record button again. A new take will appear on the Timeline, living over the old audio. The old audio is still there. Pressing T or right-clicking and selecting the appropriate menu item toggles back and forth between the various takes. Takes can also be directly monitored, by stopping playback, right-clicking, selecting Choose Active, and then clicking Play in the dialog box.

7.14   Using Takes is an efficient method of recording a section over
        and over, keeping only the best performance.

Takes can be renamed to help identify them. Takes can also be opened in the specified audio editor for further editing and then saved as a new take or saved as the name of the take opened in the audio editor. Takes can be deleted from an event as well, leaving only the desired audio in the event.

Takes can also be added to the Timeline in yet another fashion, albeit not necessarily in time. Right-click and select multiple audio clips in the Explorer or Project Media, drop them on the Timeline, and, when the menu is displayed, select Add as Takes to put all files into one take. Takes can then be selected either using the right-click method or by scrolling through takes by pressing T or Shift+T. This method is handy for just about anything, as it allows for toggling back and forth.

Takes are very handy for cutting together the best performance and for having the performer record the same piece several times and then cutting the unwanted parts of a take. Press S to split takes and then choose the best of each line. This process is known in the industry as comping. With digital audio workstation/nonlinear editor software, comping is easy and fast. In the past, engineers had to take several tracks, and using mute buttons and fader moves, comp parts of several similar performances together to a new track. With Vegas, it's all done on one track, with no difficulty like there is in the analog world, where it needs either loads of hands on the mixer or good automation.

Pre- and postroll settings are available in Vegas. Pre- and postroll also act as punch-in/punch-out settings and can be combined with takes. To create a pre- or postroll in a single event, split the event where the record in/out points are desired. Then create a loop or selection that begins before the split point and ends after the split point. Use the Loop tool if multiple takes are desired, and use a time selection only if a single punch-in/out is desired.

Then click the Record button (Ctrl+R), and Vegas begins playing at the beginning of the time selection, begins recording at the split point in the event, ends recording at the split point at the end of the event, and stops or loops at the end of the time selection or loop point.

Recording actually occurs through the entire selection. This process allows you to expand the event out in either direction if you need to get a pickup note.

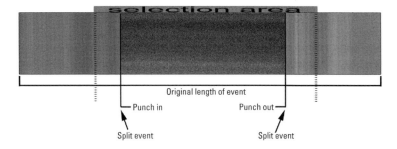

7.15   Defining pre- and postroll on a single event.

How About a Flyin' Smooth Punch?

Punch-ins have long been challenging for digital audio workstations like Vegas because of the look-ahead required to make punches smooth and clean. However, Vegas has conquered the punch-in problem and given it a total K.O.

A punch-in takes place when audio that has been previously recorded is monitored during playback, and Vegas is put into record mode during the playback process, allowing a new section to be rerecorded. For example, perhaps a voice-over (VO) has been recorded and only one word is problematic. The VO is monitored during playback, and when it comes time to replace the bad word, a punch-in takes place that allows only the bad word to be replaced. Once Vegas has gone past the punch-in region, Vegas disengages record mode and continues in playback mode.

To accomplish a punch-in:

7.16   The Record button can be punched in manually in Vegas Pro 8 with glitch-free punch-in.

1. Record a track. Assuming the track has errors, position the cursor prior to an error in the existing recorded track.

2. Locate the flawed section and using the S key, split the recorded file section prior to the error, and split again at the end of the flawed area. Create a time selection with a few seconds prior to the split, extending slightly past the split. Looping may or may not be enabled.

3. Arm the existing audio track for recording by pressing the Record Enable button found on the track header.

4. Start playback of the project or file. The original audio will be heard until the Record button is pressed.

5. Press the Record button on the transport bar or hardware device connected to the computer. Vegas will begin recording at that point. If Input Monitoring is enabled, the new audio will be heard.

6. To stop the recording process, press the Record button again. Vegas will continue rolling (postroll) for a few moments and then stop.

Vegas will also allow you to record multiple takes if looping is enabled. Press the Looping button or the Q shortcut key, and Vegas will create a new take each time the loop repeats. This provides multiple choices of various performances, allowing the best one to be chosen. Vegas will actually create regions with each take. These regions will not be part of the project, but will be displayed in the Trimmer.

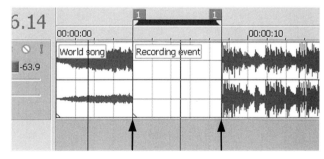

7.17   Illustration of trimmed section with pre-/postroll.

If you have multiple punch-in sections, each may be selected by holding Ctrl and clicking on each split-out section. Vegas will automatically punch in and out at these sections, allowing multiple retakes to be created over the length of the entire file.

Prior to the recording process, a file location should have been specified in the Project Properties dialog. If one has not been selected, Vegas will prompt for the file to be named and saved. If the track was named prior to the recording process, Vegas will automatically select the track name as the file name. The file may be renamed in the postrecord dialog box.

7.18   Postrecord dialog box.

Assigning Buses

Buses can be used to route audio to anywhere it must go. A bus can feed another bus, creating virtually limitless routing if necessary. Vegas is capable of handling up to 26 simultaneous buses, which is the same as the alphabet.

This fact means that up to 26 channels of audio can be streaming out of the computer at once, if enough hardware devices are owned. It takes four to eight channel converters to meet this output and to leave 6 output channels empty. The norm is to have 24 channels of output.

This feature does not mean Vegas is limited to 24 channels of audio. Not at all. Vegas is limited to up to 26 channels of audio busing, but the number of audio tracks is limited only by the processing power of the computer.

If several tracks are on the Timeline, insert buses into the mixer by clicking the Insert Bus button.

7.19   Adding a bus to the mixer.

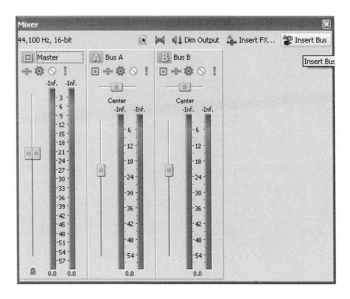

On the Track Control pane, click the small square that appeared when the first bus was inserted. Choices for busing are listed here.

7.20   Select bus routing by clicking the square on the Track Control pane.

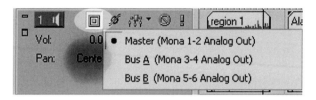

Select bus A. Audio on that track is now sent to the bus A mixer section. For example, bus A could be sent to the normal right/left outputs of a mix, or it could feed a rear channel of a surround system. Alternatively, it could feed a signal processor, such as a flanger, reverb, or delay; perhaps it's a submix that eventually routes back to the master output.

Assign the bus outputs in the Mixer window in the same manner. Click the small square that is found on the bus control. On track 2, assign the track to the same bus A output. This step routes tracks 1 and 2 through the bus A outputs.

7.21   Assigned and unassigned buses.

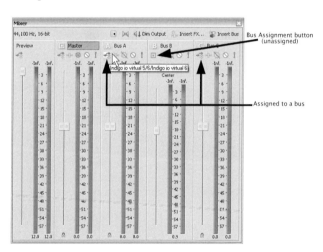

Buses can be used for submixing, such as all drums going through one submix, all keyboards through another submix, and all rhythm instruments through yet another submix. This feature is of value as then all drums can be pulled down or up in volume without affecting the mix levels of each instrument/track or all keyboards can be raised or lowered. Signal processing is less taxing on the CPU if processing is done at the bus level as well. Putting six compressors on a drum kit is much more processor-intensive than putting one compressor on a drum submix. Generally, kick and snare drums are left out of submixes, as are lead vocals. These primary instruments/tracks are typically controlled individually.

Using Buses for Routing Effects

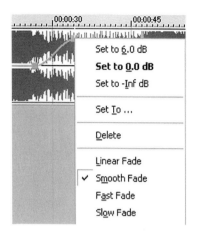

Buses can be used to route effects as well. Effects can be placed on individual tracks, but as the number of tracks grows, the load on the processor increases. It's a good idea, therefore, to place effects on buses to affect several tracks at once. This process can be done using direct track assignment or the multipurpose fader, or through assignable FX envelopes. Envelopes can be used to automate effect levels, sends, and returns.

In the Mixer window, click the Insert FX button, choose a delay effect, and set the effect to the parameters you'd like to hear. Now right-click in the Track Control pane and choose the bus to which you assigned the delay. An envelope is displayed in the track Timeline. This is the Send-to for the specified bus. Raising the line will increase the amount of audio sent to the delay and lowering it will decrease the

7.22   Inputting specific values from the right-click.

amount of it. Double-clicking the envelope places a handle/node on the envelope, allowing for automatic send changes. If a delay is needed only on a specific phrase or moment in an event contained in the track, the envelope can be pulled all the way down until that moment when the envelope will be raised to the desired level. Handles or nodes can be right-clicked, and the Set-to percentage or volume can be specified that way as well. Additionally, holding Shift while hovering over an inserted envelope allows envelope points to be drawn, just as they're created by a HUI device such as the Mackie Control Universal.

FX can be set as pre- or postfader in Vegas. This option is found on nearly all mixing consoles and is important, particularly for sound designers. This option allows audio to be sent to the processor before the fader, so regardless of where the track fader is set, even if it's off, FX receives an audio signal. Postfader is how most processing is done, in which reducing the output volume of a track also reduces the send to the FX. As an envelope fades on the track, the send to the FX fades as well. Bus sends are postfader by default. To change them to prefader, right-click the Bus Send to change it to post from the submenu that appears. You can also right-click a bus output fader in the mixer section, or select Pre/Post in the Mixing Console view (Ctrl+Alt+6).

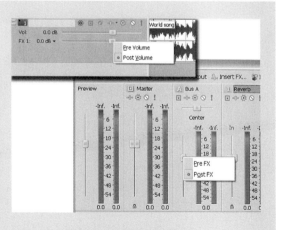

7.23   Right-click the FX Send on a track to select pre- or postfader send to the FX.

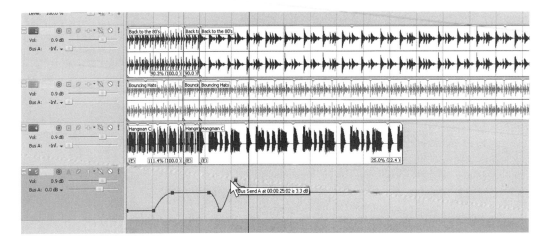

7.24   Vegas bus assignment.

Buses may be viewed as tracks for automation. Bus outputs/returns can be automated for much greater mixing power, for example, if there were several tracks with background vocals, all vocals needed to be raised in volume at once, and all required a reverb to rise with the volume. The vocals could be sent to one bus, with the reverb sent to another bus. The reverb is controlled by an inserted bus send, and the vocal levels are controlled by an envelope assigned to another bus, just like a bus routing on a typical mixing board.

With busing and automation, mixes are capable of being very deep and exacting.

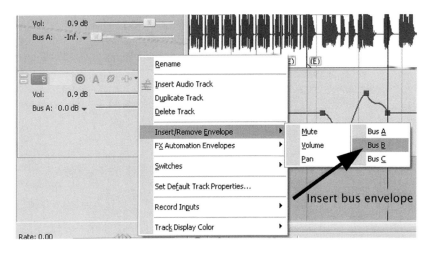

7.25a   Analog mixer bus assignment.

Could I Get a Transfer Please?

Buses are used to route audio from place to place, being used for submixes or effects send and return. However, Vegas provides the option of routing buses to buses. This allows for much easier patching of submixes. One use of this is to patch separate mixes to two different locations, such as sending one mix to a hardware device or external mixer while sending the other to a master bus. Buses may be used in a recording studio to set up master mixes while also having a headphone mix for the talent to listen to. Artists usually like to hear their performance with a little more reverb than the producer might like to hear, or perhaps they need a little more of this or that in their mix that is different from what is being heard in the control room monitors. Buses can provide all of that.

The bus panel indicates where audio is being routed to. If the [A] is seen, then the audio is bang routed to a hardware device. If the [◎] is seen, then audio is being routed to the master, and if the [▶] is seen, audio is being routed to another bus. Up to 27 buses are available.

Vegas also has a wonderful fail-safe capability that prevents a bus from being routed back to itself. If you have two buses in your project and the first bus is routed to the second bus, the second bus may be routed only to the master output or a hardware device.

Audio Mixer

The audio mixer in Vegas Pro 8 is an emulation of an analog mixer in a recording studio. Although it is a new feature, it predominantly provides a mix interface that is long overdue. This allows the user to see exactly what is incoming where and outgoing there; all buses, FX sends, channels, levels, automation, soundcards, tracks, and more are visible in this one view, and it is viewed with a layout immediately identifiable to anyone who is working or has worked in a recording studio or live sound environment.

One of the primary benefits of the audio mixer is the routing system. Older versions of Vegas could not route buses to individual audio FX. In the mixer, each channel strip will display any audio FX inserted into the channel. Inserted buses will also display any audio FX inserted into the channel, as will the master output channel.

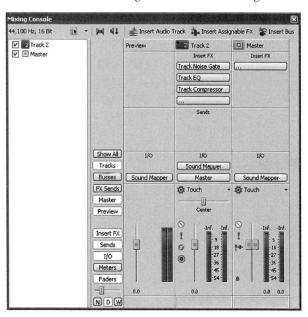

7.25b   The audio mixer found in Vegas Pro 8 provides a graphical interface familiar to audio editors and live-sound engineers.

Automation may be controlled from either the track header or the audio mixer. I believe most users will find the audio mixer to be more intuitive. Another major benefit of the audio mixer is that track headers may be minimized completely, with all track media being viewed on one screen, with the audio mixer viewed full screen on a second screen. Double-click the bar on the right side of the track headers to minimize all track headers. Place the audio mixer on the second computer screen, and in this manner, a much more comprehensive view of the project is possible.

In prior versions of Vegas, audio weighting was managed differently. In the OPTIONS | PREFERENCES, Use Legacy Track Gain has been added. If Add Channels (the default) or the Balance 0 dB pan modes are used, there is no difference. For the other pan modes that cut the signal when the pan is set to center, there is a decrease in the level (depending on which pan mode is used). When working on legacy projects (projects begun in earlier versions of Vegas), it's best to use the legacy track gain function. New projects moving forward will be best if this is left unchecked.

Notice the differences when working with panning/track modes in Vegas Pro 8:

- Add Channels (no cut)
- Balance 0 dB (no cut)
- Balance −3 dB, constant power, film (3 dB cut)
- Balance −6 dB (6 dB cut)

Audio FX panning may also be performed. If this is the goal, right-click the FX Send/Fader in the track header, and choose Link to Main in the menu.

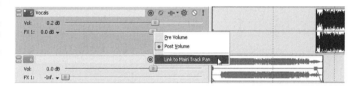

7.25c   Right-click the track FX Fader/Send to link panning to the Main output.

FX Packaging

Creating FX chains is an important aspect in Vegas. Often, presets in FX are simply not enough to recall. If multiple FX chained together with specific presets are needed, Vegas can save a chain of FX with presets. For instance, an equalizer (EQ), a compressor, and a chorus might be used for vocal processing with each of the individual FX having its own presets. Rather than having to insert and choose presets for each effect manually, all three may be saved as a chain/package complete with presets.

To create a package, perform the following steps:

1.   Click the Insert FX button in the Bus, Mixer, or Track Control windows, which opens the Plug-In Chooser.

2.   Choose the plug-ins you wish to use.

3.   Arrange them in any manner either by dragging a plug-in before another or by using the Shift Plug-In Left/Right buttons found in the upper-right corner.

4.   Click the Save As button and name the chain, which will now be stored as a package in the Plug-In Packages folder.

5.   Click OK. Your preset is now stored and can be recalled at any time.

FX To Go, Please?

Moving FX settings from one computer to another has long been a challenge for users of most any nonlinear editing (NLE) system. Vegas has a new feature that allows FX folders to be moved from system to system, permitting users to share FX chains and presets. Using the Preset Manager (available at http://www.sonycreativesoftware.com/download) you can back up and share your chains and presets across multiple installations of Vegas Pro 8. This is especially useful when you have developed a chain of FX that you want multiple editors or workstations to have access to.

This feature works the same as all the other plug-in explorer folders, but now it also works for audio FX packages, video FX packages, transition packages, and media generator packages. Newly created packages go in the appropriate top-level package folder. (You'll need to close and reopen the plug-in explorer to see the new order of FX packages.)

Using the Preset Manager to move packages from one computer system to another is simple; save the Filter Package as a .sfpreset file, then copy that file and paste it to the new computer system via a network, USB drive, hard drive, or other means. Then, open the sfpreset file with the Preset Manager on the target system and save the FX chain. The FX package will reside on the new system.

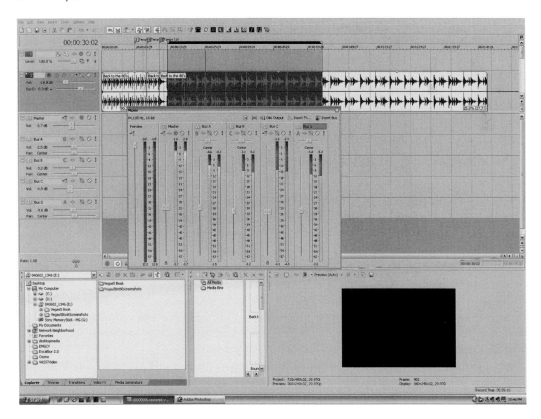

7.26   A single track feeding four buses and two auxes with automation.

Inserting Effects without Using a Bus

Effects can be directly routed and controlled in Vegas without inserting a bus. This process is similar to an aux send that doesn't return to a bus on an analog mixer.

Click the Insert FX button in the Mixer window, which calls the Plug-In Chooser dialog. Plug-ins can be viewed by All, Chains, Automatable, Sony, Third-party, or Optimized. All shows every DirectX plug-in installed in the system.

Choose the FX desired. If multiple FX are desired, press and hold down Shift while selecting FX. They will all be placed in the mixer as a series. FX selected this way cannot be individually controlled, as they all share the same send and are chained together.

FX can also be inserted individually. Every FX plug-in that is inserted in the Mixer window is also available to every track or bus. Keep in mind that this can be very processor-intensive during preview, although it will not affect the final render.

Use FX assigned to buses, as opposed to individual tracks when several tracks need the same effect. For example, a group of tom-toms, cymbals, and percussion might be able to share a reverb or delay. Rather than insert a reverb and delay on every track, send all related tracks to a bus and insert the FX, controlled by the bus.

To do this, perform the following steps:

1.   Insert FX.

2.   Insert a bus.

3.   Assign all desired tracks to the bus.

4.   Select VIEW | SHOW BUS TRACKS.

5.   Right-click the bus track and insert an FX envelope.

6.   Set envelope as desired.

Now all tracks have the necessary FX, with automation to those FX controlled from the bus. Choruses, verses, fills, bridges, other sections of a song, or sound design for a movie can be unique in the way that FX are heard and managed as a result of this method, and yet processor and RAM resources have been spared the heavy load of having many plug-ins active.

Using Track FX

Every audio track in Vegas has a chain of FX installed on it already. A noise gate, EQ, and compressor are found by clicking the FX button on each audio track. They can be heard during recording by using input monitoring, they can be removed from the track, or they can be appended to or replaced all together. These FX are optimized to keep processor resources at their peak but still place a load on the processor.

Set the default track properties by setting up the track the way you'd like it to default to. Set up an FX chain for the track FX, right-click the Track Control pane, and select Set Default Track Properties. Checking the boxes in the dialog that opens will cause the current track settings to become the default settings for future tracks inserted into the current project. Now every time Vegas opens, these track settings become the default, saving time and preventing the user from having to remember how the last mix was set up before beginning.

7.27a Set the track defaults before recording so that all audio tracks have the same settings when inserted.

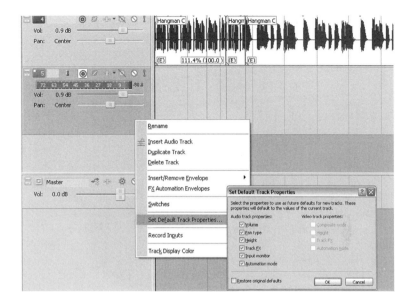

☞ Tip _____

Set up a blank project with all track settings in place, so that when a project is started, a template of several tracks is already built. Starting with 8 to 16 tracks, complete with commonly used compressor, EQ, and reverb settings, not only saves time but also impresses clients when they hear how quickly a tight sound can be dialed in. On the DVD enclosed with this book, you will find a recording interface with tracks in place that can be used as a starting place for your preferences.

Tempo-Based FX

ACID Pro offers a feature that allows users to tempo-map certain audio effects and this feature has been imported into Vegas Pro 8. It's a creative tool that allows a delay, chorus, or other time-based effect to read the tempo of the project and match the tempo when the delay is played out. This is somewhat useful for dialog only, but if music has been inserted into the Timeline or if ACID loops, Cinescore files, or other files containing tempo metadata are being used, they will significantly benefit from this feature. For example, perhaps there is a cadence to a song that has been used for editing. When the song ends, a delay that matches the beat of the song might be effective in smoothing out the decay of the song. Tempo-based audio FX might be very effective in filling out a thin audio track or powering up SFX.

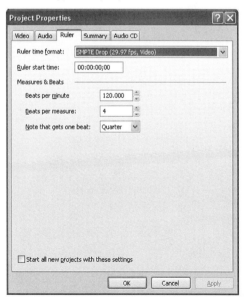

7.27b In this window, set the project tempo as the Beats per minute value.

All versions of Vegas have offered a Project tempo setting, found in the Project Properties. This is where you'll set the tempo of the project. When you are working with VASST TrakPaks, ACID loops, or other meta-rich audio, the audio's metadata will indicate the native tempo of the audio. This is the tempo that should be set in the Project Properties.

To use the tempo-based FX, insert a time-based effect such as a Sony Reverb, Delay, Chorus, or Simple Delay. When the effect dialog opens up, there will be a checkbox labeled "Tempo Sync Delay." Checking this box locks the delay to the timing of the project tempo. In the dropdown box below the checkbox, timing locks to specific musical note values may be chosen, ranging from dotted half-notes to 64th triplets, dotted half-notes being the slowest value. If Multiple Decays are chosen in the dialog, then Tempo Sync Decay lights up. Note that the same sync values apply, with the addition of syncing to Measures. This will be the slowest repeat of decay available.

When using ACIDized loops, the loops will not conform to the tempo settings of the project, unless the Import Audio at Project Tempo checkbox is selected in the OPTIONS | PREFERENCES | AUDIO dialog. Although it is very easy to set and forget this preference, some MP3 media or other non-ACIDized audio files may not play back properly. If this occurs, uncheck the Audio at Project Tempo preference.

Virtual Sound Technology

VST* is a plug-in format that often runs a little more smoothly than DirectX plug-ins but also offers a very wide array of access to various audio plug-ins that will benefit the audio user. In fact, there are a very large number of free VST plug-ins available on the web. I like the Kjaerhus audio plug-ins; they've got a Classic Series that is free, and they sound great.

7.27c

To access the VST plugs, download or install them to a directory on your preferred hard drive. I install all my VST plug-ins to a folder on my `C:` drive labeled "VST" and that's it. Vegas searches for a default directory of `C:\ Program Files\Vstplugins\`, so this is where you might prefer to install them. This directory may be shared by other applications.

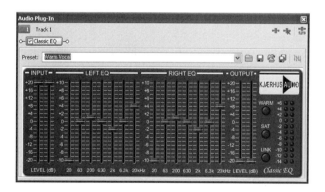

7.27d The free versions of the Kjaerhus audio plug-ins may be found on the DVD in the back of this book.

*VST is a trademark of Steinberg Media Technologies GmbH.

Now, open Vegas, and go to OPTIONS | PREFERENCES, and click the VST Effects tab. Point the Default VST search folder to the folder you've installed or downloaded the files to, if it's a location other than the default location indicated above, and then click the Refresh button. This will instruct Vegas to search for whatever plug-ins you've installed, and they'll show up in your Vegas Audio FX options in the folder marked "VST." This search could take a while if you've got a fair number of plug-ins installed. If you'd like to have alternative VST plug-ins, perhaps in the event that you'd like to sort them by manufacturer, Vegas allows for up to two separate, alternative locations for search for FX. VST plug-ins (in the Windows format) are dynamic link libraries (DLL), and the free versions of most VST plug-ins do not have an installer, but rather a Zip file containing the DLL. As mentioned, you'll want to copy or install these DLL files to the `C:\Program Files\Vstplugins\` `location`. Find free VST plug-ins on the DVD found in the back of this book, along with demo versions of other VST plug-ins.

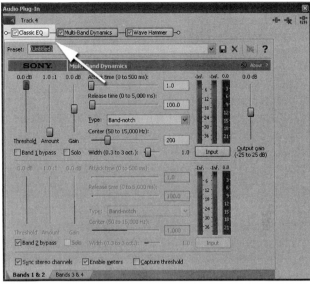

7.27e VST plug-ins can be placed in a chain with DirectX plug-ins, and they operate much like a DirectX plug-in does.

7.27f Find the VST plug-ins in the VST folder for FX.

You'll apply VST FX just as you would other plug-ins. Double-click and click OK, or single-click and select Add and then OK. Then adjust the parameters of the plug-in just as you would with any other plug-in. You can chain VST plug-ins right alongside DirectX plug-ins, and there are many automatable VST plug-ins available if you need to automate certain FX on the Timeline. Storing presets for VST plug-ins will be somewhat different, and these presets cannot be exported in the same manner as presets that are exported using the Preset Manager.

One thing to note about VST plug-ins: If a manufacturer offers both VST and DirectX installations of their plug-ins (many do), then you should install both. The reasoning behind this is that some DirectX plug-ins occasionally cause audio to drift, whereas the same application in VST form might not. The opposite may also apply; a VST plug-in may incur drift, whereas its DirectX counterpart might not.

Recording Multiple Tracks

When working with a band or ensemble, several tracks might need to be recorded at one time. A multichannel soundcard is best used in this situation. If a two-channel soundcard is used, only stereo information will be recorded, and an analog mixer will be required to manage all of the microphones. With multichannel cards, an unlimited number of microphones can be input directly to Vegas, depending on the number of cards used. (Many manufacturers of hardware cards have limits as to how many cards can be stacked.) These can be individually controlled without using an external mixing device. To select multiple inputs with an individual microphone routed to each input, assign the input of each track as mono and select either the right or the left input of the soundcard.

Remember, if your soundcard does not have preamps built in, a preamplifier is needed for every input channel.

Select a channel input for each microphone, and with every channel that has an input assigned, be sure the channel is armed. Click the Record button (Ctrl+R), and all tracks that are armed will record in sync. Enable input monitoring where necessary—the more tracks that are set for input monitoring, the heavier the processor load. Without using ASIO drivers, latency can be unreasonably high. Use ASIO drivers for input monitoring for best results.

7.28 The Echo Layla has multiple analog and digital inputs.

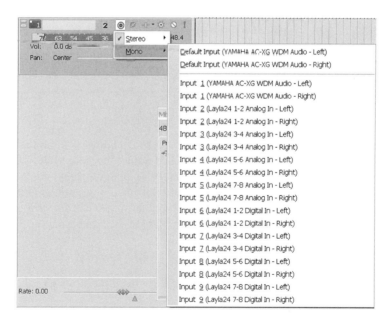

7.29 Typical session armed for recording. Double-click the right side of the track header bar to show or hide track headers.

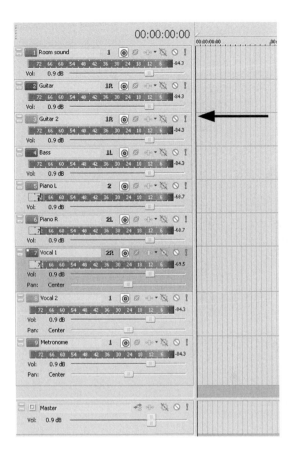

Vegas has the ability to support ASIO drivers, found in most professional soundcards. ASIO drivers are low-latency driver sets specified by Steinberg Media Technologies AG.

Tip

Pressing Ctrl + A selects all tracks at one time, and clicking the Record button on one track simultaneously arms all tracks. Clicking the Record button again after the recording is finished disarms all tracks. Use this same technique to insert volume, pan, bus, or FX envelopes on every track.

Synchronizing Vegas to External Devices

Some studio setups can call for a multitrack tape machine, sequencer, or other external device to control Vegas, or conversely, Vegas can be the master device controlling external equipment if the proper hardware is in place. To do this, a device that can convert SMPTE to MIDI timecode (MTC) is required.

Most MIDI distribution devices are capable of converting incoming MIDI timecode to SMPTE or outgoing SMPTE timecode to MIDI timecode. Most tape machines will accept either MTC or SMPTE. Some accept both.

If Vegas is to be the master device, Vegas needs to generate timecode. Set this up in the OPTIONS | PREFERENCES | SYNC dialog.

7.30   Setup of a timecode device to connect
       Vegas and external recording devices.

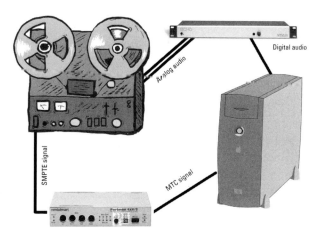

Tip _____

If you click Play in Vegas and it starts/stops an external device, Vegas is known as the master. If starting and stopping the hardware starts and stops Vegas, Vegas is the slave.

To generate a timecode that an external device can read, have the owner's manual of the external device handy so you can learn the incoming timecode specs that it requires. Most devices default to 30 frames per second, whereas other devices call for 29.97 nondrop. The standard for most professional audio equipment is 30 fps. DV has a different standard, based on American television standards.

Vegas generates timecode that is sent to the conversion device, by which it is distributed to whatever external devices Vegas needs to control. Timecode connection is necessary if Vegas will be used to edit external media that will be returned to the external recording device after edits are completed.

In the OPTIONS | PREFERENCES | SYNC | ADVANCED dialog, Vegas has an option to use either an internal clock from the CPU clock or the clock generated by the soundcard. Most instances will call for the clock to come from the soundcard. Vegas also has the ability to send full-frame messaging to external devices. Full-frame information can speed up location in some external tape machines. Not all devices can respond to full frames, and some devices can become confused. Check the documentation that came with the device that Vegas is controlling.

If Vegas is to be a slave to timecode generated by an external device, Vegas must be set to trigger from timecode. In the OPTIONS | PREFERENCES | SYNC dialog, set the trigger from the device sending timecode into the computer. Be certain that Vegas's frame-rate setting matches the frame rate being sent from the external master device. Otherwise, audio will drift ahead or behind the master when Vegas is played in time with the external master. For Vegas to operate consistently with a word clock connection, trigger must be used. Trigger refers to Vegas seeing a point in timecode, at which point it will begin to play. It is not locked to the timecode specifically. Chasing timecode means that Vegas remains synchronized with incoming timecode and follows the timecode as best as possible. Vegas has a Freewheel mode that allows Vegas to continue to play for a period of time even if timecode input is occasionally lost, playing until it sees timecode again that it should be synchronized to. If timecode is consistently lost, check the hardware or signal flow from the master device.

Sync is set up in the Preferences dialog but must be enabled in the Options menu (Ctrl+F7).

 Tip _____

> Use Vegas to edit audio from a tape machine and apply EQ, noise reduction, and processing. This process saves buses on an external machine, frees up reverbs and other processing hardware during a mix, and generally affords an opportunity to make a smaller studio have the capabilities and power of a much larger recording facility.

To view incoming or outgoing timecode, right-click the time display, which defaults to the upper-left corner of the Timeline. Choose which timecode you wish to display: time at cursor, incoming timecode, or outgoing timecode.

The timecode window is docked by default but can be moved to a convenient space on the Timeline or wherever it is most visible. It cannot be completely removed from the workspace.

7.31 Select the timecode you wish to view.

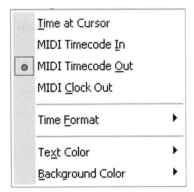

7.32

Editing Audio in Vegas

The audio editing tools found in Vegas are among the best in the world. Moreover, the audio tools in Vegas are superior to any audio tools found in any NLE system available today. Playback and recording tracks are limited only by the amount of available CPU, hard disk space, and RAM.

Placing Audio on the Timeline

Audio recorded is immediately found on the Timeline and is also found in the Media Pool. However, it's often necessary to place audio on the Timeline that might be a take, from a stock music collection, an ACID loop, sound FX, or other stored audio file.

To do this, open the Explorer in Vegas and find an audio file to place on the Timeline. Double-clicking the file inserts the file directly on the Timeline. Right-clicking a file opens several options, such as opening the file directly in the Trimmer, which allows audio sections to be trimmed before putting media on the Timeline. After audio is placed on the Timeline, it becomes an event.

7.33 The Explorer in Vegas looks similar to Windows Explorer.

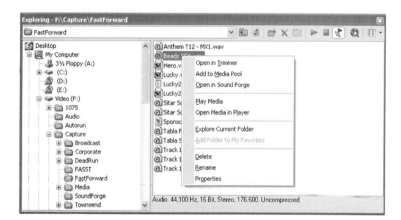

7.34 Audio opened in the Trimmer, with selections chosen to be added to the Timeline. Regions for insertion may be specified and saved in the Trimmer just as video regions may be saved.

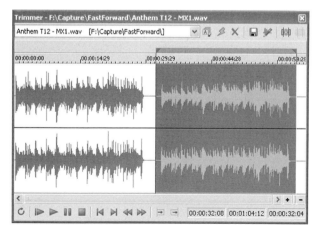

Right-clicking also offers the option of placing the audio in the Media Pool or opening the file for editing in a third-party audio editor or in Sound Forge, depending on settings in the OPTIONS | PREFERENCES | AUDIO dialog. Opening the file in the Trimmer is a simple workflow that allows phrases or sections to be marked and added to the Timeline.

After making a selection in the Trimmer, press the R key. This creates a namable region in the Trimmer that stays with the audio and will be seen any time the audio is opened in the Trimmer. After creating the region, place the cursor on the Timeline where the audio is desired and press A. This step adds the media to the Timeline, where it now is an event on a track. Selected audio can also be dragged to the Timeline from the Trimmer. Do whichever is comfortable for you.

Audio in the Trimmer can also be inserted in Ripple mode (see Using Ripple Editing later in this chapter for more details) by copying the audio in the Trimmer and enabling Ripple or by copying and pressing Shift+Ctrl+V. The audio is pasted as an event at the cursor, and subsequent events ripple down the Timeline for the length of time equal to the size of the pasted event.

Extracting Audio from CDs

Vegas provides tools to allow audio to be extracted from CDs. Whereas a single track will play back from a CD, multiple tracks or clips from a sample library that are scattered all over a CD might not play back so well, due to the limited speed of a CD or CD-R. There are two menu areas in which Vegas can be instructed to extract audio.

The first is the Media Pool. Clicking the Extract Audio from CD button opens a dialog in which users are asked to choose which tracks are to be extracted. Audio can be extracted three ways:

- By track (individual indexes can be selected)

- By time selection (a range of time for extraction can be specified)

- By the entire CD (the entire CD is extracted to the hard drive as one large file)

7.35 Clicking the Extract Audio from CD button calls up a dialog requesting information as to where files should be extracted from.

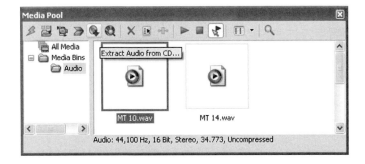

When placing any media on the Timeline, it's easy to lose focus on what the media is or where it came from. Selecting OPTIONS | PREFERENCES | GENERAL and checking 'Show active take names in events' places the name of the take on each event, whether graphic, video, or audio in nature.

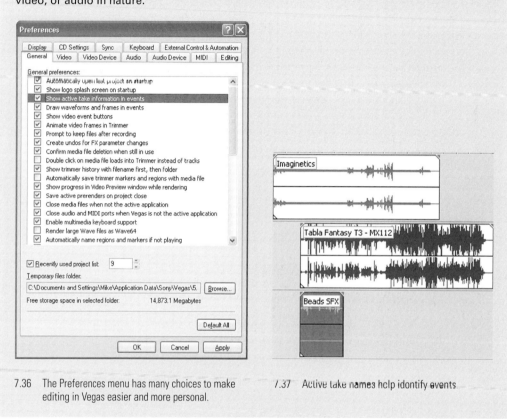

7.36   The Preferences menu has many choices to make editing in Vegas easier and more personal.

7.37   Active take names help identify events

With audio on the Timeline as events, it is ready to be edited. Basic edits would include cutting, copying, pasting, fading audio in and out, cross-fading, splitting, and moving a file.

Cutting, copying, and pasting are handled in Vegas as in most applications. To cut an event, select the event and press Ctrl+X or select EDIT | CUT after selecting the event. Events that are cut are available from the clipboard. To copy an event, select the event and press Ctrl+C or select EDIT | COPY after selecting the event. To paste an event, first cut or copy the event and then place the cursor where the event is desired to go. Pressing Ctrl+V pastes the event(s) to the Timeline wherever the cursor is located. Cut, Copy, and Paste commands are also accessible by right-clicking any file and choosing one of the commands from the context menu.

Vegas also has a Paste Repeat command that allows events to be pasted multiple times. Events can be pasted end-to-end the number of times specified in the dialog or can be spaced at intervals defined in the menu.

Selecting events to the end of the Timeline is an option when all events need to be moved up or down the Timeline as a group. Rather than Shift+clicking each file, right-click only the first file in the series, and from the menu choose Select Events to End. This process will go all the way to the end of the Timeline and select every event on that track after the cursor/selected event.

To fade an audio event in or out, it's as easy as clicking and grabbing the upper corner on either end of the event. A small quarter-circle will appear. This circle indicates that the tool is prepared to fade audio in or out.

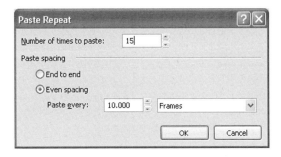

7.38 Pasting multiple instances of an audio event.

Splitting an event or series of events that are on different tracks is accomplished by placing the cursor where the split should occur. If no single event is selected, all vertical events on the Timeline will be split on the point where the cursor is. Press S to split the audio files.

If an individual event is selected, only that event will be split.

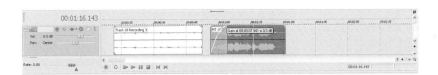

7.39   Creating a fade-in.

Fades can be customized by right-clicking the fade and choosing from the menu of five different types of fades. If one of the five fade types still doesn't provide the desired sound, use the Audio Envelope tool to create the desired fade type.

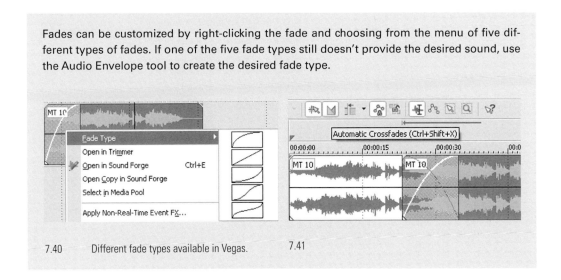

7.40   Different fade types available in Vegas.   7.41

Creating a cross-fade, in which two audio events overlap each other and one fades out as the other fades in, is achieved by sliding the two events over the top of each other for the desired length of fade. Automatic Crossfades must be enabled on the toolbar. Although defaulted to Enabled, check to be certain that the button shown in Figure 7.42 is pressed:

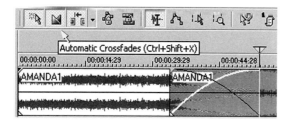

7.42

Double-clicking inside the cross-fade selects the length of the fade. The exact timing of the fade can be read in the Time Display window at the lower-right corner of the Timeline.

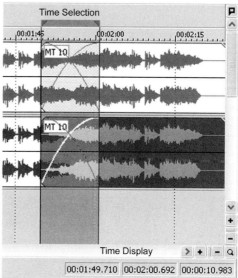

7.43 Double-click a cross-fade to make a selection. The length of the cross-fade is displayed in the Time Display window.

7.44 Vegas has many cross-fade choices available. Right-click the cross-fade to call up the Fade Type menu. Properties of a cross-fade can be adjusted by inserting a volume envelope (V) over a cross-fade.

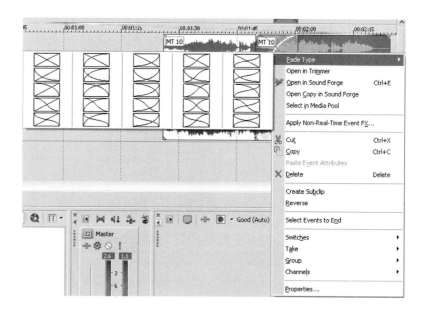

Vegas has the ability to create auto-cross-fades of a preset length. In the OPTIONS | PREFERENCES | EDITING dialog, cross-fade times can be preset. Set the desired length for cross-fades by time or by frames and select multiple files in the Explorer by pressing and holding Ctrl and selecting media by clicking them. Drag them to the Timeline, and the media will drop in as automatically cross-faded events. This same behavior applies to video files.

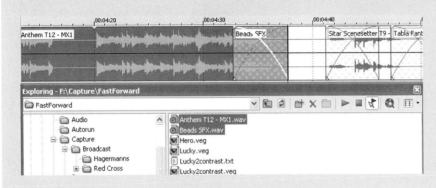

7.45　Several files can be dragged to the Timeline and automatically cross-faded by selecting several files in the Explorer.

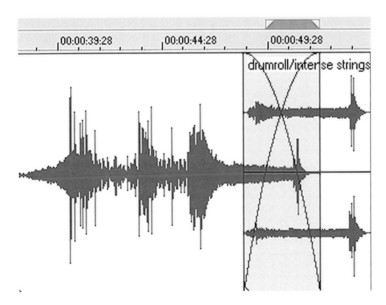

7.46　A mono event faded into a stereo event.

When interviewing with a DV cam and using one mic for the interviewee and one for the interviewer or another interviewee, the two channels are captured as one audio file with right and left information. With most NLE systems, separating channels requires editing in a separate sound editor. In Vegas, place the two-channel audio on a Timeline. Duplicate the track by right-clicking the Track Control pane and selecting Duplicate Track. Click the upper of the two identical tracks. Right-click the audio in the upper track and select CHANNELS | LEFT ONLY. Right-click the lower track and select CHANNELS | RIGHT ONLY. There are now two tracks of mono audio on the Timeline, capable of being edited and processed separately. This method is a fast means of accomplishing two tracks with separate control.

All tracks added to the Timeline are stereo. Only events are either mono or stereo. A mono signal, however, will remain mono when dragged to the Timeline. Mono and stereo signals can occupy the same track, and a mono event can be cross-faded over a stereo event on the Timeline.

Audio that is stereo, but should be mono, is quickly converted by right-clicking a stereo file and choosing Combine from the pop-up menu. Files that have been combined can be restored by selecting Both. Audio can also be selected as Right Only or Left Only, and channels can be switched by selecting Swap.

Audio that is not at nominal level can be normalized nondestructively by right-clicking an audio event and selecting Properties. Check the "Normalize" box, which will bring audio to a level normalized as specified in the OPTIONS | PREFERENCES | AUDIO EVENT dialog. On the disc in this book, a JavaScript is found that can be run as a script in Vegas, normalizing all audio on the Timeline as a script rather than normalizing all audio manually. The file is located in the \scripts\ folder as normalizeall.js.

7.47   Audio event before normalizing.

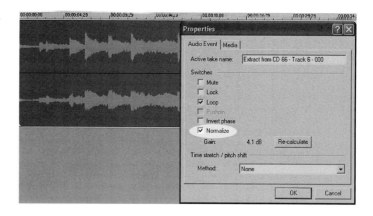

 Tip

Normalize in Sony Sound Forge as opposed to Vegas, so you can normalize on the RMS value, as opposed to the peak value.

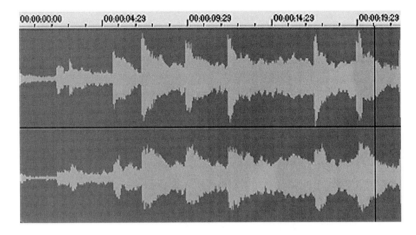

7.48   Audio event after normalizing, a 4.1 dB increase in gain. Normalizing an entire project may also be accomplished with scripting tools available for free, at vasst.com.

Audio events have an individual gain reduction on each event as well. Place the cursor at the top of the audio event and watch for the cursor to turn into a hand icon. Then click and hold, dragging the hand icon downward. Vegas indicates the gain level reduction as the gain line is pulled downward.

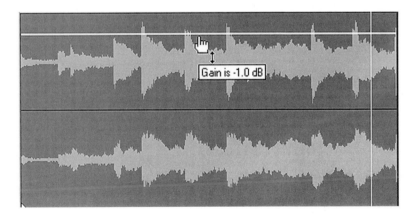

7.49   Reducing the gain of an audio event on the Timeline.

Right-clicking an audio event calls up several menu options. One of them is the ability to loop an event, which is different from setting up a playback loop for previews.

Right-click an event, choose Switches, and check the Loop box. This step allows the audio event to be dragged out infinitely, and the audio will constantly loop. Vegas inserts an indicator that looks like a small divot or carrot in the event at the point of the end/beginning of a loop. Looping is terrific for repeating sounds that might fade together or for using an ACID loop that should repeat. Looping is set to On by default.

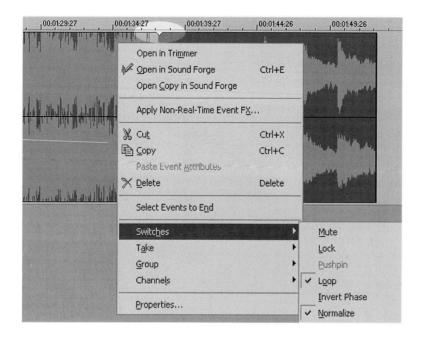

7.50   Setting an event for looped playback. Looping may also be enabled by pressing the Q key.

Looping is helpful in most situations; however, it can also work against a mix in some instances. If a reverb or delay is desired to continue reflection for a long time after an audio event ends, looping must be disabled and the file dragged out for the length of time that the reverb/delay is desired. Otherwise, the plug-in sees the end of the audio event and thinks it needs to shut off if the end of the project is reached. Dragging out an empty portion of the event with looping turned off allows the reverb or delay to continue to be audible.

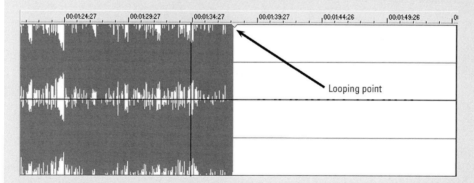

7.51   Event dragged out with looping off. Because looping is disabled and the audio has ended, Vegas treats the stretched event like empty media.

Get ACIDized!

Speaking of loops, ACID has long been recognized as one of the most valuable creative tools for composing royalty-free music for video and recorded productions. ACID uses prerecorded loops, recorded by some of the finest musicians in the world. Imagine having Mick Fleetwood playing drums for you, Rudy Sarzo on bass, Ken Jordan from Crystal Method on keys and sound design, and some of the world's best-known R&B vocalists all performing on your video soundtrack! With ACID loops and Vegas's ability to take advantage of ACID metadata, you can have these great performers and more.

Visit http://www.acidplanet.com and download some of the free eight-packs of loops. Unzip them, and start creating music in Vegas.

ACID files are .wav files containing metadata that informs Vegas of the tempo, key, and length of the audio file. Vegas will take recordings of disparate tempos and lock them up to whatever tempo is set in the Project Properties. Using the Pitch Shift functions, loop pitches may be shifted up or down to be made harmonically acceptable.

One of the caveats about using ACID loops in Vegas is that Vegas, unlike Sony's ACID application, cannot shift tempo on the fly by using tempo markers. This doesn't mean that soundtracks or underscores can't change in tempo, however. This merely means you need to work around the limitations.

In Vegas, whatever the project tempo may be, it determines the tempo of the loop. Therefore, if the project tempo is left to the default value of 120 beats per minute (bpm), then any loops dropped on the Timeline will conform to the 120 bpm tempo. However, the project tempo may be changed downstream/later in the project, and any loops dropped on the Timeline prior to the tempo change will retain their tempo of 120 bpm, whereas any loop dropped on the Timeline after the project tempo is changed will retain the new tempo value. Put another way, if you drop loops on the Vegas Timeline with the tempo at 120, any loop you drop at any point will always be at the 120 tempo. If you shift tempo later and attempt to place loops on the Timeline in sync with the earlier inserted loops, the loops will not synchronize correctly. So be sure to get your compositions correctly assembled prior to changing any project tempo in Vegas. It's also handy to save various versions of your project if you expect to be changing tempos or creating mapped tempos later on.

Vegas does not indicate the current tempo, so it's a good practice to create markers on the Timeline to indicate where tempo changes are occurring.

Another workaround is to create your project the way you want it to sound in Vegas, create a tempo change, and then reload the loops after the tempo change has occurred, loading them from the Project Media. The loops originally dropped on the Timeline will retain their original tempo information, and the loops inserted from the Project Media will exist at the new tempo.

Key changes are not possible as a global function in Vegas. Individual loops may be pitch-shifted to create key changes, but this is done only on an event-by-event basis. Vegas will not recognize the actual key of a loop, but loops may be tuned by using the pitch-shift capability found in Vegas. If Show Active Take Name is selected in the OPTIONS | PREFERENCES dialog Vegas will display the original pitch or key of the loop. (Drum loops rarely contain pitch data, and so will be blank.)

A workaround to the lack of global pitch shift is to select all loops to be shifted by holding the Ctrl key and using the minus or plus keys to shift them up or down according to desired amount.

Shifting loops in amounts of 2 semitones, 5 semitones, and 7 semitones will follow the average pop song format. There are 12 semitones in an octave. Music today is often written in what is called I, IV, V format or 1, 4, 5 format. This means that the chord or pitch changes will reflect a shift up by a fourth or a shift up by a fifth. An interval of a fourth is equal to 5 semitones, and an interval of a fifth is equal to 7 semitones. To shift a pitch down to the fifth the downward value would be −5 from the original pitch and to shift down to the fourth, the value would be 7 semitones down. It's rarely a good idea to shift a loop more than 12 semitones up or down unless a specific sound or effect is being sought. Loops in higher octaves will display less of a negative effect than a lower octave loop, because of the distance between frequency amplitude. Don't expect to shift a bass guitar loop by more than a couple of semitones without damaging the integrity of the loop.

If you have two loops of disparate or dissonant pitch, select the loop that is different from other loops or lower in pitch overall from the opposing loop. Using the hyphen or equals key, pitch the loop up or down until it is harmonically acceptable, or in the same pitch as the other loops on the Timeline.

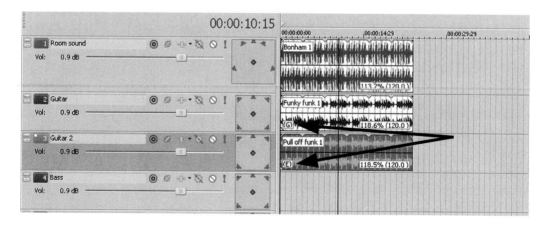

7.52   Notice that the pitches do not match. This generally will mean that the audio will be discordant and not sound correct.

Using ACID loops in Vegas is a powerful addition. This allows video editors to create rudimentary beds or sound design tools. If greater or more powerful music creation tools are required, I recommend that readers check out ACID, another of Sony's desktop media applications.

And There Goes the Pitch! (Vegas Still Hits a Home Run)

Vegas has always had amazing audio manipulation tools since the inception of version 1. Vegas 5 brought some new audio tools to the game, and one of them involves pitch-shifting on the fly. This feature is simply amazing. A weak voice-over, a music bed that conflicts with dialog, an unintelligible word or two can all be improved or even repaired just by using this feature.

To shift pitch in Vegas, make a selection of an audio event. If only a single word or section needs to be shifted, use the S key to split the audio event, singling out the area to be shifted. Create a time selection above the selected event, and press the Q key to enable looping. Start playback. During playback use the plus and minus keys to shift the pitch up or down. Pitch may be shifted up or down as much as two full octaves, or as much as 24 semitones in either direction. By holding the Ctrl key while shifting pitch, you can make changes by cents rather than semitones, giving very tight control to critical pitch shifts. Use this feature to correct an out-of-tune vocal or to thicken a doubled/duplicated track.

Any shift greater than approximately 5 semitones in either direction may have adverse effects on the quality of the audio, depending on content. Entire music beds may be shifted up or down as much as a fifth or plus or minus 7 semitones to complement dialog or make way for other audio events, whereas stingers or other special effects events might be shifted very low or high for maximum impact.

Try inserting a cymbal or other hard attack and long-sustain sound and pitch it down to −24. You might find it very powerful as an introductory sound or perfect accompaniment to a fly-in transition or graphic object. Coupling this with the new real-time reverse found in Vegas makes for a wonderful effect in some circumstances. Experiment with different sounds to learn how this effect might best suit your workflow and creative opportunity.

 Open the "dropped pitch.veg" file on the DVD in the back of this book and experiment with how the new audio-processing tools function.

Shifting stock music or other music found in the project down or up by a pitch or two will have a tremendous impact on the feel and texture of a scene and usually will clear the frequency range for a better dialog track. Experiment with this new feature, and it may well become your favorite tool in Vegas. It's definitely in the top two or three favorite features in Vegas for me.

Get the Mark Up

Vegas has improved managing of markers in a substantial fashion. No longer bridled with only 10 markers with names, Vegas now allows numbering of up to 99 markers that are autonumbered when inserted into the Timeline. Of course, all markers may be renamed and renumbered to user preference, but just having the ability to insert more than 10 markers and have the numbers stay sequential is a great thing. Earlier versions would allow for lots of markers, but only 1 through 9 were named.

Further enhancements include being able to click the Marker indicator in the upper-right corner of the workspace, causing the Marker bar or Timeline to take focus from the rest of the application. This allows the arrow keys to be used to jump from marker to marker. The left-arrow key moves cursor and playhead to the previous marker, and the right-arrow key moves cursor and playhead to next marker. Markers also move with media when a multiple selection is created and moved. Markers may be deleted individually or in groups in addition to now being able to be selectively deleted. When focus is shifted away from the Marker Timeline, the Marker tools are disabled.

To work with the new features in the Marker Timeline, click the Marker tool button in the upper right corner of the window. Now click on any marker. (Insert a few markers if you don't have any. To insert a marker, press the M key.) Notice that when the marker is clicked, it becomes selected with its number highlighted in the marker box. Click Delete to remove the marker, left-arrow to move to the previous marker, or right-arrow to move to the next marker. You may select multiple markers by holding Ctrl as each marker is selected. Markers may be moved in tandem when multiple selections occur, or multiple markers may be deleted at one time by selecting each marker while holding the Ctrl button. If you have a number of markers to be deleted, click on the first marker, hold Shift, and click on the last marker. All markers in between the first and the last marker will be selected and may be deleted with the Delete key.

7.53 The Marker button is new, allowing Vegas to focus on the Marker Timeline, providing users with several options.

Inserting Markers

Markers are often needed to indicate a specific point on the Timeline that requires an edit, to serve as a cue, to insert metadata, and for many other helpful uses. Vegas allows for three different types of markers:

- Markers—reference points to be returned to later, which identify timing or act as a reminder for later edits. Markers can be inserted on the Timeline or in the Trimmer. Markers can be named at any time.

- Regions—defined sections on the Timeline. Regions can behave as permanent indicators of a selection either in the Trimmer or on the Timeline. Regions can act as reminders of specific sections to be returned to later or can act as edit-length indicators in the Trimmer. Regions can be named at any point in time. All training materials on the DVD contained in this book are built with regions.

- Command markers—used to insert metadata in streaming media files. Text data, such as lyrics, promotional information, URL locations, and closed captions, can be embedded with command markers. (See Chapter 11—Output and Export—for more information.)

Markers and regions can remain with the audio file when inserted in the Trimmer tool. The OPTIONS | PREFERENCES | GENERAL dialog has a checkbox to save markers and regions automatically in the Trimmer tool.

To insert a marker, place the cursor where the marker location is desired. Press M, right-click the Marker bar, or select INSERT | MARKER. This step places a marker on the Timeline. Markers can be deleted by right-clicking the individual marker or by right-clicking in the Marker bar and choosing Delete All Markers. A group of markers can be deleted by making a selection on the Timeline that contains the markers to be deleted, right-clicking in the Marker bar, and selecting the menu option Delete All in Selection. Markers can be named when inserted or later by right-clicking a marker and selecting Rename. Pressing Enter or clicking out of the box on the Timeline sets the marker's name.

Markers can be navigated by pressing Ctrl+left arrow/right arrow. This step will jump the cursor from marker to marker.

7.54 Be certain that the checkbox for 'Automatically save trimmer markers and regions with media file' is checked to save the indicators in the Trimmer.

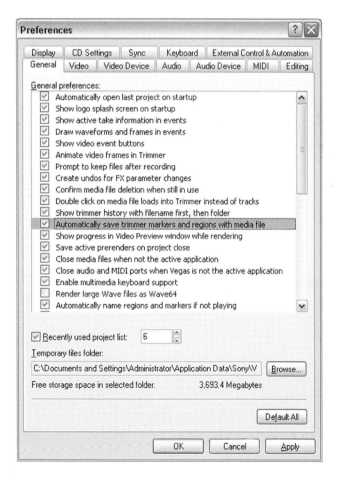

7.55 Inserting, deleting, or editing markers can be done by right-clicking the Marker bar.

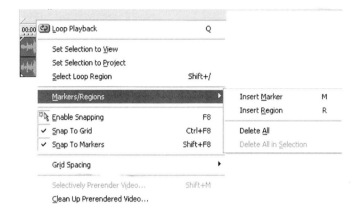

Regions are defined by creating a selection on the Timeline and pressing R or by selecting INSERT | REGION. Double-clicking an event creates an automatic selection for the length of the event. The region can be named in any way that you choose. Regions can be renamed at any point.

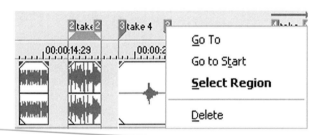

7.56 Cursor behaviors inside a region can be selected by right-clicking a region marker.

👉 *Tip* _____

Use regions to indicate miniprojects or minisections, such as a verse, chorus, or bridge. This option makes it easier to find full sections or loop full sections during the recording session. It also makes it easy to fly in a repeat chorus or bridge later on, if necessary.

Regions can be navigated or toggled. Regions can be navigated by selecting a corresponding number on the keyboard (not the numeric keypad) or by pressing Ctrl+left arrow/right arrow. This step allows rapid navigation within Vegas of various regions on the Timeline.

Command markers are created when the cursor is placed at the desired point for a metadata event to occur, and C is pressed or INSERT | COMMAND is selected. This step calls the Command Properties dialog, in which the desired type of metadata is selected.

Metadata allows for media to become rich media or media that is more than just audio. (See Chapter 12—Alternative Delivery—for more information.)

The command marker can have a name different from the properties associated with the marker. Right-clicking the com-

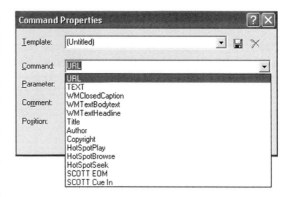

7.57   Different types of metadata that can be inserted.

mand marker provides a menu for renaming the file. Command markers can be deleted individually by right-clicking the marker and selecting Delete. Right-clicking in the Marker bar and selecting Delete All does not affect command markers.

Rubber Audio

Vegas has a feature known as Rubber Audio. Audio can be stretched by grabbing the right side of an audio event, pressing and holding down Ctrl, and dragging the event to the right. This option is useful to correct a slightly off-sync voice or to expand or compress an audio event to make it fit within a specified period. Audio that is expanded/stretched much more than 10 percent, however, will sound very strange indeed. Perhaps long stretches are valuable for a specific effect; however, the audio is quickly recognized as affected after it has gone past the 10–15 percent stretch point. Use the Rubber/Time Stretch feature only as a means of achieving sync on an out of sync and time format event or as a special effect.

 Tip

> Rubber Audio.veg is a project on the DVD that allows you to hear what rubber audio/stretched audio sounds like at various speeds and pitches.

Time stretch can also be accomplished by right-clicking the audio event, selecting Properties, and adjusting the length of the file. Audio pitch/tuning can also be adjusted in this same dialog box.

Use Semitones to move pitch in musical half-steps and use the Cents dialog to change by hundredths of semitones. For example, a pitch shift of −7 semitones is equal to a fifth interval down from the tonic, or original pitch. Shifting a pitch by +4 is a minor third up from the tonic or original pitch.

 Tip

> Sound designers will find the Pitch Shift/Time Stretch tool invaluable. Using household sounds, such as blenders, flushing commodes, gelatin being slowly sucked out of a can, and other creative sounds, coupled with the Pitch Shift/Time Stretch feature yields usable sounds for any kind of video or audio production. Adding reverbs, delays, flanges, and panning information to these sounds further enhances value and realism.

Variable-Speed Audio in Vegas

Currently, Vegas does not have the ability to gradually speed up, reverse, or slow down sound on the Timeline. If audio speed must be gradually reversed or slowed down, the file must be opened in either Sound Forge or another audio editing application. If a multichannel soundcard is available on the system, however, there is another option.

Create a new bus and route the audio to be sped, altered, or reversed to this bus. Create a new track and select the output of the new bus to feed the new track. Click Record and play away with the Playback Rate control in Vegas. This process is a lot more accurate and fun than using the J, K, or L keys or a Contour ShuttlePRO/SpaceStation AV. The altered playback shows up on the new track on which it can now be filtered, EQ'd, or otherwise processed.

This process can also be accomplished with the Windows Media Recorder by selecting the inputs from the Windows Media Mixer.

To reverse audio with no gradation in speed, right-click the audio event and choose Reverse from the submenu options. This is a real-time process, so you'll see the audio event reverse itself and redraw its waveform.

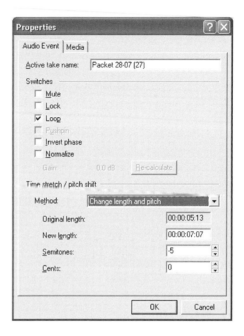

7.58   Changing pitch of an audio event can bring a slightly off-key singer into tune or create that 'news television' sound for a slightly thin voice-over.

Reverse Decisions

Ever wanted to reverse an audio or video clip? In the past, video could be reversed by using the Velocity envelope set to a value of −100 percent and video would be easily reversed. To reverse a file, right-click and select the Reverse option from the submenu that pops up. The beauty is, this reverses video too, if video is selected. Any audio may be reversed whether tied to a video event or not.

Any time audio is reversed, a subclip is created that will be found in the Project Media. This subclip may be placed on the Timeline as a separate event. An incredible use of the Reverse tool is to apply it to a cymbal that has a strong attack and a light decay. Reversing this provides a great opportunity to create a stinger or audio event that can lead up to and impact a particular scene or action in a video. The Beatles were the first to take great advantage of reversed audio, but one of the best examples is when Roy Thomas Baker used reversed tape on a piano for the "We Will Rock You" and "Bohemian Rhapsody" songs recorded by Queen. Try this on a variety of instruments, combined with the pitch-shifting tools now found in Vegas. You'll be surprised at the creative inspiration you'll find in doing this. For even greater effect in dialog, try placing a duplicate of a dialog track and reversing one of the two tracks. It creates a mess, but where the two tracks converge, it's a very interesting effect. You may want to split out one section of the dialog and do this. Alfred Hitchcock used this technique in Psycho to create a sense of babbling and underlying confusion, and it certainly worked well. It might just make your production take on a whole new meaning.

Snapping Audio Events

Vegas can snap audio events to a marker, region, grid indicator, or a butting event.
  Two events on the same track always snap together if snapping is enabled.
  Two events can also be snapped together on different tracks, however. To do this, follow these steps:

1. Double-click the event to which you want the next event to snap. This step creates a time selection.

2. On the track that holds the event to which the selected event should be snapped, move the event toward the front or back of the region or selected event. Vegas autosnaps the moved event to the first event that is selected, regardless of tracks. Several events can be snapped at once.

Events can also be snapped to a grid line. Pressing F8 enables snapping, and pressing it again disables snapping. If snapping is not enabled, timing grids are not visible. To snap an event to the grid, press Ctrl+F8. To snap an event to a marker, press Shift+F8.

7.59 Snapping several events to a
      selected track event.

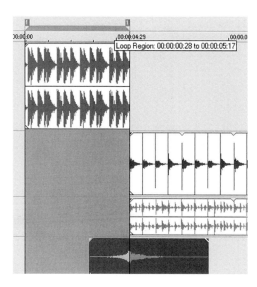

Trimming Events on the Timeline

Events can be trimmed in the Trimmer window before being placed on the Timeline.
They can be edited for length directly on the Timeline as well. Position the cursor over the start or end of an event, and the cursor changes to the trim cursor.

Grab either the start or the end of an event by clicking and holding, and drag the end of the event to the left or the start of an event to the right. The event shortens as it is dragged or trimmed.

If Auto-Ripple (Ctrl+L) is enabled, any trimming on the Timeline will result in events following the trim filling the space/hole left behind because of the trim.

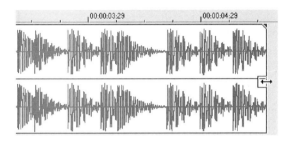

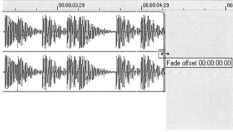

7.60   Before trimming on the Timeline.

7.61   After trimming on the Timeline.

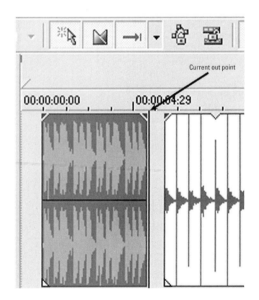

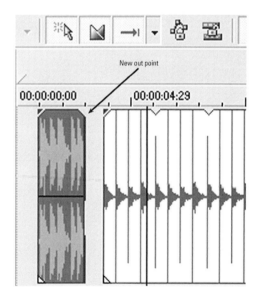

7.62   Hold down the Alt key while click–dragging within the audio event to move audio within the same time space.

7.63   Rippled on the Timeline, media following trim filled in time vacated because of trimming on the Timeline.

Another option to trimming on the Timeline is to slip or shift the contents of an event. By pressing and holding down Alt and dragging right or left inside an event, audio can be slipped forward or backward in time without moving the actual event. This feature is great for moving audio within a specified time space without having to be concerned about losing space in time. The event remains a placeholder while audio can be fine-tuned. This feature is also useful for fitting audio in a stipulated time space, when time is specified but the contents can be determined later.

Deleting Events from the Timeline

Selecting events by clicking them and then pressing Delete removes them from the Timeline. Multiple events can be selected by pressing and holding down Shift and clicking events to be deleted. Deleting events removes them from the Timeline but does not eliminate the empty space that remains unless Auto-Ripple is enabled (Ctrl+L). If an entire space in time across multiple tracks is to be deleted, make a selection on the Timeline. Select Delete (Ctrl+X). (Selecting Delete does not place deleted media on the clipboard.) If Ripple is enabled, all events remaining on the Timeline shift to fill the empty space; otherwise, the time selection remains behind and is left empty. Events or time can also be deleted by selecting EDIT | DELETE.

 Tip_____

If in the process of deleting events for which Ripple is needed but not enabled, use a postedit ripple to close deleted areas. Postedit ripple behaviors are selected in the Edit menu or by pressing F, Ctrl+F, or Ctrl+Shift+F.

Using Ripple Editing

Vegas has Ripple features that make rippling intuitive and easy. Entire tracks, multiple tracks, and individual events can all be rippled collectively or individually. Enable rippling by selecting the Auto-Ripple button.

Select Affected Tracks from the three options displayed in the dropdown menu. Drag several events to the Timeline, butting them together. Trim the outpoint of the first event. All events subsequent to the first event slide to the left, remaining butted up against the first event. At random, place markers on the Timeline. Now drag the out point of the first event back to where it was when originally placed on the Timeline. The events subsequent to the lengthened event slide forward in time for the exact length as the event being dragged moves. However, the inserted markers stay where they are.

Return to the Auto-Ripple dropdown menu and select Affected Tracks + Project Markers, Keyframes, and Envelopes. Drag the out point of the first (or any other event) to the left, and this time, when all events slide to the left, regions, markers, envelopes, and all other attributes of all tracks slide to the left as well, keeping the project Timeline intact. This process is called a ripple edit.

7.64   Vegas draws an arrow indicating the direction of the ripple that also demonstrates the length of the ripple.

 Tip_____

Notice that the Ripple tool in Vegas will give a display of the amount of time the media is being moved backward or forward in time.

Inserting from the Trimmer is easy and fast as well. Select or regionalize audio in the Trimmer and either press A with rippling enabled or, if rippling is not enabled, press Shift+Ctrl+V. The audio inserts as an event with all subsequent audio sliding down to make room for the new event. Ripple editing is useful in quickly cutting together on-air commercials, or in a musical setting, it's excellent for cutting out entire sections or bars of music.

Grouping

At times, it's helpful for entire sections or types of events to be grouped or locked together so that when one is moved, all of them move. Grouping events is quick and easy in Vegas. Select a number of events and press G. This step ties all of the events together so that when one is moved, all the others move with it. For instance, perhaps all events related to a chorus, bridge, or verse might be grouped so that when one section is moved, all related events to that group are moved with it.

To remove an event from a group, select it and press U to ungroup. Grouping can be temporarily ignored by clicking the Ignore Event Grouping button on the toolbar.

Groups are great for applying edits to multiple events at one time. To apply an edit to all members of a group, perform the following steps:

1. Press Shift+G or right-click one member of the group.

2. Select GROUP | SELECT ALL. You can cut, copy, or paste edits to the entire group. Grouped, but unselected events, are not edited together.

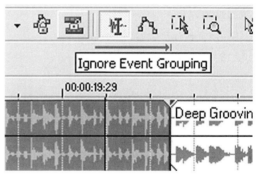

Events can belong to only one group at a time. Adding an event to a group essentially dissolves the existing group and creates a new one. As many groups as needed can be created, yet no two groups can contain the same event.

7.65   Grouping can be temporarily ignored.

Working with Audio Plug-ins

Vegas has a tremendous assortment of plug-ins that come with the application and that provide massive mixing and editing power. Particularly necessary in the digital audio world, there are multiple types of compressors and equalizers, plus reverbs, delays, flangers, noise gates, resonators, and more. As a result of the open DirectX platform, plug-ins from companies such as WAVES, Ozone, Sonitus, and Cakewalk and dozens of other manufacturers can be used in Vegas.

Sony was the first adopter of what was once called Active Movie, which later became ActiveX, which then once again changed names to DirectX. Sony supported Active Movie in their 4.0a version of Sound Forge. Because of Sony's pioneering work in the plug-in interface market, most every video editing application, as well as every audio application, supports the DirectX audio platform.

Plug-ins, such as compressors, reverbs, delays, and noise reduction, all take the place of hardware counterparts in the analog world. In fact, many software plug-ins look just like their hardware counterparts, and, in some cases such as WAVES, the software tools were so popular that the company followed up the software tools with hardware tools for the nondigital environment!

Sony offers nearly 30 plug-ins with Vegas. Rather than examine each of them, we'll look at what each family of plug-ins does.

Dynamic-range plug-ins offer the ability to ensure that audio doesn't exceed the dynamic-range capabilities of digital audio. This includes compressors, limiters, and combinations thereof, such as Wave Hammer, Sony's final-step plug-in.

Although digital audio has an extreme dynamic range, it is also less forgiving than its analog counterpart, in that the zero point in the digital world is cold, harsh, and unforgiving. In the analog world, the dynamic range is fairly limited by any comparison, ranging in the upper 60 dB area depending on the quality of equipment used. Twenty-four-bit digital recordings have a dynamic range of 138 dB, or more than double the dynamic of analog. Dynamic-range plug-ins help reduce dynamic range while maintaining most of the nuances of a fairly dynamic performance. They could be considered automatic volume controls. By limiting, or subtly compressing, the exceptionally loud portions of a performance, the performance still maintains its soft to loud moments but at the same time doesn't exceed the preset point. More on dynamic-range control is found under "Mixing Techniques" in this chapter.

Sony Dynamic plug-ins include:

- Express FX Dynamics
- Graphic Dynamics
- Multi-band Dynamics
- Track Compressor
- Vinyl Restoration
- Wave Hammer

Frequency-based plug-ins/FX function by varying the amount of volume of a given frequency or group of frequencies to change the way a recording sounds. Equalizers, wah-wahs, phasers, and similar tools work on either moving a frequency's amplitude up or down to change the audio's sound or timbre. Wah-wah and phaser sounds sweep/shift the amplitude and frequency over time, giving the sound of motion, similar to the concept of a Doppler effect. In fact, some plug-ins are written to simulate the Doppler effect.

Frequency-based plugs include:

- Wah-wah
- Graphic EQ
- Paragraphic EQ
- Smooth/Enhance
- Track EQ

The Doppler effect, discovered in about 1845 by Christian Doppler, an Austrian mathematician, demonstrates that shifts in frequency occur as the article generating the sound moves. This effect is how our ears perceive sounds coming toward us and moving away from us. Listen to a train as it approaches. The frequencies contained in the sound that the train makes shifts as it moves toward you or away. The shifting frequencies result in shifting pitch as the object moves in either direction.

Time-based plug-ins/FX are based on just that: time. Delays, reverb, chorus, and flangers are all based on delaying, recombining, and/or reflecting a moment in time. When a sound originates, roughly 40 percent of its sound that we perceive is based on reflection of sound in a given space. In other words, singing in the shower is so much more fun than singing in a closet because the reflections of the voice in the shower hit the ear much more quickly than the reflections in a closet do. Some types of music are predominantly based on reverbs and delays, used to create emotional expression and to fill holes in a song. Without long delays and reverbs, many of the ballads and arena anthem rock songs would sound empty and powerless because the lead vocal and chorus vocals would lose their presence and power through the absence of filled time and massive reflection. Time-based effects are used more than any other effect to create emotional responses. Dripping water combined with huge reverb settings is part and parcel of nearly every horror movie made, and the simulated sounds of space (space has no air and therefore sound cannot pass) also include reverbs and delays.

Time-based plug-ins include:

- Flange/wah
- Multitap delay
- Reverb
- Simple delay
- Acoustic Mirror*
- ExpressFX Chorus*
- ExpressFX Delay*
- ExpressFX Flange*
- ExpressFX Reverb*

*Optional FX from Sony

On the DVD enclosed with this book, you will find demonstration plug-ins from PSP Audio, WAVES, Ozone, and Sonitus. A wide variety of plug-ins are available for you to experiment with and enjoy.

Upgrading from Vegas 3 or 4 to Vegas Pro 8, and your plug-ins disappeared?

Use the Plug-In Migration Wizard in your Vegas toolkit. Go to START | ALL PROGRAMS | SONY | UTILITIES | MIGRATION TOOLS. Run the register DirectX plug-ins utility. This should restore all of your plug-ins to Vegas. This generally happens only once you delete an old version of Vegas, such as version 4. I recommend you leave the older version loaded for a period of time, until you are entirely familiar with Vegas Pro 8, if only for the compositing tools found in the video toolset.

Automating FX in Vegas

One of the most exciting tools in Vegas is the ability to automate FX. Many of the DirectX plug-in tools have the ability to be automated. EQ settings, delay times, reverb decays, and much more can now be controlled by Vegas's automation envelopes. Many of the high-tech sounds demanded by production music today require either several hands at the mix console or automated FX control.

For instance, if a vocal line reaches a break just before a chorus and a long delay is needed, automated FX can change the length of the delay time as opposed to using another FX send just for the vocal breaks. Perhaps an EQ sweep, just as a car passes from right to left, creating the illusion of a Doppler effect, would make the sound more believable. Frequency sweeps added to drum mixes or to a main instrument sound become part of the instrument itself, creating an unmatchable identity. Remember "Axel F," the theme song from *Beverly Hills Cop?* The sweeps heard on the bass lines in that song were created by synthesis, but the sound itself was a huge part of the song. Techno music is nearly always automation-dependent because of the repetitive nature of the music.

To hear an example of automation, open the FX Automation project on the DVD.

On track 1, you can observe an inserted automation envelope by right-clicking the Control pane and choosing FX Automation Envelopes. Notice in the Track EQ settings that the "Band3 Gain" and "Band3 Bandwidth" boxes are checked. Click OK.

7.66 Select the boxes related to the automation parameters you wish to control.

A pair of dark-colored envelopes are on the track in the Timeline. These are the bandwidth and gain controls for the EQ that you have set for automation.

7.67 Automation envelopes appear
when Automation parameters
are selected.

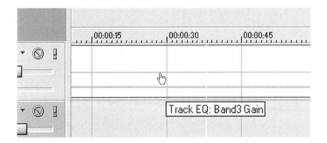

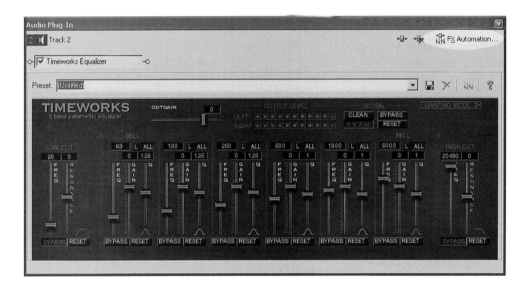

7.68 The FX Automation button opens up a dialog in which tool automation features can be viewed and selected.

Every 2 seconds, insert a handle on the Band3 Gain envelope or the envelope that appears in the middle of the track. (The project grid is laid out in seconds.) In between the handles on the Band3 Gain envelope, handles are already inserted on the Band3 Bandwidth envelope. Now drag every other handle of the Band3 Gain handles down to the bottom of the track, or −15 dB worth of adjustment. Experiment with the type of fade by right-clicking the handle and selecting different fade types. You'll be astounded at the degree of control this offers the sound.

Not all DirectX plug-ins have the ability to be controlled by automation envelopes. iZotope, NewBlue, Sonic Timeworks, WAVES, Wave Arts, and the plug-ins found in the Automated plug-ins folder are all examples of automatable plug-ins. If a plug-in is capable of automation, a selection button will appear in the upper-right corner of the plug-in. When the button is clicked, the parameters available for automation will appear.

Some plug-ins have to be added to a chain at least once before they are recognized as automatable. Don't be alarmed if you don't see them in the automatable folder right away.

Working with Other Types of Plug-ins

Noise Reduction

In 1995, Sony released a product called Noise Reduction 1.0. This new tool revolutionized the music industry. In the past, only very expensive hardware tools or the Digidesign Intelligent Noise Reduction tools found in ProTools or No Noise from Sonic Solutions were available. One was too expensive and only occasionally effective, the other not satisfactory in extremely noisy circumstances. Sony's Noise Reduction tool gave working musicians the ability to clean up poor-sounding rooms or environments.

Noise Reduction uses an algorithm known as Fast Fourier Transform (FFT) as part of the power behind how it functions. This algorithm is large, requiring millions of calculations based on information selected in the noisy portion of the file. A basic explanation is that when noise is present in a sound file, the noise can be isolated in sections between words, between instrument attacks, or in heads or tails of a file. The noise is then sampled, and the algorithm is applied to the rest of the audio file, removing the sampled sounds but leaving behind the original sound. Sometimes, if the sample is too large or contains too much information (sounds other than noise) or if the noise sample is frequency unstable (sound is moving), the process can remove some of the original, prenoisy sound, resulting in artifacts. These artifacts often resemble the sound of rushing water or a waterfall. Other times, it has a metallic, robotic sound. In fact, some films have used this extreme noise reduction technique to create alien sounds. In this section, however, we're interested in removing noise to make a file sound cleaner. In short,

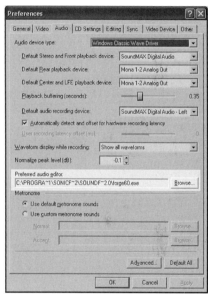

7.69 Select the Preferred audio editor in the PREFERENCES | AUDIO menu.

Noise Reduction is similar to a frequency-dependent noise gate that is divided into several hundred bands. The noiseprint determines the threshold or open level of each gate, and any time the volume of a frequency is below that threshold, it is suppressed/silenced.

Noise reduction is particularly effective when trying to remove a constant noise source, such as an air conditioner, refrigerator, or AC hum. It is least effective on moving sources, such as constantly passing traffic, running water, or varying wind noise.

A demonstration version of Noise Reduction is located on the DVD in the back of this book. Install it now, if it has not already been installed.

To apply Noise Reduction to a file, first open the file in a DirectX-capable audio editor by right-clicking in Vegas and choosing "Open copy in (audio editing application)." This option should already be configured if you followed the steps in Chapter 1. If you have not done so, select OPTIONS | PREFERENCES | AUDIO and use the Browse button to locate the executable for your favorite audio editor. It is located in the C:\Program Files directory in most instances.

On the audio file, select a very small slice of audio that contains only the noise that needs to be removed. When selecting a noise sample, less is more. Fewer frequencies in the sample make for a more accurate reduction in those frequencies.

Now open Noise Reduction from the DirectX plug-in host (for Sound Forge it is TOOLS I NOISE REDUCTION), and the screen shown in Figure 7.72 will be displayed.

Check the "Capture noiseprint" box and click the Preview button. This step allows you to hear what section has been selected. At the same time, a noiseprint has been captured. Click the Noiseprint tab if you wish to see what the noiseprint looks like. Thousands of handles are on the

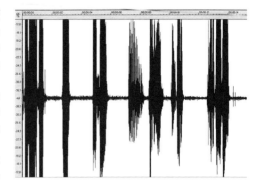

7.70   When the file opens up in the sound editor, it looks something like this. Notice the noise between words spoken.

noiseprint, so that custom or exceptionally accurate control of the noiseprint may be had. It is generally best to allow the plug-in to function automatically, however. Playing with these handles does offer the opportunity to create some fairly inventive and radical sounds.

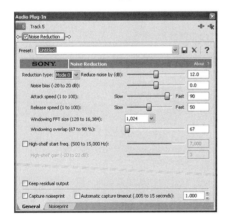

7.71   This is the main window for Noise Reduction, where all control of noise removal takes place.

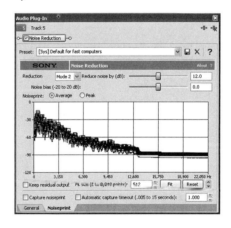

7.72   A view of how Noise Reduction interprets the noise information.

After the noiseprint has been captured, the area that the filter should be run on must be selected. Noise Reduction allows for selectable time spans, entire files, regions, or specific areas to be processed. Generally, files will be the entire area, but you can specify an area if so desired. Generally, choose the entire audio file, because if noise is present in one area, it's typically present in the entire file. (Other host applications can operate differently.) In Sound Forge 9, click More to select the start and end points for applying noise reduction.

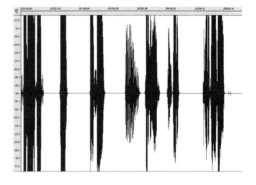

7.73   File after noise reduction applied.

Trying to use large noise samples is counterproductive, damaging wanted information while possibly ignoring unwanted information. Use small samples multiple times rather than trying to use a larger sample one time. Noise Reduction can be run as many times as necessary to remove noise from the file, and using small selections usually has little impact on the desired sounds.

7.74 Select the smallest space possible for noise sample.

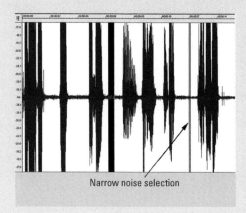

Narrow noise selection

Click OK when you have determined what time selection of the file should be affected. Now you'll be able to move the Reduce Noise By slider, listening in realtime as Noise Reduction processes the noise out. Typically, it's rare to get more than −50 dB of noise out of a file, but occasionally more aggressive settings will work.

A useful feature in Noise Reduction is the "Keep Residual Output" box. Checking this box inverts the signal, so that the information being reduced/eliminated is heard and the audio that will be kept is masked. This process allows you to hear if too much of the original signal is being affected.

After the desired level of noise is reduced/eliminated, click OK. The Noise Reduction plug-in will process the file. Closing the file in Sound Forge will prompt you to save the file. Save the file, and it will be deposited on the Timeline in Vegas in the exact place that it came from, but it is now named the original filename with "Take (number)" in the filename. It can be toggled back and forth from the original audio file for comparison.

Some files require multiple passes of Noise Reduction to obtain the best results without affecting the original audio/desired audio.

 The DVD in the back of this book includes a project called Noise Reduction Project. Open this file. You will see two video files; the first has had no noise reduction on it, the second has been noise reduced. If you monitor the project through a good set of speakers or through any headphones, the hum in the background is very clear. The noise source is a refrigerator, three rooms from where the interview was being conducted. In the case of the second file, −70 dB of noise was taken out, without creating artifacts in the desired audio file. Even if you don't have speakers that can accurately reproduce the noise, pay particular attention to the master meters.

Practice on the first file. If you don't capture a small enough segment for your noise file, you'll most likely create artifacts in the speech. FFT processing doesn't require a large slice; use a 100-millisecond slice of noise at most for your sample.

> Noise Reduction can be used for other purposes, such as creating unique sounds over a drum loop, voice, or sound effect. Experiment with it and find what works creatively for you. Drastically removing the high end by sampling the decay of a high hat or snare can give unique personality to the sound of any drum loop. Try using Noise Reduction on a heavily compressed speech file and make any human sound become more robotic.

Noise Reduction is not intended to be used as a real-time effect. It is exceptionally processor-intensive, and all but the fastest computers with loads of RAM will stutter and pop. This plug-in is best used as a destructive edit, as a take over original audio, or in an audio editor as a destructive or take-based event. It's common that noise reduction will require multiple passes to reduce noise to a satisfactory level. To accomplish this in Vegas will require several instances of the Noise Reduction plug-in on the offending track, whereas by using Sound Forge, it's very fast to process and provides immediate results with no hit on the processor.

Fingertip Mixing: Using the Mackie Control (and Other Control Devices in Vegas)

A significant barrier to using Vegas in the all-digital recording studio was that until version 5, Vegas was incapable of working with any hardware device except the Contour ShuttlePRO, which offered no mixing capabilities whatsoever. Since Vegas 5, Sony has provided direct access to external surface control with the Mackie Control and Frontier Tranzport devices and with generic controllers that can be programmed to work with Vegas. For instance, for fading and panning, no mouse is needed, simply use the Mackie Control in the same manner as you'd mix with any mixer. Accessing all parameters of FX such as compressors and EQs is very simple and intuitive with the control. Any generic device such as the M-Audio Oxygen keyboard or a

7.75 The Mackie Expanders and Control together make a very powerful control for Vegas as well as many other audio applications. The console housing for the Mackie Control was built by Omnirax and contains many racks for external audio gear.

Tascam 424 can be set up to function with Vegas as well. Once you've mixed with a mixer, mixing with a mouse becomes extremely irritating and almost painful.

To set up a Mackie Control within Vegas, you'll need:

- A Mackie Control.

- A MIDI interface device (many soundcards can manage this).

- A Mackie Extender. This is a nice addition, but not necessary. The Extender expands the capabilities of the Control so that the Control, for instance, manages channels 1 through 8, and the Extender manages channels 9 through 16. However, the Mackie Control can manage up to 128 channels of audio at a time. Switching from one channel set to another is a minor inconvenience; the video editor might not find it cumbersome nor inefficient in the same manner that an audio engineer or mix engineer might.

Connect the MIDI input of the Mackie Control to the Output MIDI connector of your soundcard or MIDI input/output (I/O) device. Connect the MIDI output of the Mackie Control to the MIDI Input of your soundcard or MIDI I/O device.

7.76   Connect the Mackie Control to the MIDI interface device.

Select OPTIONS | PREFERENCES | EXTERNAL CONTROL AND AUTOMATION. This opens the dialog of the external control parameters. This is where Vegas will be instructed to access the Mackie Control hardware interface.

7.77   This dialog, found in the track header, is used to tell Vegas how to read or write any automation or level settings from the Mackie Control.

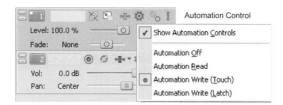

In this dialog, select the Available Devices dropdown menu and choose the Mackie Control from the dialog. Then click Add to add the Control to the Active Control Devices dialog. This should cause the Mackie faders to move to indicate that the device is communicating with Vegas. (If it doesn't respond, don't be concerned. The next step will determine communication.) When the device shows up in the dialog, double-click the box containing the Mackie Control.

This opens up the Configuration dialog, which allows Vegas and the Mackie to be set up not only to be compatible, but also to be as efficient and powerful as you'd like it to be.

Click Scan in the Configuration dialog. This will instruct Vegas to scan the MIDI connections to see what is connected to the ports. If you have Mackie Extender devices attached to the MIDI interface, they'll show up here as well.

Each device must be configured separately, but the engineers at Sony and Vegas have done most of the work for you. However, you'll need to instruct the Configuration dialog to set up the channels on the various devices. For instance, if the system is set up for one Expander and one Control, the Control can be set up to be channels 1–8, or 9–16, and the Expander can be set to control whatever channels the Control is not controlling. Since I'm righthanded and find my need to access the Control more imperative than reaching the Expanders, I set my system up as follows:

- Expander 1: channels 1 through 8
- Expander 2: channels 9 through 16
- Expander 3: channels 17 through 24
- Mackie Control: channels 25 through 32

Notice in Illustration 7.75 that the Control is set up to the far right of all the Expanders. (Expander control should soon be available for Vegas.)

After clicking Scan and setting up each device for its controlled channels, click OK. Now click the Apply button in the External Control and automation dialog. All is set for Vegas to know what to do, except one last detail.

Close the Preferences dialog and go to OPTIONS | EXTERNAL CONTROL, and click on External Control. This will place a small check mark next to the External Control words. This tells Vegas that you'd like to control the application externally. Of course you'll still be able to operate Vegas via the keyboard and mouse, but this tells Vegas to accept information from the Mackie Control.

Vegas will automatically be mapped to all the knobs on the Mackie Control, so nothing more is needed. The Mackie Console should have come with a Lexan overlay that you can stick to the surface of the control. The Lexan overlay is specific to Vegas,

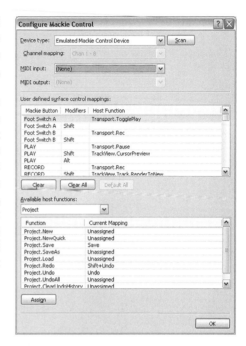

7.78 Set Vegas and the Mackie Control up to behave exactly as you'd like them to behave in the Configuration dialog.

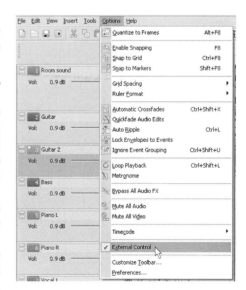

7.79 Enable External Control from the OPTIONS | EXTERNAL CONTROL dialog.

indicating how each push button relates to Vegas and what it controls. As mentioned earlier, you may customize the key mapping to set any button to perform a specific task in Vegas.

A single Mackie Control may be set up to operate as many as 128 channels at a time on a single device, but this does require a lot of paging through various views to look at each channel past the eight that are automatically displayed. Because most of my audio mixes require me to have immediate access to all channels, I find it more efficient to use a series of Extenders and Controls. One powerful side benefit of the Mackie Universal Control (and any other controlling device) is that the device may be used as a video switcher as well, providing access to color-correction plug-ins and other plug-ins found in the Vegas filter set.

Other Controlling Devices

Any MIDI control device may be set up to control Vegas. For example, the M-Audio Oxygen keyboard has eight generic control knobs that may be accessed within Vegas and may be used like a mixer via generic surface control.

Some MIDI devices won't use a MIDI connection, such as the Oxygen. Control data is passed back and forth via the USB connection.

To use generic surface controls, the setup is very similar to the Mackie Control setup. First install the device drivers and connect the device to be used as a generic surface control. Open the OPTIONS | PREFERENCES | MIDI dialog. The generic device should appear in the dialog box. Tick the boxes related to the connected device, telling Vegas which devices you'd like to use as a control surfaces.

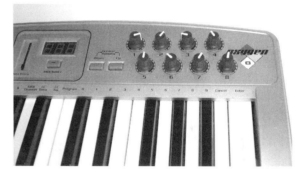

7.80   The eight knobs on the Oxygen may be assigned as controlling devices for Vegas.

Click the External Control and Automation and select Generic Control from the dropdown in the Available Devices dialog box. The dialog below will display the generic devices. Right-click or double-click the Generic Control and open the Configuration dialog. In the Configuration dialog, you'll need to map the keys and controllers to specific functions within Vegas. Some devices may be ready to roll with Default Mapping. Devices such as the Tascam 424 and the eVolution U Controller should link up fairly quickly, although no mapping has been created for the device. You can locate the files for surface controllers in the C:\Program Files\Sony\<Vegas Dir>\External Control Drivers\Generic Control Maps folder.

Locate the Quikmap.xml file on the vasst.com/login.htm web site, which will set up all automation needs for the M-Audio Oxygen. You will also find other controller parameters on the VASST site.

Audiomation?

Even if you don't have HUI devices connected to Vegas, you can still take advantage of the automation found in Vegas. Each audio track header's automation button contains several options. Right-click the automation button to view the options.

The Automated Mute feature allows audio to be muted during the recording of automation during playback of a file.

To insert an automatic mute into your project, place an audio file on the Timeline. Click the Automation button and select Show Automation Controls from the submenu. This will insert the Automated Mute button into the track header. Click the Automation button again and choose Write (Latch) or Write (Touch) from the submenu.

Begin playback, and while the playhead is moving down the Timeline, press the Automated Mute button. Vegas will insert an automated mute point into the Timeline, and each time the playhead crosses this point the audio will be muted. Press the Automated Mute button again and the audio will be unmuted.

Audio may also be mixed on the fly with Vegas using a mouse, clicking on the track and inserting envelope points during playback. Choose a track header, press V to insert a volume envelope or P to insert a pan envelope. During playback, click the volume or panning envelope. This will insert an envelope point or handle into the Timeline. Moving this envelope point or handle will modify the volume or pan position of the track. All movements of the volume or panning envelope will be remembered and recalled automatically for future mixing. Setting up a time selection and loop will allow mix points to be tweaked on the fly.

Training Vegas

Vegas can be trained to work with most standard controller devices. To train Vegas to accept input from your MIDI Controller device, open the OPTIONS | PREFERENCES | EXTERNAL CONTROL AND AUTOMATION tab. Double-click the Generic Controller, or right-click and select Configure from the submenu. The Configuration dialog will open.

In the Configure dialog, click on the parameter you wish to control.

Touch any controlling device button, slider, or knob. This will cause the Learn button in the dialog to light up. Tick the "Learn" box, and turn, slide, or press the parameter knob, fader, or button to instruct Vegas to link it to the specific parameter. Repeat this step for each parameter you wish to control. Be certain you save the map so that it's available for your next session. (Maps are saved as XML files.)

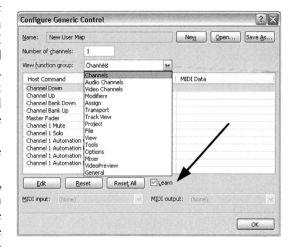

7.81a Select the parameter that you'd like to control by clicking on it and then moving, sliding, or pressing the controlling device, knob, slider, or button. You'll need to tick the 'Learn' box.

Every Breath You Take, Every Move You Make!

Automation is the act of the host application remembering every move made on the external control device. In past versions of Vegas, automation was entirely controlled by a mouse. Although intuitive and functional, it is certainly nearly impossible to generate an inspired mix with a mouse. Music is supposed to be inspired by the whim of the moment, and sometimes generating mixes by hand at moments of random will spark the most amazing muse and mixes. Moreover, being able to recall random mixes at will and create multiple mixes to play back for a director or producer is a wonderful thing.

Nearly all parameters of Vegas's functions may be automated and recalled. With a higher-end controller such as the Mackie Control, you can access parameters of all effects, bus sends, auxiliary sends and returns, reverbs, and compressors.

Automation in Vegas is a wonderful thing to experience because of its simplicity with underlying complexity.

To automate, even a small Griffen knob can be used. It's a little challenging to set up, but once the controller is set up, here are the steps to automate a mix:

1. On the track to be automated, click the Automation settings button.

2. Choose Automation Write in one of the two modes offered, Touch and Latch.

3. Click Play or press the spacebar, and start to twist knobs, slide sliders, or push buttons.

4. Stop playback. If you are pleased with the mix, it may be put into Automation Read mode, in which no movement will be taught to the application; it merely will read the moves previously input with the controlling device.

 *Tip*_____

If you are an experienced audio engineer, you can mix all tracks live just as you would with an analog mixer. Select all tracks in Vegas before putting a track in automation mode, so that when one track is placed in automation record mode, all tracks are put into automation record mode. You can always go back and overwrite all fader moves quickly on individual tracks if necessary. If you have a hardware device such as the Mackie Universal Control, it's fast and easy to write a full mix and then go back and tweak later. If you have more audio tracks than you have fader control over, enable automation only for the tracks you have faders for, then switch the faders to the remaining tracks, writing automation and tweaking as you go. Remember, you can always reorder tracks in Vegas by dragging tracks to where they are most convenient in layout and priority.

Touch Me, Latch Me! Automation Modes
There are two forms of writing automation. One is Latch mode, and the other is Touch mode. Each has its benefits, and each is fairly common to automated studios. Generally the workflow between the two processes is managed in a specific order. For most recording scenarios, you'll be working with Vegas by starting in one mode and finishing in another.

7.81b

For a fresh mix with no automation moves inserted, start in Latch mode. Play the mix by pressing the spacebar or clicking Play or by pressing the Play button on your controlling device. Move knobs or faders during the playback on however many tracks you have in automation mode. This creates a "rough mix" as it's called in the industry. Now Vegas will remember all movements you made regardless of **wheth**er they are volumes, pans, or FX automation movements. This is usually done with **all tracks** in record mode, but just because it's usually done this way doesn't mean you have to do it this way.

Latch mode will continue writing settings regardless of whether you are making fader movements or not and will overwrite any existing movements that you may have created earlier, making Latch mode excellent for writing over an entire mix or an entire track if you are dissatisfied with the mix or want to create an alternative mix.

Following the mix set up or rough mix, the mix can be either fine-tuned by individual track or tweaked with all tracks still in automation mode. However, switching tracks over to Touch mode is best. In Touch mode, keyframes and control points are created only when you are touching or adjusting the parameters of the track. As soon as you stop moving sliders or knobs, Vegas quits writing movements, and the already existing movements you inserted in Latch mode or the first write of automation take over again. This is why Touch mode is best for tweaking a mix.

On each track header, there is an Automation icon. You can see it next to the Mute and Track FX button. Click it and a submenu appears.

Automation is found on all track headers and may be set up for all tracks at once or set for individual tracks.

In the submenu, you can select Show Automation Controls, and this will cause the Automation icon to display the mode that the specific track is in. This is handy if you find yourself wondering why a specific track is behaving in a particular way.

Mutes may now be automated too. A device like the Mackie Control or the eVolution 33 has Mute buttons on it. Mutes may also be inserted by clicking on the Mute button found on the track header or by pressing the Mute button found on the controlling device. Automated muting

7.82 The four icons that indicate track status are Off, Read, Touch, and Latch. Notice that Read and Touch are very similar. The Read icon is green and the Write icon is red.

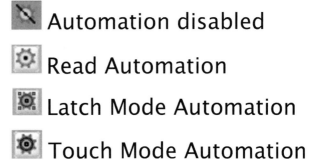

Automation disabled

Read Automation

Latch Mode Automation

Touch Mode Automation

is very handy for music or dialog composites, in which various sections and takes are on multiple tracks and you want to comp together all the acceptable parts of different tracks to create one final track.

Feeling Fat? Get Thin!

Automation will write literally thousands of nodes, also known as handles or keyframes, during a write. This can be exceptionally tasking on the CPU if left on its own. However, Vegas has a feature known as thinning by which the number of nodes and keyframes can be thinned out, controlled by the user. In the OPTIONS | PREFERENCES | EXTERNAL CONTROL AND AUTOMATION dialog, there is a checkbox for thinning. Thinning will be necessary on slower machines that are used for large mixes. Otherwise, the thousands of envelope points generated by fader motion will be more than the processor can handle.

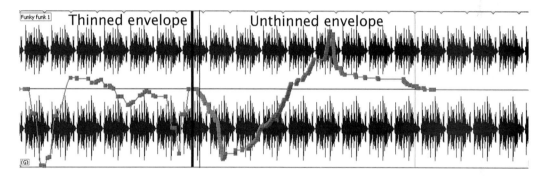

7.83   Use this menu to reduce or increase the amount of thinning of keyframes and handles found in a mix.

Video editors may or may not find the nuances of thinning necessary to control. Musicians will demand to have as much control as possible and so will want to set this to preference. If you still feel that thinning is missing or hitting an area that doesn't feel just right, you can always manually adjust handles by using a mouse and clicking and moving the node or envelope point until it is sitting just right in the mix. One suggested workflow is that the mix be created in Latch mode with Thinning enabled. Turn Thinning off, and tweak or fine-tune the mix using Touch mode. Use Touch mode only on the areas that need fine-tuning or you may end up rendering the earlier-thinned sections moot.

Though it may seem odd, various controllers may send differing amounts of information and some may insert far more values or fewer values than necessary. Experiment with your controller device to determine whether thinning is necessary for your mix.

The small marks inserted either manually or with a controlling device may be called nodes, handles, keyframes, grips, envelope points, and or rubber band markers by various applications. All of these names mean the same thing. Sony calls them envelope points.

Tip_____

If you need extreme control over complex mix sections, do a rough mix and get things as close to finished as possible, then turn off Thinning in the OPTIONS | PREFERENCES | EXTERNAL CONTROL AND AUTOMATION dialog.

Faders Flying Everywhere

Fader movement can be viewed on or off; the question becomes one of whether fader movement is distracting to the mix or too much information for a lesser video card to draw movement for. With a complex mix of more than 16 channels, viewing fader movements might be too big a load on a 4 or 8 MB video card. Any 16 MB or larger VRAM video card should easily draw fader movements. If by chance your video card can't write the movements, visit the OPTIONS | PREFERENCES | EXTERNAL CONTROL AND AUTOMATION dialog. In this dialog, uncheck "Animate Screen Faders during Playback." If you have a flying fader device such as the Mackie, faders will move on the device regardless of whether the screen is drawing the movement or not. This is a very sexy and impressive event for those not familiar with fader movement. Watching faders move, meters bouncing, and all functions doing what they do while the user is hands off is quite exciting.

Another great reason to use a device like the Mackie for an external control surface is that metering can be viewed on the LCD screen of the Mackie Control. Sony has made this work in such a manner that you don't have to look constantly at the computer monitor while setting a mix up on the Mackie, as the meters are very accurate and laid out above each channel strip, making it easy to see and familiar to audio engineers used to viewing metering on the console. The meters will show up as long as the Mackie is in I/O mode, found on the console view section. Also, the Mixing Console view in Vegas is adjustable as to the level of detail you'd like to observe in the meters.

Mixing Audio in Vegas

Mixing audio is a practice based entirely on personal preference, but some standards and techniques are used by most engineers and producers to achieve mixes that meet with industry expectations. Each person's ears are different; this is what makes one producer more popular for various kinds of music than another. Mutt Lange, a very well-known producer of heavy metal music and pop rock, is one of the few to jump from one musical style to another. (Marrying country legend Shania Twain didn't hurt.) Peter Gabriel is renowned for his production of world-pop music, just as William Aura is known for his adult contemporary work. Alan Parsons, Tom Lord-Alge, Ross Collum, and Danial Langios are all unique and well-known producers/mix engineers. All of them credit their years working with the equipment and producers in the studios they cut their teeth in as third engineers, janitors, or receptionists. All of these producers got to where they are not only because of their inspired sense of what people want to hear and how to bring an artist's talents to the fore but also because they knew the basic principles and practices of mixing audio. Knowledge and a practiced ear are the two most important things to creating a great mix. Knowledge is easily found. Having a practiced ear can take years. The basic principles of understanding a mix are fairly simple; from there, it simply becomes a matter of expanding on experience.

Mixing Techniques

Setting up a mix is entirely dependent on the contents of the track, whether it's instrumentation, bed music with a voice-over, Foley, sound design, or full-blown orchestra. Bass frequencies tend to be more centered in a mix than are high frequencies, in which a right-to-left spread is more evidently heard. Bass frequencies below 250 Hz aren't really even directional but rather omni-directional. Higher frequencies are very directional, which is why bass drums and bass guitars/synthesizers are generally mixed to the center of a mix and higher frequency sounds are spaced throughout the right-to-left areas of a mix. An easier way to think of it is to look at a photo of a beautiful mountain vista. The mountains form the base of the image, and the eye is drawn to the bugling elk in the forefront, slightly off center. You notice the green trees and the stream or brook flowing through the picture. The primary subject of the picture is the elk in the foreground, but without the surrounding beauty, the elk looks rather stark. Creating a good mix is just like that: lots of individual elements that draw the ear to a primary element. Try to picture a mix visually with the score or performance in your mind's eye, which will help achieve the end goal.

Fine-tune mixes by holding down the left mouse button and use the 2 or 8 key on the numeric keypad to fine-tune any envelope up or down. The 4 or 6 key moves a node forward or backward on the Timeline. The amount of control is determined by the depth of track focus. With maximum zoom, superfine envelope increments are possible. The Quantize to Frames (F8) option might need to be disabled to have accurate access at maximum zoom.

The same keyboard trim features affecting the video Timeline are also found in the audio toolset. Use the 7 or 9 key on the numeric keypad to select an event edge; use the 1 or 3 key to edit longer or shorter by samples. The depth of track focus determines how fine the keyboard edits are made. Zooming in deep on a track causes up to sample-by-sample edits; zooming out on the track edits larger sections of audio. (See Chapter 3 for more information on keyboard editing.)

Some mixes are built from the bottom-end elements first, finishing with the primary element, and other mixes are built starting with the primary element and the other sounds are built around it.

For working with a dialog-based mix for film or video, this is a good way to start, getting the voice to a level that is comfortable. It should be loud, but never crossing the −3 dB mark so that room exists for other elements to maintain their dynamic expression. Adding a compressor to the primary element is fairly standard practice. If the primary is a voice, start with light compression settings of 1.5:1, or 2:1, working with the threshold to suit the mix. Be cautious of squashing the sound too much, as this element is the most out-front part of the mix.

Next, begin to place the foundation elements, such as static walla, traffic, or background noise. In a musical context, these elements would be the kick drum, bass guitar, or other bottom-end elements. If the bottom sound is muddy or tubby, remove some of the frequencies in the 300 Hz region. In a musical mix, add a little 1.5 kHz for some snap in the kick drum and bass guitar. In a mix for video with dialog, leave some of the upper frequencies out, perhaps even dampen them a bit, so as not to fight with the frequencies in the primary element/front voice. Use a compressor, starting with a basic setting of 3:1 or 4:1, and work with the settings from there to keep the mix from becoming too dynamic in the low frequencies. Send all the bottom/foundation elements to one submix/bus, with an additional compressor if necessary on the bus.

> The term walla stems from the early days of radio, when extras were brought in for a radio or film show, and actors would say "walla-walla-walla" over and over, with just a few people saying the words out of sync with each other to create the sound of a murmuring crowd. No individual words were spoken at all. To this day, background dialog is called walla, but actors no longer use the fixed-word format.

Sound design comes into the mix next, with motion and depth filling the speakers with moving elements that can be musical or not. Either way, the sound should be a filling sound that underlies the other pieces of the mix. In a music-oriented mix, this is the rhythmic element. Try to avoid panning this sound hard right or left if possible. More of a 9 o'clock and 3 o'clock is the ticket, washed wide rather than being too loud, so as to take away focus from the aural subject. Guitars, synths, and background vocals all fit into this space too. Be cautious of wanting too much sparkle or bottom end in these elements and leave room for the primary sounds and foundation sounds. Use reverbs or delays to wash these sounds across the sonic canvas, rather than increasing the volume of an individual instrument. These sounds contribute a sense of color or timbre of the musical element. If everything were taken away except this element and the lead element, there would still be something worth listening to. If inconsistent sounds are in this element, try to bring them in and out gently rather than with surprise. Otherwise, they'll detract from the front elements.

Next placed are the special FX or signature sounds of a piece. In the musical context, this is the moving sounds of a synth that has a signature to mark the song, rather than a synth that is emulating a traditional keyboard. In a video context, these sounds are the cannon fire, bullets flying, spaceships, aircraft swoops, or other action sounds. These should be placed to move right to left or front to back in a surround mix. These are the exciting elements of a stereo or surround mix.

Remember, these tips are mere rudiments. From here, the mix can be tweaked according to the individual ear.

Compression

One might say that it is simply impossible to do a good digital mix without compression, yet compression is one of the most misunderstood parts of the mix and audio process. First, it's important to understand the difference between a compressor and a limiter.

A limiter prevents audio from passing at a predetermined volume. Any audio that attempts to pass the preset level is squashed to fit the preset level. Limiters are generally not good for music or audio for video mixes but are more suited to situations in which not all elements of the media can be controlled.

7.84 An overhead view of mix elements.

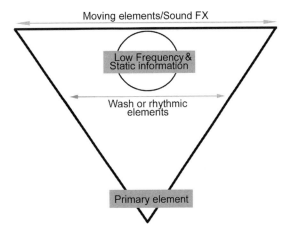

7.85 Audio before being limited.

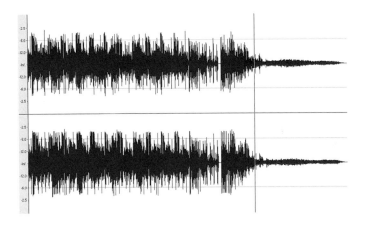

7.86 Audio after being hard limited.

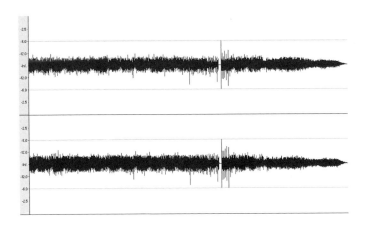

There are hard limiters and soft limiters. The difference is how much of a dynamic the limiter might be set at before the hard limit point. In other words, a limiter might be preset to ensure that nothing greater than −3 dB is allowed to pass, but the majority of the audio information is at −5 dB with lots of dynamic that wants to go much louder than the −3 dB allowable maximum. Using a setting that instructs the limiter to start reducing levels at −9 dB allows some dynamic feel to remain in the audio track. Limiters often squeeze the high end and life out of a mix, making it dull and boring. Television commercials are often hard limited and compressed to give maximum volume (one of the annoying things about the overall volume of a television commercial).

The term soft limiter is really just drawing a comparison to a hard compressor. Most compressors also have limiting ability built in.

Compressors operate a little differently compared to a compressor limiter, being more elastic or malleable only in the way they control dynamics on release. A limiter is a compressor with a ratio of 10:1 or greater but usually with fewer adjustable attributes than a compressor. Compressors can make audio louder, while at the same time making sure that the dynamic range is reduced. Generally, a compressor is used to keep dynamics as accurate as possible, while at the same time preventing audio from crossing a chosen threshold. This feature makes it easier to get an event/signal louder in a mix, while still maintaining control over the apparent signal.

For example, compression might be required for a singer or voice-over artist in the studio who moves toward and back from the microphone. Recorded levels are not consistent. Perhaps the same vocal artist has very quiet to very loud passages in their speech. A compressor evens out the differences between the two sections.

A compressor is used by guitar players and bass players to maintain the sustain of a plucked or strummed note/chord. A compressor smoothes down the attack on the strings and then opens up/releases gradually by allowing the note/chord to appear as though it is going longer than it would have otherwise been heard.

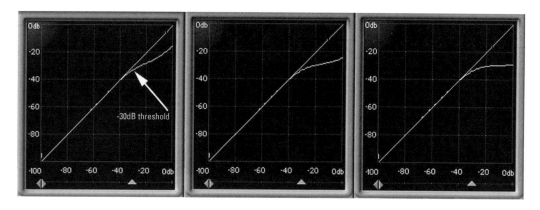

7.87   Threshold set at ?30 dB, with variable compression ratios: 2:1, 5:1, 10:1. Notice the compression curve at the different settings.

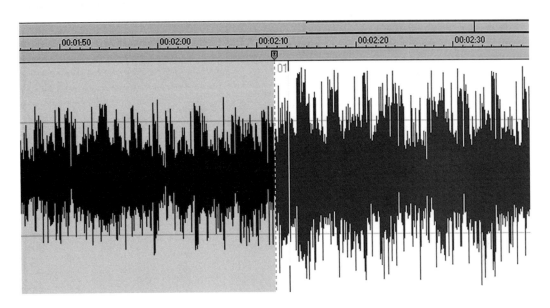

7.88 Mastering level compression at 2:1, with threshold at ?8 dB, allows the signal to be louder overall because of the reduced dynamic range.

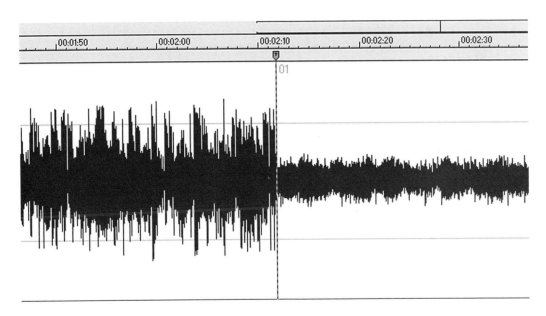

7.89 Compression applied at 2:1, with threshold at ?24 dB. Beginning the attack earlier in the signal with a lower threshold makes a huge difference in the behavior of the compressor.

Here's how a compressor works. Comprehending the ratio, threshold, attack, and release are the most important pieces to understanding compression.

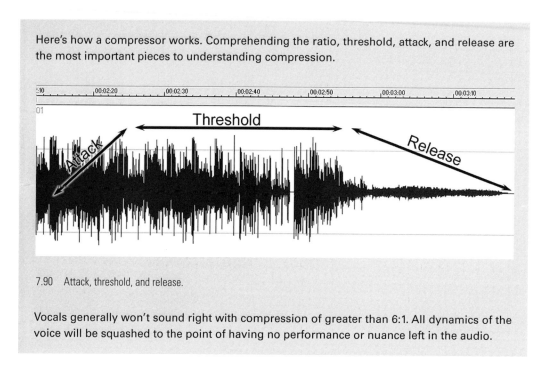

7.90   Attack, threshold, and release.

Vocals generally won't sound right with compression of greater than 6:1. All dynamics of the voice will be squashed to the point of having no performance or nuance left in the audio.

On the DVD included in this book are five demonstrations of audio and audio for video. Listen to the differences in how the audio cuts through on the repaired sections.

Sony provides a multiband dynamics processor in their plug-in arsenal. This multiband tool is a combination of four compressors with frequency-dependent settings. Rather than compressing an overall instrument or mix, individual facets of the audio can be affected while leaving other portions alone. For example, a snare drum might be exactly the sound you want but is too loud at one particular frequency or range of frequencies. The multiband dynamics plug-in, or EQ-based compressor, gives the ability to compress only the offending frequency or range of frequencies without affecting the rest of the audio information.

De-essing

A component of both spoken and sung word is sibilance. Sibilance is the hissing sound made when speaking or singing S or SH. Difficult to repair, this issue, known as "essing," creates distortion or apparent distortion on cheap speakers and high-end systems alike, regardless of how much compression or EQ is applied. In fact, EQ is the last resort to repair essing, and compressors are only one step ahead of EQ when it comes to de-essing sound. A de-esser is just a band-specific compressor.

When sibilance from S's gets in the way of the mix, open up the Sony Multiband Dynamic plug-in and start with the De-Ess preset. Reset the attack time to 5 milliseconds. Reset the decay time to 40 or 50 milliseconds for a male voice, set the frequency center to 5 kHz, and for female vocals, set the frequency center to 6.5. True sibilance is usually centered between 8 and 10 kHz. Both of these settings are starting points. It might be that further adjustment is required.

7.91 Saving the De-Ess preset
setting preserves it for
another session or for other
de-essing in the same project.

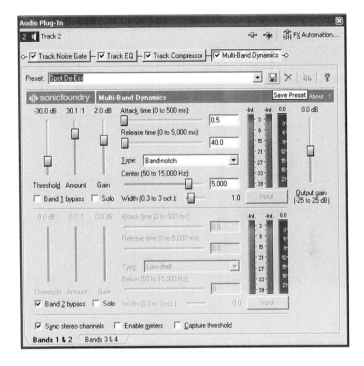

The compression ratio should be set at 30:1, to start with, and the threshold set at −30 dB. Now start a loop over a section where sibilance is present and adjust the multiband settings as the loop is heard. Be cautious of applying too much of a ratio; a singer or voice-over can quickly gain a lisp if it's set too high. Sometimes as little as 6:1 is enough. Experiment with raising the threshold and reducing the ratio until the desired fix is found. Save this setting as a preset by typing a preset name in the Preset box and pressing the icon that looks like a floppy disk. This preset is now part of your toolbox.

Using Equalization

Equalizers, also known as EQs, are one of the most oft-turned-to tools in the plug-in arsenal. EQs are used to cut frequencies of fat sounds that occupy space in the audio spectrum that other sounds can also occupy, creating confusion about what the ear is hearing. EQs are also used to correct problems with a tracking room or poor frequency balance in a microphone or sometimes simply to enhance a performance or characteristic of an audio event. While invented initially to flatten sound over the telephone, today's EQs are predominantly used to unflatten sound, and so in jest, some engineers call these tools unequalizers.

The use of an EQ must be judicious. Too much boost of any frequency can cause overload of the outputs, can cause a compressor to work harder than it needs to because of excess volume boost, or can even create distortion in the harmonics related to a sound.

EQs typically come in two formats: graphic and parametric.

7.92   Graphic equalizers set
       at octaves.

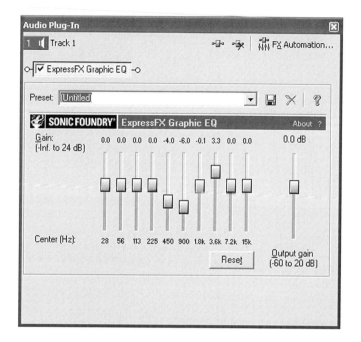

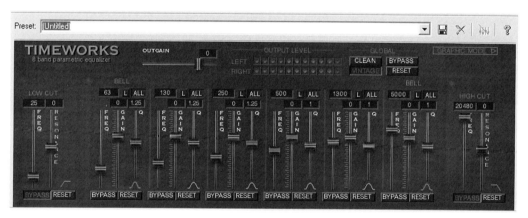

7.93   The Timeworks parametric EQ resembles a graphic EQ. However, frequencies can be selected, and the bandwidth or Q of
       the frequencies can be defined.

With graphic EQs, frequencies are preset, and only the gain of specific frequencies can be increased or reduced. It is found in octave, half-octave, and one-third octave in most instances. An octave is determined by a frequency multiplied by 2. The octave of 125 Hz is 250 Hz, the next octave being 500 Hz, and so forth. The half-octave of 125 Hz is 187.5 Hz, and the one-third octave of 125 Hz is approximately 160 Hz. Frequency centers are set by the International Standards Organization (ISO).

Vegas has four different graphic EQs available as plug-ins.

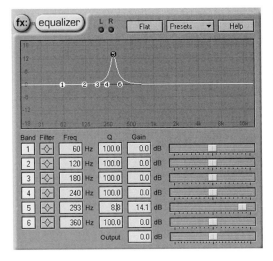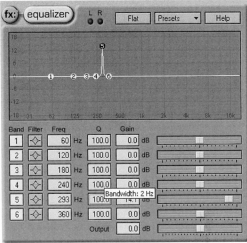

7.94   The Q is fairly wide, affecting frequencies on either side of its center.

7.95   The Q is very narrow, affecting only the immediate frequency selected.

With parametric EQs, users can select a specific frequency center, select the amount of bandwidth that the frequency has control over, and control the gain or reduction of that same frequency band. Usually parametric EQs allow several frequencies to be specified and controlled.

A derivative of both graphic and parametric EQs, paragraphic EQs are mixed-mode equalizers that generally have fixed frequencies for the bottom and top frequency spectra and midrange frequencies that can be shifted. This type is rarely seen in software-only forms.

Tight Q is useful for cutting out a specific frequency that can be a hum, distortion, or simply a problem frequency. Tight Q is also valuable for enhancing specific frequencies, such as boosting presence in a vocal to give an airy quality to obtain the pop vocal sound that is popular today.

Tip

On the DVD, open the Equalization Demonstration project. The file contains the same event in duplicate. The first version is the broadcast version; the second has presence and compression added to it using a parametric EQ with a boost at 4.1 kHz. Notice the difference between the two. Either of these two mixes is acceptable for final output, but a difference exists in how the two are perceived.

Using Reverb

Reverb can be used for any kind of audio mix, whether for video or audio, spoken word or music. It is also one of the most overused effects in the palette of tools available. Reverb is used to reproduce various room environments artificially. In the past, music had to be recorded in large chambers or in rooms with large reflective areas. The reverb created in such large rooms helped blend sounds together, creating a cohesive yet individual expression of instruments or vocal authority. Ever notice how the voice of God in film or recording always is accompanied by a large reverb? As technology and creativity grew in the music industry, reverberation was emulated in tubes, springs, complex room systems, eventually electronics, and now in software. Reverb can express a vastness and spatial distance or be part of an intimate communication, made unique by how certain consonants, syllables, or instrumental inflections sound within a reverberant sound. Every environment common to the world has a sound. What makes up this sound is the reflections within that environment. Singing in the shower makes even a poor voice sound rich, whereas that same voice singing in a closet sounds dull and lifeless. The shower is full of hard surfaces, while the closet is full of soft surfaces. The hard surfaces effectively create a doubled voice sound that the ear hears immediately, whereas the soft surfaces absorb nearly all sounds, preventing almost all reflections and making the sound harder to hear. Large rooms with reflective surfaces, such as cathedrals, auditoriums, and long hallways, not only reflect the sound, but reflect it repeatedly, expanding and elongating the sound, all the while softening the sound, giving an illusion of infinity.

Somewhere between the sound of a closet and that of a cathedral, there are reverb settings useful to nearly every situation. Vegas has lots of great reverbs built in, and incredible software reverbs are available from several third-party manufacturers, such as PSP Audio software, WAVES, iZotope, Anwida, and more.

 Tip

Several reverbs are included on the DVD with this book, including freeware from PSP Audio software.

Overused or overly loud reverb can wash over too much of the audio spectrum, making the audio sound muddy and without clarity. Use carefully.

Consider using reverb in very short, quiet settings for interviews that might be too dry from being in a very tight, quiet room or that might have some ambient noise that can't be washed with other sounds or beds. Reverb is also useful for making a mono audio signal appear to be stereo by creating artificial reflections that reach the ear at different times. Feed a mono voice or instrument into a bus or FX send that is only the reverb and then route back to the master output. Make sure the reverb is fairly short and has very little predelay. Panning the reverb/sending the reverb to the same location as the dry sound also is a great technique for keeping the sound large, but located. Pan the original signal to where it sounds right in the mix before adding reverb. Use an FX send to route the dry sound to the reverb. Pan the reverb to the same space. This technique works well with vocals mixed with a music bed, as well as with single-instrument sounds, such as guitars, snare drums, keyboards, and other single-point-source instruments.

Be cautious about reverb sounds that are too bright. Although they usually warm up a voice, bright reverbs also tend to elaborate sibilance and can easily create distortion in the high end. Use a de-esser or EQ before the reverb if this problem occurs.

When mixing audio, sometimes a need arises to lower the audio volume quickly, whether for a phone call or visitor or because it's too loud for a conversation. Vegas provides a Dim button that dims audio by 20 dB. This option ensures immediate volume reduction without changing the audio output level sliders and without affecting render output. The Dim button is found just above the Master Volume slider or can be enabled by pressing Ctrl+Shift+F12. Of course, with Vegas's key-mapping feature, you can map the Dim button to be any key setting you'd prefer.

Mixing for 5.1 Surround Sound

Surround-sound mixing brings an entirely different perspective in prepping and setting up a mix. Rather than being concerned with just two speakers in a stereo field, there are now six speakers, all individually controlled. The term 5.1 is derived from there being a right and a left speaker for the front and the rear, a center channel, and a subwoofer (the .1 of 5.1). Each speaker has its own input, and setting the mix for each speaker can quickly become a challenge, as the stereo field all of a sudden becomes small. Moreover, having extra sound points excites most any engineer who hasn't had experience in the surround realm, and it's very easy to create an over-the-top mix, which, while sounding exciting in the control room, loses its excitement in the listening environment. Sometimes mixes don't even make sense to the ear when taken in the context of a nonvisual setting. In short, it's easy to overemphasize the rear channel speakers simply out of the novelty of having them.

Vegas has the ability to do 5.1 channel surround mixing. This type is the standard for most DVDs, and many music recordings are moving into the realm of 5.1 surround. The Eagles' *Hell Freezes Over* CD was one of the first immersed-experience CDs on the market and is an excellent example of a 5.1 surround-sound audio recording.

The room must be set up correctly for mixing in 5.1 surround. Having a 5.1 sound system from the local office supply and a 5.1 surround card is barely going to suffice and will not suffice at all if the room is not set up correctly.

7.96 Wiring the surround system properly is important. Use high-quality cables to connect speakers to a soundcard.

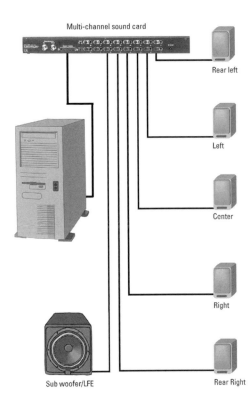

Multi-channel sound card

Rear left

Left

Center

Right

Sub woofer/LFE

Rear Right

7.97 Select the surround setting to create buses for the surround mix.

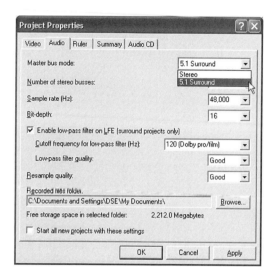

On the DVD contained in this book is a test clip, which allows audio to be tested on the output of all speakers in the room. It's critical that they all be equal in volume to achieve a balanced mix. Use these tones to test the output.

Do this process by placing the tone as an event on the Timeline of Vegas and then open the FILE | PROPERTIES dialog. Select the Audio tab, and, in the Master Bus Mode drop-down list, select 5.1 surround.

This process automatically inserts buses in the Mixer docking window to allow for mixing levels to front, rear, and center speakers, plus a low-frequency enclosure (LFE) control. It also adds a surround panner to each audio track on the Timeline.

Set levels on the soundcard's mixer at 0 dB to ensure that Vegas is the only mixing device being used to control levels. Otherwise, it's possible that rendered files will not be accurate to what is being heard. Having unequal soundcard mixer settings guarantees an unbalanced mix.

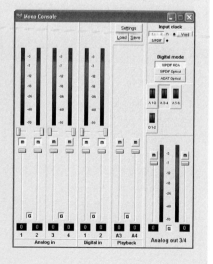

7.98 Some soundcard mixer control levels outside of Vegas. Check this carefully for accuracy in the mix.

This panner control is how Vegas maneuvers audio around the audio space. Notice that five speakers are in the panner. Clicking the LFE button in the upper-right corner of the panner control sends the channel only to the LFE output.

Audio is panned from front to rear and from right to left using keyframes. Vegas uses keyframes in the audio tools slightly different from how it uses keyframes in the video tools. Automatic mixing makes this very effective and powerful; rather than using hardware to set up the mix, audio positioning can be exactly keyframed and edited at any point in the mix, with Vegas graphically showing the placement of audio at any point.

After opening the Surround Panner, right-click the Track Control pane associated with the open Surround Panner. Select Insert/Remove Envelope (Shift+P) from the menu and then Surround Pan Keyframes from the submenu. This process allows for keyframes to be placed on the Timeline, instructing audio to pan to wherever you wish it to be, at any point on the Timeline.

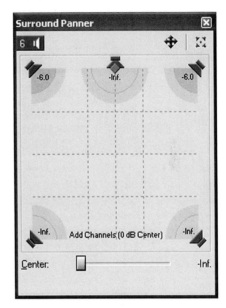

7.99a, 7.99b   Double-clicking the Surround Panner on the Track Control pane splits it off as a movable window, making panning easier to define.

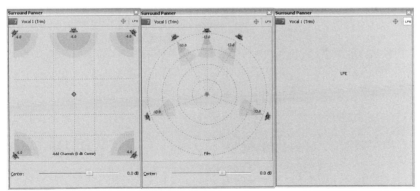

Normal Surround Control   Film Mode Surround   Low Frequency channel

7.100   These are the three surround pan modes in Vegas. Right-clicking the first/default pan mode allows selection of film style or LFE control, shown to the right. Selecting the LFE button sends audio only to the LFE channel output.

With the Surround Panner open, follow these steps to move audio in the listening space:

1. Place the cursor where movement should occur or should finish, if the location is different from the default front-center position.

2. Move the orange dot found in the Surround Panning box to where the audio should be at that moment. Audio will slowly pan to this point from where it originated at the first keyframe. Notice that the reference position is followed by small dots, indicating how the audio will move.

3. Place the cursor on the next time point to which audio should be moved.

4. Move the reference position in the Surround Panner to the desired point.

5. Repeat until all panning is complete for the project on that track. Keyframes/audio position can be edited later.

When panning stereo signals, moving right to left can create problems when audio becomes louder on one side than on the other side when audio is off balance during a pan. Add Channels, the default setting, can easily create distortion. The Constant Power setting moves audio around the audio spectrum at equal volume with no change in volume at any point. Notice that Vegas displays the relative volume for each channel in the Surround Panner tool. Experiment with various settings during panning operation if audio seems to jump in volume during a pan.

Vegas has separate control of the center channel per track, rather than assigning it to a bus as some 5.1 systems do.

Right-clicking keyframes in the Surround Pan Timeline opens a menu, which shows choices for the velocity attributes of how the keyframe will move sound. Hold freezes audio until the next keyframe. Smooth gently speeds up as it leaves the keyframe and slows down as it approaches the next keyframe. Fast ramps the audio quickly to its next keyframe. Slow ramps the audio to the next keyframe fairly slowly. Linear provides a straight movement. This is the default keyframe setting in Vegas. Although not always easy to see, the various keyframe settings draw the audio path differently in the Surround Panner window.

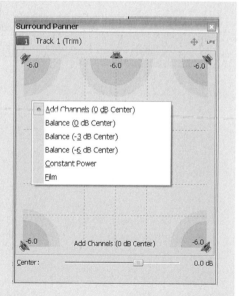

7.101 Right-clicking the Surround Panner offers choices regarding the audio power at a specific point in the pan.

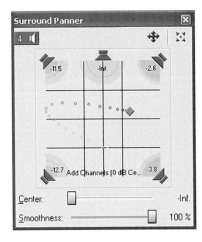 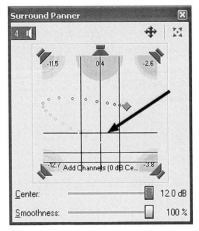

7.102, 7.103   Center channel is at 0 dB by default. Notice how the sound field draws to the
rear as volume from the center speaker increases.

The center channel is at zero volume by default. As the volume is increased in the Surround Panner window, however, notice that the sound grid draws backward, as the power/volume increases in the center channel.

Vegas has surround modes that may be accessed by right-clicking the Surround Panner and choosing Film from the submenu that appears. The Film panner mode more closely simulates the theater environment for more accurate mixing of surround. Notice that the center channel is now defaulting to 0 dB rather than the −Inf. position that it defaulted to in earlier versions of Vegas. This will have an impact on currently existing projects, so monitor carefully, as your monitoring environment may not have changed, but you may not have had an accurate mix.

7.104   Film panning more closely resembles a theater sound system, and you may find it easier to mix in this mode.

When using motion in the center channel, experiment with the Smoothness setting. If dialog or center audio is fairly transient in nature, such as intense dialog, fast-attack guitar playing, or other sharp sounds, and the smoothness is set too high, the audio will sound very slow moving from center channel to the left or right. If set too low, audio will appear to "jerk" into other speaker fields. This issue varies with the listening environment, which again demonstrates the necessity of having a good monitoring system. Users of earlier versions of Vegas will appreciate the changes made to the panning ratios in Vegas Pro 8.

☞ **Tip**

In versions prior to Vegas Pro 8, audio weighting was managed differently. In OPTIONS | PREFERENCES, Use Legacy Track Gain has been added. If Add Channels (the default) or the Balance 0 dB pan mode is used, there is no difference. For the other pan modes that cut the signal when the pan is set to center, there is a decrease in the level (depending on which pan mode is used). When working on legacy projects (projects begun in earlier versions of Vegas), it's best to use the legacy track gain function. New projects moving forward will be best if this is left unchecked.

Notice the differences when working with panning/track modes in Vegas Pro 8:

- Add Channels (no cut)
- Balance 0 dB (no cut)
- Balance −3 dB, constant power, film (3 dB cut)
- Balance −6 dB (6 dB cut)

If you prefer the older format, or are working with legacy audio projects, in OPTIONS | PREFERENCES | AUDIO, check the "Use Legacy Send Gain" tick box.

The room should be set up with equal distances between audio speakers (audio monitors), and it should also be damped and have reflective surfaces minimized. Monitors should be equidistant to the listening space, measured from where you'll be sitting.

Try to set the room up similar to a home listening environment, as this environment is how most recordings will be heard.

It is possible to mix through a typical home stereo system, if the receiver allows for separate audio channel inputs. Vegas does not send a decoded AC-3 stream, so you'll need to have connections that allow for line input. Many receivers/amplifiers today do. Run cable from each output on the soundcard to the inputs on the receiver back. Using high-quality cable is critical if radio frequencies and other noise in the room is to be avoided. Mix in the room, perhaps referencing a favorite or similar DVD.

Additionally, many professional soundcards have TOSLINK outputs/optical outputs that can feed consumer receiver/amplifiers for monitoring over home theater systems. This process is not advised, as home theater systems are anything but flat, and it is very difficult to create a quality mix on anything but reasonably flat speakers.

The primary elements of a surround mix are:

- Dialog
- Music
- Sound design
- Effects

Dialog is obviously the most important consideration in most situations. Typically, it is in the center channel and should receive attention first. When setting up the mix, find the peak point of the dialog and then lower the dialog by −6 dB relative to the peak. This process allows for head-room/increase in the dialog channel, as it usually is needed after the final mix is prepared. If the peak is lower than −3 dB, consider normalizing that event or perhaps raising the level at the track.

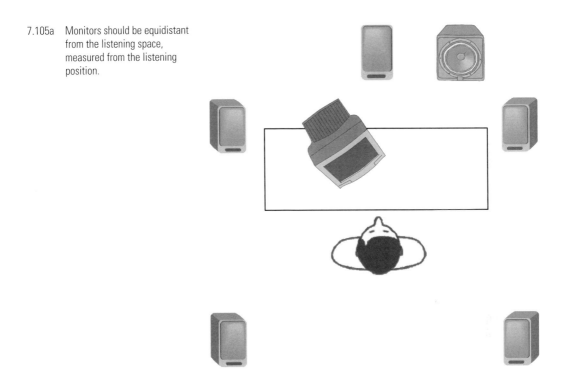

7.105a Monitors should be equidistant from the listening space, measured from the listening position.

Conversational dialog or direct dialog belongs in the center channel in most instances. Working with the center channel presents some challenges, particularly in music mixes. If sound isn't properly handled in the center channel, listeners on a stereo system or a four-channel system missing the center speaker will hear strange artifacts in sounds mixed for the center channel. Adding a slight reverb to the center channel is always good practice, even if it's merely a small room bounce with no predelay. Walla or background conversation goes in the left/right or rear left/right, so it won't be brought into the mix at this point.

The next element is music in most instances. Music typically is placed in the front right/left monitors, with some elements moving to the rear speakers, depending on the point of view or movement of the camera, the sound design, or moving dialog.

This point is where the actual mixing starts. Bring the music up to the level that it should be, monitor at a comfortable level. Listening too quietly makes the mix out of balance in both levels and equalization. Listening too loudly means your ears fatigue fairly quickly. Low-quality speakers also tire the ear, so use the best monitors that you can afford. Active monitors are typically cleaner, flatter, and easier to work with in a surround environment.

Begin bringing in any sound design underneath the music, leaving the dialog channels alone for the time being. Mix the music and the sound design, working the sound design to the rear channels. Be cautious of too much movement in the rear channels as it quickly becomes distracting to the ear.

As an example of a mix, we'll take a cityscape shot with a dialog in the foreground and examine some of the aural potential, as shown:

- Center speaker—contains dialog between two people. Low frequencies rolled off/high passed from 120 Hz and above.
- Left/right front speakers—contain traffic, walla, moving audio, bed music, and sound design. Low frequencies rolled off/low passed from 120 Hz and above.
- Left/right rear speakers—20/30 percent sound design, 10/20 percent bed music, traffic noise panning from front at camera movement or when dialog permits. Motion front to back related to transitions in video. Music moves to rear speakers during dialog, as scene elements require.
- Subwoofer/LFE—contains dialog elements, bed music elements, and sound design. High passed at 120 Hz by default in Vegas's surround setup and as ISO. Although this is a standard, experience suggests that a high-pass filter, rolled off at 24 dB per octave, starting at 80 Hz, be inserted in the LFE channel.

Be cautious of moving audio into rear speakers during dialog.

In this scenario, when dialog is the focus but music is required along with traffic and walla, move the music to the rear before moving traffic and walla to the rear. Cut midrange in walla and traffic to make room for dialog. With dialog taking place, the cut frequencies are not noticeable unless the midcuts are too drastic.

Use smooth keyframes for sound design and music that is moving to the rear. Don't be afraid to use hard keyframing/abrupt shifts in audio placement, based on hard cut editing. Smooth visual transitions call for smooth aural transitioning. Hard visual transitions can use either hard aural transitions or smooth transitions, based on what is happening on-screen.

Overall, do not tread on the dialog mix. As keyframes start to fly bed/design/FX audio right to left or front to rear, it's easy for the dialog to get lost. This point is when the extra 6 dB of headroom left in the early stages of the mix is invaluable. If you find that 6 dB isn't enough, something is not correct in the other audio mixes.

View buses as tracks in Vegas. Doing so provides automated mixing of the buses, offers easier surround control, and is visually more comprehensive to follow. Assign dialog, bed music, FX, and sound design to separate buses. If a single track doesn't provide enough control of a sound/series of events, duplicate a track and keep the volume out of the track until it's called for in two aural locations. At that point, raise the duplicate track volume assigned to the correct bus.

When planning a project that will include a surround mix, camera shots can be a consideration as well. Panning the lens toward and away from a scene makes an easy transition both visually and aurally. Dollying into a scene makes a wonderful rear-to-front transition. Panning from the bottom of a scene with upward motion or panning down from above a scene into the subject makes a wonderful visual transition that sound readily enhances.

Do not remove all low end from the right/left/center/rear mixes. If there is no bass in these mixes, listeners in a collapsed environment (stereo only) will hear no low end. Most everything in the mix goes into the LFE mix anyway, but if there are exceptionally important low-frequency elements, such as gunfire, cannons, and extremely low end in sound design, it's advisable to duplicate those tracks, roll the low end out of one copy of the tracks, and roll the high end off of the other copy. Send the copy that has high end removed to the LFE channel to supplement the bottom, while not distorting the other surround speakers and ensuring that audio collapses properly in a stereo listening situation.

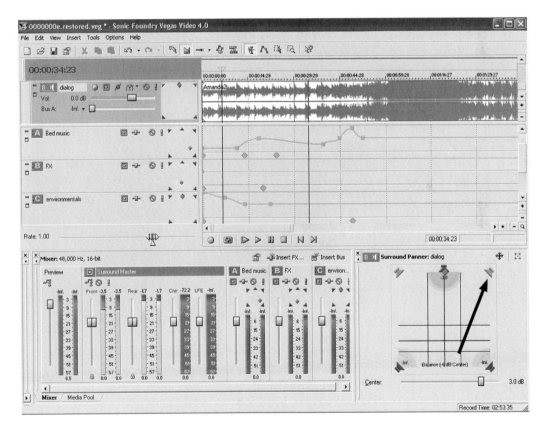

7.105b   Viewing buses as tracks offers tremendous control. Notice each bus in the mixer and that the left/right speakers are disabled in the dialog bus.

Surrounded by FX: Surround Plug-ins

Yet another feature of Vegas is to bring specific plug-ins to the surround-sound toolset. Vegas 4 provided surround-sound tools to the desktop editor, but effects could be placed only on the individual tracks and buses that made up the surround project, thus making a controlled mix a challenge. Vegas 5 not only provided the ability to place FX on the master output but also provided customized plug-ins specifically for a 5.1 mix. As mentioned earlier, Vegas Pro 8 offers new envelope settings.

Digital audio requires very tight control of outputs. Sony now offers the Wave Hammer tool, first made popular in Sound Forge, in a 5.1 surround-sound formatted tool. This 5.1 plug-in allows users to control the output levels on all buses in the surround environment, preventing distortion on any output and making it easier for editors to create a robust, yet clean, surround audio signal. The Wave Hammer plug-in may be enabled or disabled per channel of audio by checking or unchecking the checkbox found in the Routing tab of the 5.1 Wave Hammer.

There are three components to the Wave Hammer 5.1 plug-in tool.

First is a compressor. The compressor can be used to smooth out dynamics and add power to the overall mix. Used improperly, it can also create a somewhat warm distortion in the signal, but this is rarely desired in a surround mix. Wave Hammer's presets are set up quite well for most video-mix situations, but you may want to experiment with the settings to find what works best for you. Refer to Chapter 3 and Chapter 8 to learn more about using dynamics processing in Vegas and video applications. Particularly in a surround mix, be sure to keep the threshold set fairly high and the overall compression levels set low. Using a fair amount of compression starting at low trigger levels will nearly always create

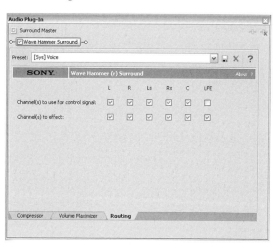

7.106 Enable/disable the Wave Hammer on individual surround channels by checking or unchecking these boxes.

distortion. Particularly for video-output mixes, leave the "Auto Compensate for Output Levels" checkbox unchecked. This will nearly always result in distorted signals that will be obvious with dialog.

Wave Hammer now allows for either peaks or RMS levels to be scanned for processing. Either scanning method works fine, but be aware that setting this to RMS may allow fast transients such as gunshots or other fast and hard sounds to escape processing, creating distortion that you may not be able to hear easily but that clip beyond the output level of 0 dBFS.

If very light compression is used, it's a good idea to turn on "Longer Look Ahead" for best results. This allows the plug-in to scan audio farther ahead in the file for information, usually creating a smoother attack when slow attack times are used. However, if a large transient is encountered it can sometimes create a fade-out or breathing or pumping effect just before the transient, so monitor transients carefully if the Longer Look Ahead is used.

Next is the Volume Maximizer, found in the second tab of the Wave Hammer plug-in. This could easily be one of the most important plug-in tools for any broadcast-destined audio for video mix. The Volume Maximizer works exactly as its name implies. It maximizes volume of an audio track or bus without creating clipping on output. When using the Volume Maximizer, any levels that go beyond the threshold are limited to whatever level the threshold is set to. Audio not crossing the threshold is managed and increased in overall level. Because digital audio does not have the flexibility for going beyond zero in the same manner analog does, this is a terrific means of maintaining maximum output while ensuring that at no point will audio exceed the output level. More importantly, using the Wave Hammer tool provides the ability to have a house-standard level of output as part of a final render process. If files are destined for AC-3 output, this also ensures that the AC-3 encoder receives maximum information for the best possible encode. I recommend using the Wave Hammer set to the "Master for 16 bit" preset on virtually all audio for video mixes. In the absence of my favorite WAVES Ultramaximizer plug-in, this is the next best thing and is the only plug-in available for a 5.1 surround output.

The Routing tab is next in line on the Wave Hammer plug-in. Although this seems to be a simple row of checkboxes, it's much more than it appears to be. For example, a setting that instructs the Wave Hammer to begin compression on the surround speakers when the center/dialog channel reaches a specific point might save an otherwise muddy or loud mix. Any one of the 5.1 output channels may be used to determine the point at which other channels will be ducked or compressed.

Also available as a 5.1 surround plug-in are the Track EQ and Dither tools. EQ is important as it allows editors to fine-tune the EQ of individual surround buses as opposed to inserting EQs on the individual tracks or mix buses. This not only saves processor power but also prevents EQ settings that may conflict with one another. Track EQ does not provide a specific EQ for each bus, but rather provides a master EQ that affects all buses. You may enable or disable the track EQ from affecting a specific bus or buses.

Use the Track EQ settings to create a tighter mix signal in your surround, repair muddy or weak areas, or balance the overall signal. Automation may be applied to Track EQ found on the surround bus, including the enabling and disabling of the EQ on specific buses. Therefore, if you have an EQ setting in place that should affect only a specific portion of a mix on a specific bus, you may enable the EQ on that bus only via automation. The 5.1 EQ is the only automated 5.1 effect that Vegas has available.

Generally you'll want to have the EQ precede the Wave Hammer in a final output or mix. Otherwise, the Wave Hammer will not

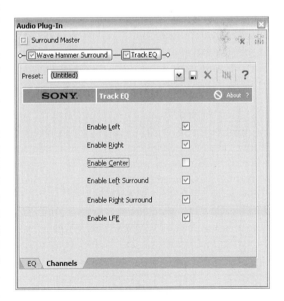

7.107 Track EQs can be automated while in 5.1 format in Vegas. By selecting or deselecting these checkboxes, individual buses may or may not be affected by EQ settings.

have the equalized signal information and won't be able to react appropriately. This could easily lead to distortion as well, if the Volume Maximizer is used prior to the EQ and the EQ is being used to boost any frequencies in the audio signal.

Dithering is the process of adding noise to an audio signal to mask or hide quantization noise. With surround, this is particularly useful on mixes that contain a lot of high-frequency information to keep the information clean in fade-outs. See the Dithering guide on the DVD found in this book for more information. In most instances, however, you'll be using a Rectangular or Triangular dithering shape.

Mixing Surround or DVD Audio

Musical DVD is an entirely new soundstage with surround sound, offering musicians, producers, and engineers entirely new methods of presenting their art. The quality of digital versatile disc-audio (DVDA) finally goes past the consumer-hype words of "CD quality." CDs are 16 bit/44.1 kHz, whereas DVDA is 24 bit/48 kHz.

Mixing audio only for surround presents new opportunities, while also presenting new challenges. Caution must be taken with placement, EQ, and sonic spacing to keep the mix cohesive and credible. One major advantage of surround is that it requires far less compression as currently called for in a stereo-only environment.

In a recording of a vocal-based group, the lead vocal takes center space. It's very important, however, that the lead vocal not be assigned exclusively to the center channel, or collapsed listening environments (stereo only) will hear artifacts and ghosting of the vocal. Using a slight reverb on the vocal helps dilute this phenomenon, if the reverb is added to the right/left mixes.

Percussion, acoustic guitars, and ethnic instruments all share the listening space of left/center right/center quite well, which opens up more frequency space for vocals or lead instruments.

Picturing the soundstage as it would appear to a concert-goer helps build the mix. Drawing the mix in advance can't hurt and often provides a great visual reference for an engineer.

Consider pairing left/center and right/center, rather than thinking of left/right as separate elements. Treat the rear speakers predominantly as assignments of the reverbs, delays, and audience responses. Audience members don't often sit in the middle of a stage, so placing much musical information in the rear speakers is not often a good practice. Placing the audience, however, where a lead vocalist might stand is a wonderful place to be. Save the rear surrounds for effects and aural surprises.

Mix the bass guitar/bass synth to all speakers, without regard for the LFE. If more low-end punch is needed, bus the bass and any other low-frequency information to a separate output, feeding the LFE. Whereas the bass channel in a surround system has 12 dB more headroom than the remainder of a surround system, few consumer-grade subwoofers are able to handle the extreme volumes of low end, so be mindful of your listening audience. Save the LFE for exceptional low end, such as the five-string bass or synthesizer that really needs the punch. Kick drums should be sent to the LFE with caution.

Feed reverb returns to the rear speakers, along with any vocal or instrumental effects. Sending the vocal to two reverbs or delays with similar settings allows for separate control to front and rear speakers, giving listeners a more intimate seat in the listening experience.

Use the rear channels for any audience information, such as applause and walla. Don't forget to feed a little to the front speakers as well, or stereo-only listeners will hear odd anomalies at the end of songs in a live environment. Panning reverbs and delays to the rear as part of an effect makes the rear speakers become part of the art of the mix. Keeping the rear speakers at full volume, full of a surround element can quickly dilute the value of a surround mix. Use the rear speakers as a paintbrush, not as a canvas.

Always check a surround mix in a stereo-only environment as well to ensure that it is collapsing correctly. Headphones are great for checking this out. (Remember never to mix in headphones.)

Blue Man Group's self-titled CD, the soundtrack to the movie *A.I. Artificial Intelligence*, the Eagles' *Hell Freezes Over Tour*, or Jon Anderson's *Deseo* CD are all excellent examples of surround sound in nonvisual settings.

Surround sound is part of the future, and eventually nearly every facet of video and audio production will call for it. Artists like surround productions because they are harder to pirate. Consumers enjoy 5.1 because it's a sweeter entertainment experience. Radio stations are starting to broadcast in surround, and surround systems are becoming fairly common in the car as well. All in all, the industry has many motives for moving in this direction. Engineers with surround chops will find their talents more and more in demand.

I'm All Mixed … Down! Down-mixing in Vegas

Mixes on DVDs are often 5.1 these days, yet many viewers of DVDs don't own speaker systems or receivers capable of playing 5.1 surround sound. Furthermore, some viewers have only mono televisions. Most systems have a feature in them that allows for audio to be down-mixed so that the viewer is capable of watching the show even though it's not being heard in the original mixed format of 5.1 or stereo. However, whether the mix is down-mixed correctly is the responsibility of the editor and engineer. No playback system can repair a bad mix when the six channels are collapsed to be heard over stereo speakers or even a mono speaker. Even the small DVD players that are used for flying or automobile viewing can't accurately play back 5.1 mixes that are not correctly assembled.

7.108a   Vegas provides a tool allowing editors and engineers to monitor their mixes for all playback situations: mono, stereo, or 5.1.

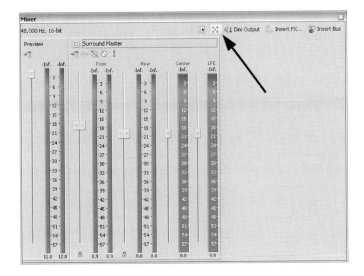

Down-mixing is not an arbitrary process; it is controlled by information embedded in a metadata stream contained in the AC-3 file. This metadata is present in all AC-3 bitstreams. For example, the dialog channel sets the normal information for the stream. This is what tells the program how loudly it should be played by way of the information being received by the Dolby Decoder in the system. In a down-mix to stereo or mono, this information is combined and modulated to allow it to be heard on a standard stereo or mono system.

Needless to say, if the mix isn't correct, or if there are parameters out of whack in the 5.1 mix, the down-mix at the viewer's end will also be strange and could mask dialog, lose bottom end entirely, or create an overburden of bottom end. Other information may be either lost or overbearing, depending on the way the mix was managed in the authoring stages.

To allow Vegas users to combat this issue or at the least address it, Vegas provides a DownMix button that allows users to hear what their mixes sound like in stereo or mono and compensate for those scenarios during their 5.1 mix session. Users of earlier versions of Vegas will need to convert their mixes to mono or stereo by changing the project properties, but this won't provide the same sort of information.

To use the DownMix feature, click the DownMix button, found on the master bus in Vegas.

Broadcast Wave Format

Vegas supports BWF files, or Broadcast Wave files. These are used as a packaging format by various recording devices such as the Studio Devices and Edirol recording products, among others.

Although the average user might not find these valuable, filmmakers, radio stations, television broadcasters, and users of high-end recording devices will appreciate this new feature. The Broadcast Wave file format was developed to foster a format of audio interchangeability by EBU Project Group P/DAPA (Digital Audio Production and Archiving), with significant input from the audio industry. An easy way to think about BWF files is as standard wave files with a metadata layer.

The BWF file metadata contains several parts not found as part of the standard wave file format. Included are:

- Broadcast Extension Chunk
- Compulsory Chunk defined by Microsoft
- The Broadcast Wave file
- Audio Data

Broadcast Wave files are the same as WAV formats, which you're likely already familiar with, except that a BWF file can contain metadata about the file, such as the author, the length of the file, and logging information that will allow the file to be logged for broadcast and copyright or performance royalty needs. It also allows for time-stamped files to be laid onto a Timeline in exact position. To add all this data to the file format, a new chunk, or layer of information, is added to the wave file. BWF files also support the MPEG audio format, and an additional layer of information is added to the MPEG file where the BWF metadata resides. Only linear PCM and MPEG audio files may become BWF files. If the file is a not a PCM file, an additional chunk, known as a "fact chunk" will reside with the file.

The Broadcast Extension Chunk may contain:

Description   Title information
Originator   Name of the author or producer
Reference   A reference number issued by the author or recordist
Date and time   When the file was created
Coding history   A record of the signal coding, e.g., linear PCM or MPEG.

If you have BWF files, you can import them several different ways. Import them in alphabetical order, import them by time stamp, import files as a single Timeline track, or create a new track for each file imported. The latter is critical if you've got multitrack projects from recording devices that generate BWF files. You can find demo BWF files for import on the DVD in the back of this book.

To import a BWF file:

1. Choose FILE | IMPORT | BROADCAST WAVE.

2. Browse to the device containing the Broadcast Wave or to the location at which the Broadcast Wave is stored.

3. Determine whether you wish to add the file across tracks or across time.

4. Determine whether you wish to order tracks by time stamp or filename. (This applies only when you are adding across tracks, not adding across time.)

5. Determine whether you'd like to place the file based on where your cursor currently is placed or based on Ruler time.

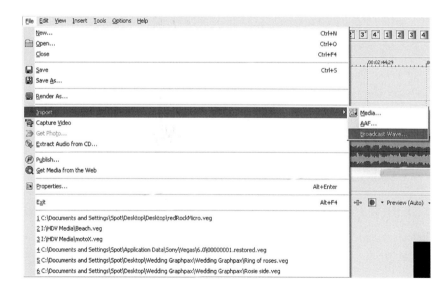

7.108b

Encoding Audio to AC-3

Encoding audio to AC-3 is included in Vegas Pro 8. AC-3 is a compressed audio format that allows audio for DVD or DVDA. DVDA typically doesn't use AC-3; it uses meridian lossless packing. The whole point of the separate format is to allow ultrahigh-quality audio to be compressed to fit six channels of information onto a DVD for video or audio. This process allows for greater bitrates of video on a DVD and allows for higher sampling rates for audio on a DVDA. AC-3 stands for Audio Coding–Third Generation. AC-3 is licensed from Dolby and follows their specifications. Sony became one of the first licensees in the PC environment with their Soft Encode product in 1996.

After a mix is finished in Vegas, it's a simple matter to select the AC-3 encoding option in the FILE | RENDER AS dialog. Audio is output that is then imported to a DVD authoring application. If you are working with DVD Architect, AC-3 becomes a selection in the final creation of the DVD or can be imported as a separate stream. Vegas does not allow the monitoring of AC-3 files, so be certain that the mix is correct before encoding.

Creating and distributing an AC-3 file technically requires any packaging to contain the Dolby Digital trademark. For more information, visit www.dolby.com.

7.109 Select the AC-3 format in the FILE | RENDER AS dialog, which has a stereo or 5.1 option.

7.110 Dolby and the double-D symbol are registered trademarks of Dolby Laboratories.

Tip _____

When rendering audio to AC-3, consider trying setting the dialog normalization level at −31 and setting the Preprocessing Line and RF modes to None. This will often more closely approximate what's being heard from the Vegas Timeline. Sometimes encoding audio from uncompressed files to AC-3 doesn't have quite the robust sound once encoded, so experiment with audio files to see what most closely approximates what is coming off the Timeline.

Other Compressed Formats

Vegas offers encoding to virtually every major audio codec available, ranging from a variety of MPEG codecs (including MP3) to high-definition, uncompressed audio. With car audio, online distribution, embedded audio in web pages, etc., new codecs are constantly becoming available.

Vegas Pro 8 offers FLAC, or the Free Lossless Audio Codec, as an encoding option. FLAC is gaining ground across the Internet as a means of sharing full-resolution audio and as an archiving format. FLAC is much like a Zip file for audio; there is no loss when files are compressed to the FLAC format. Be aware that having many FLAC files on a Timeline, i.e., a multitrack project of length, can cause an older/slower system to bog down and stutter. FLAC files may be played back in some personal electronics devices and home audio equipment; support is expected to grow as several recording labels and distributors are now beginning to support FLAC as a distribution/download format.

To access the FLAC codec, browse to FILE | RENDER AS | SAVE AS TYPE | FLAC. Templates ranging from 22 kHz mono to 96 kHz stereo are available.

More information on FLAC may be found at http://flac.sourceforge.net/

How Come the Audio Cats Get All the Cool Stuff?

Actually, they don't. With mapping, all audio features can also be made to apply to video. Muting tracks, fade-outs, compositing envelopes, and transition modes may be automated using a controlling device. Control of playback and rewinding can be controlled with a Mackie or other controlling device. Fade to Color and Compositing Envelopes come to mind as two of the most common uses for automation in video editing. This is an exciting new paradigm and possibility for video, even to the point of copying audio movements and tracks and applying those envelopes to a video track. In Vegas, the following parameters may be automated and controlled with an external surface controller:

- Video envelopes and compositing envelopes
- Video bus track envelopes
- Track FX parameters
- Parent overlay modes
- Track level mask generators
- Track motion keyframes

Thinning will apply to video envelopes as well. They may be thinned after the automation input, with as much or little control as necessary. Automation is accomplished on video tracks the same way as audio tracks are managed. Click on the Automation icon found on the video track header to determine how you want the automation to work. This will set up the automation to work the way you'd like it to function. For those audio folks that have a Mackie Universal Control or other MIDI controller connected to Vegas, try doing automated camera/composite fades just as you would do with a live switcher. This is a fabulous way to automate shots between camera scenes on the Vegas Timeline.

7.111　Pressing the Automation icon will give video editors an entirely new toolset for working with video. You might surprise yourself how much you may be inspired by using these tools to create composites. Experiment with a controller and see what it does for your creativity.

Creating Titles in Vegas Pro 8

Titles are an important component of every video project, and Vegas Pro 8 provides a multitude of title-generating options. Vegas offers two internal titling tools, and users can import motion graphics from third-party titling tools or from Flash-generating apps. Static graphic titles may be imported with alpha channels and animated in Vegas using various compositing tools.

The ProType Titler is a new tool found in Vegas Pro 8, adding to the existing standard titling tool. Each has its advantages. A major benefit to the ProType Titler is the ability to save titles with characters, making title modifications very easy, regardless of the complexity of the title. In projects that have a repetitive title placement, style, and theme, this single feature alone is a tremendous time-saver.

Be sure to keep titles within the title-safe areas indicated in the Vegas Preview window. The title-safe overlay may be toggled on/off by clicking the overlay switch in the Preview window. The dropdown menu offers either title-safe overlay or a Grid overlay. Select the Safe Areas option. If titling components are not kept within this safe area, some television displays may chop off characters at the top/bottom/sides of the display. This is less of an issue with flat panel displays, but is still a good practice when creating titles for broadcast or DVD delivery. Title-safe spaces are not an issue when delivering media directly to the web.

The ProType Titling Tool

This new tool is filled with opportunity at various levels of complexity. Simple titles may be created in seconds, or very deep titles taking several hours or days may be created.

8.1 The ProType Titler is an exciting, innovative, and powerful tool for Vegas Pro 8 users. The ProType Titler may be opened via the Generated Media menus.

The ProType Titling tool is opened via one of two methods:

- Drag it from the Generated Media tab and drop it on a video track.
- Create a selection on a video track, right-click it, and choose INSERT GENERATED MEDIA | PROTYPE TITLER from the menu.

The second method is my preferred method, as it allows users to set the length of the title prior to the title being inserted. The first method requires that the title length be manually input.

8.2

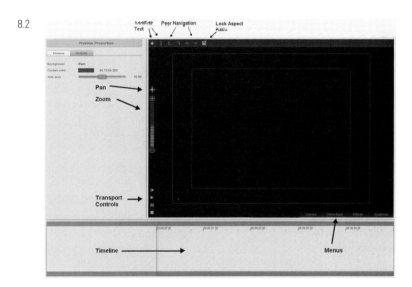

Tip

Text may also be formatted in a text editor such as WordPad. Copy the text using standard Windows Copy commands, and paste the words into the ProType Titler using Ctrl+V. Additionally, right-clicking a title while in the Text Edit mode allows all punctuation and symbols associated with the selected font to be seen and inserted. This is handy if a trademark symbol, copyright symbol, or other commonly used symbol is needed, without knowing the keystroke associated with the desired symbol.

Let's start by using the titling application at its most basic level.

Open the ProType Titler using one of the above-mentioned methods. When the title tool opens, double-click in the title tool workspace. This will insert the words "Sample Text." (You may need to resize the window to see everything.) The text will be highlighted in blue. For the moment, we'll ignore this text; click the maroon bar at the top of the title tool, and this will deselect the text. If by chance the text is now surrounded by a sizing boundary, simply click in any blank area surrounding the text. This will also deselect the text.

Notice the tabs to the left of the workspace. The tabs will have changed to a two-tab configuration labeled "Preview" and "Defaults." In these two tabs, the default fonts, font sizes, safe areas, and background colors in the titling tool are defined.

Select a font that you'd prefer as a default font. Arial may be just fine, many video editors prefer the Verdana variant. Unless you're working with unique colors for title overlay, it's recommended that the background color be left black or neutral gray (RGB values 150, 150, 150). This will help in identifying any aliasing that may take place with serifed fonts (it's generally not a good idea to use serifed fonts in video titling) or other detailed fonts.

8.3

Safe areas should be left to default settings in most instances. This is less of an issue when creating content for plasma and LCD displays, particularly widescreens, yet care should always be taken to avoid titles or graphics being too close to the bezel/overscan area of any display.

☞ Tip_____

The "safe area" is the area of variable edges found particularly wide on cheaper consumer televisions, but also on LCD and plasma panels, where portions of the actual signal are not displayed due to bezels, scanning, conversion, or other causes. Titles or graphics placed too near these edges may be fully displayed on some monitors/displays, yet cut off on others. For this reason, it's a good practice to be cautious about title and graphic placement. Title safe and Action safe are not the same value. Content destined for HD display needs less than 5% title-safe area, whereas 4:3 television requires approximately 18% safe area.

Once defaults are set, click the words "Sample Text" and a border with sizing handles will appear around the words. These handles can be used to resize the text from its default size. If the "Lock Aspect" checkbox is checked in the titler toolbar, the title will keep its aspect ratio when being sized. Holding the Shift key while resizing will disable Lock Aspect temporarily. For this exercise, hold Shift while stretching the words "Sample Text" vertically.

8.4

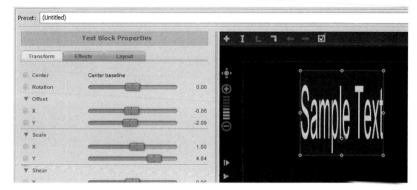

This gives an idea of how the text may be stretched; more importantly, look on the left side of the title tool in the Transform tab (by default the first view in the titler) and watch how the parameter controls for Scaling are moving as the text is resized. If the Shift key is not held, the horizontal and vertical parameters move equally. When wanting to scale titles in aspect ratio, dragging the handles is the best way to resize, particularly when setting up automation … more on that later.

 Tip

> Any control slider in the ProType Title tool window may be reset to its default value by double-clicking the control, just as with any parameter control in Vegas Pro 8.

Notice the small dot in the center of the title. This indicates the center point around which the text can be rotated. The dot may be moved by click–dragging to any desired point, thus changing the center of rotation. Placing the target in the middle of the first or last letter in a title is a common center point for many titling sequences. For this exercise, click–drag the dot to the middle handle on the left side of the text (should be the middle of the letter S).

Now choose the Effects tab. In this dialog, enable Drop Shadow and check the "Gradient Fill" checkbox. The title should turn to a white/orange gradient. If you wish to change the two shades of the gradient, set the first gradient color by clicking the small diamond on the left side of the gradient selector bar. Set the second color by clicking the small diamond on the right side of the

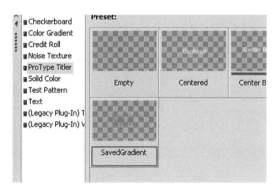

gradient selector bar. Insert additional gradient points by double-clicking in the gradient selector bar and setting the color. Bear in mind that gradient points will combine, and colors may blend. If this happens, click–drag the gradient points while previewing the text in the Vegas Pro 8 Preview window. You can also delete gradient points by right-clicking them and choosing Delete. If you find you particularly like the gradient you've created, click the Save To Collection icon, enter a name for your gradient, and press Enter to save the gradient to your library.

8.5

Now that you've created and saved a custom gradient, let's apply a different gradient to the text. Open the Gradients library at the right bottom of the titling tool. Notice that the previously saved/named gradient appears in the library. To use a gradient from the Gradient library, drag and drop a library gradient from the library over to the Gradient selector bar. This will apply the preset gradient to any selected text.

OK, now we've sized and added a gradient to the text and added a shadow. Let's add a couple more shadows to the text. Click the Effects button at the right bottom of the titling tool, and drag–drop a shadow to the left side. Then drag another one. Three Drop Shadow parameters should now show in the left side of the Effects window. Choose the Expand triangle in the left side of the first Shadow dialog. The Shadow dialog will expand to show:

- Blur amount

- Horizontal offset

- Vertical offset

- Shadow color

8.6

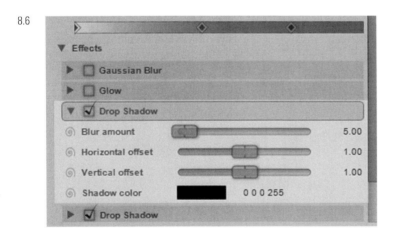

In the top shadow, leave the offsets at default, and set Blur to a value of 16.00. You can do this by click–dragging the slider or by clicking in the numeric field that has defaulted to 5.00 and typing 16.00. Set the shadow color to 255, 255, 255, 80. This will increase the transparency of the shadow. Click the Expand triangle to collapse the parameters of the first shadow, and then select the Expand triangle of the second shadow. In this shadow, set Blur to 20.00, set the Horizontal and Vertical offsets all the way to the right side for a value of 100 on each parameter, and set the shadow color to 255, 255, 255, 44. Collapse the parameters for the second shadow.

Expand the third shadow parameters. Set the Blur to 10.00, Horizontal and Vertical to −100, and the shadow colors to 255, 255, 255, 25.

There are now three shadows associated with the words "Sample Text."

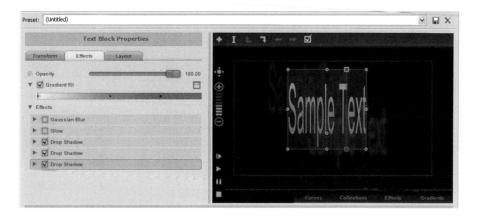

8.7

Select the first tab in the title tool (Transform). In this tab, the angle of the text and related shadows may be set off-center, sheared, or offset to right/left/up/down. Remember earlier when we set the target center? Click and drag the Rotation slider to the left or right. The text will rotate, but will center around the S in "Sample Text." Notice that in the Center dialog, the preset selected is "Custom." To reset our text, double-click in the Rotation slider to set it back to 0. This will reset the target point to the center of the title.

At this point, the Offset, Scale, and Shear parameters may be collapsed; if so, expand them by clicking the Expand triangle at the left of the parameter. Note that the Scale parameters are not equal; this parameter was changed when we vertically stretched the title earlier in the exercise.

Experiment with the Shear parameters to understand how this feature may be used. It can be used to "bounce" text as it enters or leaves the screen when animating text.

Finally, select the Layout tab. In this tab, text may be displayed vertically (this is especially useful when setting up rotated displays), tracked, spaced (similar to leading in the old text tool), Selected (fades text on/ off screen), and placed on a path.

In this dialog, we'll discover the automated keyframe tools for animating text on a screen.

In the Tracking parameter, enable the automation tools by clicking the small "spiral" icon found to the left of the parameter control. Notice that an automation track named Tracking has been added to the titler keyframing Timeline. Each time you enable automation by clicking on a spiral icon on the left side in the dialog, a new keyframable automation track is added in the Timeline below.

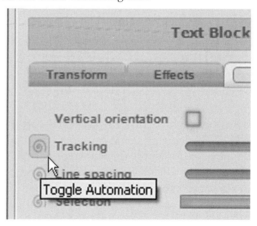

8.8   This icon is the autokeyframe tool. Enabling it will allow for creation of keyframes in the titler Timeline.

With this function enabled, we can now animate the title. We'll be animating several parameters throughout this next section.

By default, the cursor for the titler Timeline should be at the beginning/far left of the Timeline. If not, place it there by clicking and dragging the Current Time Indicator (CTI) in the top of the Timeline. In the Tracking parameter, set the value to 10.00. This will spread the letters far across the screen. Move the CTI to the 3-second point (third tick in the Timeline). Double-click the Tracking slider. This will set it to 0, or default. A new keyframe has been generated and is seen in the titler Timeline.

8.9

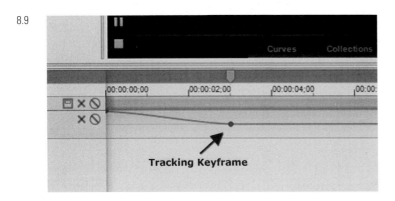

Take note of the double triangle in the Tracking level of the titler Timeline. Selecting this double triangle will further expand/collapse the keyframe/envelope tools found in the titler Timeline. This function is available for all automated Timeline parameters. Expanding the Timeline is very useful when working with Bezier curve controls of fine or tight Timeline areas.

8.10 Expanding the keyframe Timeline will allow very fine control of Bezier curves.

Press the Play icon (or spacebar) in the titler preview window, and the title will play. The title should now display a widened start point, narrowing to a normal Tracking setting, illustrating how the automation functions. Setting the resolution of the Vegas Preview window to DRAFT | AUTO will give a higher frame-rate playback.

Let's add more automation. Click the Effects tab and check the Gaussian Blur checkbox. Expand the Gaussian Blur parameter set and enable horizontal blur automation by clicking the automation icon found to the left of the Horizontal Blur parameter.

Place the CTI at the far left/start point of the keyframe Timeline. Slide the Gaussian Horizontal Blur parameter control to the far right for a value of 100. In the keyframe Timeline, move the CTI to the 3-second point (the same point as the previous keyframe) and then double-click the horizontal slider in the Gaussian Blur parameter. This will cause the text to be horizontally blurred at the start of the title, moving to a clean view as the tracking brings the letters in the text together.

In the top of the Effects tab is the Opacity function. Moving the CTI back to the far left/title start point, enable the Opacity automation. Set the Opacity value to 0 and then move the CTI to the 2-second point on the Timeline, and then set the Opacity value to 100. The title will now begin at full transparency and fade to full opacity.

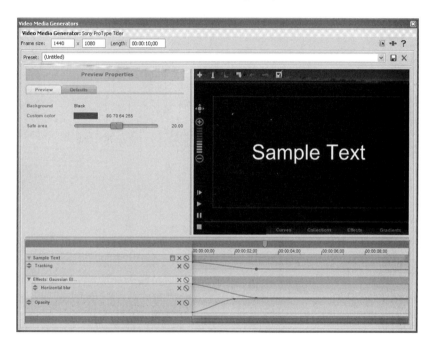

8.11 Note the tracking, blur, and opacity curves.

Close the title tool by clicking the X in the upper-righthand corner; trim the event to be 4–6 seconds in length, and double-click the new title/generated media on the Timeline. This will create a selection; use Shift+B to generate a RAM render. Preview the title.

Reopen the title tool by either clicking the small green Generated Media icon or right-clicking the title and selecting Edit Generated Media. This will reopen the ProType Titler.

Inserting a second title in the same title tool is very easy, and this second title may have any of its own behaviors.

Double-click in the title tool preview area, and a new text instance will appear. This too, will say "Sample Text." The text should already be highlighted; if for some reason it is not, highlight it. For this exercise, change "Sample Text" to read "Flying Letters." While the text is highlighted, change the font to something different from the "Sample Text" title. If the text has become deselected, double-click to put the text back in Edit mode, and rehighlight the text, or click the Edit Text I-beam icon on the text toolbar. When in Text Block mode, clicking the I-beam icon puts you in Text Edit mode. When in Text Edit mode, clicking the maroon toolbar at the top of the Preview window or pressing the Esc key will put you back in Text Block mode.

Once the font is changed, and perhaps resized, we'll animate this text. Select the Layout tab in the Text Block Properties dialog. In this tab, enable the following automations: Selection, Fade Selection, and Position on Path. In the Selection Type option, click and select Character from the dropdown menu. Underneath Fade Selection, click the checkbox for "Path." The path should change, causing the letters to be wavy.

Moving down to the titler Timeline, place the CTI at the far left side and click the Expand triangle next to the words "Sample Text." Note that this will cause the "Sample Text" keyframed parameters to collapse. Now expand the keyframe parameters for "Flying Letters." Moving the Position on Path slider to the left (back in the Layout tab) will cause the text to move across the path to the left, just as moving the slider to the right will cause the text to move to the right. It may take a moment or two for your system to redraw this display, so experiment by moving the slider just a little at a time to see the results.

We're now going to move the text around. Start with the text block object "Flying Letters" in the middle of the Preview window. Slide the Position on Path slider to the right to a value of 1.4. This puts it predominantly off-screen. We'll modify the path, but need to zoom into the Preview screen first.

The titler Zoom tool is found on the left of the titler Preview screen. Click–dragging will zoom in/out on the Preview screen/work area. Zoom in deeply enough to see the path associated with "Flying Letters" clearly.

Click and hold the target dot on the left end of the curved path, and drag it farther to the left. Grab the target dot from the associated Bezier curve and extend it, pointing it straight up. This puts a pronounced "hump" at the left side. Click and drag the right target dot (at the base of the F), and use the associated Bezier curve to flatten out the title path from the right side.

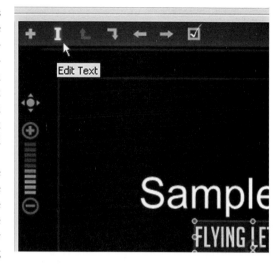

8.12   Select this icon to edit a selected text object. If only one text object exists in the titler, then that text object will be available for editing.

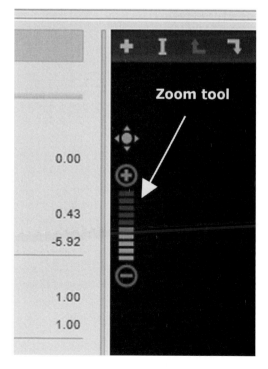

8.13   Click–drag the Zoom tool to increase/decrease the preview size. Alternatively, press/hold the plus and minus keys.

8.14

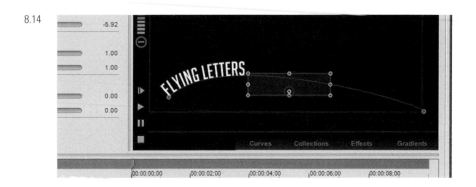

Move the CTI in the title Timeline to the 5-second point (five tick marks from the left). Use the right/left arrow keys if it seems difficult to achieve precision. Notice that the "Sample Text" title created earlier has now appeared on the screen at its ending position. In the Layout tab, set the Position on Path value at .25 (remember that you can click and edit the value directly). This should nearly center the text. On the keyframe Timeline, right-click the newly created keyframe and select Linear from the menu that opens.

Let's add another keyframe, but with the same position value. Place the CTI at the 8-second point on the Timeline. Double-click the keyframe envelope in the Position on Path envelope to create a new keyframe. Alternatively, move the Position on Path slider away and back, being careful to move it back to the same .25 value. Setting two keyframes to the same value provides an amount of time for the animation to remain stationary, in this case for 3 seconds. Right-click the newly created keyframe and set this value to Linear in the menu (these keyframes don't actually need to be set to Linear, a part of this exercise is to become familiar with various keyframe options within the title tool).

Now move the CTI to the 11-second point and set the Position on Path value to −.75. This will take the text to the left and off the screen at the bottom of the Preview window. Return the CTI to the far left of the Timeline and hit the spacebar or click the Play button in the titler Preview window to preview the title.

Return the CTI to the far left of the Timeline. In the Selection Type dropdown menu, be sure that Character is displayed. If not, click the button and select Character from the dropdown. In the Selection Bar, click on the far-right side of the bar and drag to the left until only the letter F is visible. Notice this creates a fade in the "Flying Letters" object? Place the CTI at the 7-second point, and slide the Selection Bar all the way to the right so that all characters in the "Flying Letters" object are revealed. Play the title from the beginning (Shift+spacebar).

Curves Presets

In the Presets toolbar (lower right in the titler Preview window), there are the four preset options. On the left side, open the Curves presets by clicking on the Curves tab. The Curves presets will display.

8.15 There are several prebuilt keyframe curves available in Vegas Pro 8, and you can save your own to the library.

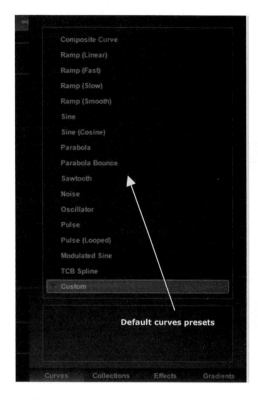

Here is where you can easily add serious life and creative punch to your title objects. Click and drag the Parabola preset to the second keyframe in the Position on Path keyframe on the titler Timeline. This will create a highlighted block section surrounding the keyframe itself.

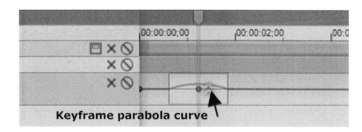

8.16 highlighted block area indicates that a Curves preset has been applied to a keyframe. Notice the double up arrow. Clicking this arrow will open the preset parameters.

Play back the Timeline now. Notice that the "Flying Letters" object will "bounce" as it reaches the second keyframe. This is probably too bouncy for any real purpose, it is easy to modify this preset. In the preset block, either click the small double up arrows or right-click and choose Properties. Either action will open the Properties dialog for the Curves parameter.

8.17

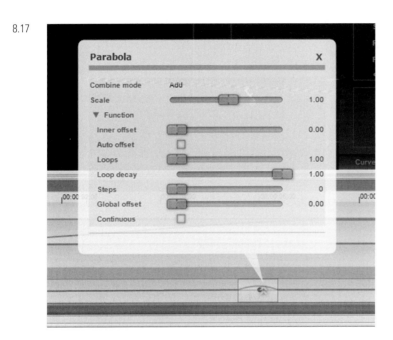

Set the Scale value to 0.09. This will make the bounce much smaller. Observe the way the keyframe waveform changes inside the keyframe block. Negative values will bounce the text object to the left, positive values will bounce the text object to the right. Close the Properties dialog, and click–drag the right side of the highlighted block. The block may be enlarged or shrunk to the right or left. Click–dragging in the middle of the highlighted block allows the entire block to be moved without resizing.

Now that a title has been created, there are some other tools that you should become familiar with.

Other Basic Tools

Double-click on either of the text objects in the titler Preview window. This will put that text object into Text Edit mode. On the left side of the title tool, the span properties have changed back to text editing tools such as Font Type, Size, Weight, Centering, Color, Slant, and more. Selecting text by click–dragging over letters allows those letters to be changed.

8.18

For example, in the "Flying" example created earlier, it is possible to highlight the first letter of each word and change the font or font weight. Perhaps the first letter of each word should be bolded, italicized, underlined, or all three. Each character may have its own color, stroke, weight, strikethrough, or underline. Additionally, each character (or all of them) may be backed with a specific color block if desired.

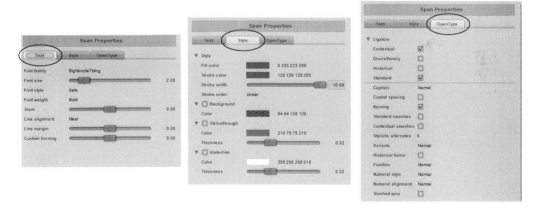

8.19   In these menus are found controls to affect individual characters or entire text objects. Double-clicking the Span properties will also insert a new text object.

In the OpenType tab, take note of the specialized text options such as determining whether a fraction should be displayed as a slashed or stacked fraction, or perhaps the number 0 should display with a slash through it.

Also noteworthy in the OpenType options is the ability to create subscripts, superscripts, or other variants, as well as the ability to specify how capitalized letters are displayed.

The functions found in the Span properties such as fonts, weights, text color, underlining, and OpenType features are not keyframe controllable.

Advanced Titling Tools

There are several additional tools found in the ProType Titler that aren't apparent at first glance.

Controlling individual characters is a powerful feature; this is managed through parent/child relationships. Don't confuse the parent/child relationships in the ProType Titler with the Parent/Child tools found in the Track Compositing modes of the Timeline.

A full sentence or group of characters may be considered as the "parent." Each word in the sentence or group of characters would be one of the "child" levels. Each individual character in a text object would be the smallest "child" in the title object.

8.20   In this example, word and individual characters are selected as children of the larger text (sentence) object.

Navigation between sentences, words, and characters is achieved either using shortcut keys or clicking icons on the titler tool bar. Shift+Enter navigates downward until the lowest child level (a character) is achieved. Using the Esc key will navigate backward from the child to the parent. When a child is selected, navigating to the next child (called a "peer") is done with the Shift+right/left arrow keys.

8.21

Each child may carry its own keyframe attributes, in addition to the keyframes assigned to the parent the child belongs to. When a child is selected, note that the Span dialogs change to Word dialogs and Character dialogs. These dialogs contain all of the keyframable parameters that a selected child may access. Experiment with changing opacities and character sizes for interesting titling effects. These may be made more interesting and creative by adding various Curves presets from the Curves library. Curves may be dragged and edited for individual characters just as they may be added to word or full blocks/spans of text objects.

Here are some exercises that will quickly show the power of the advanced tools found in the titler:

- Keyframe opacity of individual letters, increasing opacity in an odd order, such as last letters first.
- Keyframe a shift in gradients per word.
- Add a stroke to a word, adding blur to the stroke via the Gaussian Blur tools.
- Stroke a different word in the span with a different stroke color and thickness.

Transferring Titles

Titles may be saved, shared, and transferred from one computer system to another. Titles are generated internally using XML, so they are very easy to copy and send in an email or zip as a collection. To export/save a title with Windows XP, use the Windows Explorer to browse to C:\ Documents and Settings\{username}\Application Data\Sony\Titler 1.0\Collection.

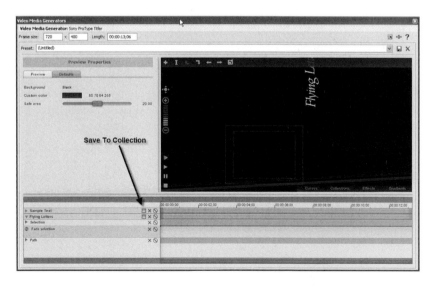

8.22 Vista users will find these files in C:\Documents and Settings\{username}\Application Data\ Sony\Titler 1.0\Collection.

8.23 In this image, note that the two collections have been zipped for sharing.

Title collections may be zipped up, exported, emailed, shared on a disc, or stored on a web page. Simply unzip (if the file has been zipped) the file and extract it to the file location mentioned previously. Collections may be shared on the VASST web site as well (www.vasst.com).

Using the Vegas Titler

In addition to the ProType Titler, Vegas offers a legacy titling tool that is still quite useful for many titling styles and techniques. The legacy titles also tend to render slightly faster, so if speed is an issue, the Vegas Title tool may be your best bet.

To insert a title over an image, first place a visual event on the Timeline. Right-click the Track Control pane and select Insert Video Track or select INSERT VIDEO TRACK.

In the new video track, right-click the Timeline and choose Insert Text Media from the menu.

The Title tool opens with the Edit tab displayed, showing the words "Sample Text" inside. This area is where the words found in the title are inserted. Text size, font, and attributes, such as bold, italic, and justification, are also selected here. These attributes and the Edit window work just like a word processor.

> Get your title to exact length the first time. Create a time selection in the project that is the desired length of the title. In the track where you'd like the title to live, right-click and choose Insert Text Media. A title dialog will open up, set to the length of the selected area. This will override the default title lengths in the OPTIONS | PREFERENCES | EDITING dialog.

8.24 Right-click brings up this menu, then choose Insert Text Media to insert a title.

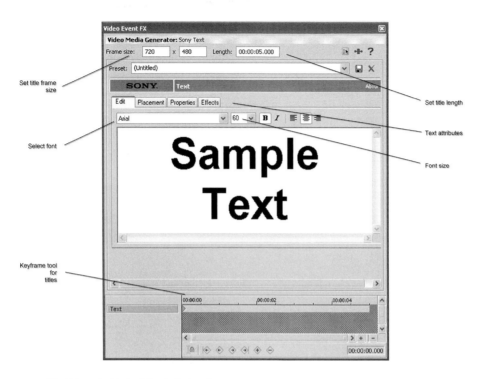

8.25   The Title tool with the Edit tab displayed.

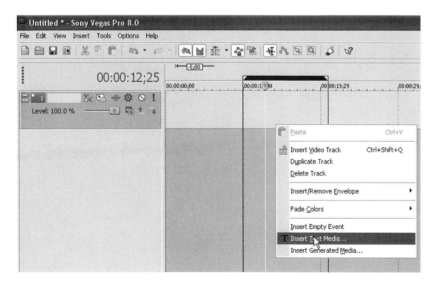

8.26

The frame size can be selected at the top of the titling tool. In Vegas, generated media always defaults to 720 × 480 (nonsquare pixels), but appears correct as to frame size. (If you are creating titles outside of Vegas for NTSC DV, the frame size should always be 655 × 480, and for PAL the frame size should always be 704 × 577.) This factor compensates for the nonsquare pixel aspect ratio of DV.

The media length is set by default to whatever the length of stills is set at in the OPTIONS | PREFERENCES | EDITING dialog; however, the length of the media can also be selected in the top of the Title tool, overriding this value.

8.27   The Editing tab found in the OPTIONS | PREFERENCES dialog allows users to preset title and still default lengths.

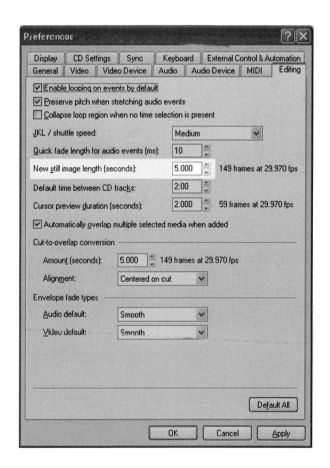

Often, the setting in the Options menu is for stills, yet titles need to run longer. It's speedy to extend a title by specifying a longer title in this dialog. Titles, of course, can be looped to any length. Presets are available in the titling menu. These presets are there to assist you in creating great titles out of the box, but for truly powerful and professional-looking titles, you need to learn the features of the rest of the titling tool.

Titles can be positioned anywhere on the Text Placement dialog, which is under the Placement tab.

To place a title manually, click the text in the window of the Edit tab and then drag the title to the desired location. By default, a safe area is defined at 10 percent. This safe area indicates the area in which a title should live if it's being shown on television. Televisions have an area that is partially covered by a bezel in addition to being unscanned. This area hides approximately 10 percent of the video signal. Some televisions cover more and others less. The safe zone can be defined from a zero size area to a 30 percent safe area, by clicking in the Safe Zone text box and entering the desired safe area size. Ten percent is a typical safe area for NTSC and PAL video. Streamed media requires no safe area.

Title placement can be keyframed if the title should move onscreen.

8.28　Titles can be manually placed anywhere, or presets can be used to place a title.

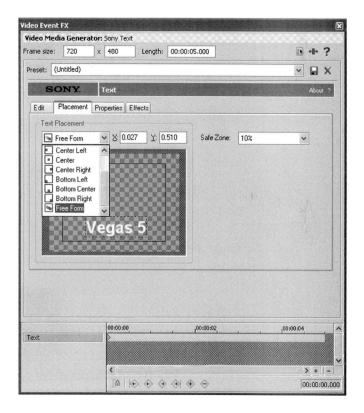

Title Properties

Under the Properties tab, the color, tracking, scaling, and leading of the title can be controlled. Selecting the color is done by placing the cursor in the color palette and clicking. The cursor changes to a small target icon that can be dragged inside the color selector.

If a specific color is desired, the RGB values of the specific color can be entered into the color value boxes. Vegas also offers a color picker, which allows you to use the Eyedropper tool to select a color or range of averaged color. The Eyedropper tool can be applied to any image on the screen. If a commercial color set is available, exacting color selection is possible.

Color can also be selected based on hue, saturation, and luminance (HSL) by selecting the HSL button just above the Eyedropper tool.

A background color can be specified if necessary. If the title is overlaid on a video image, a background color probably shouldn't be specified and should be left transparent instead. This feature can be used as an effect over video, and if the opacity of the background color is reduced, the visual image will show through the color, causing the background color to act as a color filter. All color aspects are keyframe-controllable.

The Text Properties area of the Properties tab in the Title tool allows for adjustment of the kerning, leading, and spacing of text. By default, autokerning is disabled. Check the button to enable it.

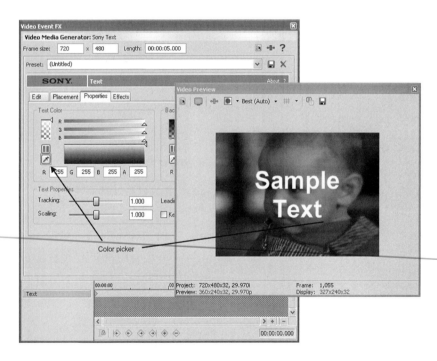

8.29   Using the Eyedropper to match the color title to the flower on the shirt.

Tracking controls the distance between letters in the text/title field. Leading controls the space between two lines. Leading fine-tunes a single line of text up and down. Scaling controls the sizing of the letters. All three text controls are keyframable. Scaling tends to be jerky in the scaling of text, so use with caution.

8.30 Selecting a background color's transparency/opacity.

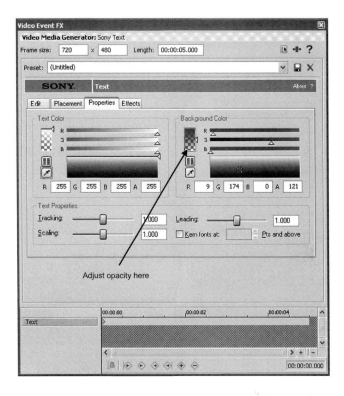

8.31 The tracking control.

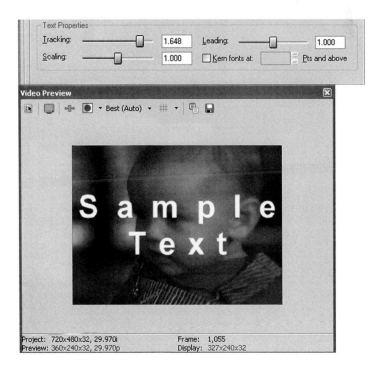

8.32   The leading control.

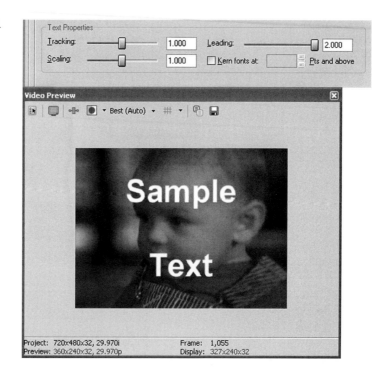

8.33   The scaling controls.

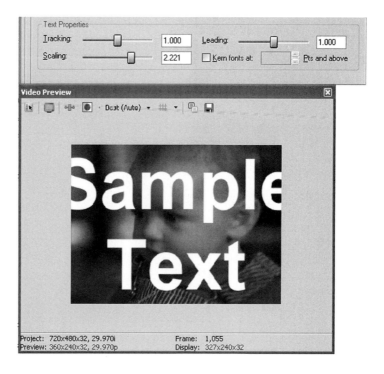

A checkbox is available for automatic kerning of letters above a preset, user-controlled size. Kerning is the specific spacing between a pair of characters. Some letters take up more space than others, and without kerning, sometimes letters appear to be too far apart in a word. Kerning generally alleviates this problem, although some fonts use more space than others.

Adding Effects to Text

The Effects tab offers a number of options to edit and enhance text. Effects often are used to make text stand out on otherwise busy visual screens or to create a specific mood.

Adding a glow to text can make letters show up when the underlying media is of a similar color. Glow is also often used to give text an image of depth, such as coming out of a vacuum. Clicking the Draw Outline checkbox adds a glow to the text. This effect is great for outlining light-colored text with a slightly darker color, creating a slight illusion of 3D.

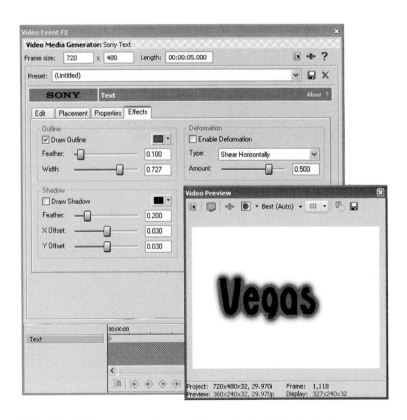

8.34   Using Outline to create a glow around text causes the text to stand out.

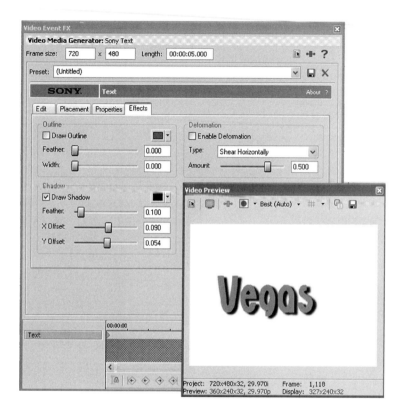

8.35 Adding a shadow adds depth and dimension to text.

The outline can be feathered, which smoothes out the transition between the text and the underlying media and softens the edge of the glow. Use this effect to add a bit of flair to text that might otherwise be dull.

Drop shadow, or shadowing, is one of the most useful tools in the Effects tab. Click the Draw Shadow checkbox, and a shadow will appear beneath text. This shadow can be colored in any color found in the palette by clicking the Color button and then either selecting a preset color or choosing a custom color by using the color picker/Eyedropper to select a color.

Shadows can be keyframed to add depth to a title, moving in a direction opposite the original text, which creates an image popular in Hollywood titles today. Colors and opacity can be keyframed and combined with glow to create very rich and deep title attributes. Feathering smoothes and softens the edges of shadows and adds perspective to the depth of the text.

The Deform tool can shear, bend, squish, or compress text. Text can be wrapped around images by curving, or text can be used to give the impression of urgency by keyframing a fast bend as the text comes on or off the screen.

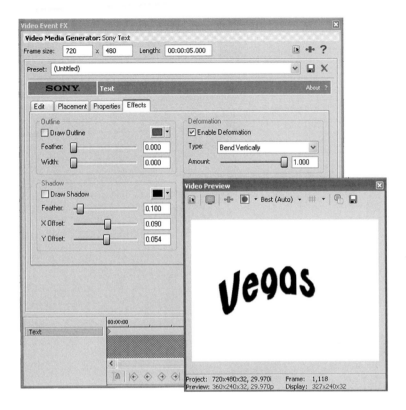

8.36   Bending text around an image can create an illusion of text and image being one image.

You can keyframe text with any one of the many effects in the tab and create flowing text that appears to be very deep, particularly when combined with other text effects.

Each of the three effects sections has slider controls for different text features. Double-clicking a slider returns the slider to its default "null" position. Clicking on the slider activates the effect, and the control can be either controlled with the mouse or, if active, moved with the right arrow and left arrow keys for more precise control.

Learning to manipulate titles is an introduction to compositing, and titles are one of the most creative and yet difficult aspects of film and video production. In the past, complex applications were required to do in-depth titling, but today Vegas contains many tools that accomplish the same applications as the more complex tools offered in the past. With some creativity and inspiration, Vegas can be used to create Hollywood-level titles. In fact, several Hollywood-level films and television productions contain title work created in Vegas.

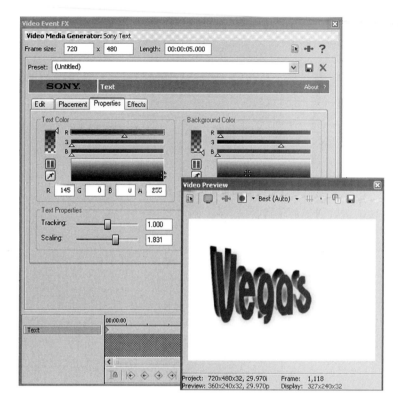

8.37   Inserting a mix of effects can create complex titles.

Flashy Titles

Titling is extremely important in any video production. Some would argue that titling sets up the viewer for what he or she is about to see and therefore makes the difference between a good film and a great film. Titles can take a lot of artistic development time, and a lot of creative energy as well, and therefore titles are often farmed off to editors or artists who specialize in nothing but titling sequences. One of the formats for titling in video is Macromedia's Flash format.

> When importing Flash files into Vegas, they must be from Flash 5 or earlier. Flash MX files contain metadata types that Vegas cannot correctly read and import to the Timeline.

Vegas supports Flash import, and .swf or .fla files may be dropped directly on the Vegas Timeline. Although these files don't always play back at full frame rate, they provide unique opportunities for users to import powerful sequences of images. Flash files containing ActionScripts, audio, or motion video may not be inserted into the Timeline, nor may Flash files created in Flash MX. Only files created in Flash 5 or older may be loaded onto the Timeline.

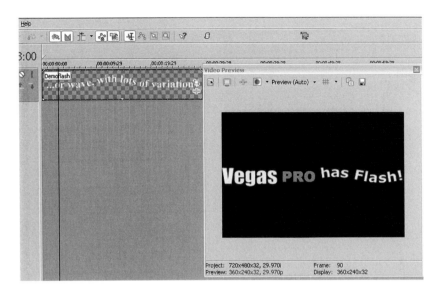

8.38   With Flash now importable to Vegas, the titling and animation possibilities are greatly expanded.

Flash is also a powerful animation tool for product presentation, for lower thirds, or for portraying a specific type of image from a web site or other multimedia presentation. Many companies have Flash introductions or menus on their web sites. These may now be set up and used with productions created in Vegas. Graphs, charts, and spectacular titles are all part of the Flash graphic format that may be imported to Vegas. Interactivity with Flash files will not carry over into Vegas.

Flash is often used for creating instructional media, giving an added edge when combined with video presentations. However, CoffeeCup Software and Swish are both available for creating excellent Flash files and are substantially easier to learn and use. Learn more about these products at http://www.swishzone.com and http://www.wildform.com.

You can also download demo files from these sites to practice working with the Vegas Timeline. Find the demoflash.swf file on the DVD in the back of this book. Drop it on the Timeline, laid over an existing video file, and you'll see how clean the Flash file can be. If you are unsure of whether the Flash is showing at the project property size (it should always scale to the project property size), then double-click the header or title bar of the Preview window to set the Preview window display to the project properties. To gct a better understanding of how this function works, reset the project properties to a new setting, such as changing the project properties to a PAL setting, and you'll see the Flash project scale to the new project property settings.

> Vegas does not scale Flash media cleanly when the Pan/Crop tool is used to zoom in on the Flash file, suggesting that the vector information in Flash may be ignored. Create your Flash projects at full size and resolution for best results. Vegas will properly scale them to project resolution. In summary, this is a problem only when zooming in on the Flash file with the Pan/Crop or Track Motion tools.

Importing Static Graphics

When importing static images from PhotoShop or similar applications, create the title images at the full resolution set for square pixels in the graphics editing application. Otherwise, the title may be stretched.

For example, a static graphic for an HD project would be imported to Vegas at a true resolution of 1920 × 1080 or 1280 × 720. Even though an HDV project setting is 1440 × 1080, bear in mind that the pixel aspect ratio is 1.333 for HDV, meaning the pixels are stretched.

Import stills at the following resolutions for nonstretched results:

DV 4:3 NTSC = 720 × 480

DV NTSC widescreen = 873 × 480

DV 4:3 PAL = 720 × 576

DV PAL widescreen = 1049 × 576

Note that these are different from when importing still images that are to be pan/cropped.

Pan/Crop, Track Motion, and Basic Compositing in Vegas

What Is Compositing?

Compositing is the combination or interaction of two or more graphic or video images to create a single finished image. Compositing can be as simple as laying a title onto a visual image or as complex as combining hundreds of photographs, video, and animated elements to create complex images.

Compositing in its most complex forms is absolutely an art; there are compositing artists all over Hollywood, Austin, New York, Sydney, and other major cities that do nothing but create complex imagery for major networks, film, and corporate media departments. The fantastic imagery seen on ESPN and CNN and in most major motion pictures is the result of these artists' work. It is most likely that not one major motion picture has been released in the past few years that didn't contain significant compositing, whether it's titling, green- or bluescreen work, or overlaid imagery. *The Matrix* is an amazing example of how greenscreen work is brought to the big screen through the creative use of composited images, as is *The Lord of the Rings* and even the heralded *Titanic*. Many of the full ship images in *Titanic* were composited together, including animations of people walking, driving, and loading the ship. Most of the scenes including fish were composited and animated. So in short, compositing is very much about eye candy and illusion.

Using the Pan/Crop Tool

Vegas has a Pan/Crop tool that can be used on any video event. This powerful tool can be used to correct camera depth, create motion on a still image, match aspect ratio, or crop out unwanted material from an image. Although simple in use, this tool is extremely powerful. Open the Pan-Crop.veg project so you can follow along visually with this section. After the video is captured and placed on the Timeline, each clip will contain a small Crop symbol. Notice that in Figure 9.1 the image in the monitor screen does not entirely fill the video preview area. Clicking the Crop tool opens a dialog that allows the user to fill the Preview screen entirely and match the image view to the aspect ratio of the Preview screen.

This feature is particularly useful when creating videos of scanned-in still photos or cropping unwanted content from a video image. See Chapter 3 for details on photo sizes and scanning.

With the Crop dialog open, right-click the image inside the Crop window and select Match Output Aspect.

9.1 The photo does not fill the entire Preview window.

This action causes the image to be cropped to a size that will completely fill the preview area. Now, the Preview window is completely filled with no black background showing. The aspect ratio of the photo, however, appears to be correct even if the photo itself really isn't. This aspect ensures that all imagery mixed with DV and other graphics can be made to fill the viewing screen completely at all times, matching the aspect ratio of the project. This accomplishment, however, isn't without its specific issues. For example, we no longer can see the entire image that comprises the photograph shown in Figure 9.1.

9.2 Selecting the project aspect ratio crops too much of the image out in some instances.

Notice that the full frame of the cameraman is not visible in Figure 9.2. The viewers can now see only the part of the camera operator that the editor allows them to see—useful in some situations, but not in others.

Wouldn't it be great if the still image could move, almost as though a camera had been used to capture the image rather than a scanner?

We can create that movement by the use of keyframes. Right-click again and select the Pan/Crop tool or click the Crop tool icon found on every clip or image on the Timeline. Now, move the Selection/Crop window to a new position. The Keyframe tool automatically inserts a keyframe, telling the Timeline that at a specified time, the photograph should be cropped differently. Zoom in on the photo and zoom out of the photo, placing keyframes at each point of movement. Notice the added keyframes in Figure 9.3.

Producers of PBS specials, BBC documentaries, wedding videos, and broadcasts apply this same technique to create the illusion of movement. Even if the image is exactly the correct aspect ratio, no one really likes looking at a static photo on a computer or television screen. Even the smallest bits of movement are far more interesting to watch than a static photo.

In the past, tracking cameras, or remote control-operated cameras that mount on a rail, shooting motion images over a still photo have been used to create this effect. Ric Burns, celebrated filmmaker/documentary genius of *The Civil War, The Way West, New York*, and others, has employed still images coupled with motion to change the entire face of documentaries. This effect can now be easily accomplished with a scanner and the Pan/Crop tool. This tool is tremendously powerful and useful for putting together slide shows, wedding montages, or other photo-heavy presentations.

Another application uses the Pan/Crop tool to correct bad camera movement. It can also be used to generate camera movement when the camera is static or not moving at all. If the clip of a soccer game, for example, is tripod-shot and static the camera movement could be generated to tell the viewer where they should be looking. A word of caution: don't zoom in too far, or the pixels will become too large and the detail of the event will wash out. This tool should be used in a subtle way for video. It's a terrific precursor to a transition.

Still images can usually handle deeper zooms if the resolution is set high enough on the original photo. Typical sizes of photos generally are considered best at 72dpi for video; in most cases, saving photos at double the standard resolution provides a clean image for zooming and panning. However, preview stills in your scanning software to ensure the best resolution for your needs.

In addition to the Match Output Aspect menu in the right-click dialog, additional choices include the following:

- Restore—restores pan/crop boundaries to the edges of the image. No pan/crop takes place.

- Center—centers pan/crop boundaries around the centering dot found in the middle of the crop boundaries.

- Flip Horizontal—flips images horizontally, making the right side become the left side. (This feature is great for changing a view. Open multicamera.veg for more information.)

- Flip Vertical—flips images vertically, causing most images to be upside down.

- Match Output Aspect—matches the image aspect ratio to the settings in the FILE | PROPERTIES dialog, which is usually 720 × 480 for DV editing.

- Match Source Aspect—matches the image aspect to the original aspect ratio. Use this setting when applying full photos over other montages and when it is acceptable for the photo's borders to be seen. This feature will still allow an image to be resized smaller; however, the aspect ratio is that of the original image, not of the project.

 Tip

Having photos at too high a resolution creates artifacts on the video image, containing too much information for a video image.

Standard-size graphic images, such as titles, backgrounds, and generated graphics, should be created at no higher than 300 dpi, or double the maximum zoom, and should be sized at 655 × 480 for insertion into a DV project. This configuration compensates for the non-square pixel issues found in DV. Always reduce interlace flicker for photos and consider using the Broadcast Colors filter on stills if they are beyond legal colors. The Broadcast filter can be dropped directly on a still image event, or if the Timeline contains a large number of stills, the filter can be dropped on the Project window instead. Instead of a Broadcast filter, you might want to try a Levels filter, set to convert Computer RGB to Studio RGB. Set this by reversing the Studio RGB to Computer RGB settings, which will ensure that the entire dynamic range is passed. (See Chapter 6 for more information on legal colors.)

9.3 Notice the keyframes created to build the illusion of a camera-shot still photo.

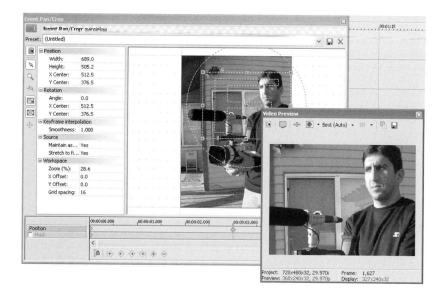

The Pan/Crop tool can also be used to create 3D-like imagery. By spinning an image, whether video, photo, or graphic, the illusion of 3D can be created by adding a glow or shadow to the image. Of course, with the 3D Track Motion tools, this merely becomes an added bonus.

In the second section of the Pan-crop.veg project, a flip or rotation is found on the project. Glow, shadow, and keyframed motion of the pan/crop are applied to the image.

Use the Pan/Crop tool to flip images horizontally or vertically or to squeeze an image onto the screen. Partnered with the Spherize plug-in found in Vegas, this process is one means of creating unique titles or animations of transitioning video.

Masking with the Pan/Crop Tool

Users of early versions of Vegas will find the masking tools to have a slight learning curve, but once understood, the power of this toolset in the Pan/Crop tool is fabulous.

> If the Pan/Crop icon isn't visible on each video event, go to OPTIONS | PREFERENCES | SHOW VIDEO EVENT BUTTONS, and tick the checkbox there. This will cause the Pan/Crop and FX buttons to be visible on each media event. If you are working with single-frame events, you may want to turn this feature off. You can always access Pan/Crop and FX by right -clicking any video event.

Place a video event on the Timeline. This can be a generated media event or a video event. Insert the Pan/Crop tool by selecting the Pan/Crop icon found on the event or right-clicking the event and choosing Pan/Crop.

9.4 The improved Pan/Crop tool in Vegas Pro 8.

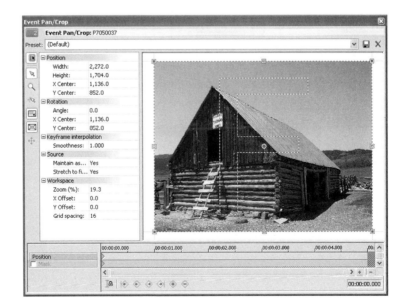

The Pan/Crop tool is slider-based. A parameter is chosen and the slider used to set the parameter. For example, notice the Zoom option. Check the word "Zoom," and the slider next to the parameter lights up. This allows you to zoom in more deeply on the image in the Pan/Crop window and work at fine detail levels without the Pan/Crop preview window requiring a shift in size as it did in previous versions of Vegas. I find that setting this to a level of 50 is a good starting point for most Pan/Crop motion work. As with all of the Sony tools, double-clicking the parameter slider or button resets this to the default. The default setting for the Pan/Crop tool is 100, which may prove to be too large for some work spaces, such as a laptop.

The Pan/Crop tool still may be manually moved in the workspace as in previous versions of Vegas, and values may be inserted using the keyboard as previously possible. But the slider tool found in this latest revision may prove to be more creative or intuitive for some users. I grew used to it very quickly and find it a great way of getting my images to position or size very quickly.

Open the Pan/Crop tool the way you usually do, and you'll see a control in the Pan/Crop keyframing tool labeled "Mask." The Mask allows Bezier curves to be drawn in the Pan/Crop tool as masks, opening up an entirely new creative realm.

Click the Masks indicator so that Masks is selected in the keyframe tool. Now hold down the Ctrl button, and this will cause the cursor to turn to a Pen tool in the Pan/Crop preview window. Left-clicking the Pen tool in the Pan/Crop Preview window will insert a point in the window. Now move the cursor to a new location, hold Ctrl, and left-click again. This will create yet another point in the Pan/Crop preview window. Create at least three points, joining one to another. As the Pen tool is rolled over the first point in the mask, a small circle will appear, and all mask points will turn yellow, indicating that

9.5   Close-up view of the Pan/Crop tool with all tools expanded.

the mask is a completed path. A selection is now made. Pressing the Alt key and clicking on any of the yellow anchor points will select all anchor points. Clicking on any single anchor point allows it to be selected and the Bezier curve to be adjusted to work with the angle or curve you'd like to create. These curves and selected areas are completely keyframe controlled, so this sort of selection may move with any object or subject that you might have in the video image. Multiple selections may be made in the Pan/Crop window, allowing for multiple objects and selections to be cut out and defined.

But How Is This a Mask?

On the left side of the Pan/Crop tool, you'll find a new interface and control set. In this control set is a setting labeled "Path." Click on the Path Mode dialog or on the + symbol next to the word "Path," and a dropdown menu appears with the choices "Positive" and "Negative." When Positive is chosen, the area inside the curve is visible and the remaining space is transparent. When the Negative option is chosen, the area inside the curve is transparent, and the area outside the anchor points and path is visible. This is a great tool for removing a subject from a background, placing it in a new background, or removing a background from a current scene and replacing it. One way to consider this tool is that it's like a chroma key tool that will work regardless of the number of colors found in the background. At many levels, this feature brings some of the tools found in rotoscoping tools to Vegas.

The opacity of the mask may also be controlled via the new Pan/Crop Bezier tool. Opacity, like all other aspects of the Bezier tool, is keyframe-controlled. One benefit is that masks may be faded in or out over time by using the keyframe tool to create the type of image needed to complete the composite or overlay.

Open the Path dialog by clicking the + symbol next to the word "Path." Note the Opacity parameter in the Path dialog.

Opacity may be controlled by entering a value via the keyboard, sliding the Opacity slider, or using the spinner controls next to the Slider tool. Use the Page Up and Page Down keys for coarse control, moving the value in increments of ± 10, and use the up and down arrows for fine control moving in fractional values. For example, setting the first keyframe in the masking Timeline to a value of 0 causes the mask to be transparent, or invisible. Setting the next keyframe to a value of 100 will cause the mask to be completely opaque. This may be used to fade the mask in or out of the image composition.

> Values in the Pan/Crop and Track Motion dialogs may be controlled by the keyboard or a programmed HUI device. Use the Page Up and Page Down keys for coarse control of parameters in these two dialogs. This shifts the value in increments of ± 10. Using the up or down arrows shifts values by single-digit increments. You can also use the Tab key to scroll downward through the attributes of the dialogs and use Shift+Tab to scroll upward.

Next in the list of power tools found in the new Pan/Crop tool is the Feathering tool. This allows you to blend the masking lines created in the Bezier mask with the background. When working with moving media, this is exceptionally helpful as it can assist in blending moving images against a moving backdrop.

Feathering can take place either inside the mask or outside the mask or in both directions.

To take advantage of the Feathering tool, first create a mask as described above. Open the Path dialog by clicking the + symbol next to the word "Path." Note the feathering dialog beneath Opacity.

Choose how you'd like the path feathered. Experiment with all three feathering modes to determine what works best for the mask.

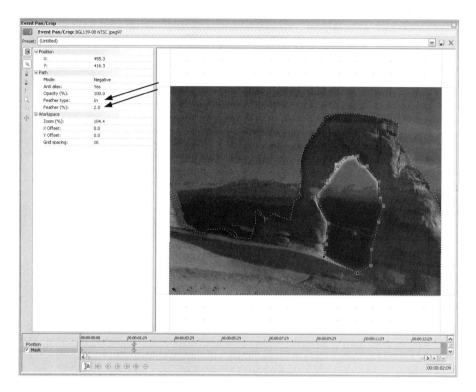

9.6   Use Feathering in the Pan/Crop tool's masking toolset to blend the mask with the background if the lines seem too visible. Feathering may be either inside or outside or in both directions from the mask line.

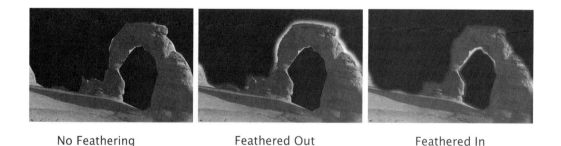

No Feathering   Feathered Out   Feathered In

9.7   Three examples of feathering with the Bezier masking tool.

Masks created in the Pan/Crop tool may be copied and pasted to other events. The most common method of copying or pasting a mask is to copy an event containing a mask contained in the Pan/Crop tool, right-click on the destination event or video clip, and select Paste Attributes from the submenu that appears. However, if the destination image is of a different size or aspect

9.8   To copy mask attributes from a source image that is different in size or aspect
      compared to the destination image, copy the keyframes from the source image
      rather than using the more common Copy and Paste attributes. This will ensure that
      regardless of the aspect ratio of the image being pasted to, the aspect of the mask
      will remain correct rather than scaling to fit the aspect of the new image.

ratio compared to the original, this will not apply the mask correctly in the destination image, as Vegas will interpolate the position based on the value of the source image. For example, if a mask has been created by drawing points around a .jpg image and the mask is copied or pasted to an .avi file of a different size, the mask will not paste in the same location or aspect as created in the source .jpg. The correct method of copying and pasting a mask attribute from differing file types is to copy the keyframes from the source image and paste them into the keyframe Timeline of the destination image. This will ensure correct aspect and location.

Using Track Motion in Vegas

On each video track, Vegas assigns a Track Motion tool. This tool is exceptionally powerful and goes far beyond its initial impressions.

The Track Motion tool in its most basic form can be used to create a picture-in-picture presentation, allowing one motion video event to be placed over another motion video event while reducing the size of either event and allowing both images to be visible simultaneously.

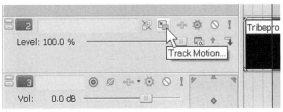

9.9   The Track Motion button is found on every video track in Vegas.

9.10 The Track Motion dialog has many choices with which to manipulate an image.

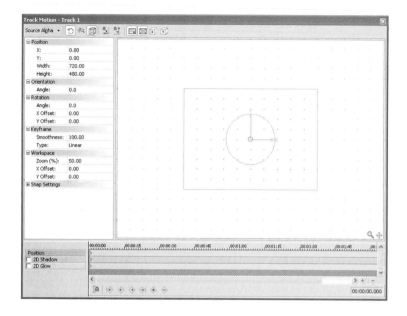

9.11 A shadow applied with the Track Motion tool.

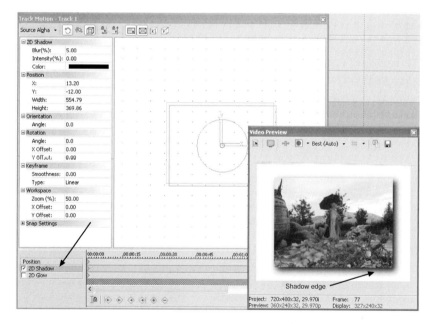

Clicking the Track Motion button opens a dialog that is similar to the Pan/Crop dialog. In fact, these two tools share many of the same attributes but accomplish completely different tasks.

As an example, a shadow can be applied with the Track Motion tool, as shown in Figure 9.11. Shadow can be applied to any image with the Track Motion tool, even if the resize or motion features of the tool are not used. This fact will be useful when using text as masks as shown

9.12, 9.13 Similar settings in the Pan/Crop tool (9.12) and Track Motion tool (9.13) frame windows, but very different results in the Preview window. Try inserting a Border filter with the Soft Edge preset on this sort of composited shot.

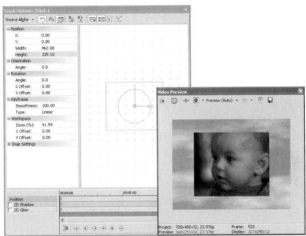

later in this section. It's also a simple task to apply shadow to a still image or graphics with a transparency by using this tool.

Starting with the top-left corner, a number of tools are found within the Track Motion dialog. The Show Properties button hides and shows the position, angle, zoom, and other views found on the left side of the Track Motion tool. The Normal Edit button, just below the Show Properties button, is the tool predominantly used to size, rotate, and manipulate the images in the Track Motion frame window.

The Zoom tool, which looks like a magnifying glass, allows for tight zooming on the frame window area and is very helpful when trying to align images in the frame to a small grid space or when creating exacting keyframes.

Enabling Snapping causes the frame in the Track Motion tool to be snapped to the nearest grid and is also useful for accurately locating the frame during editing.

The Lock Aspect Ratio in the Track Motion tool functions in the same way as the Pan/Crop tool. Unlike the Pan/Crop tool, however, the Track Motion tool causes the frame in the Preview window to remain in the correct aspect ratio, but with reduced size.

The Lock Aspect Ratio function should be used in most operations of Vegas so that the vertical and horizontal aspects of the image remain equal. The aspect ratio, however, can often be used as part of a creative edit. Turning off the aspect ratio and adjusting generated media, for instance, is great for creating lines or other shapes. (Generated media is discussed later in this chapter.) By default, these buttons should be enabled.

The Size at Center button found on the top side of the Track Motion tool to the right of Lock Aspect Ratio causes the frame and subsequent view in the Preview window to center around the dot found in the middle of the Track Motion frame. When you move the dot to another location, right-click, and then choose Center while this button is enabled, the dot will return to the center of the Track Motion frame. In addition, the frame image will move with it while keeping the dot where it was moved to in relation to the original center of the frame. The center dot is actually designed to move a frame off-center during movement, providing a pivot point for rotation of the frame.

Track Motion is where most users become acquainted with the concept of deeper compositing, as opposed to just creating titles overlaid on images. Another common use of Track Motion is

Sizing a frame down to one-fourth screen and snapping at the centerline causes the frame to be part of a quad image on a screen. Figure 9.14 shows three images reduced in size and snapped to centerlines of grid. The gradient is generated media with a title overlaid.

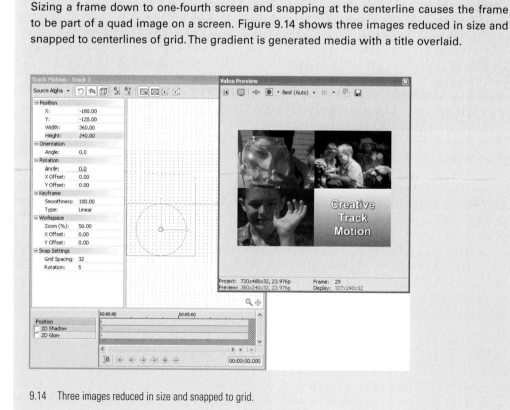

9.14   Three images reduced in size and snapped to grid.

to create a picture-in-picture image. Creating a picture-in-picture is fairly simple and is a good exercise for getting started with manipulating images.

To create a picture-in-picture image, create two tracks of video, with events on both tracks. Place the cursor in the middle of the two events. Track 1 is the overlaid event that will become the picture in the picture. Select the Track Motion button on track 1.

Make sure Lock Aspect Ratio is enabled, grab the lower-right edge of the frame in the Track Motion frame view, and reduce in size, watching the Preview window as the frame and preview image are reduced. Reduce the track 1 event to the size of X = 317.0, Y = 210.0. (Size is displayed near the cursor during resize or can be directly input in the Track Motion Properties dialog.)

In the Properties Center dialog, input a value of 180 for the left box and a value of 120 for the right box. These settings will place the video slightly to the right of extreme left and slightly below the top of the screen.

Preview the image by pressing W (rewind) and the spacebar (play).

The track 1 event will be previewed in the upper-left corner, while playing over the top of track 2's event. If both tracks are video tracks, full motion will be seen in both events.

Be sure that the Sync Cursor button is disabled when working with this exercise unless the desired effect is to shrink the track 1 event to the proscribed size. Otherwise, the first keyframe, which in most cases will be a full-frame view of track 1, will gradually shrink the track 1 event until it reaches the second/new keyframe generated by shrinking. It is easy to create unwanted keyframes accidentally during the Track Motion or Pan/Crop actions. In the event of a second keyframe being created in the Track Motion dialog, right-click the first keyframe found in the keyframe dialog and select Delete from the menu. This step will then cause the second keyframe to be the initial size of the event. You will quickly create a workflow based around your personal preference for managing these two tools.

9.15   Picture-in-picture images are very fast to create with Track Motion.

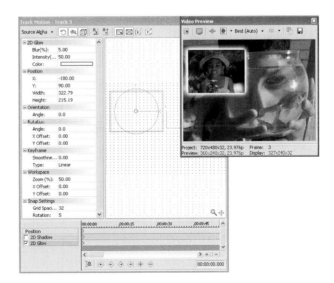

The picture-in-picture image might seem flat or without dimension, as the two images are at exactly the same depth of field. To create a depth of field, insert a shadow.

Shadows can be inserted in any color, at any opacity, and in any size within Vegas. Open the Track Motion dialog again by clicking the Track Motion button on track 1. A checkbox for a shadow is located at the bottom of the dialog on the left side of the keyframe Timeline. Checking this box adds a shadow to the frame in the Preview window. One of the more creative uses of the Shadow tool is to turn off the aspect ratio of the Track Motion tool when applying shadowing and to create shadows that stretch, move, shrink, or rotate while the image that the shadow falls from remains in aspect ratio. To disable aspect ratio on the shadow, which is enabled by default, press Ctrl while moving the shadow about the screen. To disable it for the duration of the editing process, click the Lock Aspect Ratio button, turning this tool off. If the image on the Timeline has an alpha channel, the shadow will work with the opaque image. This method is one way to create layered shadows under PNG, TGA, GIF, AVI, or other alpha-capable image formats. Shadows are keyframable for opacity, color, size, and position.

9.16 Shadow applied to a PNG file containing an alpha channel.

9.17 Glow can be subtle.

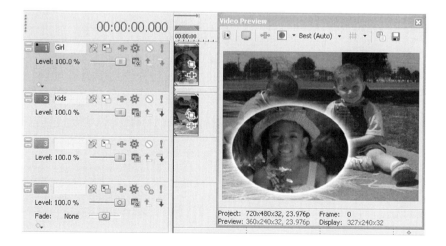

9.18 Glow can be exaggerated.

Glow may also be applied to images in the frame. Glow on its own, or combined with shadowing, allows for very complex image manipulation. Glow is adjustable in opacity, color, and size. Glow can also be feathered to blend into background or other composited images.

Using glow in a subtle manner around letters whose color properties closely match a background color can help offset the letters from the image underneath. Glow is keyframable for opacity, color, size, and position and can be used in a way similar to shadow in that it can have a separate path from the image to which it is assigned. Using a combination of glow and shadow allows for two separate moving images beneath a single event.

The project seen in Figure 9.19 is on the DVD in this book, labeled compositel.veg. This project can be used as a template.

The Track Motion tool can be applied to just about any project in some form or fashion, splitting screens, creating multiple screens such as seen in the opening of the Brady Bunch television series, flying titles in or out, or any number of other creative uses.

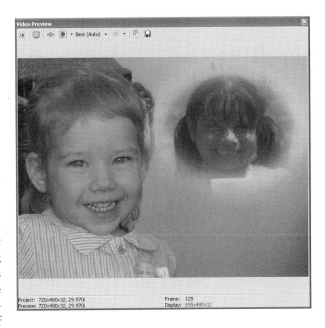

9.19 Glow combined with a mask and shadow makes for a seamless transition between the foreground and the background events.

9.20 Mask soloed to demonstrate the cookie cutter, blur, glow, and shadow combined.

The project displayed in Figure 9.21 can be found on the DVD in this book and is labeled composite2.veg.

9.21 The split screen is achieved quickly with the Track Motion tool.

The Next Dimension: 3D Track Motion Tools

Early versions of Vegas took a great leap into the next level of creative power by offering a few 3D creative tools. If you've worked with the PluginPac from DebugMode for earlier versions of Vegas, then you are more or less familiar with how this tool is going to work for you; however, the Sony 3D feature is embedded in the Track Motion tool. Access to all planes of movement may be keyframed from within the Track Motion tool.

9.22 The new 3D feature is great to use with text to create alternate planes and angles for text.

The new Track Motion tool feature set will be unfamiliar to previous users of Vegas, as it marks a departure from the interface that users are familiar with. However, to accomplish some of the features now found in Vegas, these changes were clearly necessary.

To get started with the new Track Motion tool, create a new video track and drop a video event on the new track. Select the Track Motion button on the track header. A new dialog opens up, showing the new Track Motion appearance.

Notice that in the upper-left of the dialog there is an option for Source Alpha modes. This is where you'll access the 3D behaviors for Vegas. Click the dropdown menu from the Source Alpha Modes button and choose 3D Source Alpha from the menu choices. A new dialog opens up within the Track Motion tool.

In the lefthand side you'll find several controls for the 3D parameters. The primary controls are for X, Y, and Z axes. Manipulating the X axis moves the media along a right or left horizontal plane, manipulating the Y axis moves the media placement up or down along a vertical plane, and manipulating the Z axis moves media forward or backward.

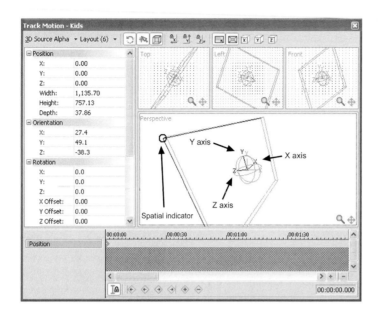

9.23 The three planes are accessible in the Track Motion workspace. Zoom in for greatest control if you are moving planes with the mouse rather than using the spinner, slider, or dialog box.

Notice that there are controls for Position, Orientation, Rotation, Keyframe, Workspace, and Snap settings. Each of these control groupings may be minimized or maximized by pressing the plus or minus sign next to the parameter control heading.

In the Position group, select the X parameter. (You may need to maximize the group by pressing the plus symbol if the group is not fully visible.)

When the parameter is selected, a small dialog containing numeric value, a spinner control, and slider control opens up. Position value information may be input manually by typing a value into the numeric dialog, or values may be determined by moving the spinner or slider values up or down, allowing preview of the media position. For the purposes of this exercise, set the value to 1.0. This will move the media to the right, nearly half-way.

Select the Y parameter and set the value to 00.00.

Now select the Z parameter. It will adjust in exactly the same manner as the X and Y parameters. Set the Z parameter at a value of −100. This will cause the media to zoom forward.

To adjust the 3D placement, enlarge the Orientation dialog if it's not already open. (You may wish to minimize the Position dialog by pressing the minus button next to the Position indicator.) Select the X plane.

Adjust the value of X to 148, the value of Y to 50, and the value of Z to 130. This adjusts how the image floats in 3D, but these positions are also keyframable. Place the cursor at the out point of the video on the Timeline. Enable the Sync to Cursor button in the Track Motion dialog.

Notice how the cursor moved in the Track Motion keyframe Timeline, to a new location that matches the location of the cursor on the workspace Timeline.

Here's where you can learn another method of manipulating how the parameters are controlled in the Track Motion dialog.

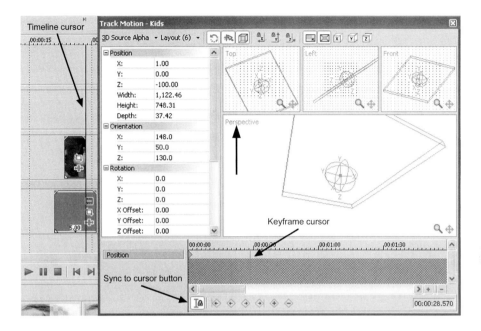

9.24 The window view may be varied by selecting the window description in the upper-left corner of the dialog. Notice the Sync to Cursor button in the lower-left corner of the keyframe dialog. This will sync the cursor in the Track Motion keyframe dialog to match the location of the cursor on the Timeline.

In the lower portion of the Track Motion dialog, the Perspective window is found. When the cursor is rolled over the center, or location of media, a box will highlight. This box indicates the X, Y, and Z axes of the media.

Roll the cursor over the edge of this box, and a small circle will appear in the corner of the spatial indicator box. Click and drag on this circle, enlarging the image. Notice how the numeric values in the Width, Height, and Depth dialogs change in the Positioning window.

Drag the corner of the spatial indicator box until the Z value reaches 3732 in size. If you try to input the numeric value, the aspect ratio of the media will change unless you have Lock Aspect Ratio enabled.

Beneath the Orientation group, you'll find the Rotation group. In this group, the media may be rotated on any of its three axes. For this exercise, click on the keyframe that was newly created in the previous step, in which the size of the media was dragged larger. Now select the Z plane in the Rotation dialog, and input a value of −60 by manually entering the value, using the spinner, or using the slider to set the value.

Like all other tools within Vegas, double-clicking the slider will reset the slider to default value. This is very useful when finding yourself a little lost in the early stages of learning the 3D tools.

Double-click the file and press the spacebar to begin playback of the file. Notice how it flies across the Preview window and rotates.

To see an example of how this functions, open the 3D#2.veg file found on the DVD in the back of the book. It may also be located on the vasst.com web site.

3D composites will greatly slow the rendering process, and working with 3D media in nested VEG files can be hard for even the fastest CPUs to process. I recommend rendering 3D media whenever possible.

Nesting Composites

Another great feature found in Vegas is the nested compositing tools. In earlier versions of Vegas, the compositing tools were powerful but were limited in creating in-depth composites. Vegas can have multiple tracks entirely controlled   by one parent track. Individual tracks may have their own motion in space using 3D or 2D tools, with a master composite track controlling all tracks beneath it that are assigned to it. This is great for building monster composites and having one final track control them. In the audio world, this is similar to a mixdown, with a master volume, pan, and effects. The tracks of video are all controlled by the master. In the case of nested tracks, even the master track may have its own 3D properties, as well, that affect all tracks nested, or acting as children to the parent or master.

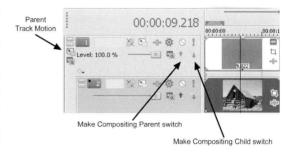

9.25 For those familiar with earlier versions of Vegas, parent/child switching is slightly different, due to the nested compositing modes.

Follow these steps to understand the basics of parent/child tracks:

1. Create four new video tracks (Ctrl+Shift+Q).

2. In tracks 2–4, place either video or generated media.

3. On each track, open the Track Motion dialog, turn on 3D Alpha mode, and create 3D motion in each track so that all three tracks reveal themselves at some point in the project.

4. In each track header, there is a Parent/Child switch. Press the switch to cause all tracks to act as child tracks beneath the parent.

5. In track 1, open the Parent Track Motion dialog, and enable the 3D Alpha mode on the parent track.

6. Create movements on that track, using X, Y, and Z planes; orientation; and rotation. All three tracks beneath the parent will respond to the parent track motion regardless of their own motion.

7. In the parent track, insert text or other form of media.

8. In the track header of the parent track, click the Track Motion button. Enable 3D Alpha Channel mode in this dialog. Assign 3D motion in this dialog as well, creating keyframes to animate the track. This track animation is independent of the other three tracks that are children to the parent track, yet the parent track controls this track's motion as well.

So in the composite created above, there are five track motion elements occurring at one time. Each of the four tracks has its own track motion element, with the parent track controlling each of these tracks in a separate motion path. You also may need to move the parent position by a few pixels to see the shadow or glow beneath the child tracks.

As you are working on individual tracks, notice that the track header number contains a small blinking indicator signifying which track is being affected by whatever process is being applied. This is particularly helpful when working on parent/child comps, as this makes it clear as to which track is currently selected. Even when multiple tracks are selected, only the number of the track whose properties are going to be affected will blink.

Effects may be set up to be pre- or postprocess in the Keyframing tool for that particular effect. Pressing the Pre/Post toggle button in the effect will instruct Vegas when to process the media with that specific filter. Tracks in 3D mode may not be pre- or posttoggled.

Select the Pre/Post toggle button in the Keyframing tool for each effect. Vegas will automatically reroute or reorder filter position for you.

9.26a If the triangle points left, it's precompositing, and if it points right, it's postcompositing in behavior.

Parental Guidance/Shadows and Glow

Another benefit of a master parent track is that all child tracks may be assigned a master shadow or glow. This allows for a more cohesive composite as opposed to creating separate shadows and glows individually.

In the composition created earlier, open the Parent Track Motion, and disable the 3D Alpha Channel mode.

To the left of the keyframing Timeline in the Track Motion dialog is a checkbox for Shadow and for Glow. Enable the Shadow, and you'll see that the child tracks have shadow showing where the background allows it to be seen. You may need to create a nonchild track at the bottom of the Timeline that contains a white generated media slug to see the shadow, depending on the color of your shadow and media content.

You can also insert a white slug on the parent track, and insert a compositing envelope on the parent track. This will allow the parent track to control opacity of all nested media. Open the

Rings-opacity.veg file found on the disk in the back of this book. Notice how the parent tracks control opacity of tracks nested as child tracks. Move the handles on the composite envelopes on the tracks to get a feel for how this works.

To insert a composite envelope to control nested tracks:

1. Create the composite as you'd like it to appear.

2. Insert a new video track above the composition.

3. Parent the new video track to the tracks beneath.

4. In the new parent track, choose the compositing mode tool in the header, and select Multiply/Mask mode.

5. Choose the Parent Track Motion button in the parent track. In this track, you'll assign 3D motion (or any other motion) to the child tracks. Assign any motion you would like, if any. Otherwise, right-click the track header and insert a compositing envelope. Double-click the compositing envelope to assign handles to the envelope, allowing the opacity or transparency of the track to be adjusted.

Glows and shadows will be cleaner in the 32-bit modes available in Vegas, but beware of the hit on render times.

Ten-Bit Color and 32-Bit (Floating) Processing

Vegas Pro 8 users will enjoy the addition of 10-bit color sampling and 32-bit float processing. The addition of 10-bit capability has been long desired.

Ten-bit color sampling adds an additional 2 bits per color channel when ingesting video. This represents the number of levels per color channel. Older versions of Vegas offer 8 bits per channel (the same as most cameras shoot), which equates to 256 levels of color per channel; 10-bit offers 1024 levels per channel, or four times more brightness levels than 8-bit offers.

However, the availability of 10-bit video doesn't immediately mean that your video quality will increase.

Where 10-bit video offers some significant benefit is when video is captured as 10-bit and is to be color corrected, composited, or worked within an SDI (serial digital interface) workflow for broadcasting or higher-end postproduction workflows. Ten-bit is the standard in all midlevel to high-level postproduction houses and in all broadcast facilities.

To benefit from 10-bit video sampling, a hardware card that supports 10-bit video is required. Currently, the AJA Xena LH and the Xena LHe are the only fully supported cards. The Blackmagic Design DeckLink cards have offered 8-bit support in Sony Vegas since version 5, and at the time of this writing there were no drivers for Vegas Pro 8. Blackmagic Design have stated that they'll release drivers for their products for use in Vegas Pro 8.

Video shot on an 8-bit format such as DV, HDV, XDCAM, and HDCAM will still benefit when captured as 10-bit video, due to how the codec will work with the video and how the codec will respond to color correction and other processing.

At the end of the day, this can be said: 10-bit video simply looks better than 8-bit video. The question of whether to go 10-bit isn't about the quality, but about the associated costs of building a 10-bit workflow. Ten-bit video will require more hard drive space, faster hard drives, an

HD/SD SDI card, and perhaps an HD/SD SDI monitor, depending on workflow. All of these additional requirements may easily increase the cost of an editing system by a factor of 10.

One of the immediately visible benefits of the 32-bit floating point process is seen if you're shooting sky, water, or any other large area that contains a single graduated color. In 8-bit processing, the image will display banding at some point, but with a 32-bit float, the banding disappears.

Thirty-two-bit floating point is a different feature; no hardware card is needed for users of Vegas Pro 8 to benefit.

Thirty-two-bit floating point is a processing function. The primary benefit of 32-bit floating point is a far more precise processing of frame information. What this means in layman's terms is that gradients will be smoother, edges of blurred edges or motion information will be softer, and fades will be smoother. Transitions that blend information will also be better overall. Thirty-two-bit processing will use significantly more system resources than 8-bit processing, so be prepared for longer renders and slower previews.

Vegas Pro 8 offers three modes of working with media (these processing bits should not be confused with color bits):

- 8-bit processing (this is the standard of previous versions of Vegas)
- 32-bit processing with 1.00 gamma
- 32-bit processing with 2.222 gamma

The 32-bit mode with 1.00 gamma may decode video differently, depending on the source media. XDCAM, HDV, and AVCHD format media will all decode differently. This may create problems if you're not sure exactly what the footage should look like. Additionally, the footage is decoded to computer RGB vs studio RGB. This means that rather than being confined to the broadcast standard of 16–235 RGB, the video will be decoded to 0–255 RGB. This isn't going to be a problem for media destined for DVD or the web, but it could potentially create problems for media heading for broadcast. Additionally, bear in mind that previewing on an external broadcast monitor will not deliver accurate results, as the media is being converted back to 16–235 (IRE standards) on output.

Additionally, some of the FX in Vegas will not function accurately when working with 1.00 mode; experiment with various FX to get an idea of how they may function. Dissolves, crossfades, and similar transitions will be smoother and more cinema-like. Titles will be richer and deeper in color and may blend better with underlaid video, but the transparency level of the titles may behave differently as well.

Some of the FX that ship with Vegas, and most of the third-party FX available for Sony Vegas, are 8-bit only. The 8-bit FX are indicated by a small blue square next to the FX in the FX window. Using these FX will always force the video stream to be processed in 8 bits.

HDV, AVCHD, MXF IMX and HD, Sony YUV (8- and 10-bit), and uncompressed RGB floating point formats read directly into 32-bit floating point without going through 8-bit first. HDV, AVCHD, MXF IMX and HD, and Sony YUV (8- and 10-bit) formats may render without passing through 8-bit. Video FX and transitions with blue squares appearing next to the FX/ Transition name are not floating-point capable, and the image will be reduced to 8-bit before using these plug-ins.

The decision to work in 32-bit modes in Vegas Pro 8 is one that should best be made prior to beginning a project. FX and some transitions may display different results between the 1.00

and the 2.222 gamma modes. To get an idea of how this may affect you, create a Timeline and place a couple of HDV, AVCHD, or XDCAM files on the Timeline. Create cross-fades with them, and add color correction to the files or track. Switch between the gamma modes in the Project Properties and observe the changes. Choose one mode or the other prior to beginning the project for consistent results. A good rule of thumb when choosing 32-bit is to start with 2.222 gamma, as this has a color profile similar to that of standard 8-bit. But, try alternate settings for the most appropriate look.

9.26b   The Levels filter set to 2.222.

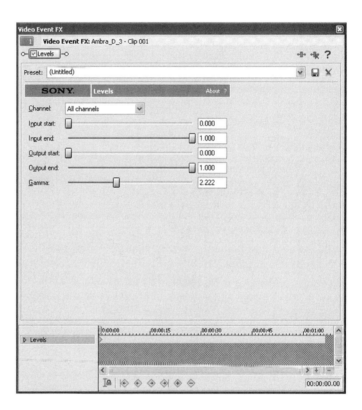

The Levels filter may be used to correct media that isn't correct in a 1.00 gamma project. Be sure the Pre/Post toggle is set to Pre (facing left).

There are some workarounds to working with 1.00 gamma projects that may be creating problems. If the 1.00 gamma project offers the desired results in compositing, creating blurs, diffusion, or effects that benefit from the linear light processing found in the 1.00 mode, build those segments in a 1.00 gamma Timeline and nest this Timeline in a 2.222 gamma project. Another option is to work in a 1.00 gamma project, but apply the Levels filter with a gamma setting of 2.22 at the track level. Place media that should receive linear light processing on one track, and create another track for media that, when processed, doesn't meet the desired appearance with the 1.00 gamma setting. When you drop the Levels filter on the track, you'll want it to process first in any chain or spatial change made to the media (such as Pan/Crop) so select the Pre/Post switch in the plug-in chain.

When will you see absolute benefit from 32-bit floating point processing?

As mentioned before, HDV, AVCHD, and XDCAM projects become richer as a result of the difference in decoding. Additionally media from AVCHD and HDV camcorders that offer XV color will also be significantly more rich and saturated. If the 10-bit YUV codec is used via an AJA Xena card, this media, too, will benefit from the 32-bit floating point process. Standard DV will benefit when you color correct and push color; the banding normally associated with pushed DV/8-bit disappears.

Rotated Display Functions

It's hard to go through an airport, nightclub, office building, or other high-traffic area without seeing vertically mounted displays. The Rotated Display tools in Vegas Pro 8 make this type of content creation very easy and fast. Media can be rotated +90, 180, or −90° in angle.

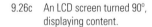
9.26c   An LCD screen turned 90°, displaying content.

Rotated projects begin in the Project Properties settings. Open the Project Properties by browsing to FILE | PROPERTIES | VIDEO. In the upper portion of the Properties dialog is a dropdown menu.

Note that there are three options; the 90° angles are the most common angles for creating display media and the 180° angle is most commonly used for editing footage that has come from footage recorded using a 35mm adapter on the lens, such as the RedRock Micro adapter (these

9.26d Project Property settings
for rotated displays.

sorts of adapters turn the video upside down during the recording process).

Set the rotation to the desired angle in the drop-down box and select Apply. This will rotate the display in the Preview window to the desired angle (if 180° was chosen, no visible change will occur).

Producing Rotated Media

The best method for creating vertical content is to shoot at a 90° angle. Many professional tripods

9.26e RedRock Micro M2 mounted on a camera.

allow for a camera to be rotated to a 90° angle. Shooting in this manner allows for a stable video recording and will provide for a higher-quality finished product. Handheld shots are much more noticeable in a vertical display than in a horizontal display due to the unique nature of the display and the difference from what the eye is familiar with.

Any media on the Timeline will maintain the original aspect ratio; it will simply become smaller in the display.

Nonvertical files placed on the Vegas Timeline will require some additional attention if you want the file to fill the vertical screen. There are two methods of managing the video.

Right-clicking the video event and selecting Properties from the menu displays a Rotation option in the Media tab. Set the media to rotate and match the Project Properties setting. If the video was created using a rotated camera, this is the method best used.

Another option is to right-click the file and choose Pan/Crop (or use the Pan/Crop shortcut button found on all video events). In the Pan/Crop dialog, right-click the open area and choose Match Output Aspect. This will crop the video so that it fills the

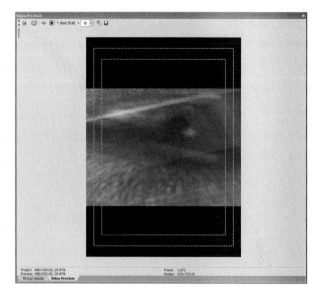

9.26f

display. Be aware that resolution will be lost in the process and video may look soft.

Graphics may be created in any image editor; simply change the rotation in the image editor to match the Project Properties after the rotation has been applied. Generally, images will be 480 × 655 or 576 × 702 when working with SD media and 720 × 1280, 1440 × 1080, or 1920 × 1080 when working with HD media.

Titles created in Vegas after Project Properties have been established will be of the correct aspect/rotation angle (regardless of working with the ProType Title tool or the legacy title tools found in Vegas). Be aware of the narrow restrictions in this mode.

9.26g

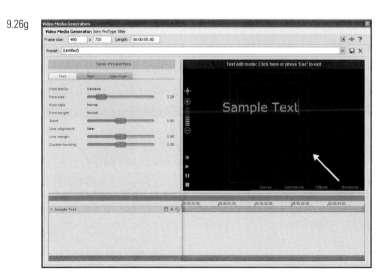

Optimal Preview is achieved by tearing the Preview window from the docked area and double-clicking the header bar of the Preview window.

9.26h   Vegas Preview window in a
          Rotated Display project.

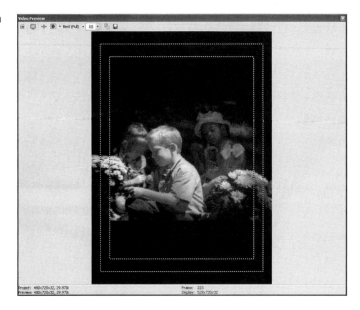

When working with Cookie Cutter and other masking FX, the aspect of the mask may need to be changed, as most masks and FX are designed to function horizontally. Either modify the mask in a graphic editor or use Track Motion tools to modify/stretch the mask to fill the vertical display.

Playback of rotated media should be at full frame rate or frame rates identical to similar media playing in horizontal modes.

Generated Media

Vegas has the ability to create or generate media using nothing but plug-ins (no physical file is required) that can generate titles, solid colors, noise, gradients, checkerboards, and other graphic elements. You can quickly and easily generate colors for inserted media, masks, filling backgrounds under titles that don't have associated video or graphic events, and many other uses.

To learn how to create generated media, insert a new video track on a new project by right-clicking the Track Control pane and choosing Insert New Video Track or by pressing Ctrl+Shift+Q. Right-click in the Timeline area of the new track and choose Insert Generated Media from the menu. The Generated Media dialog opens.

9.27 The Solid Color dialog box is used to define solid colors on the Timeline.

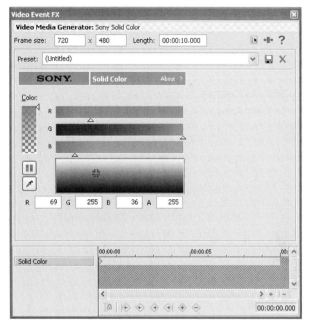

Select Sony Solid Color. The Solid Color dialog box opens, and you can select the color of choice. For this exercise, choose black.

After setting the color, set the length of time that the event should last and close the dialog by clicking the X in the upper-right corner of the dialog. A black event now appears on the screen.

Click the Event FX button found on the event, or right-click and choose Event FX.

From the FX dialog, select two plug-ins: Add Noise and Black Restore. Both can be selected at the same time by pressing and holding Ctrl down while selecting the second FX plug-in. On the top/header of the plug-ins dialog, you should see both FX names displayed.

Click the Add Noise box. In the Add Noise plug-in dialog box, uncheck the "Animate" check-box, and slide the Noise Level slider to 1.0. In the Black Restore dialog, set the threshold for 0.600.

You have just created a star field from nothing more than computer-generated media.

To add more media to the star field to make it more realistic or interesting, insert a new video track above the existing track. Right-click in the Timeline area and choose Insert Generated Media just as you did before.

Now follow these steps:

1. Choose Sony Color Gradient.

2. Select Sunburst from the menu. Notice that by moving the target marker around in the Gradient Preview screen, the curve of the gradient can be adjusted.

3. Define the length of time that the event should occur. This length of time should be the same length of time as the previous event created. Now close the dialog.

The new gradient now covers the entire Preview screen. To show only the portions that are to be actually seen, select the Video FX tab on the bottom left of the screen or click the Event FX button found on the new gradient. Choose the Cookie Cutter FX plug-in.

In the Cookie Cutter dialog, select the Arrowhead in the Shapes menu. The screen can still be covered with the Sunburst image. Using the Size slider, size the arrowhead so it is not filling the entire Preview window. A size of around 0.050 is a good choice. Close the Cookie Cutter dialog.

Now open the Track Motion dialog on the track with the arrowhead. Place the cursor on the upper-left corner handle of the frame. The cursor will change into a circular shape, indicating that the Track Motion tool is prepared to rotate the frame.

Rotate the frame so that the arrowhead in the Preview window is pointing at the lower-right corner of the Preview window.

Click and hold in the middle of the Track Motion frame and slide the frame to the upper-left corner of the frame window. The arrowhead in the Preview window will move to the same location and should remain pointed at the lower-right corner.

Enable the sync cursor in the Track Motion Keyframe section. In the Timeline, place the cursor on the right edge of the generated media event. In the Track Motion tool, move the frame to the lower-right corner. A new keyframe will be inserted in the Timeline as a result of the sync cursor being enabled.

9.28 The cursor changed to a rotating cursor, used for rotating the frame inside the Track Motion tool.

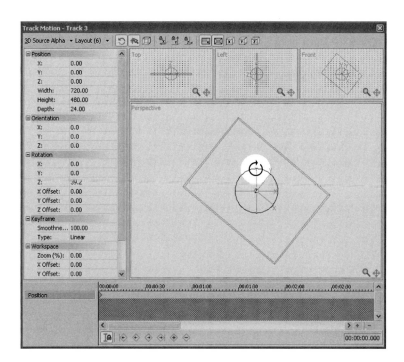

Now press the spacebar or click Play on the Transport control. You should see the arrowhead flying across the star field, and if the loop is enabled (press Q), the arrowhead/starship will fly across the screen from the upper left to the lower right.

9.29 Flames created with glow give a realistic edge to the starship.

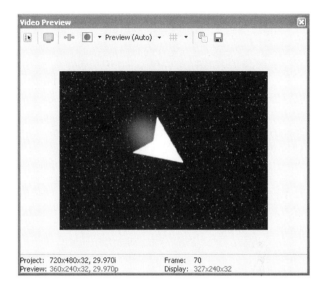

Adding an orange glow and sizing it to cover only the back of the arrowhead will create a flame coming out of the back of the arrowhead/starship. By animating the feather, opacity, and intensity of the glow, the flames can come to life, moving at different depths and opacity, giving a realistic sense of video to an otherwise static image.

This project can be found on the DVD included in this book and is labeled composite rocket.veg. The keyframes animating the flame are also found on the VEG file.

Credit Rolls

Inserting a credit roll is one of the generated media options in Vegas. Credit rolls are used for more than only titling at the end of a video project; they are great for showing specific product information, creating introductions to a video, or creating fast-moving numbers or letters for a specific effect, particularly when used at reduced opacities.

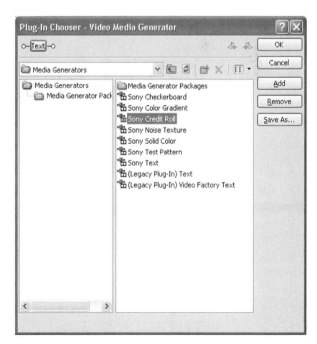

9.30 The Credit Roll plug in is found in the Generated Media chooser.

Insert a credit roll by right-clicking a track and selecting Insert Generated Media from the sub-menu. In the Generated Media chooser, select Credit Roll from the listing of available generated media types.

The Credit Roll plug-in offers many choices to manage text in the credit roll. Three text settings are allowed in the roll: a Title Text (headline), Subitem Text (main topic), and Item Left/Item Right (subtopics). Each of the three settings can have its own font size, color, style, and position.

The type of line can be adjusted by clicking next to the field in which the text will be entered. For example, a single line of text can be either a Title Text field or a Subitem Text field.

✍ Tip

You can also use the standard title tool and the Pan/Crop tool to create credit rolls. Simply type text into the Text Generator for its full length, then use the Pan/Crop tool to pan up/down the generated text, creating a very controllable credit roll. This method offers more options than the standard credit roll function.

The type of text is selected by clicking the small box next to the input field. Clicking in the field allows you to input text into the field.

In the Style dialog, kerning, spacing, and connecting styles, such as dashes or dots, can all be specified. All aspects of the credit roll can be keyframed. Because of the nature of the credit roll and generated media, there is no sync cursor ability.

The length of the event determines the speed of the credit roll, and the number of lines determines how fast the roll moves through the length of time. Longer event lengths with fewer lines create a very slow crawl, whereas short event lengths with several lines scroll more quickly.

From the Properties dialog, a timed sequence can be created. In a timed sequence, titles can be zoomed in and out, faded in and out, and slid from the bottom, top, and side depending on the selection in the menu. The number of lines and length of credit roll event determine the length of time of each title image on-screen.

By default, credit rolls are of transparent background. Background colors, transparency, and letter colors, however, can all be adjusted. Shadows and glows are not options in the Credit Roll.

Using the 3D Track Motion tools, DebugMode 3D plug-in, a bump map, or a height map (discussed later in this chapter) can add a number of options and creative ability to the credit roll.

✍ Tip

To add a shadow or glow to a credit roll, open Track Motion. Leave the track position at default but check the "Shadow" or "Glow" (or both) checkbox. These settings add a shadow or glow to the characters on the credit roll. These can be keyframed on or off or for position if the shadow or glow is desired to flow different from the direction of the credit roll.

✍ Tip

If credit rolls have jagged edges or aliasing, try resizing the generated media to double size, or 1440 × 960, and reducing opacity of the credit roll to 98 rather than 100 percent. Don't use fonts with serifs or fine linens. Adding .001/.002 of Gaussian blur can sometimes help clean up soft edges on credit rolls, as can the Unsharp Mask filter.

9.31 Selecting the Styles tab allows parameters for each of the three styles to be adjusted. Clicking the Style button on the left side of the Credit Roll plug-in chooses which text style the line will present.

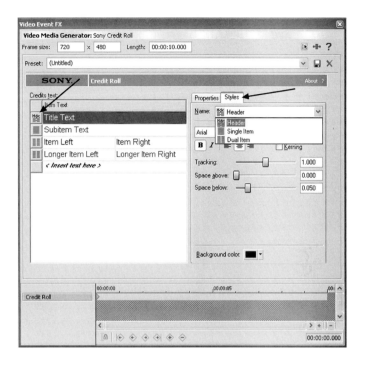

9.32 Connect the left and right credits on the scroll with dashes, dots, or lines.

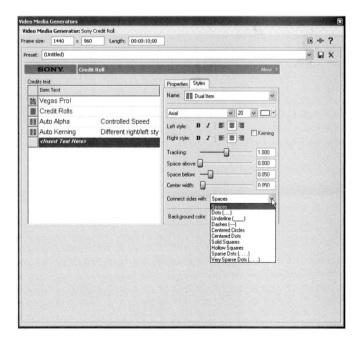

9.33 Using Track Motion in 3D mode(or using the DebugMode3D LE plug-in), text can be angled on the screen, resembling a wall or doorway. Height mapping can be used to wrap the text on a textured surface.

Creating/Using Masks in Vegas

Masks are exceptionally powerful tools for creating composited media. The generated media project created earlier contained a mask, inserted with the Cookie Cutter plug-in.

Masks can be made from just about any photo editing tool, font, or shape that exists. Vegas autosenses an alpha channel from most images that contain them and has options to force recognition of an alpha channel if it is not automatically sensed.

To force Vegas to recognize an alpha channel if it is not seeing the channel automatically, right-click the event containing the alpha channel. Select Properties from the submenu that appears. Select the Media tab in the Properties window, and at the bottom is a menu labeled Alpha Channel. Next to this, locate a dropdown list that offers several choices. Select Premultiplied from the menu.

An alpha channel defines the areas you want to be transparent. Each image on the video screen comprises four channels: red, green, blue, and alpha. The alpha channel acts as a mask, instructing the other channels on how the pixels should blend or merge. Alpha channels can have gradations, allowing the blending of multiple images on top of one another at various levels of transparency. Another way to understand how an alpha channel functions is to imagine a stencil laid over an object and a can of spray paint. The alpha channel reveals the events beneath, much as a stencil reveals the object beneath. Alpha channels usually display transparent areas as white space, whereas hidden areas are displayed in black.

Masks can either hide or reveal information/images in a video project, allowing image areas to be defined within an event. Another name for a mask is a matte or a key. All terms mean the same thing: hiding or revealing an area so another image can show through, or hiding an area so that another image can be composed over the top of it. In any definition, a mask, matte, or key defines the transparent pixels of an image for superimposing or revealing another image.

Just as titles are one of the simplest forms of compositing, they are also one of the most viable uses of masking. Titling is an excellent method of learning exactly how a mask works.

9.34 Right-clicking and selecting PROPERTIES | MEDIA allows alpha channel recognition to be forced if an alpha channel is present.

Open a new project in Vegas. Insert three new video tracks. Choose a video or still file to serve as a background. To create the mask, place the video or still image on track 3.

Place a title on track 1. Do not use fonts that contain serifs or small lines. A font such as Impact or Arial Black will serve best as you learn this technique.

On track 2, place a video file that has high motion with bright colors for the best effect in the learning stage.

The text is a mask but is not seen as such just yet. On the extreme left side of the Track Control pane, there is a small arrow pointing upward, which is the Make Compositing Child (parent/child) button. Clicking this button will cause all areas of track 2 to become transparent. The only portions of track 2 that are seen are seen inside the letters of track 1. Click this button.

The event on track 2 disappears and becomes visible only inside the title letters. The letters are a mask; the letters become the parent, and the event beneath becomes the child. This process causes the parent to instruct the child how to be shown. Multiple tracks can be the child, but only one track can be the parent. As many parent and child relationships as necessary can exist across multiple tracks; however, no child track can have more than one parent. If multiple parents are required of a child track, the child track must be duplicated.

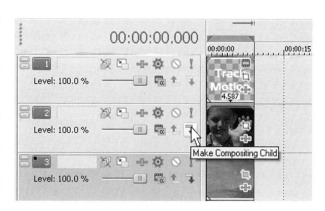

9.35　The Parent/Child button is found on the left side of every video track.

To gain a better understanding of the masking process, change the color of the text on track 1 to black. It will cause the letters to become invisible. Reset the color of the title to white to continue this section.

This process is masking in its most basic form. Any image that contains transparent/alpha information can be used in place of a title. To continue the concept of manipulating the title appearance, however, keep this project on the Timeline.

In track 1, right-click the title to edit it or click the Edit Generated Media button found on the title event. The Title tool opens. Navigate to the Effects tab and select a shadow on the text. The shadow can't be seen. Changing the color of the shadow will result in the shadow being seen.

9.36　The video of track 2 (the child) shows through the letters of track 1 (parent track).

To place a shadow on the mask, or to place letters in this instance, select the Track Motion tool on track 1. In the Track Motion tool, check the "Shadow" checkbox. A shadow will appear beneath the mask/letters on the Preview screen. This shadow can be keyframed in exactly the same way that a shadow in a normal track motion instance would be keyed. Color, size, feathering, transparency, and position can all be user-defined using keyframes.

Open your favorite photo editing application. In the application, create a new project/photo image that is 655 × 480 pixels for NTSC or 704 × 576 for PAL. Flood the entire work area with black.

Paint a design or shape in the work area, using white as the color. Save the design as a PNG file for best results. A GIF, JPEG, TIF, or Targa will also work.

Open a new project in Vegas. Create three new video tracks. Place the new image on the Timeline on track 1. The Explorer might need to be refreshed to see it in its newly saved location. Refresh the Explorer by clicking the Refresh button on the Explorer toolbar.

Insert the media that should be showing through the mask on track 2. The length of the event doesn't matter, as the length of the parent event determines how long the underlying event is visible. (Of course, if the child event is shorter than the parent event, the child will not be seen for the full length either.)

On track 3, insert an event that contains video or a still image that functions as the background image.

9.37   You can have fun while learning to make masks.

9.38 Adding a shadow to the mask with the Track Motion Shadow tool. Glow can also be added to a mask.

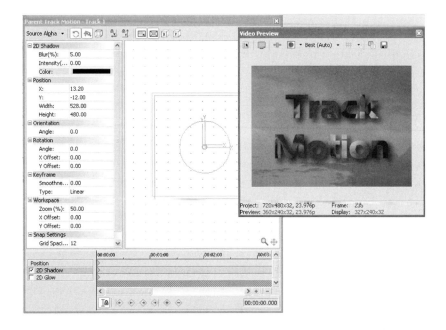

9.39 Any shape can be used to create a mask, so long as it contains a mask and an alpha image.

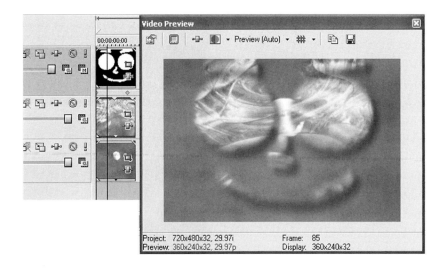

In a gradient mask, white areas are revealed, whereas black areas are hidden. When using other colors as the mask, the closer a color is to white, the more revealed it becomes, whereas just the opposite is true for gradient colors approaching black in value. However, when using other colors in a mask, those colors reduce the opacity of the underlying image.

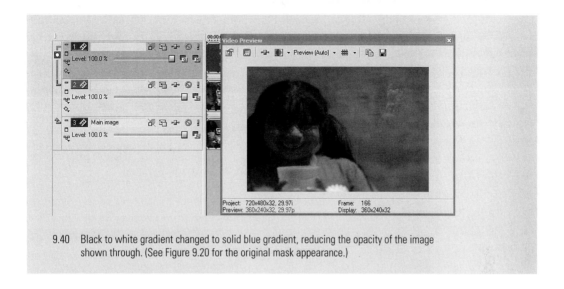

9.40   Black to white gradient changed to solid blue gradient, reducing the opacity of the image shown through. (See Figure 9.20 for the original mask appearance.)

Now click the Parent/Child button on track 2, and the image you created becomes transparent, except the visible mask areas, which now show the event on track 2.

Filters can be applied to the events on the child track, which will affect how the events on track 2 are shown. Applying blurs will blend the mask into the underlying events.

Another means of creating a mask in Vegas is to use generated media to define what will be masked out. One useful way to do this process is to create a mask that splits the screen in two or three parts, using blur and mask to create a completely smooth transition from one side to the other.

To create a split screen with a seamless transition:

1.   Insert three video tracks. Track 1 is for the mask, track 2 for one half of the screen, and track 3 for the remaining half of the screen.

2.   Insert the desired events on tracks 2 and 3.

3.   On track 1, insert generated media by right-clicking in the track 1 area of the Timeline and selecting Insert Generated Media. In the Media Generator plug-in dialog, select Sony Solid Color and choose white as the color.

4.   Select the Pan/Crop tool on the generated media by right-clicking or by clicking the Pan/Crop button found on the media. In the Pan/Crop Preview window, slide the frame to the right until it divides the frame in half. (The Center should be at 720 and 240.) Close the Pan/Crop dialog box.

5.   On track 2, click the Parent/Child button on the right side of track header. This step will cause the screen to split in half, showing track 2 on the left side of the screen, as it is being masked by track 1 and the pan/cropped image. If the images on tracks 2 and 3 are not centered, the Pan/Crop tool should be applied to the images to center them.

6. With the screen split, apply a Gaussian blur to the event on track 1 either by dragging the blur to the event from the Video FX docking window or by clicking the Event FX button on the solid color event on track 1. Apply the blur to the desired setting.

7. This process can also be applied in a series of two transitions as well, by adding two more tracks to the project. This step will display three split sections. Pan/Crop will need to be applied in opposite directions and in thirds of the screen.

☞ Tip

The project shown in Figure 9.43 can be found on the DVD in this book. The filename is 3screen.veg.

9.41 Splitting the screen with the Parent/ Child feature.

9.42 Splitting the screen into three parts is fast and simple with masks made from Generated Media.

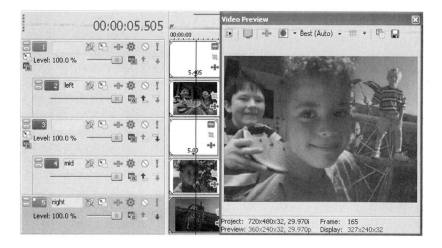

9.43 Access the Mask Generator by clicking the Mask FX button found on any parent/child combination.

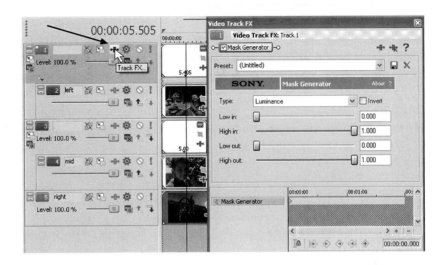

Vegas also has a Mask Generator for every video track parented to another.

Five different mask modes are available in the Mask Generator dialog. Each mode blends or masks media differently, based on color or luminance found within the parent image, and they are described here:

- Luminance—uses luminance in the image to determine transparency.

- Alpha—uses an alpha channel to determine transparency.

- Red channel—uses the color red to determine transparency.

- Blue channel—uses the color blue to determine transparency.

- Green channel—uses the color green to determine transparency.

Open the colorchannel.veg file on the DVD included with this book.

Use the Low in/High in sliders to limit or delimit the information in the child events in the parent/child relationship. These attributes are keyframable and can be used to limit/delimit transparency of a channel over time. Use this tool as one alternative to animate lines on a map, create handwriting on an image, or mask out a color channel over time.

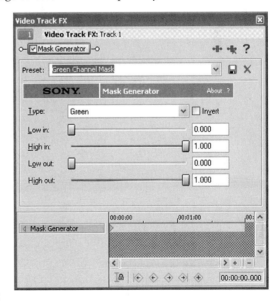

9.44 Specific color channel controls determine the transparency of that color's channel.

There are many creative ways to use masks in Vegas. Using masks, a reflection of text can be quickly composited.

Open a new project. Insert six video tracks. Do the following steps in order:

1. On track 6, insert a background image. For purposes of this exercise, use generated media, preferably a color gradient.

2. Double-click the media on track 6 to create a selection. On track 5, right-click to insert text media. For this exercise, keep the text to one single line. Use a creative font for best results.

3. On track 4, with the selection still active from double-clicking track 6, right-click and select INSERT GENERATED MEDIA | SONY COLOR GRADIENT. (If the selection is not active, double-click track 6 again) In the Gradient dialog, select the Linear White to Black from the menu. In the Aspect Ratio Angle dialog box, enter a value of 37. In the keyframe Timeline of the Color Gradient dialog, click the Last Keyframe Button to move the cursor in the dialog to the end of the selection/event. Rotate the Aspect Ratio Angle to −180.0, which will cause the gradient to rotate in the project. Now select the Parent/Child button on the right of track 7.

4. Right-click the text on track 5 and select Copy. Right-click in track 3 and select Paste. Vegas will ask if you wish to create a reference to existing media or if you wish to create a new copy. Select New Copy.

5. On track 5, select the Track Motion button. In the Track Motion dialog box, right-click in the Track Motion Preview window and select Flip Vertical. The "F" in the Preview window will now be upside down in the Preview window. Now resize the track preview to 947.1 × 568.3. Center the image at 360.0 × 360.0.

6. Still working on the event on track 5, insert the following event FX: Add Noise, Gaussian Blur, Deform, and Light Rays. These plug-ins create the illusion of a reflected surface. Set the Add Noise plug-in to 0.168, with MonoChromatic and Gaussian Noise boxes checked. In the Gaussian Blur dialog, set the Horizontal value at 0.023 and Vertical at 0. In the Deform dialog, set the Amount to 1.00. Check the "Center Image" box. Leaving the Left and Right sliders set at 0, set the Top slider value to −0.209 and the Bottom slider value to 0.510. Finally, set the Light Rays to the values shown in Figure 9.45.

7. Place the cursor in the center of the Light Rays keyframe Timeline. Set the Strength value to .550 and move the Light Source indicator to the center of the Preview box. Move the cursor to the end of the keyframe Timeline in the Light Rays keyframe Timeline. Set the Strength value to .250 and move the Light Source indicator to the far right of the Preview box.

8. Right-click the mask on track 4 and select Copy. Paste this copy on track 2. Once again, Vegas will ask whether a new copy should be created or a reference to the original file should be made. Create a new copy. Click the Edit Generated Media button found on the generated media on track 2. In the Aspect Ratio Angle dialog, on the first keyframe, enter a value of 0.0. Now click the last Keyframe button in the keyframe

9.45   Light ray values.

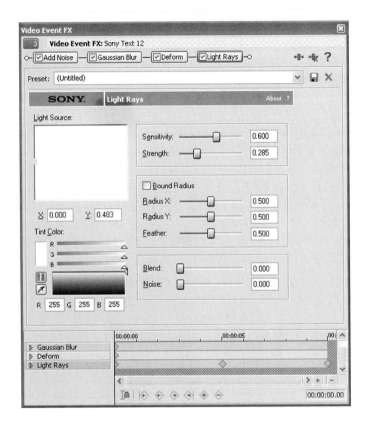

9.46   Settling values.

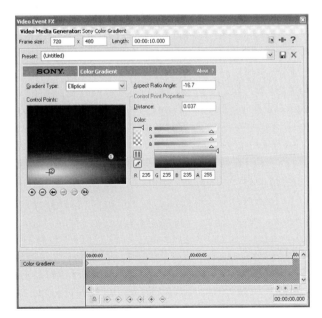

Timeline and enter a value of −180.0. On track 3, click the Parent/Child button to cause track 2 to be a parent to the text event found on track 3.

9.   Create a selection again by double-clicking any event on the Timeline. On track 1, place a Sony color gradient. In the Gradient dialog box, set the values to the settings shown in Figure 9.46.

9.47   Creating a reflective surface is very fast and requires no additional plug-ins.

Use the RAM Preview Render setting by creating a selection of all the media and pressing Shift+B. Vegas will take a moment to render the project to RAM. Be sure that RAM preview is set to the maximum available amount in the OPTIONS | PREFERENCES | VIDEO dialog. The default setting is 16MB of RAM. To render this project, you'll need at least 300MB of RAM available.

Compositing Modes in Vegas

Vegas has 14 different compositing modes. Source Alpha is the default mode, whereas additional modes can be used for a number of image manipulation and creative settings.

9.48   Compositing Mode button on each video track.

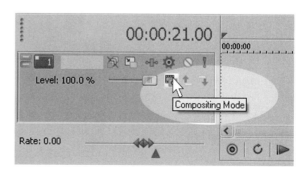

9.49   Various compositing modes in Vegas.

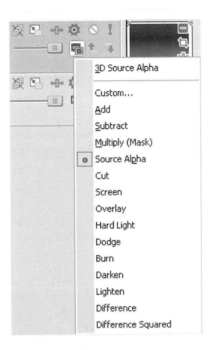

9.50   Original foreground and background events.

Compositing modes define the manner in which a higher track combines with a lower track. As higher-level tracks dominate, for purposes of reference, the higher-level tracks are referred to as foreground, and lower-level tracks are referred to as background.

Compositing Mode tools allow for rapid access to creating multilayered images quickly. Compositing mode parameters are not adjustable. Using compositing envelopes allows you to adjust compositing level, or color management plug-ins can be used to provide opacity, chroma (color), and transparency control over all events. For instance, in the Add mode, using the Color Correction Secondary plug-in, combined with blur, creates a moving sonic wave. Using the Screen mode creates a more organic property in the sonic wave, almost as if it were a moving cloud.

When tracks become parented to one or more lower tracks, a new icon will appear in the Track Control pane of the uppermost track of the parent/child set. This is the Parent Track Overlay Mode button.

The Parent Track Overlay Mode button provides options to manage masked events above other events.

Out-of-focus video is sometimes an issue with even the most experienced of videographers. Using the Hard Light composite mode and a plug-in or two, marginally out-of-focus video can be brought to a faked focus or, at the least, a more sharpened image.

Place the problem footage on a track and duplicate the track. On the upper track, apply the Convolution filter and the Sharpen preset in the Convolution filter. Reduce the opacity of the upper track to approximately 50 percent. Various settings will apply to individual events. On the lower track, apply a Hard Light compositing mode.

Some events with good color balance can also benefit by applying a Hard Light overlay mode in the compositing modes selection.

9.51   Before and after applying Hard Light and Convolution Kernel filter.

9.52   Parent Track Overlay Mode button.

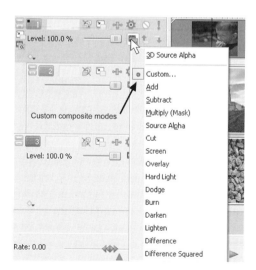

9.53   Parent Track Overlay
mode.

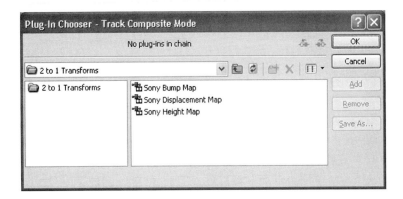

When you select this button, there are two menu choices. The first is the default Multiply mode, and the second is Custom. Selecting Custom opens a dialog offering three compositing overlay modes: Displacement Map, Height Map, and Bump Map.

Displacement Map

This mode uses the parent image as a controller to offset the pixels in the composited child tracks along the X and Y axes. This process uses a two-channel displacement. In other words, pixels are displaced to the left, to the right, up, or down depending on their relationship to colors in the mask. The displacement map is also useful for following contours of shapes.

9.54

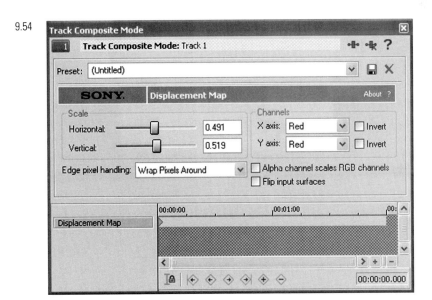

This plug-in can be challenging to control. Working with solid colors or gradients as masks will yield the best results, particularly when learning how to use this tool.

9.55   Using a red mask causes the image to shift in a clean four-way split.

9.56   Using a blue-to-green mask causes the image to shift all pixels to the right, creating an extremely wide-angle appearance around the center of the screen without the associated rounding of the image, or vignetting.

9.57 Ordinary clouds shift to streaks of movement using the height map to shift pixels farther from their original position.

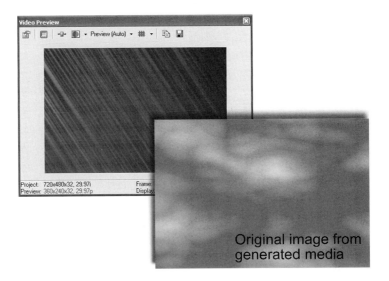

9.58 Three tracks are required to create the project illustrated in Figure 9.57.

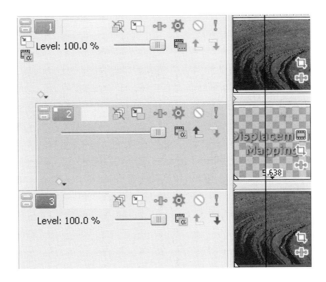

To learn more about the displacement map, create two video tracks and place the stone.png image (from the DVD) on track 2. Create a title using a bold font on track 1. Duplicate track 2 and slide the new track so that it is track 1, the text is on track 2, and the original image is on track 3. Now make track 1 parent to track 2, which will cause the text to be masked.

Check the Composite Mode button and choose CUSTOM I SONY DISPLACEMENT MAP from the menu that opens.

In the dialog box, change both channels to Red. In the Horizontal axis, set the value to −0.018, and set the Vertical axis to 0.027. The appearance of the text in the Preview window will vary depending on the font used. Experiment with the slider values to find the appropriate setting. Notice how the lettering conforms to the rocks in the photo. Using a text color slightly lighter in hue over the rocks completes the effect.

Height Map

This mode uses the parent image as a controller to cause pixels in the composited child tracks to appear closer to or farther away from the viewer. Adding a height map is a great tool for creating the appearance of moving water or viewing an image through glass or water, creating shimmers, fire, or smoke over another image. This mode can be added to gradients, masks, or other images above lower images.

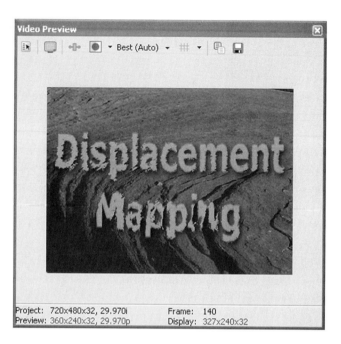

9.59   Three tracks were used to create this effect.

To learn more about the height map, create a new project. Insert two video tracks. Place the image rings.png from the DVD in this book onto track 1 and place a video or generated media event on track 2. Now make track 1 parent to track 2 by selecting the Parent/Child button on the left side of the Track Control pane. On track 1, click the Compositing Mode button. From the menu, select CUSTOM | SONY HEIGHT MAP.

Enter the following settings in the dialog box:

- Amplitude: 0.023
- Elevation: 0.319
- Height Scale: 0.320
- Smoothness: 11
- Source Channel: Intensity (menu selection)
- Edge Pixel Handling: Wrap pixels around (menu selection)

Add a pan/crop to the event on track 1, zooming in by 40 percent. Experiment with the Amplitude and Elevation settings in the Height Displacement dialog box to understand better how this plug-in functions.

Any track-level keyframes can be viewed, moved, and edited directly from the Timeline. By expanding the keyframes in the track view, keyframes can be slid forward or backward in time and double-clicked to open the track motion or compositing keyframes This feature provides a visual reference at all times when there is track motion or compositing information on a track, which allows for cursor placement on musical beats or specific musical or dialog points or simply provides a reference to what is being seen in the Preview screen.

9.60   The Expand Track Keyframes button opens a keyframe pane directly on the Timeline.

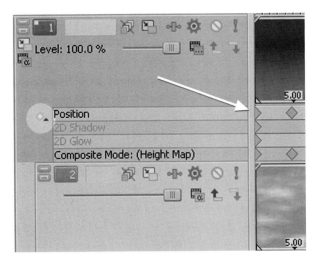

In nearly all of the previous projects, a gradient mask is used. Gradients and other generated media forms are very useful as masks. As an example, try this method of creating a mask:

1. Insert a gradient mask.

2. For mask shape, select rectangular.

3. In the Gradient Preview window, slide the color placement control points so that they are lying over top of each other with very little overlap.

This process takes some attention, because if the control points are not placed correctly, the mask will reverse itself and change from an outer mask to an inner mask. This element can also be used as a valuable tool. A color with reduced opacity can also be added to the mask's outer area, acting as an overlay, if desired. This type of mask is similar to the way the Cookie Cutter filter functions; however, this method has greater flexibility in some instances.

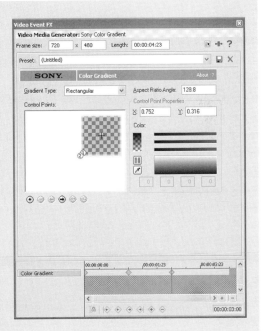

9.61   Masks can be any shape at all.

Practice using the black-to-white gradient as a mask in projects, as it is one of the most power-ful masking tools Vegas offers.

Open the file called jellyfishswim.veg from the DVD in this book. It is a fairly complex project and contains many attributes found in Vegas. Let's look at each track individually.

- Track 1—contains generated media and height map and is at 20 percent. The generated media acts as a guide to shift pixels generated on track 2.

- Track 2—contains generated media from the new Noise Texture generator. The Noise Generator is shifting in bias, causing it to create ripples on the "water."

- Track 3—is a gradient mask over track 4. It's composited in an Add mode, which brightens the image and adds contrast to allow the jellyfish to stand out over the other elements.

- Track 4—is another Noise-generated event, with color shift and pan/crop to create motion in the water.

- Track 5—is a simple blue generated media overlay at 50 percent opacity.

- Track 6—is another gradient, in Subtract compositing mode, acting as a mask for track 7. This feature helps bring out the colors in the jellyfish by masking brighter color values. With some work, a similar effect can be had with a secondary color corrector.

- Track 7—is a Noise-generated event, shifting across the Frequency, Noise, Offset, and Amplitude settings. Masked by the gradient on track 6, this color sets the shimmer over the jellyfish.

- Track 8—is the still image of the jellyfish, using pan/crop to move the fish, whereas two instances of the Spherize plug-in create the motion in the jellyfish. There is also a minor adjustment to the color of the still, reducing the exposure of the flash in the original shot. It also contains a height map to give the jellyfish texture and shine and is mapped to the event on track 9.

- Track 9—is a Noise-generated event, creating a texture of movement under the water, beneath the jellyfish.

Underneath all these layers is a motion blur added only to the jellyfish and Noise-generated layer found on track 9. Motion blur is applied at a value of 15 percent.

With this project open, change the compositing modes, opacities, and generated media gradi-ents or colors. See how these changes affect the jellyfish appearance. This demonstration pro-vides a visual overview of the function of each aspect of the tools.

Bump Map

This mode uses the texture of the parent image to create a map of light and dark information. This tool is very handy for creating 3D titles, creating textures over an event, and mapping a texture to an underlying event.

Lighting angles are definable with the Lighting Type menu. Use the Intensity slider to increase or decrease the presence of a light. The X, Y, and Z parameters can be controlled by inputting values to the input field or by moving the target dot in the Bump Placement window. Reset the X–Y parameter by double-clicking the yellow dot or by right-clicking in the Bump Placement window and selecting Reset.

9.62 In this image, the stone creates a texture, mapped to the outlines of the cowboy, creating a hand-drawn effect.

9.63 In this image, a simple text event takes on 3D attributes with definable lighting, depth, and bump height.

9.64 Controls found in the Bump Map dialog box control light, focus, depth of mapping, and light displacement.

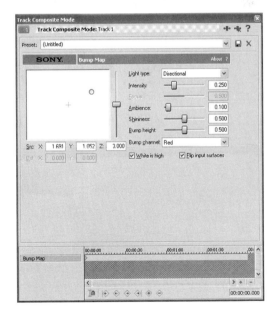

The Z slider (vertical) controls the height of the light on the mapped image. When Spotlight is selected from the menu, the distances of X and Y are controllable, and the Focus slider is enabled as well. Focus controls the tightness or breadth of the light image. Omni-directional and Directional menu options automatically disable the Focus and X–Y distance controls. The Destination of X–Y can be adjusted by moving the X in the Bump Placement window.

The Shininess slider controls the reflective surface of the map, and the Ambience slider controls the amount of light seen in the mapped image.

The "White is high" checkbox causes the bump map to view white areas as the highest areas of the bump texture. Leaving this box unchecked causes the black areas to define the high areas of the texture.

Finally, flipping the input surface reverses the two images, causing the upper and lower tracks to flip images.

Open the bumpmap.veg file found on the DVD in this book for examples of the bump mapping shown in the images earlier.

Learning to work with these tools helps build titles, scene atmospheres, and magical shots quickly and powerfully. Compositing itself is an art form and requires a great deal of time and experimenting. Vegas has some of the most powerful compositing tools in its class of editing systems and, overall, has more compositing tools than any NLE system that doubles as a finishing editor. On the DVD in this book, several compositing projects are available, although not described in this chapter.

Using Chroma-Key Tools in Vegas

Chroma key, also referred to as greenscreening or bluescreening, is an art form that must first be practiced at the camera and shooting stage of a production. Even fairly weak footage, however, can be usable in Vegas when filtered with the color-correction tools and chroma-key tools.

Chroma (color) and key (mask) come together to create a mask from a selected color(s). A quality mask or key can also be made from nearly any color or reasonable gradient of color. Selectable colors/chroma can be keyed or masked out, so that other events can show through those sections. Although industry tradition uses a screen of blue or green, any color can be keyed. Due to the luminance and chroma sensitivity of the bright green used in screens, however, in most situations, green is the best choice for DV.

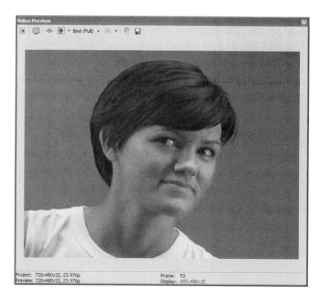

9.65   A clean greenscreen shot, with no spill on the face of subject.

(For more information on the relationship between chroma key and DV, visit http://www.sundancemediagroup.com/tutorials/ChromaDV.htm and read the tutorial on 4:1:1 DV.)

Shooting a clean screen is critical to having a relatively smooth experience with keying. Many tutorials are available on how to shoot a clean screen, and the Sundance Media Group VASST training course teaches this as well (www.vasst.com). Some basics to know are presented here to assist the inexperienced cameraperson/editor in creating a clean shot to be keyed in the editing stage.

Use Rosco green paint or a commercially produced greenscreen. I recommend the Photoflex dual-color screens that have flex hoops in them for easy storage. When shooting on DV, green is the only safe choice. Blue can be used in analog shooting.

Good lighting is critical. To shoot a clean screen requires at least three lights: a key light for the talent and two lights for the screen itself. A reflector for the key light to light the opposite side of the subject is valuable too, as are flags (masks) to keep the key light from spilling onto the screen.

Shoot the subject at a minimum of six feet from the screen. This practice is necessary to prevent green reflection from spilling onto the subject. This kind of reflective spill is very difficult to remove in editing, regardless of the application used for creating a key or matte.

Vegas has excellent chroma-key tools that allow for rapid and clean keying of colors. A successful key, however, is also dependent on practice and experience on the part of the user.

From the DVD, open the greenscreen.avi file on the Timeline in Vegas. Select the Event FX on the file and open the Sony Chroma Keyer tool.

In the Chroma Key dialog box, uncheck the checkbox in the upper-left corner. The Chroma Key dialog defaults to blue, and unchecking this box allows Vegas to sample an accurate replacement

9.66 Chroma Key tool at default setting. Uncheck the "Chroma Keyer" box in the upper-left corner.

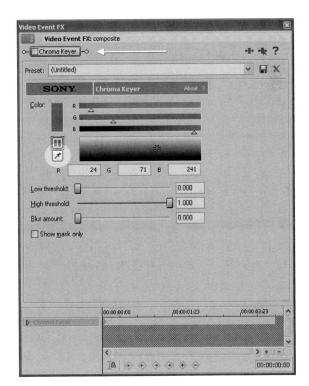

9.67 Draw or click in the Preview window to select color for removal.

color. Select the Eyedropper tool, found in the left center of the Chroma Key dialog. With the Eyedropper enabled, click the color to be removed from the event in the Preview window.

Enable the Chroma Key tool by placing a checkmark in the checkbox in the upper left of the Chroma Key dialog. A portion of the selected color will immediately change in the Preview window. Now the Chroma Key tool must be adjusted to create a clean key.

Start by placing the event to be seen beneath the keyed event. This process helps adjust the key for best matting. Generated media is great for this, especially generated media that is a color similar to that of the replacement event. Of course, the replacement event can also be used. If it's a fairly busy event with lots of detail, however, it is sometimes difficult to create clean lines, as the detail in the background event hides lines during the key process.

 Tip

Viewing the key process on an external monitor is helpful to ensure a clean key process. During the color selection, however, the preview must be on the computer screen. After the key color is selected, video can be sent to an external NTSC or PAL monitor.

After an event is placed beneath the event being keyed, slide the Low Threshold slider to the right and slide the High Threshold slider to the left. On the greenscreen.avi file, a clean key will be achieved with the Low Threshold slider at 0.400 and the High Threshold at 0.800. The Blur setting is dependent on the background media used. In the instance of the greenscreen.veg file found on the DVD, the Blur setting is at 0.015 to soften the harsh transition between the background color and the edges of the key. Some keyed events require a fair amount of blur, whereas others can require no blur whatsoever.

Creating a Garbage Matte in Vegas

A garbage matte or mask is a simple mask, created from an event or image in Vegas, which removes one element from other elements on the screen. By definition it gets the "garbage" out of the image. This option assists in the keying process, particularly where more than one color must be keyed out. The earlier project does not require a garbage matte; however, many instances exist in which a garbage matte is beneficial.

To create a garbage matte, click the "Show mask only" box in the Chroma Key tool. This step displays the areas being masked and quickly shows a clean or unclean key. This matte/mask can be rendered to a new track, which is then parented to the original event, saving processor time and allowing multiple masks to take place on the Timeline/project. To render the matte to a new track, solo the track containing the mask. Double-click the event to be rendered to a new track, creating a selection. Select TOOLS | RENDER TO NEW TRACK. In the dialog box, select Custom and select the Audio tab. Uncheck Include Audio.

A popular effect is to create an image that is entirely black and white, except for one or two colors. This is part of a color pass, which allows a color to pass through an image that is otherwise black and white.

To create this effect quickly, place the events on the Timeline to be color passed. Duplicate the track so that two identical tracks exist. On the upper track, insert a Chroma Key and Black and White filter in order.

Using the Eyedropper in the Chroma Key tool, select the color to be passed, or allowed to be shown. Use the "View Mask Only" checkbox to see what areas will be knocked out in black and white. Adjust the Black and White filter to the desired level of black and white blend. For maximum effect, the lower track can have a slight blend of black and white with the color. This option reduces the amount of contrast between the color and the black and white areas if this is the desired effect.

Although this is one method of color passing in Vegas, see the section on color correction in Chapter 6, which discusses alternative methods.

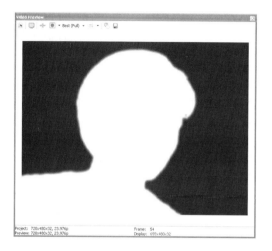

9.68   A clean and simple garbage matte/mask.

9.69   An improper mask/matte.

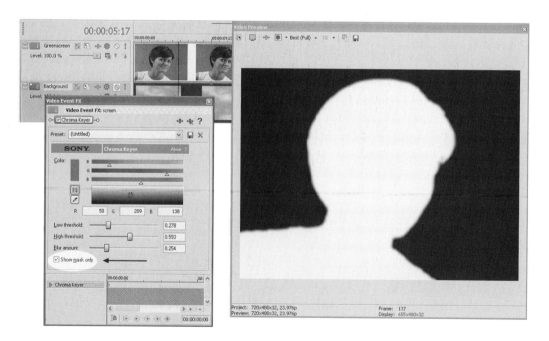

9.70   Track 1 soloed and with "Show mask only" enabled in the Chroma Key tool. This process is done to render a matte/mask to a new track.

After the new track is rendered, it should be parented to the original track. Click the Event FX button on the original track and disable the Chroma Key tool by unchecking the checkbox in the upper left of the Chroma Key tool. Parent the mask event to the original event by clicking the Parent/Child button to the left of the original track.

9.71 Parent track 1 to track 2 by using the Parent/Child button on track 2.

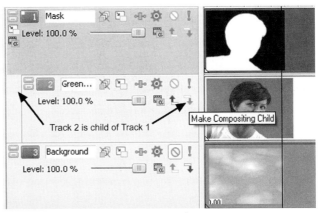

Track 2 is child of Track 1

Make Compositing Child

9.72 A clean composite.

The two events over the third track, which contains the background information, create a clean composite over the background image if all parameters are adjusted correctly, as illustrated in Figure 9.72.

The original image can be color corrected, blurred, or otherwise filtered for creative presentation if desired. Figure 9.73 shows three problem areas in the screen.

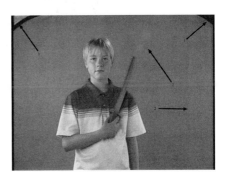

9.73 Identifying problem areas in a screen isn't always easy or obvious.

1. The corners of the screen are visible. These areas will not mask cleanly.

2. Lens flare/reflection shows across screen. This will not mask cleanly.

3. There is spill getting past a flag, allowing backlight spill on the screen and creating two colors of green. This will not mask cleanly.

These problems can be overcome, but the time involved, coupled with the loss of resolution, quickly demonstrate the necessity and time savings of having media shot correctly in the production stage.

To see how to correct the poorly shot footage, open the badscreen.veg file on the DVD in this book.

A clean mask has been rendered to track 1. This garbage matte is required to create a clean composite. Track 2 is parented to the mask/garbage matte, which is similar to the way the first greenscreen project was done. To be able to create a clean mask, however, a secondary color corrector and black restore were used to cause the mask to render cleanly. The event is also panned/cropped to remove the corners from the scene and to create a clean masking area. Still the original event requires color correction to blend into the background with a believable presentation. The original settings for the color correction and chroma key have been left in place on the original event in region 1. Click the Event FX to enable these two FX, allowing you to see how the mask was created. Color correction has been added to the event as well. Disable this by unchecking the checkbox in the upper-left corner of the FX dialog. A very small amount of blur has been added to the mask to smooth over the transition from the masked area to the background area.

These are two examples of how a chroma key can be used to repair a background image or to insert new media. There are other instances in which a screen is valuable, however.

Open the tvscreen.veg file on the DVD in this book.

The tvscreen.veg file contains a still image: tvshot.png. This image is an old photograph of a child watching television. The television screen has been replaced with green, allowing for a motion picture to be placed in the television screen. This method can also be used to replace screens in television studio-type shots or military establishment-type shots to create a sense of realism. There are more examples of this sort of masking on the tvscreen.veg file. Play with them and notice how the Track Motion tool is used to fill in the masked sections.

Never be afraid to experiment using various FX, Track Motion, Pan/Crop, and other tools on composited media. Turn lots of knobs, slide the sliders, and check the checkboxes. Various combinations turn up lots of artistic possibilities, and, as mentioned at the front of this chapter, compositing is an art form. Be creative!

Create a Holograph in Vegas!

Remember the beamed holographs seen in *Star Wars* episodes? At the time the movie came out, this was an exceptionally cool thing, never seen nor conceived before. *Star Trek* had a simple transporter beam effect that used masks to create the look of being transported, but the holograph was a method of communication and projection never before seen. Playing around in Vegas on a VASST tour, I was working with a piece of footage and realized how simple this would be in Vegas. To accomplish this look you'll need to shoot against a solid backdrop, preferably green if you are shooting with DV. (See my tutorial on why green

9.74 The original image is shot against a green background.

is better.) Shoot your footage with your actor dressed in imaginative clothing, but color of the clothing won't matter much, as we'll be applying a blue filter over the original footage to mask most color detail. Just be sure the clothing doesn't contain colors that are the same or fairly similar to the background color. You'll have the most effective look if your actor is shot full-body, but even half or three-quarters works acceptably well. However, to mimic the *Star Wars* look, you'll want to do a full body shot. Remember, if this is to look like a communication transmission, your actor should look at the camera just as though he or she can see a video or holographic representation of who he or she is speaking to.

First, I used the secondary color corrector to pop my blues, allowing for better extraction from the background, which has a few gradients, as we didn't use the cyclorama's full lighting system. I then added a Chroma Key tool, and using the "Show mask only" checkbox, I cleaned up my output. The project.veg file has left these two tools in place, merely turned off, so you can work with the demo media to see how I popped the blue and cleaned up the output. I then used the Pan/Crop tool to create a 16:9 letterbox and used the Track Motion tool to stretch the body and create a thinner and off-aspect appearance to the shot. After getting the mask set up, I found a background .jpeg that I wanted to insert the original image into. In this case, it's a shot of a living room.

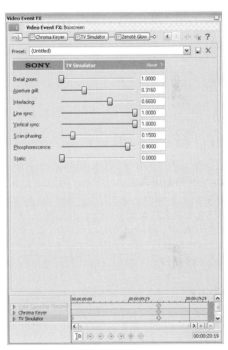

9.75   Match the sliders in this screenshot to create fast pulsing sync lines.

Next, I rendered a new track with the "Show mask only" box still checked. I unchecked "Include Audio" from the RENDER | CUSTOM options, as I wanted the new mask track to lie directly above the original track with no audio, and the audio from the original track was used in the project, removing the need to have a second, duplicate audio track. This allowed me to create a garbage mask or matte to be used as a parent to the original image. Don't create the mask or matte until the Pan/Crop and Track Motion attributes have been determined. Be sure Ripple is disabled before rendering to a new track. On the original track, remove the Secondary Color Corrector and Chroma Key from the original. With the matte above the original track, parent the matte to the original by pressing the Parent/Child button on the original track. This will allow the original track to show through. At this point, you should see a fairly clean image over top of the selected background. Set the opacity of your matte to 75 percent for starters. This will allow the background to be seen through the hologram.

Using selected filters, we'll now create the image of the hologram. Drag the Gaussian Blur filter to the matte. Set the values for both horizontal and vertical blur to approximately .025 for starters. This will likely be tweaked later. (The project VEG is set to .027.) The blur helps create a soft edge on the original media. It also washes out the screened edges and blends the image into the background a little more smoothly.

Drop the Secondary Color Corrector onto the original video track. Choose the Desaturate All but Red preset for starters. Slide the Saturation slider to the right, to a value of 3.000. Now slide the Limit Hue value to the full right, to a value of 360. Slide the corrector target dot to the lower left in the color wheel, setting the track to a blue color. Set this to the desired level. This should blow out the edges of the original media. This step is not necessary for creating this particular look. I simply wanted to blow out my edges.

Now drop the TV Simulator on the original media. Select the TV Look preset. Slide Line Sync, Scan Phasing, and Phosphorescence all to the right to create a fast scan image. Add a tiny value of Static if you'd like to distort the image a little further. If you want less interlacing (the horizontal lines in the image) reduce the Interlacing value to 0. For a unique look, keyframe Line Sync and Scan Phasing value movements to make the picture break up every now and then. Notice there are no keyframes in the project. I left these blank so you could experiment with these values on your own.

Now drop the Brightness and Contrast filter on the original image, setting the Brightness value to .22. That's all there is to it. The project is ready to be rendered.

Some options you might want to try, depending on source footage if other than the media used in the training file:

- Drop the Glow filter on the footage. (The Zenoté plug-in was used for the original render seen in the demo footage. It's an excellent tool for smoothing out the highlights.)

- Drop a Film Grain filter on the original along with the TV simulator to create noise in the file.

- Use the Convolution filter to create unique effects. This won't work for all looks but is a great look for some effects.

9.76   Here is the look of the final product.

9.77   Motion blurred at full value with the Motion Blur tool.

Motion Blur

Vegas has a feature called Motion Blur that allows you to apply an envelope controlling the duration and shape of the blur applied to the motion of video. What makes Motion Blur unique is that it applies blur at the frame level, creating a blur over time (temporal) as the video shows movement. This option makes zooms, pans, and motion in the image blur smoothly. A standard blur applies a blur in 2D space or a spatial blur. A motion blur acts more like a wide-open shutter, allowing for a greater exposure time.

Applying the envelope is performed by selecting VIEW | VIDEO BUS TRACKS (Shift+Ctrl+B) and then right-clicking the video control pane and inserting a Motion Blur envelope. Double-clicking the envelope and adding handles/nodes controls the amount of blur.

Applying this filter to sequences of still images, fast or slow motion video, and animations can add a sense of realism to the media. It can also be inserted with great intensity to generate a dream-like quality.

One really great effect to try with Motion Blur is to render an event with lots of motion to a new track and to add a motion blur to suit the eye. In that new track/event, right-click and select Undersample. Undersample the event by at least .750, which will create a unique and stuttered look with blur shifting. The most unusual effect comes from using an extremely low undersampling/frame rate in which the frames skip enough to cut the blurred frames to the point at which they are almost unrelated in motion.

Another terrific use of this tool is to blur a camera pan when transitioning from one scene to another. A motion blur, coupled with a velocity filter and transition, is a good combination for the popular effect of stuttered motion or stopped-motion blurring during a pan into another scene or shot sequence. Motion blur does add considerable time to a rendered section, so make sure the envelope is completely off when not being used.

Every track will be blurred when this envelope is up, unless the Bypass Motion Blur button is chosen. This option allows you to blur tracks selectively. The button is next to the Scribble Strip on each video track in the Track Control pane. Leaving it enabled causes the video track to be blurred.

Supersampling

Supersampling resamples each pixel of video information in Vegas and significantly improves the smoothness of the pixel edges and matches to adjoining pixels. This feature is primarily valuable when used in conjunction with the Motion Blur envelope but is also beneficial when used in

9.78   The original image from Thomas Edison's 1900 film *The Kiss.* Notice black edges to be cropped out, bringing the image to correct aspect ratio.

upsampling smaller resolutions to DV or higher levels. Supersampling will not be as noticeable with video containing high motion or with video that is not being changed in output size or resolution. Use supersampling in connection with Motion Blur, when upsampling small-resolution video, or when working with extremely low resolution stills. It works exceptionally well when shifting the aspect ratio from one size to another, such as converting video that is 160 × 160 to 720 × 480.

9.79   The same image after cropping and supersampling at a value of 2 frames.

The way this works is that Vegas creates interpretive frames based on the difference between the project frame rate and the frame rate of the media or the computer-generated imagery. This process also creates smoother flow and edges for generated behaviors, such as Pan/Crop, Track Motion, Transitions, and other new media created in the Timeline during the editing stages.

Insert a Supersampling envelope in the same manner as inserting a Motion Blur envelope by selecting VIEW | VIDEO BUS TRACKS (Shift+Ctrl+B) and inserting a Supersampling envelope. Use the envelope to control how many interpolative frames are created. For instance, by using an envelope setting of 4, four times as many frames are rendered as existed in the original event. This means that render times are significantly slowed, so don't plan on doing a supersample while you are answering a phone call or grabbing a quick bite to eat. Supersampling, however, is a fantastic tool when shifting resolution, frame rate, or both. It often is beneficial to add a small amount of Gaussian blur as well, to shift the image spatially. Supersampling won't benefit media that isn't changing aspect ratio or frame rate, if it merely is being employed to go from one format to another format of matching dimension.

Media Manager

The Media Manager is a powerful search and retrieval tool used for quickly finding media. It provides a way to catalog all of the video, audio, and still images used in your projects or anywhere on system hard drives and organize them into multiple categories for instant identification. It also provides three ways to search and find media quickly.

Conceptual Overview

It is important to understand that the Media Manager does not contain any media. The media is still on the hard drive after adding it to the Media Manager. The Media Manager merely catalogs where the media is located and displays the content in one place, much like a phone book catalogs phone numbers and shows them all in one place. Similar to how the phone number in a phone book is a pointer to a person; the Media Manager maintains pointers to all media wherever it may be.

There are two ways in which you can use the Media Manager. It may be used to catalog stock footage, motion backgrounds, royalty-free music, ACID loops, etc., and used as a library. Or you can allow it to dynamically catalog every piece of media that you have ever used in a project. In the first case you add media manually and deliberately and only the media that you add gets into the Media Manager. In the latter case, media is added to Vegas simply by placing it on the Timeline of a project. Each use has its benefits and you should consider how you best want to use the Media Manager as you read this chapter.

It is also important to understand that you can have multiple Media Manager databases. This means that you can have some that are libraries of stock media and others that are collections of media you have used in your projects. You can also decide to make several smaller databases that are good for particular kinds of projects. For example, you might have a Media Manager database with documentary media, and another with news media, and another with wedding media. The possibilities are endless.

User Interface Layout

The layout of the Media Manager interface is shown in Figure 10.1.

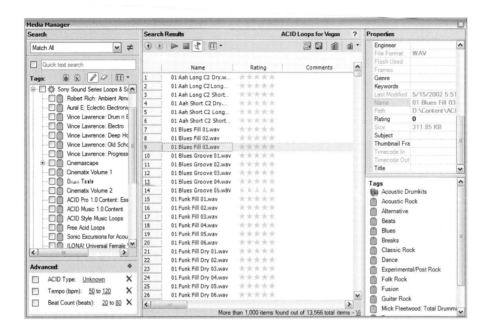

10.1   Media Manager interface.

On the left, from top to bottom, is the quick text search (keyword search), the tag tree (the organizational heart of the interface), and the advanced search. The center of the interface shows the main interface toolbar at the top and the search results in the middle. Notice at the bottom is says "More than 1,000 items found out of 13,566 total items." It would be difficult to browse through 13,566 pieces of media so this view is limited to a subset, which you can control in the preferences. Normally you would see fewer files because a query would restrict the view to only those files that match the search criteria. On the right top are the properties of the currently selected file and the right bottom shows any tags associated with that file. Tags are discussed under "Organizing Your Media with Tags" in this chapter.

At the top of the center search results area is the Media Manager toolbar.

The icons on the left allow you to cycle through the previous/next queries; play, stop, and autoplay the selected media; and change the search view from a grid to a list or thumbnail view. The icons on the right allow you to add media, save the tags to the media, open the reference library, and create/load new libraries and change the options.

10.2   Media Manager toolbar.

Setup and Preferences

Starting with Vegas Pro 8.0, the Media Manager is an optional installation. Make sure that you have it installed from the Vegas Pro 8 DVD or download package. You also want to be sure that it is enabled in Vegas.

To enable the Media Manager:

- Select OPTIONS | PREFERENCES | GENERAL tab
- Check "Enable Media Manager" (requires restart)

If this option was not previously checked, you will have to restart Vegas to activate the Media Manager, just as is done with the XDCAM Explorer.

Another important option on the General Preferences tab is "Save media-usage relationships in active media library." If you would like to use the Media Manager to catalog stock media and not have your project media added, you should *uncheck* this option. If you don't have this unchecked,

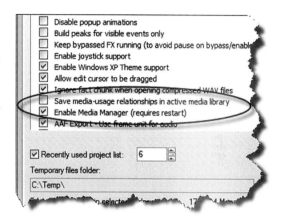

10.3   Enable Media Manager in the General Preferences.

every piece of media that you drop on the Timeline or into a media bin, whether you use it or not in the final project, will get cataloged. This is not desirable if you are creating a stock media library. However, if you want Vegas to dynamically add the media that you use in projects to the library, keep this option checked.

Changing Options

The Options dialog is accessed by the icon on the far right of the toolbar called the Media Library Actions button. Selecting this toolbar button will give you a number of choices. For now we will select the one marked Options.

10.4   Menu options.

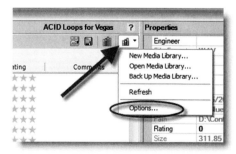

If you plan to add any Sony media (such as ACID loops) to your library, make sure that you have the Sony Sound Series Loops and Samples reference library enabled. This is an optional download and installation is available from the Sony web site.

10.5 General options for the Media Manager.

Create a New Library

The Media Manager creates a library called "Default" when it is first installed. You can add all of your media to this library or you can create a new library.

To create a new media library:

☞ Select MEDIA LIBRARY ACTIONS | NEW MEDIA LIBRARY.

10.6 Create a new media library from the Media Library Actions icon.

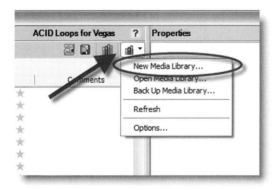

You will be prompted to give this new library a name. Name it something meaningful so that you will know what's in it. In this example we will create one with motion backgrounds and royalty-free music suitable for titles and DVD menus.

10.7   Give the new library a
        meaningful name.

You may have as many Media Manager libraries as you want and easily switch between them. The default folder to hold them is in the \My Documents\Sony Media Libraries folder but you can place them anywhere you'd like on your hard drive or even on a network drive to be shared among editors.

10.8   The library name is
        displayed on top.

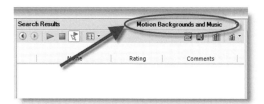

If you want to know which media library you have open, just look at the top of the Media Manager interface and you will see the name above the toolbar to the right.

Adding Media to the Media Manager

Once you have your options set and a new library created, it's time to add your media to the library. The term "add" is a bit of a misnomer because the media does not go into the library; rather it is *cataloged* by the library. This means that a pointer to the media is added to the library so it can be found later, much like a card catalog at the library points to books on the shelves.

To add media to the library:

☞ Press the ADD FILES TO MEDIA LIBRARY button.

10.9   Use the Add Files to
        Media Library button
        to add media.

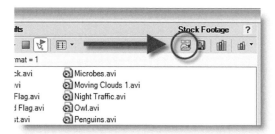

You will be prompted to browse for the folder that you would like to start searching for the media. If your media is in multiple folders you want to start one level above. If your media is all in one folder then just select that folder.

10.10 Select the folder to start scanning for media.

This calls up the Add Files to Media Library window.

10.11 Add Files to Media Library window.

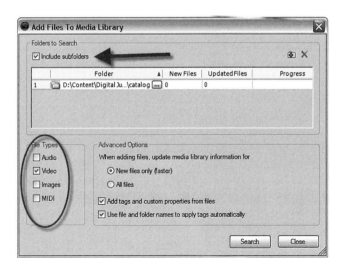

If you have selected a starting folder that has subfolders and you want those subfolders to be searched for media, make sure you have the "Include subfolders" option checked (this is the default). It is also important that you select the file types to search for if your folders have more than one type of media and you want only certain types to be found. In the example, each folder contains the video media and a still image thumbnail of the video. Because the Media Manager will automatically show us thumbnails of the video, we do not want these still images imported, so only the Video type has been selected.

In the Advanced Options you can elect to have only new files added or to rescan all files, which will take considerably longer. The first time you are adding files from a folder it doesn't matter which you select because all of the files will be new. On subsequent runs, you would want to scan for all of the files only if you changed the files and want the new changes to be picked up.

The "Add tags and custom properties from files" option will import any tags that were saved with the files and will save you hours of tagging the media manually. You will learn how to save your tags with the media later in this chapter. You also may want to check the "Use files and folder names to apply tags automatically" option. This will match file folder names to any tags in the library with the same name and it will tag the files as being part of that category. For example, if you have a tag called Backgrounds and the scan finds a file in a folder called .\Backgrounds it will automatically add the Backgrounds tag to the file in the library.

You may have the Media Manager search more than one location on your hard drive.

10.12 Add a folder to search.

To do this, press the Add Folder icon at the top right of the Add Files to Media Library window. This will bring up the Browse Folder window again and you can add more folder locations to search.

To start adding media:

☞ Press the SEARCH button.

10.13 While searching you will see the number of files found and percentage complete.

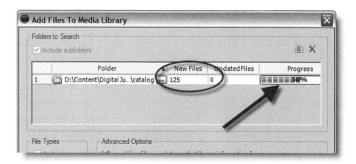

Once the search is complete, press the Close button and you will see all of the media listed in the center window of the user interface. To make this view more interesting you can change it from a list view to a thumbnail view:

☞ Select CHANGE SEARCH RESULTS VIEW icon | THUMBNAIL.

10.14 Change to Thumbnail view for video or image media viewing.

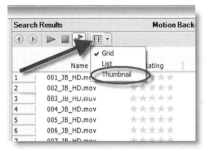

The thumbnail view is great for video files and images because it allows the contents of your media to be viewed as picture icons. If you hover your mouse over a thumbnail it will enlarge, allowing for a better view.

10.15 Enlarge thumbnails by hovering over them.

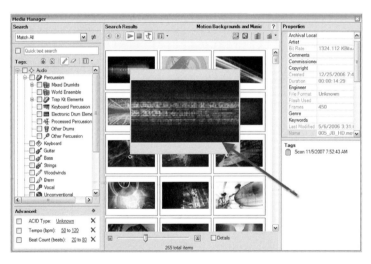

Once the enlarger is active, you can move your mouse over the other files and they will each enlarge without delay. You can also display the filenames by checking the "Details" checkbox.

10.16 Add filenames to thumbnails with the "Details" checkbox.

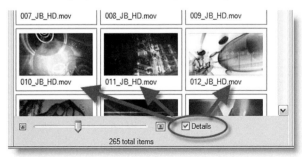

Organizing Your Media with Tags

Organizing your media is the key to finding it easily. You can organize before you add media or after you've added media, it's up to you. In this example we are going to organize before we add media to a new library called "Stock Footage" so that we can take advantage of the option to "Use files and folder names to apply tags automatically." We will build a tag tree that matches the folder names of the files we are going to import. This will allow the Media Manager to tag the files automatically as they are added to the media library.

You can add new tags to the existing Audio and Video tree or you can create new top-level tags. To add a new tag:

☞ Right-click any tag and select New from the pop-up menu.

10.17 Right-click any tag to add a new tag.

You can name this tag anything you want. In this example we will call it "Stock Footage." You can also assign a new icon to it to distinguish it from other tags easily. To do this:

☞ Right-click on the tag you want to edit and select Edit from the pop-up menu.

10.18 Change the tag icon by right-clicking and selecting Edit.

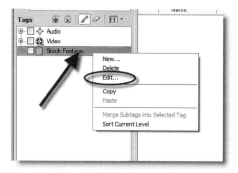

The Tag Editor window will appear, in which you can change the name and select a new icon.

☞ Click on the new icon and press OK.

10.19 Select a new icon from the Tag Editor.

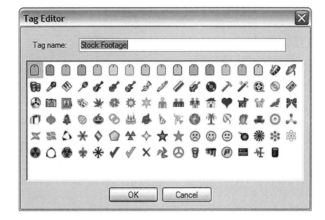

Continue adding tags by right-clicking and selecting New. You can drag and drop a tag under another tag to make a hierarchy of tags so that Stock Footage is the parent tag and all others are the child tags.

Continue to add tags until you have made categories for all of your footage.

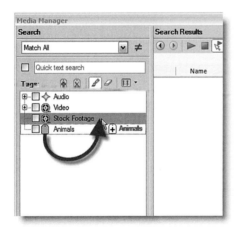

10.20 Drag tags to form a hierarchy.

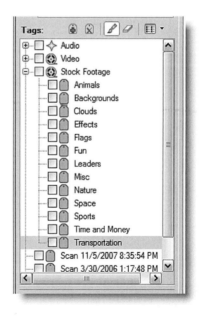

10.21 Create a hierarchy by adding tags and dragging and dropping into place.

In this example, when we add media to the library, the Media Manager will assign all of the media from the Animals folder to the Animals tag and all of the media from the Backgrounds folder to the Background tag, etc. This allows you to click on a tag and see only the media that is assigned it. In the example in Figure 10.22, the Clouds tag is checked and only media that has been assigned to the Clouds tag is shown.

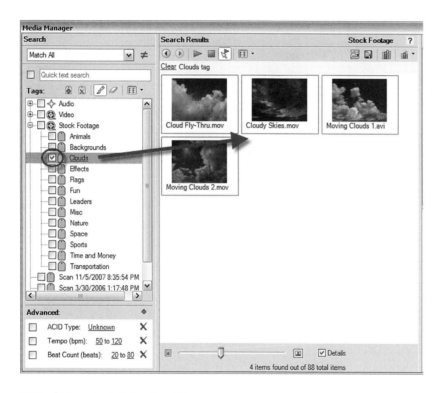

10.22   Click on a tag to find media quickly.

Once you have your media library organized and all of your data tagged, it is very important to save the tags with the media.

10.23   Save tags with the media so you can reuse them.

The reason it is important to save the tags with the media is so that you can create a new media library and not have to retag the data. Once you save the tags with the media, you can reimport that media into a new media library and the tags will return, leaving all of your media automatically organized the way you want.

Seek and You Shall Find

The real power of the Media Manager is in its search capabilities. You have seen how you can use tags to perform a search simply by clicking on the tag. In this section we will learn two more powerful ways to search.

At the top of the search pane is an option that affects all searching (quick text, tag, and advanced). The choices are Match All, Match Any, and Not Equal (≠).

When you select:

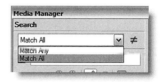

- Match All—the search will return the media that matches all of the search criteria. For example, if you select two tags, only the media that is associated with both tags will be returned.

- Match Any—the search will return the media that matches any of the criteria selected. For example, if you selected two tags, the media returned can be associated with either one of the tags.

10.24 The Match option affects all searches.

- Not Equal (≠)—the search will return the opposite of the search criteria. In other words, it returns all of the media that does not match.

It is important to understand how Not Equal will affect the match criteria:

- Match All+Not Equal—the search will contain none of the criteria. For example if you selected the tag "Cloud" and the keyword "Fly," you will get media that does not have the Cloud tag and also does not contain the keyword "Fly."

- Match Any+Not Equal—the search will contain some of the search criteria. For example if you selected the tag "Cloud" and the keyword "Fly," you will get media that either does not have the Cloud tag or does not contain the keyword "Fly." This means that some of the media that has the Cloud tag but does not contain the keyword "Fly" will be returned because Match Any says that it can match any of the criteria.

Tip_____

Before doing any search, press the Clear link to clear any previous search.

10.25 Press the Clear link before doing a new search.

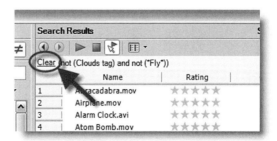

Quick Text or Keyword Search

The Quick Text or, as it's sometimes called, "keyword" search will search all of the fields in the library. When you use the grid view you will notice that there are several columns that have information in them, such as filename, file format, size, bit depth, path, copyright, tags, and comments. The keyword search looks in all of these. Be mindful of this when you do your search. If you want to search only a specific column or set of columns use the Advanced search.

To use the keyword search:

- Type the keywords to search for into the keyword entry field (you can use the words "and" and "or" in your search).

- Check the checkbox to make the search active.

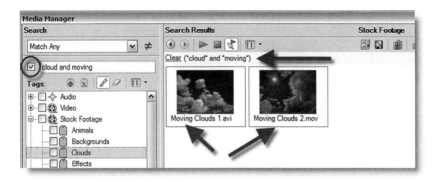

10.26   Use the keyword search checkbox to turn the search on and off.

In the example we used the keywords "cloud and moving" and the search returned two files with Moving Clouds in the name. Notice that the media matched even though the words in the filename were reversed. This is because it looked for each keyword regardless of the order in which it was entered. If you really wanted to find media with the words "cloud moving" you would leave the "and" out and add quotes around the keywords. If you are ever unsure of what the search criteria are, just look next to the Clear link. The search is always displayed there when active.

Advanced Search

The advanced search looks in individual fields. You can enable and disable the criteria by using the checkboxes to the left of each field just as you did with the keyword search. You can also remove criteria entirely and add new criteria. Let's start by removing any existing criteria.

To remove advanced search criteria:

☞ Click the red X in the Advanced search section.

10.27 Click the red X to remove a criterion.

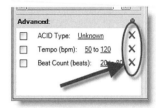

To add a field to search:

☞ Click the green + to add a field to search.

10.28 Click the green + to add a field to the Advanced search.

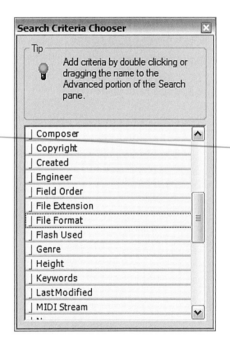

This will bring up the Search Criteria Chooser, in which you can select any of the available fields and add them to the search.

• Double-click or drag–drop the field you want to search on.

• Click on the value to select a new one.

• Check the checkbox to activate the search.

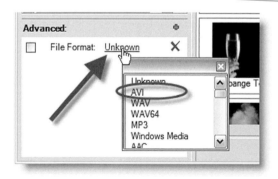

10.29 Drag–drop a field into the Advanced search.

10.30 Select a value to search by and check the checkbox to activate.

It is important to understand that all three searches can be active at the same time. This means that you can select a tag and add a keyword and use the Advanced search to really fine-tune the criteria by which media is returned. You use the checkboxes to control which search is active and the Clear link to uncheck them all.

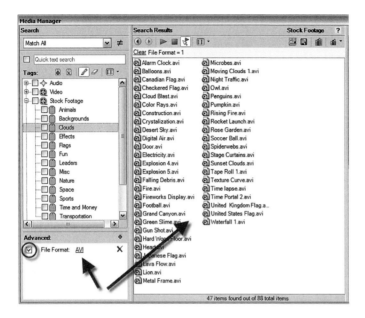

10.31   Search results from File Format AVI.

Conclusion

The Media Manager can be a real time-saver when searching for a particular piece of media. It does take some time to set up the way you want it, but once you are organized you will more than make up that time in productivity gain. Don't forget to save the tags with your media and *always* press the Clear link before starting a new query so that you get back the media you wanted.

Output and Export

Last Steps with Vegas

Vegas is unique in that it is currently the only end-to-end NLE or digital audio workstation (DAW). Vegas contains tools for output to every web format, CD/VCD format, serial digital interface, high-definition broadcast quality, and multiple audio format. Vegas is formidable. No wonder it's the choice of many large encoding and finishing houses!

As mentioned previously, Vegas started life as an audio-only tool. As a result, the audio features in Vegas are what first brought attention to the application years ago. Development for audio has continued, and Vegas is currently one of the most open-ended output DAW systems in existence on any platform.

Output Formats

After a mix is completed, it needs to be output in a format that others can hear or distribute or that a replicator can work with.

Open a multitrack mix in Vegas. Assuming all parts of the mix are satisfactory, the multichannel mix needs to be mixed to a two-track mix that can be put on a CD and prepped for distribution. This process is called the mixdown. Mixing down multiple tracks is the next-to-last step in the finishing process.

To mix the multichannel mix to a two-track mix, select FILE | RENDER AS and render the mix to a Stereo WAV mix.

When rendering the multiple tracks to a final two-track mix, be certain that if any buses were used they all point to the master output. This issue occurs only if multichannel hardware has been used, with outputs assigned to other devices.

11.1   Rendering multitrack to a two-track mix, ready to be mastered.

If the project has been recorded at any sample rate other than 16 bits, 44.1 kHz, the mixdown process is not where the sample rate should be dithered to 44.1. Keep files in their higher resolution state where applicable. They'll be dithered to a 16/44.1 state later in the process.

After this process has been performed with each song, or multichannel audio project, the multiple two-track mixes are ready to be mastered. Vegas has excellent mastering tools—tools that have been used to master/produce my Grammy-winning and Grammy-nominated recordings.

Mastering

The mastering process is not to be taken lightly. This stage is the final one before sending the master disc to a replicator. It is generally advisable to do the mastering in a familiar room, using familiar monitors. It's rarely a good idea to master on the same monitors that were used in the mixing stage, as it is entirely possible for monitors to mask or enhance problems in a mix. The entire point of mastering is to discover anomalies or errors in a mix and to bring all cuts of a project to a state of consistency so that regardless of sequencing, tracks complement each other and flow comfortably from one cut to another. Mix on a different set of speakers if possible. Move to a different room, if possible. If nothing else, check the mastered mix multiple times on different stereo systems to ensure a consistent and balanced master. In one studio years ago, we installed an FM transmitter that was fed by our master tape deck. We then went out to the car in the parking lot and listened to the mix over an FM receiver. To this day, all mixes at Sundance Media Group are checked on an old Craig boom box, a standard home stereo system, and a high-end car audio system before being sent off for replication.

Mastering is not mixing. Mixing is blending several channels of audio together, placing elements in different portions of the sound field while using EQ, reverb, delay, and other tools to create a sense of depth and space. An analogy might be that mixing is like baking a cake, whereas mastering is the decorating part that pretties things up.

Mixing is an entire book in itself, so this section covers mastering only. See Chapter 6 for more information on mixing.

Mastering is taking the two-channel, four-channel, 5.1, 7.1, and 16.1 final mix and finishing it for the audio space/delivery mechanism. The primary preparation is making sure that all audio is of maximized level, in phase, and properly faded in/out, with all hum, pops, and noises removed, proper compression applied where/if needed, relative level adjustment between cuts of audio matched, and other tweaks applied to give the audio that final sparkle. Mastering is rarely done in the same room as the audio mix was done in, as a different set of speakers in a different environment tells the tale when poor audio practices, sneaky noise, or other anomalies were present but were not heard in the original recording environment. Mastering is also generally done by a mastering engineer, rather than by the engineer who mixed the audio. A fresh set of ears is invaluable at this point, even if it's just a friend with good ears who can make comments on how something sounds.

If you'll be mastering for surround 5.1 or 7.1, be certain that you have a high-quality audio tool, such as the Echo Audio Layla, Mona, M-Audio Delta Series, or a similar tool. A low-quality audio card will create problems in any instance at this point. Higher-quality cards allow for synchronous playback of multiple channels of audio, whereas a low-end soundcard with surround ability will have slur and phase issues in most instances. Worse still, many low-end audio cards induce noise into the audio path. (With Microsoft's Windows Media 9, you'll need a surround-capable card to prep audio for the new codec/delivery tools.) Remember, this stage is the last stage in preparing your audio for the world to hear. If you've worked hard to make a mix, video, or other project that sounds great, you'll want to put your best foot forward, especially when presenting the product for sale or broadcast.

11.3   Echo Audio Layla (back view).

11.2   Delta 1010.

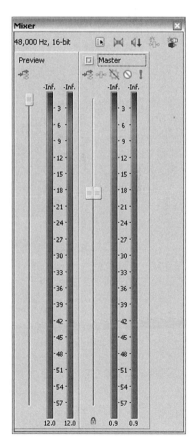

Meters are critical to this endeavor. Vegas has two meter display spaces: one is the master and the other is for buses/ auxes. For this section, we're concerned only with the master volume meters. Notice the small lock icon on the master meters. This locks right and left together, so that both channels are identical. They may be unlocked by clicking the icon.

Ideally, during the mix process, the audio was mixed to a level not exceeding 0 dB and not less than −6 dB at peaks, which are the loudest points in the audio mix. Audio that is too quiet won't be heard well over the television or stereo system on which the video is played or on which the CD is played. In addition, in the event of poor playback equipment, audio that is too quiet can cause any noise associated with the poor playback equipment to shine through, making your finished product sound unfinished or of poor quality.

Many ways exist to bring up audio levels in the digital world. One is to apply a simple volume adjustment. In Vegas, volume can be increased by 12 dB at the track slider and decreased infinitely to the point of no volume whatsoever. Vegas's track pane setting for volume is 0 dB, at which point there is no increase or decrease in the volume of the audio.

Another means of raising volume is to normalize the audio levels. Normalizing in Vegas instructs the application to search the various peak levels of the audio information and set the loudest point to a prespecified level. To normalize in Vegas, right-click the audio file and select PROPERTIES | NORMALIZE. This step can also be done by selecting EDIT | SWITCHES | NORMALIZE from the Vegas menu bar.

11.4   Disable locks on master faders if separate control of right/left channels is necessary.

Change the Normalize Default Level in the OPTIONS | PREFERENCES | AUDIO dialog. Normalize defaults to −.1 dB in Vegas.

Yet another method to bring audio to the maximum level is to use a maximizing tool, such as Sony's Wave Hammer or the industry favorite, WAVES Ultramaximizer. Maximizers are fantastic for bringing audio to an optimum level without distortion. These are usually applied last in the chain, however.

11.5 WAVES Ultramaximizer plug-in is great for mastering output levels.

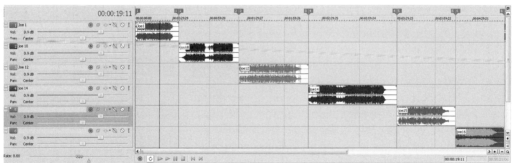

11.6 Having all audio cuts on separate tracks provides the greatest control.

During mastering, effects such as delay and reverb are rarely applied. These are more mix tools than master tools. However, EQ, compression, and audio wideners are all commonly applied. Filters/processes can be applied either at a track level or at an event level in Vegas. Generally, it is best to apply filters at the track level, only for purposes of maintaining consistency and clear processing paths.

To begin the mastering process, place all audio to be included in the final output on the Timeline in the desired order. This process can be done either with each event on its own track or with all events on the same track. It makes no difference other than catering to individual workflow preferences. Leave exactly 2 seconds of blank space at the head of the first track, if the audio will be burned to a Redbook/duplicatable CD. Vegas can autoinsert these 2 seconds as well, which is defined in the OPTIONS | PREFERENCES | EDITING dialog. Audio CDs have specific areas for specific info, such as the first 46 mm of the CD, where the lead-in occurs. Lead-in is where indexing, table of contents, data information, logical block address, and length of track information are stored. If anything more or less than 2 seconds is defined at the head of the CD, Vegas will give an error message indicating that the error must be repaired.

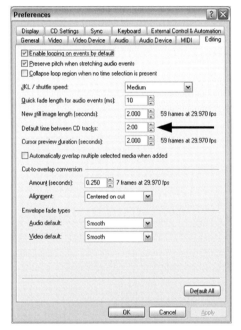

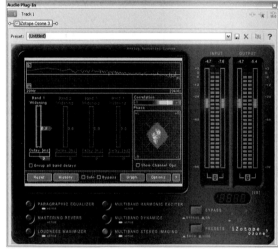

11.7   Set default time between tracks at 2.00 seconds in the OPTIONS | PREFERENCES | EDITING dialog.

11.8   Ozone contains tools specifically for video editors and voice-over artists, as well as being very musical and warm.

Listen to the timbre/tonal differences between pieces of audio. Perhaps one has more or less bass than another, or more high-end or less midrange information. This might be desirable or it might not be. The first part of the process is to determine how to make each event complement the next, without appearing to have jumps in bass, midrange, treble, volume, or pan/right–left information. The transition from one event to the next should be fairly seamless, regardless of whether it's musical or not.

To add EQ to an event at the event level, select TOOLS | AUDIO | APPLY NON-REALTIME EFFECTS, choose an EQ, and click Add. Graphic or parametric choices are available and depend predominantly on the engineer's requirements. Graphic EQs are broader in terms of frequency adjustability, and parametric EQs allow for specific frequency controls.

Here is where plug-ins really shine. Although Vegas does come with a selection of audio plug-ins, many third-party plug-ins are available. For instance, the WAVES Q series or Renaissance plug-in tools are very natural, yet powerful tools. They are very musical and have great control.

Ultrafunk also has some great plug-ins available as well, and their EQs are very musical and warm sounding. Apply EQ sparingly and lean more toward smoothing out harshness, rather than attempting to fix a problem with the overall EQ from the mix. If the track requires a tremendous amount of EQ at this point, it's probably a good idea to revisit the mix. If the master file is audio from a video file, pay attention to the weaknesses in EQ and compensate in future times with better mic techniques and attention to room acoustics.

Applying a touch of bass at the 150 Hz setting will add punch to the mix, whereas adding any frequencies below 90 Hz will most likely enhance any low-end rumble or noise. It's generally a good idea to roll these lower frequencies off with an EQ, using the high-pass filter setting. Adding 1 to 3 dB of gain in the higher ranges, 8 to 12 kHz, will give a little sparkle to the overall mix, but again, too much can create resonant frequencies that are painful to the ear and difficult to control. Watch for harshness in the 1 to 2 kHz regions. When working with audio recorded in a large reflective room, such as a warehouse, bathroom, or conference room, pay close attention to the frequencies around the 500 Hz point. This combination often creates a boomy sound in the audio and should be compensated for or removed if overt and noticeable to the average listener.

Listen to the applied filter and determine if the sound is to satisfaction. If so, then move on to the next event. Notice that when the non-real-time plug-in is applied, a new file is written for the event. Track-level mastering/processing becomes valuable at this point, as real-time effects can be applied without writing a new file. To apply filters/processing at the track level, open the track filter/processing dialog by clicking the FX Filter button found on the Track Control pane. The dialog box will show a noise gate, compressor, and EQ already in place, with check marks showing that the processors are selected. There is also a Plug-In Chain button in the upper-right corner, which allows you to insert other real-time effects and processes. Click this button to add a real-time effect, from the Cakewalk, Sony, WAVES, Ultrafunk, iZotope, or other DX plug-in. Keep in mind that this effect will affect every piece of audio on the track, which is why placing each piece of audio on its own track is a good idea for the mastering process.

When all audio is finished, it is ready to be output. To output to an MP3 format file, select FILE | RENDER AS, and choose MP3 from the Save As Type dropdown menu. The file will be rendered as an MP3 file. Using this same method, Vegas can output AIFF, Ogg Vorbis, or Windows Media Audio files.

11.9   The Plug-In Chain switch/button in the Vegas plug-in chooser.

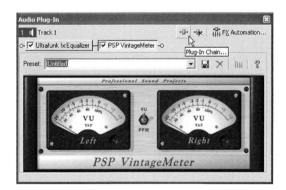

Burning to a Master CD

With all tracks processed to satisfaction, all levels checked, compression at correct settings per cut, and a master compression or EQ setting for the overall project (if it needs a master compressor or EQ), the project is nearly ready to be burned to a CD. Track indexes must be inserted so that listeners have track numbers to skip around to. This process is quite easy in Vegas; just double-click each audio event/track event and press N for a new index point. If subindexes/chapter markers are required, use Shift+N to insert subindex markers. Index points can also be laid out automatically in Vegas Pro 8. Select TOOL | LAY OUT AUDIO CD FROM EVENTS.

Vegas will inspect events on the Timeline and autocreate index markers. However, if events overlap, Vegas will not see the individual beginning/end of events and therefore not assign a track index marker. Check each event beginning to ensure it has a track index marker if this is desired. Autolayout can also be achieved by right-clicking the Marker toolbar, visible only when at least one marker is on the Timeline.

11.10   The Burn Disc-at-Once Audio CD dialog offers speed, testing, and performance options.

11.11   Vegas is capable of automatically creating track indexes for audio CDs.

With markers inserted to indicate track indexes, Vegas is ready to burn a CD. Vegas is capable of Disc-at-Once (DAO) CD burns or Track-at-Once (TAO) CD burns. If a Redbook Master is required for duplicating, DAO is the only option. Redbook standards do not support TAO-burned discs. (Redbook is a mastering/duplicating standard.)

 Tip

All CDs have errors, which is a fact of digital media creation regardless of the authoring application used. However, errors can be minimized. CDs destined for a duplicator will contain fewer errors when burned at lower burn speeds. Although errors cannot usually be heard, they are seen by replicating equipment in most professional duplication houses. Minimize burn errors by burning CDs at the 1× speed where possible.

Audio CDs have specific areas for specific information, such as the lead-in in the first 46 mm of the CD. For burning a Redbook-compliant CD, there must be exactly 2 seconds of dead space/silence before the beginning of the first track. Some burners will allow more than 2 seconds but all require not less than 2 seconds of blank space. Up to 99 tracks are allowed on a Redbook-compliant CD.

Track-at-Once CDs

TAO CDs can be burned from Vegas. TAO burns are handy for capturing tracks as they are mixed for reference purposes or when merely getting the audio to a CD is necessary.

11.12 Track-at-Once burns are efficient for getting a session burned to disc for referencing the session's work.

To burn a TAO, have the track/cut to be burned to a disc on the Timeline and select TOOLS | BURN DISC | TRACK AT ONCE. Select the burn speed and burn device, and finish.

In TAO mode, Vegas can also burn a region to a disc from the Timeline. Select the "Burn Loop Region Only" checkbox. This option is useful for authoring Sony's ACID loops, for sending an advanced digital recording loop section out, or for burning a section of a track that needs to be reviewed without cutting and pasting sections of the track.

Mastering Audio for Video

Mastering for video broadcast is different from mastering for audio CD or DVD. Broadcast standards require deep bass and ultra highs to be rolled off or they'll be chopped off at the limiter/compression stage at the broadcast facility. It's better to have control over the amount of cut off and roll off at the editing/mastering stage than to be unhappy about processing during the broadcast stage. Although no set standard exists for audio roll off in the NTSC or PAL broadcast world, the average is −18 dB per octave roll off at 80 Hz and −9 dB per octave roll off starting at 12 kHz in most houses. Going beyond these ranges almost ensures that you'll have frequencies cut off and compressed at broadcast. DVD and CD playback allows for almost any level of audio, so long as levels don't exceed 0 dBFS. (See Chapter 5 to refresh yourself on the differences between analog and digital zero.)

Using Compression in Vegas for Video

Audio for video should not have a dynamic range of greater than 20 dB. Generally, a dynamic range of less than 15 dB is preferable, depending on the content or attitude of the video and the desired effects. A scary visual might call for a 20 dB dynamic range, going from sublime to extreme to elaborate a particular shot, but in the general norm, dynamic ranges for video should be fairly limited.

Vegas comes with a good compressor. Here again, however, is where a third-party tool can really shine. The Ozone compressor from iZotope has a very warm and broad sound, as they use analog emulation in their application. The maximizer, stereo widener, and compressor alone are worth the price of admission with this tool.

Ozone has to be the sexiest-looking plug-in around, worthy of a Hollywood appearance. Sonic Timeworks' Compressor is also fantastic, with a warm sound, soft or hard compression, and a great look and ease of use too, as are the WAVES, Ultrafunk, and Cakewalk plug-ins.

Compression must be used sparingly at the mastering point; generally settings of less than 3:1 are used at the mastering stage, as audio should have been compressed in the mix stage if the mix process was done to standards. Compression is applied to smooth out dynamic range. If desired, a compressor can bring quiet passages up to a nominal level, while reducing loud passages to a manageable point. Compression is used to get maximum levels while maintaining control over distortion and output levels.

A compression tool can be used at this stage as well when only one or two frequencies are causing the audio to go beyond rational norms. A dynamics compressor, which is a compressor that works only on specific frequencies, is invaluable at this point. Troublesome frequencies can be specified, and the amount of compression of those specific frequencies can be controlled. This option helps smooth out sibilant or plosive sounds from a poor interview mic or helps take down the overdriving pulse of a train that might be in the background of a wide shot mic'd with a handheld or shotgun.

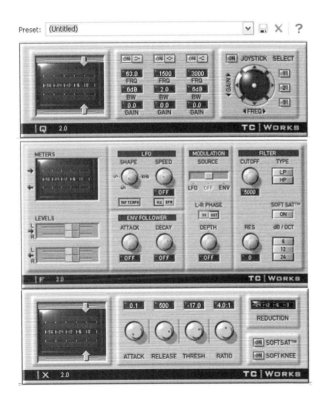

11.13 TC Works has great plug-ins, and they are quite reasonably priced. These tools will tremendously improve the quality of your audio whether for audio production or audio for video.

11.14   A dynamics compressor is excellent in the finishing stages to suppress irritating frequencies, particularly from background sounds interfering with primary dialog or primary audio information.

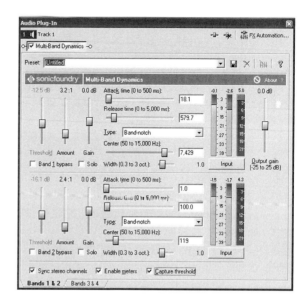

To tune a compressor, listen to the audio closely and notice the peaks and valleys in the spoken word or music. These can be watched at the same time as being listened to. Notice how the peaks seem to jump out and how the valleys need special attention to be heard.

The space between these peaks and valleys is dynamic range. Too much dynamic range creates fatigue on the ear and creates a sense of overdriven sound, even though the audio might be clean. It's a quick way to tire out listeners.

Using Equalizers

A touch of EQ may be added at the final stage as well to bring the overall product to a consistent EQ attitude. The addition of EQ at this last stage, however, should be very minimal and used only to balance out inconsistencies that might arise or to create a final personality in the mix. Most professionals, however, do not add a final EQ as the proper EQ will have been applied during the initial stages of mastering. Keep in mind, there have been two previous opportunities to add EQ to each event/track in the mixing and mastering processes, and it's usually a mistake to apply much EQ to a final master stage. Often, EQs are mistakenly used here to compensate for error in the initial master, mix, or recording stage. If EQ is used in the finishing/mastering stages for video, it should be sparing and applied as an overall mix setting.

Dithering Audio in Vegas

Dither is valuable when audio is going to be printed to a CD, and the original recording was at a sampling rate higher than 44.1 kHz or at a bitrate other than 16 bits. Of course, this is valuable when working with audio for video as well, rather than simply truncating bits in the sample rate change. This process is not the same as resampling but is part of the resampling process. Sony has a dithering plug-in, and a demo of the iZotope Ozone plug-in is on the DVD in this book.

The dithering plug-in should be applied to the master bus to ensure that the last audio process is dither.

Sony's dithering plug-in is Type triangular and the noise shape high-pass contour should be similar to the Ozone Type 2, simple shape. The Ozone Type 1 is rectangular; Type 2 is triangular. Triangular is recommended regardless of which dither you're using, and high-pass shaping is good in both plug-ins. For more advanced noise shaping, the Clear shape for acoustic stuff is highly recommended. It's not as aggressively shaped as the psychoacoustic shapes. The Clear shape sounds natural, but it still has less perceived noise than a simple high-pass shape.

Fade-in/out will be the most noticeable applications of dithering. Highlight the last part of a fade, turn it up fairly loud, and compare right when the audio fades into the noise floor. With the in/out checkboxes on plug-ins, it's pretty easy to A/B. No dither (just truncation) will make the end of the note fade sound like a buzz, like harmonic distortion, or metallic. It will most likely have a zipper sound before it fades out completely. Add dither and get a smoother tail but more noise. Add dither and some noise shaping, such as the Sony or Ozone Type 2, Clear shape, and you'll get a smooth tail but less noise on the fade. (iZotope has excellent information on dithering on their web site at www.izotope.com. There's also a dithering guide from iZotope on the DVD found in this book.)

Rendering Options in Vegas

Vegas is amazingly flexible when it comes to outputting video, whether to tape, a CD, a DVD, the Internet, or a hard drive. AVIs, QuickTime, Windows Media, REAL Media, MPEG-1, MPEG-2, MPEG-4, and any other codec installed on the computer can be used for output. (See Chapter 10 for information on outputting streaming media files.)

Vegas has the option of either rendering an entire project or merely doing a print to tape. The difference is that with a print to tape, Vegas temp-renders sections of the project that require recompression. These sections are written as multiple AVI files. A full render writes an entirely new file as one long file. Either method works as well as the other, and the choices are up to the user's workflow and time constraints. A video that needs to be moved off the hard drive and back to tape quickly might be best handled as a print to tape. For final archiving or for multiple file-type outputs, a full render is recommended. If the same media will be output to Windows Media, QuickTime, REAL, and DVD, all of these processes will go much faster if working from an AVI file, rather than from a project file.

Save the file before rendering, just as a precaution. Writing long video files is taxing on a hard drive and processor, and some older systems cannot handle multiple drives, getting very hot, and will shut down.

11.15   The Render As dialog box provides a choice for the rendered file. Notice the Network Rendering option for Vegas Pro 8.

Rendering to an AVI

Select FILE | RENDER AS to render to an AVI format file. In the Render As dialog box, click the Custom button.

In the Project tab of the Custom Template dialog, select Best. This option will slow down the rendering time slightly, yet ensures that the best rendering options will take place. Under the Video tab, the "Create an OpenDML compatible file" checkbox may be unchecked. Unchecking this option will prevent users from rendering a file larger than 2 GB. You might need to uncheck this box to be compatible with some third-party applications. Leave this box checked if the file contains alpha channels that will need to be accessed later in another editing session.

For a standard AVI file to be printed to tape using the Vegas Capture tool, leave the settings under the Audio tab, including the codec and aspect settings, at their default positions for a successful print to tape. The video must be 720 × 480 for an NTSC-DV print to tape and 720 × 576 for a PAL DV print to tape, and audio must be 48 kHz/16 bits. Otherwise, the camera, converter, or whatever is being used to get the video to a DV tape will not be capable of accepting the media.

To print to tape without rendering the entire project, select TOOLS | PRINT VIDEO TO DV TAPE. This option opens a series of dialogs that make sure the project is prepped correctly to print.

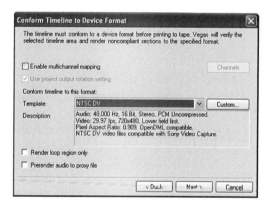

11.16   First dialog box in the print-to-tape process. Be sure you have the entire region selected if leaving the "Render loop region" box checked.

11.17   Second dialog box in the print-to-tape process. Here is where colorbars and test tones are chosen.

Clicking Next in the first dialog leads to the second dialog. In the second dialog, test tones and colorbars can be specified. Colorbars are standard SMPTE colorbars, and the test tone is a 1 kHz test tone, output at −20 dB. Colorbars can be substituted for any test pattern by using the choices in the menu in this second dialog. These bars and tones are necessary, even required by most replication houses and broadcast houses. If this is a print to tape for personal use or to a VHS tape deck, the tones/bars are not required.

Click Next in the second dialog; a third box is displayed. This box asks whether you want automatic control of a tape machine or manual control. Automatic control will start printing to tape after a series of prerenders is finished, wherein all recompressed media on the Timeline is written to a temp file. This option should be selected when long prerendering times are

The tones in Vegas 2, 3, 4, and 5 were at −12 dB.

Vegas Pro 8 has output tones in alignment with the new Advanced Television Standards Committee output standards (www.atsc.org). If any products are calibrated to the old output standard, recalibration will be necessary.

anticipated. This option is useful for the overnight renderer, or for those users who edit during the day or evening and then render and print to tape late at night while all the world is sleeping.

Manual tape control is useful for DV decks that cannot be controlled by the computer or for printing to an analog tape deck, such as a VHS or Beta deck. Selecting the manual option still allows users to walk away from the computer during renders, as Vegas gives a countdown option to printing manually.

After this selection is made, click the Finish button. Vegas then does one of two things:

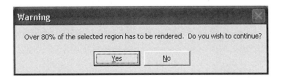

11.18 Vegas warns users if the render process appears to be a lengthy task.

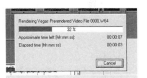

11.19 The rendering progress window indicates how long a render will take.

- Vegas will start to print to tape immediately if no prerenders are left to complete, or if there are very few prerenders, it will complete those and begin the printing or countdown process.

- Vegas will give a warning that more than 80 percent of the project must be rendered and will ask if you wish to proceed. In either event, instruct Vegas to complete the process.

Click OK from the warning, unless a standard render is determined to be more time-efficient.

After Vegas has completed the render process, if automatic control was selected in the Print to Tape dialogs, Vegas will start the DV machine automatically and print the project to tape with no further input/involvement from the user. In a situation in which manual control has been selected in the Print to Tape dialog, Vegas will prerender

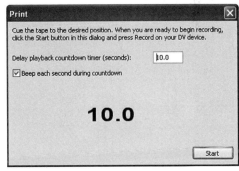

11.20 Vegas allows users to define the length of a countdown.

the recompressed sections and then wait for a click in a countdown box. Vegas will then count down from 10, providing a beep at each second, until it reaches 3 seconds. It will then start to print to tape. To use this manual feature effectively, allow Vegas to count down and, when the counter reaches 3 and no more beeps are heard, click Record on the tape machine. These steps usually provide enough leader time for various tape machines to get up to speed and begin the recording process.

Exporting Events to Third-Party Applications

Sometimes it is necessary to export video events from Vegas to use in a third-party application, for compositing, color grading, etc. When exporting, files should be exported at the best possible resolution, and choices are therefore limited. If files are exported from Vegas using the standard NTSC-DV settings, most third-party applications can read the files, but until Sony opens their codec up to other applications to use, those third-party applications can't write back to the Sony codec. Using the Microsoft codec really isn't a solution either, as it limits quality output too much. Therefore, an uncompressed codec is the answer.

In the FILE | RENDER AS | CUSTOM dialog, an uncompressed setting can be chosen. Understand that using this output method will exponentially increase render times.

Be certain to uncheck the "Create an OpenDML compatible file" option. Most third-party applications cannot read these file types yet.

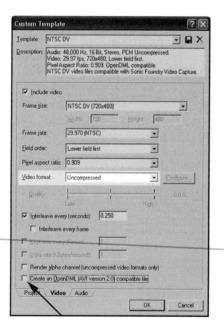

11.21   Select Uncompressed in the Video tab in the rendering options. This option also allows the uncompressed file to retain an alpha channel, should one exist or have been created in the editing process.

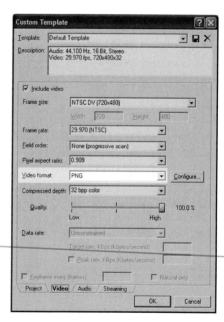

11.22   Rendering to a PNG/QuickTime format is a high-quality output method for exporting to a third-party application.

Another option is to use QuickTime for output, with its numerous options. A few users of Vegas have found great success using the PNG codec as an output option that both Vegas and most third-party applications can read. The PNG format is a lossless compression format that keeps file sizes more manageable and render times slightly faster than using a standard uncompressed output.

To render to the QuickTime format and its various codecs, select the part of the file or event that requires export. Select FILE I RENDER AS, and choose QuickTime/.mov from the Save As menu. Click the Custom button. In the General tab, select Best. In the Video tab under the Video Format menu, select PNG. Adjust the quality slider to 100 percent.

Animators and rotoscope artists often require Targa files (TGA) for their editing applications. Render to QuickTime format, select the Video tab, and select FORMAT I TGA. Set the frame rate, pixel aspect, and frame size in their menus according to the requirements of the importing application.

If audio is part of the export and sync is important, move to the Audio tab and change the default output sample rate to 48 kHz/16 bits, rather than 44.1/16 that QuickTime asks for.

Files exported and imported in these formats will be clean and without quality loss. Using any codec or compressed format between applications runs a risk of loss of quality, so experiment with various outputs to discover what is best for each particular situation. Upsampling/downsampling is a foolish thing to do, as video always loses some information in the up-/downsample. Some applications upsample imported DV as 4:2:2 or 4:4:4. Use caution and check files carefully for color accuracy when upsampling or downsampling between images.

My personal preference to ship frames from one application to another is to output from Vegas as an XDCAM file. The XDCAM MXF file format may be read by virtually every NLE available. The XDCAM format is also great for outputting HDV-acquired 24p streams for import to Final Cut Pro (as of this writing, FCP does not support 24p GOP streams). In the Render As dialog, choose Sony MXF from the Save As Type dropdown. In the Template dropdown, select the template that fits your format.

EDLs and Vegas

One of the perceived weak points in Vegas is the lack of OMF and advanced EDL support. Before saying anything else, I'll comment that Vegas is a finishing tool. It's designed to be used as a start-to-finish solution.

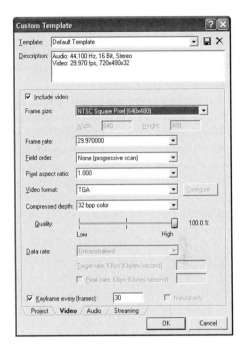

11.23 Render a Targa file by using the QuickTime option in the Render As dialog. The QuickTime authoring tools must be installed on the system to access this menu.

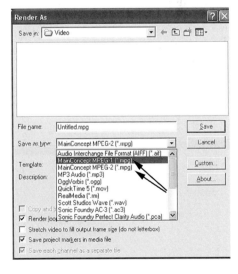

11.24 Select the MPEG format you wish to work with from the Save As Type dropdown menu.

That said, Vegas provides scripting tools for CMX 3600-style EDL export and AAF export that will support standard editing functions. Several steps must be taken to have accurate EDL value.

First, make sure your tapes are clearly and cleanly labeled, as the third-party application will likely require recapturing of the media on the tape. Most applications will not be able to read the timecode from Vidcap.

Second, edit the media as a cuts-only project. Most systems will not be able to read wipes and color correction. Set your project up as a drop-frame project rather than non-drop frame.

Third, use the TOOLS | SCRIPTING | EXPORT EDL feature. This will generate an EDL to be provided to whoever will be using the edits to finish their final project.

On the audio side, there are those times that something must be imported or exported from ProTools, Avid, SAW, SadIE, and other applications. Perhaps someone is sending you a file generated in another application and you want to use their EDL information in Vegas, or perhaps you prefer to work in Vegas but your coworker prefers another application. This used to be a problem. However, there is now a new product available from Cui-Bono Software that will convert most any format of EDL to another format of EDL. This company, based in Germany, has perceived the difficulties of all the various studio formats out there and has created a killer product that works for more than just Vegas users, because this is an industry-wide issue.

EDL Convert Pro is a great application that no professional studio should be without. It's capable of dealing with fades, markers, and in and out points and is basically just a series of clicks. EDL Convert Pro will examine the project settings of the original EDL and set up the conversion based around those settings. You need to alter these settings only if you are taking the EDL to a project that has different settings, but in most instances, you'll use the default properties.

This tool will work in most any format you can imagine, converting Vegas files to or from Samplitude/Sequoia, Audition/Cool Edit Pro, SAW, Wavelab, SADiE3 and 4, Sonic Studio,

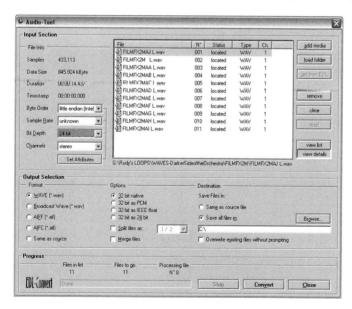

11.25a   This tool will allow you to convert most any audio EDL to a format that Vegas can read or a format that Vegas files can be read in.

Discreet edit, AES31, OpenTL, and OMFI formats. If you are working with a SONAR user, you'll use the OMFI format to import and export for Vegas.

Check out the demo on the DVD in the back of this book or visit the Cui-Bono web site: http://www.cuibono-soft.com/Products/products.html.

AAF Import/Export

No, this isn't related to the band Alien Ant Farm. AAF, or Advanced Authoring Format, is one of a few current standards by which various DAWs and NLEs can share project files. AAF export from Vegas works very well with Adobe Premiere Pro CS3, for example. Using AAF, basic project information may be shared. You can export a project from Vegas and open it in Premiere Pro, Final Cut Pro, Avid products, and a few other NLE systems via AAF, but it's not a perfect transport format protocol. Don't expect things like composites, color-corrected video, or the majority of your transitions to open. It's primarily a means of getting the media onto a new Timeline in exact placement with a few additional granules of sugar thrown on top for sweetness, but it's not the total answer.

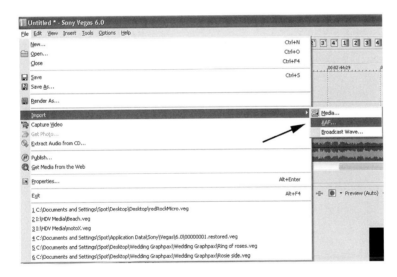

11.25b   Browse for the AAF file that you'd like to import via the FILE | IMPORT
         dialog.

To import an AAF project format, choose FILE | IMPORT | AAF. Browse to the location of the AAF file that you'd like to import. This will import all media associated with that project file. Note the word "media." Any nonmedia file, such as generated titles or masks that are from a specific application that is not in graphic format, will not be imported. Bars and tones are also not imported if they have been generated by an application-specific process.

Transitions (other than cross-fades), color correction, any special filters, audio processors, and composites will also not be imported, as this is not part of the AAF format. Basically, AAF allows an application to locate assets *outside* of the application along with its relevant in/out points on a Timeline.

This is one of the drawbacks of the AAF format. AAF is a cuts-only transportation format from one application to another. Although more robust than a typical CMX EDL export/import format, it doesn't provide perfect translation from one application to another. Let's hope that Vegas supports the more robust MXF, although somewhat complementary to AAF, in the very near future.

To export an AAF for import into After Effects, SaDiE, Final Cut Pro, Avid Express, Cakewalk, or other AAF-supported applications, choose FILE | SAVE AS. From Save As Type, choose Edit Protocol Compliant AAF File. Use this format for most exports. You'll likely want to check the "Embed Wave/AIFC media" box for audio export in the Wave or AIFC codecs. You'll also note that there is an Avid Legacy AAF File option. Use that for exporting to older Avid software tools. The "Embed Wave/AIFC media" checkbox is not available for the Avid Legacy AAF File option.

Another option to check is that the default checkbox for "AAF Export — Use frame unit for audio" in the OPTIONS | PREFERENCES, General tab, is enabled. Otherwise, audio is exported in sample units rather than frame units. Many NLE systems will not be able to read the AAF project file correctly if video is in frame units and audio is in sample units. Therefore, to ensure maximum compatibility, check this box.

11.25c   Choose FILE | SAVE AS to create the AAF file for export.

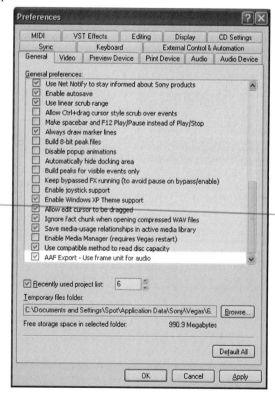

11.25d   Find the "AAF Export—Use frame unit for audio" option in the OPTIONS | PREFERENCES, General tab. Use this as a default for exporting AAF files.

Outputting Other Than AVI Files

Vegas has output capability for nearly every output format, including MPEG-1 and MPEG-2.

Although Vegas does a reasonable job of outputting MPEG-1, the primary MPEG format output focus is on MPEG-2, which is used for DVD encoding and authoring. The primary benefit of an MPEG-1 file is that although it's an old codec and not of top quality, MPEG-1 files do indeed play on just about any player in the world.

Tip

If working with DVD Architect to author DVDs, rendering to an MPEG file is not necessary at this point of your project. DVD Architect works with multiple file formats, and users of Vegas +DVD might find it in their best workflow interest to work with AVI files or native file formats until the project is ready to burn. All versions of Vegas since version 4 provide a render template for DVD Architect in the render settings, whereas DVD Architect has encoding qualities similar to those of Vegas Pro 8.

MPEG Rendering Improvements

Vegas Pro 8 has an excellent MPEG rendering process that provides options for two-pass encoding, among other new features. Two-pass encoding allows the encoder to scan the media in the project, allocating bits for which sections need more attention in the encoding process as opposed to single-pass encoding, which merely encodes what is put into the encoder.

Two-pass encoding is much slower than single-pass encoding, but for high-motion or high-contrast video projects, it's well worth the end result.

To use the two-pass encoding process after you've edited your video, go to FILE | RENDER | MPEG-2 and press the Custom button in the render dialog. Then select the Video tab.

In this dialog, you'll see several options. To access the two-pass encoding, you'll need to select the VBR (variable bitrate) radio button. Notice the checkbox for two-pass encoding. Check this box, and set the rest of the encoding parameters to desired settings.

In the two-pass encoding process, Vegas will first scan the project and write a log file containing information about what's in the project media, noting what's found in the project media. It then begins the scanning process again, encoding the media based on information contained in the log file. Static media, media that contains little movement or little contrast, will not substantially benefit from two-pass encoding. It's a good idea to render short sections of your project to see if there is a discernable difference between the two-pass and the single-pass process of encoding. In most instances, there should not be a large difference from one to the other. If your project contains a lot of still images, remember to set the video rendering quality to Best. This will lengthen the render time, but will provide a cleaner encode quality.

MPEG-2 file types are fairly ubiquitous, and it is the file format of choice for DVD. Vegas uses the MainConcept codec to encode files to the MPEG format, although the Sony version of the MainConcept codec should not be confused with other applications using this codec. Each group of software engineers from the various NLE manufacturers has written individual interfaces to the codec.

To render to MPEG codecs, select FILE | RENDER AS and choose MPEG-1 or -2 from the Save As Type dropdown menu. Selecting MPEG-1 renders an MPEG-1 format video that can be placed on a CD or on the web for download. Selecting the MPEG-2 option renders the MPEG-2 file for use on CD or for sending to a DVD authoring application. (When using Vegas with DVD Architect, files are not required to render to MPEG until DVD Architect prepares the media for the DVD burn.) Audio files in the MPEG-2 format are rendered to an MPEG-2 audio format.

MPEG files can be rendered as progressive-scan or as interlaced files. MPEG files should be rendered to a progressive-scan output for best appearance if the targeted display is a computer screen or progressive-scan television. If the file will predominantly be played on television sets, leave the file interlaced. If the primary target is for computer viewing, set the file format as progressive scan. In the event that a progressive-scan file is displayed on a television that does not have progressive-scan settings, the television or output device will interlace the video. The settings for progressive scan/interlaced are found under the Custom button in the Render As dialog box.

The bitrate (encoding depth) can be selected in the Custom dialog as well. This option is found in the Video tab. Bitrate for standard DVDs should be 8Mbps variable bitrate (VBR). Using VBR allows the encoder to determine the quality of frames based on motion in the various frames.

Some DVD authoring applications require separate video and audio streams. Vegas can output separate streams to meet these requirements. To output separate video/audio streams, select the FILE | RENDER AS | MPEG-2 | CUSTOM | SYSTEM tab.

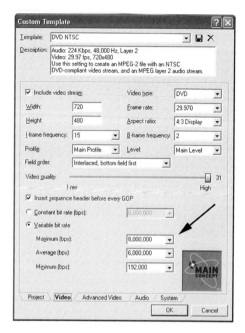

11.26   Bitrate can be selected in the CUSTOM | VIDEO tab.

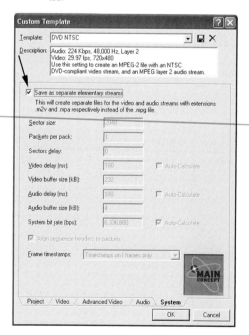

11.27   Create separate audio/video streams for DVD authoring applications that require separate streams.

Place a check mark in the "Save as separate elementary streams" box in this dialog. Vegas will create two separate files: one labeled m2v for the video stream and one labeled mpa for the audio stream. Import these two streams into the DVD authoring application.

Unless you are exceptionally well informed about MPEG encoding functions, you shouldn't change anything else in the MPEG output settings. For more MPEG setting information, see the Sony MPEG white paper on the DVD included with this book.

Outputting an AC-3 Format File

One of the features of Vegas is the ability to output AC-3 audio files. AC-3 is a compression scheme devised and overseen by Dolby Laboratories (www.dolby.com). AC-3 can be output in stereo or 5.1 channel format. The primary benefit of AC-3 is that it allows for audio to be compressed, leaving more space for video on a DVD. AC-3 audio delivers high-quality audio in an encoded format that most consumer and computer DVD players can decode. This option gives viewers the best possible audio experience.

To output AC-3 files, select FILE | RENDER AS and select AC-3 from the menu. Vegas will ignore the video file and render the audio as a stereo or 5.1 audio file, depending on project settings. If the project is a stereo project, audio will be rendered as a stereo/two-channel AC-3 file. If the project is a 5.1 surround project, the AC-3 file will render as a 5.1 file.

For most purposes, the AC-3 presets in Vegas are designed to function as they are built. Experienced AC-3 encoders, however, might find some of the menu options quite valuable for creating a better listening experience. Changing AC-3 settings could possibly create an invalid render in the output file, so experiment on projects that are not time-critical.

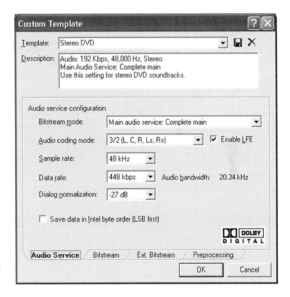

11.28 Stereo or 5.1 surround, Vegas offers a number of choices for output formatting.

 **Tip**

Create a custom template for AC-3 files by setting the Dialog Normalization to −31 dB and setting the Preprocessing Film setting to None. This will cause the AC-3 file to approximate more closely the audio heard during the monitoring process.

Creating a VCD/SVCD

Burning a super video compact disc (SVCD) or video compact disc (VCD) is a one-step process in Vegas, with or without a rendered project. VCD is capable of reading only an MPEG-1 file. SVCD is capable of reading several file formats.

With a project on the Timeline, rendered or not, select TOOLS | BURN CD | VIDEO CD. This selection will open a dialog that allows either a nonrendered project or a previously rendered project to be specified.

If the project has not been rendered to an MPEG-1 format file, Vegas will render to this format automatically when it is instructed to burn a VCD. The new file will need to be named, which will be the name/title that appears in the header file of the burned CD when it is complete. Vegas will indicate the required amount of disc space that the finished render will use. If the file size exceeds the amount of disc space, Vegas will indicate this before the burn.

The menu choices in the VCD dialog are few, as the VCD spec is very narrow. The only options are to burn an NTSC CD or a PAL CD.

Burning an SVCD is a much more open option. QuickTime, REAL, Windows Media, AVI, MPEG-1, and MPEG-2 are all SVCD-capable formats. To burn the SVCD, the project does not need to be rendered separately from SVCD authoring. The file will require rendering in its final format; this can be done directly from the SVCD burn dialog. Select TOOLS | BURN CD | MULTIMEDIA CD.

In the dialog that opens, select the destination for the final render. Then select the file format to which the SVCD file will be rendered. Select a file template based on the file type chosen. NTSC and PAL variants are available for AVI and MPEG file formats.

As with all other render formats, a loop region can be defined as the only area to be rendered. Defining a loop region allows you to select a smaller area of a larger file to be rendered without splitting, copying and pasting, or rendering new sections.

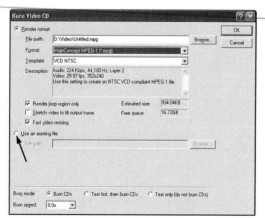

11.29   Select the "Use an existing file" checkbox and browse to locate and burn a previously rendered MPEG-1 file to create a VCD if the project is finished.

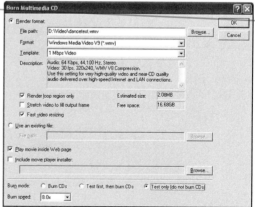

11.30   Menu options include playing video inside a web page and including a player/installer with the SVCD.

11.31 The video can be played inside a company web page or inside any form of HTML document.

If including a player/installer on the disc to be distributed, be sure that the executable file (EXE) is the extension seen on the file. Players can be found at www.microsoft.com, www.quicktime.com, or www.real.com or at several third-party player sites. For any distribution other than personal/internal distribution, a license is required from the appropriate owner of the player software.

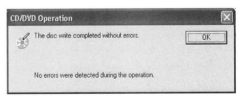

11.32 Viewers of the file who do not have an appropriate player will receive this message complete with links to downloadable installers.

11.33 When the disc has been burned, a successful burn message is displayed.

Additional Rendering Options

Vegas has additional rendering options available, giving users a wide variety of choices. As an example, a loop region can be defined on the Timeline by creating a selection and pressing Q, which will turn on the Looping tool. In the Render As dialog, rendering only a loop region is an option that is valuable when only selections need to be rendered out.

Another option is to stretch the video to fill the screen. This option prevents black bars from being added to the top, bottom, or sides of a video render that has an aspect ratio different from that of the project. Check this box in the Render As options if you want to stretch to fill the aspect ratio.

11.34 Defining a loop region for rendering allows select sections to be rendered for output or export.

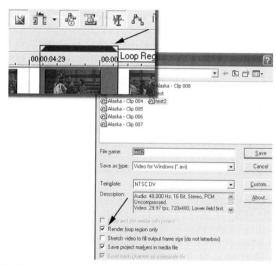

11.35 Pillar Boxed rendered for RGB output/Windows Media.

11.36   Stretched image, using the Stretch to Fill Screen option.

Network Rendering

A favorite, fantastic, and powerful feature in Vegas that everyone will be excited about is network rendering. Sometimes this is referred to as "render farming" because processors from multiple computers are used to render a project, or rather, pieces of the project are "farmed out" to other locations to "grow" the final project file.

If you're a typical computer geek, you likely have more than one machine and will have a network of some sort installed in your office or home. Vegas can now take advantage of all the processors on your network, saving hours of rendering time. This allows you to keep working on a project in Vegas while rendering is taking place in the background, over the network, with very little load on the host machine.

It's as though each computer on the system is taking part in the render and the host machine (on which your editing version of Vegas is installed) assembles all the small rendered sections from the various computers into one finished file. The host machine decides which computers on the network receive which portions of a file for rendering. Vegas uses two different types of workload distribution for network rendering. The first is nondistributed network rendering, which behaves much like a single rendering machine. This format is best used for streaming or other encoded renders requiring multiple bitrates. Using this type of rendering distribution instructs one assigned computer to complete the entire rendering process on a file. In nondistributed rendering choices, multiple files may be queued up for rendering as single files on each machine. However, projects may not be broken down so that portions of a file are rendered on various machines.

Nondistributed renders are also best for audio-only projects, as Vegas renders video first in a rendering process.

> Vegas sets render tasks in either distributed or nondistributed assignments. Use distributed rendering for DV and uncompressed file types for fastest rendering results. Each machine on the network will render small portions of the Timeline and the host machine assembles the small pieces into one finished file.
>
> Nondistributed rendering is best for encoding to .mpg, multiple bitrate, or audio-only render tasks. This uses one machine per finished file, with no portions being rendered separately, and no portions being assembled or stitched together to form a complete file. (MPEG, AC-3, and MP3 files cannot be rendered on a client-only license of Vegas.)

Distributed rendering causes Vegas to send out small packets or portions of a Timeline to be rendered over various machines on the network. The host, or parent machine, then assembles all of the various rendered portions in to one large, finished file. This is best for .mpg or .avi file formats to be rendered quickly.

> If you intend on using this feature regularly, you should find it beneficial to set up a "File Server" on which all files for projects are stored. Not only will this allow for multiple users or machines to access the same files easily, it also will allow for a fast and simple set up for the Network Render feature.

Setting Up the Rendering Network (Render Farming)

The components of a render farm are critical to the system functioning correctly. Without all components set up, render farming will not work. You need:

- A minimum of two computers, each with at least 256 MB of RAM. More RAM is advised. At least one machine must have a full version of Vegas Pro 8 installed, and other machines must have either full versions or render-client-only versions of Vegas installed on them.

- A switched network. A wired hub will not work; go purchase a switch. They cost slightly more money, but they're necessary, as a switch will not determine workflow speed like a hub will.

- A wired 100 Mbps network. Using a wireless network, sexy as they are, simply will not function for this. There is too much data that needs to pass through the network. If you have a gigabit network, it's all the better for rendering speed.

- Shared folders to hold the VEG file, all media, and all assets to the project to be rendered over the network. All folders must have permissions set to read, write, delete, and create files on the network.

Rendering Clients

The machines used for rendering that are not the host machine are known as clients. Each client machine must have either a full version of Vegas installed or a render-client version of Vegas installed on it. Render-client licenses are available from Sony, the cost of which was not determined at the time of this writing. MPEG, AC-3, and MP3 file formats cannot be rendered on render-client-only machines due to the way files are stitched together, so if you plan on rendering a number of these licensed file formats, you'll do best to purchase full versions of Vegas for each client machine. (Just prior to printing of this book, Sony announced that these file types may be rendered over a network; see Sony's web site for more information.)

Install the software on the client machines.

On the rendering-client machines, start the rendering service. It may take a moment to load, as the application is going to search for any machines connected to the network prior to displaying the user interface. This application will determine how the network renders your project files. You'll need to be logged in to each machine to be used on the network prior to rendering. Start the VegSrv50.exe application. You can create an icon on the desktop for this. Simply browse from the Desktop shortcuts menu to the C:\Program Files\Sony\Vegas Pro 8 folder and locate this file, and an icon will be created on the desktop. When you run the application, an icon will appear in the system tray. This may also be used to determine how a network render will function.

You do not need to start the rendering service for each rendering job, but as mentioned previously, you'll need to be logged on to each client prior to rendering. Once logged on, if the client or host machine sees a project, it will automatically be ready to start working for you.

In the Rendering Services application, you should see each machine that is able to be used as a client machine logged on to the network. Click the Renderers tab to select which machines will be used to render the project.

Depending on your network configuration, you may need to modify TCP settings on the host machine. This is rarely necessary; however, some systems may require it. If you are unsure of what to do, consult an IT person in your company, or call an IT specialist to help you set up the rendering network.

The following steps may be necessary for some systems:

1. Exit the Vegas Network Render Service application if it is running.

2. Open the NetRenderService.config file in a text editor such as Notepad. This file is located at C:\Program Files\Sony\Vegas Pro 8.

3. Edit the <channel ref="tcp" port="53704"/tag in the file to reflect the port you want to use.

4. Save the modified file information.

5. Relaunch the Vegas Network Render Service.

You'll need to know the name of each computer on the network to assign and access it from within the Vegas Network Render Service. To locate the name of each computer on the network, right-click the My Computer icon on the desktop or in the application menu and choose

Properties. Choose the Computer Name tab, and the computer's full name will be displayed. You can copy and paste this name into the Renderers tab of the Network Render Service dialog to connect the client machine to the host machine.

To connect the client machines to the host machine, select the Renderers tab. In the Host dialog box, input either the IP address or the computer name you wish to add to the render service. Press Enter and the Render Service application will then communicate with the client machine. If the machines communicate successfully, the Render Services application will show "Ready" in the Status box. If the two machines fail to communicate, a "Failed to add" dialog will open up. If this error occurs, double-check the IP address or name of the client machine you are attempting to connect to, and try again. Be sure you are logged on to the client machine. If the client machine is in a room far from your host machine, log on to the client machine and use Ctrl+Alt+Delete to lock the machine while communicating with the client machine via the host machine.

To set up a distributed network render:

1. Save the project.

2. From the File menu, select Render As.

3. Use the Render As dialog to determine the file type and location where you want to save your finished project file. The location of the finished file must be in a shared folder.

4. Select the "Render using networked computers" checkbox in the Render As dialog, and click the Save button. The Network Render dialog will be displayed.

5. Select the "Distribute Rendering among Peers" checkbox in the Network Render dialog.

6. From the Stitch Host dropdown list, choose the computer you want to use to assemble the rendered segments. If you are planning to be working on the host machine during network rendering, it's advisable to select another machine as the Stitch Host for best results during the editing-while-rendering process.

7. Choose a file format for your rendered segments.

8. Select the "Use Final Render Template" checkbox if you want to render segments using the format you chose for your final output in the Render As dialog.

   Use this option when you're working with DV or uncompressed files. In this case, using the rendering template for rendered segments makes the final stitching process fast because the segments are copied and assembled without being reencoded.

9. Clear the "Use Final Render Template" checkbox and choose settings from the Save As Type and Template dropdown lists if you want to render segments using a format other than your final output format. You can create your own templates for final output, and these custom templates often come in handy.

Use this option when you're rendering to a format that uses temporal compression, such as MPEG, QuickTime, REAL Media, or Windows Media. Rendering segments as uncompressed or DV AVI files allows transitions and composited tracks to be rendered in a high-quality format. When the segments are stitched, the project is reencoded using the format you chose for your final output in the Render As dialog.

At the time of this writing, AC-3, MPEG-2, and MP3 rendering was not supported over the network because of recompression issues. Due to the method in which these file types are created, segments may not be stitched together without recompressing the file, causing a loss in quality.

10. Click OK to start rendering. The segments of the project will begin rendering on the various machines as instructed in the Network Rendering Services application dialog.

For nondistributed network rendering:

1. Save the project.

2. If you want to render only a portion of the project, create a time selection that includes the segment to be rendered.

3. From the File menu, choose Render As.

4. Use the Render As dialog to choose the file type and output location where you want to save the finished file. The location of the output file must be in a shared folder.

5. Select the "Render loop region only" checkbox in the Render As dialog if you want to render the selected portion of your project.

6. Select the "Render using Networked Computers" checkbox in the Render As dialog, and then click Save. The Network Render dialog will be displayed.

7. From the Render Host dropdown list, choose URL or location of the renderer you want to use to render your project.

8. Click OK to start rendering.

9. To add a project to the queue, open the project and repeat above instructions.

You can select a different render client for each project or time selection if you want to render the files at the same time on separate machines. If you choose the same client, the rendering jobs will be queued to run sequentially on that machine.

Monitoring the Rendering Progress

You can monitor the progress of a project render by right-clicking the Network Services icon found in the system tray and choosing Show from the submenu. The Rendering Services dialog will open and show the rendering progress on the system. Details or a summary may be viewed by selecting Detail or Summary from the Progress dropdown menu.

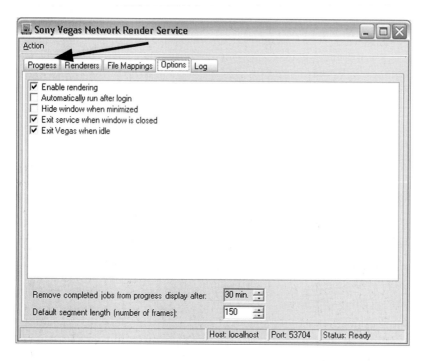

11.37   Monitor network renders from the Render Services application.

File Mapping

File mapping tells render clients where to locate media assets used in a project. When you import media assets from a local disk, the file paths saved in your project are usually valid only on the local machine. This can be the case even if the media resides in a shared folder. Generated media needs and contains no such location information.

Use the File Mappings tab to map local folders to universal paths.

1. Right-click the icon in your system tray and choose Show from the menu to display the Sony Vegas Network Render Service window.

2. Select the File Mappings tab. The tab displays a list of local folders and their universal paths.

3. Click on a blank row in the table.

4. In the Local box, type the path to the local folder (C:\media, for example).

5. In the Universal box, type the UNC path or mapped drive letter to the folder. An example might read similar to \\project file\media\.

Do not place media in a root directory. Network rendering will not be able to locate it and the render will not complete.

If you get a Failed To Initialize Network error:

1. Open a DOS window.

2. From the Start menu, choose Run to display the Run dialog.

3. In the Open box, type CMD.

4. Click OK. A DOS window will be displayed.

5. Type ipconfig at the command prompt; press Enter.

6. Your Windows IP configuration information is displayed. Note the connection-specific DNS suffix setting in the display.

7. Update your machine's DNS suffix: Right-click My Computer on your desktop and choose Properties from the shortcut menu (or press the Windows key+Pause) to open the System Properties dialog.

8. Select the Computer Name tab.

9. Click the Change button to display the Computer Name Changes dialog.

10. Click the More button to display the DNS Suffix and NetBIOS Computer Name dialog.

11. In the Primary DNS suffix of this computer box, type the DNS suffix you recorded in step 2.

12. Click OK to close all dialogs, then restart your computer.

Keep in mind that your End User License Agreement does not permit running Vegas on more than one machine at a time, so you'll need to choose a machine on the network that will be used for network rendering and that you won't be editing with. One system needs to be loaded with the client-only version of Vegas. Additional licenses may be purchased from Sony on its web site.

Additional Functions of the Network Rendering Application

The Network Rendering application has several options that you can specify to make the rendering process as efficient as you'd like it to be. For example, the local host may be used as a rendering machine or not. You make that choice.

To access these choices, right-click the Network Rendering icon in the system tray and choose Show from the submenu that is displayed. This will open the dialog.

At the time of this writing, the Network Rendering feature is still undergoing testing and writing. Please check the Sony Media Software web site for updated information.

Network Rendering Options

Enable Rendering	Select this checkbox if you want the computer you are working with (local) to be available as a rendering machine.
Automatically Run after Login	Enable this feature if you want to start the service automatically after logging in to Windows.
Exit Service when Window Closed	Clear this checkbox if you want to keep the service running after closing the window. If the checkbox is cleared, the service is minimized and found in the system tray when you exit. Unless you use network rendering a lot, leave this checked.
Exit Vegas	When Idle Select this checkbox if you want to close the instance of Vegas software that is launched by the network render service when no jobs are set up to be rendered. If the checkbox is cleared, the application continues running until you close it or exit the service.
Remove Completed Jobs from Progress Display after:	Choose a setting to indicate how long jobs should be maintained on the Progress tab of the Sony Vegas Network Render Service window. The default is 1 hour; lengths as short as 5 minutes may be specified.
Default Segment Lengths	Choose a setting to indicate the number of frames per segment when using distributed rendering. Adjusting this value can increase performance slightly depending on the complexity of the project and the speed of the rendering clients.
	If the setting yields more than 90 segments for a rendering job, the segment length for that job is automatically increased to limit the number of segments.

High-Definition Video

Vegas also offers the ability to edit and output high-definition media in 720p, 1080i, and 1080p formats. Refer to Chapter 2—Capturing Video—for details and specifics on ingesting the various flavors of high-definition media using Vegas Pro 8.

11.38 Project properties in Vegas include high-
definition settings.

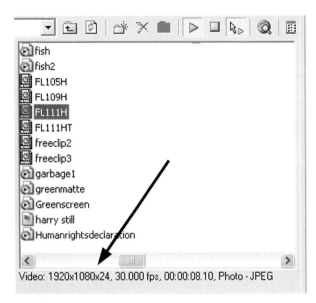

Video: 1920x1080x24, 30.000 fps, 00:00:08.10, Photo - JPEG

24p has some very significant benefits and support in Vegas. Transitions, titles, and filters are optimized in Vegas for 24p. Vegas also has specific support for the Panasonic DVX100 camera and cameras with similar features. Vegas autodetects 2-3 and 2-3-3-2 pulldown at capture and previews and prints to tape in the 24p format when the Panasonic DVX100 camera is used. The 2-3 and 2-3-3-2 pulldowns are performed on the fly in Vegas with no additional hardware required. Vegas also allows for preview on external monitors at 24p.

On the output side, Vegas can output a still image sequence up to 2048 × 2048, is capable of outputting 1080i or 720p at the 24p frame rate, and can print to tape at 24p as well. Windows Media 9 has support for 24p/HD, and streaming file sizes are smaller at 24p than at 29.97. 24p also offers up to 25 percent additional disk-space savings on a DVD.

Given that 24p renders twice as fast as 60i (standard NTSC frame rate) and that 24p offers a look closer to film, this format will continue to grow.

Vegas edits and prints media at 720p with frame rates of up to 60 fps, at resolutions of 1080p with frame rates of 24 and 29.97 fps, and at 1080i with frame rate of 60 fps (29.97 interlaced). With the output capability of 24 fps/progressive scan, video shot with 24p will stay in its native format with no pulldown.

When working with high-definition media, full-frame-rate playback is very difficult to achieve because of the load on the processor. Be aware that playback at full frame rate is unlikely on all but the fastest systems. On a Pentium 3 with 1.8 GHz processor and 1 GB of RAM, the best playback achieved was less than 15 fps. Rendering to RAM allows for full-motion playback; however, for most circumstances, a different workflow may appeal to most users.

With Vegas's ability to recapture media via the Project Media or to work with originally captured media, try to capture using a dual-stream card where possible, so that a low-resolution/

When working with high-definition media, current IDE and some SATA drive speeds will prove to be unsatisfactory for most users. SCSI drives/RAIDS with a 320-controller card are considered good starting points for most high-definition editing practices.

11.39 Rendering/output settings include high-definition capability in Vegas.

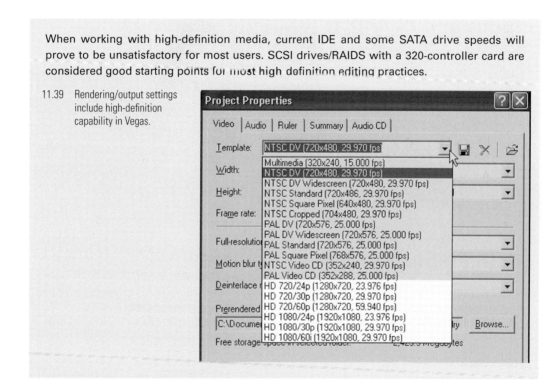

compressed capture takes place at the same time as the high-definition media is being captured. Most high-definition cards allow for this to take place. Edit on the Timeline using the lower-resolution media and replace media with the high-definition video in the Project Media when you finish editing. This process will allow editing to take place with full motion and full resolution without taxing the processor as heavily as native high-definition media. Rendering to a RAID, the media can then be printed to tape either using a high-definition card, capture tool, and high-definition tape machine or using the RAID delivered to a service bureau for final print and replication for distribution. This is a form of offline/online editing but can be done natively with Vegas as both a rough-cutting and a finishing tool. By using the Super Sampling Envelope tool, even DV can be effectively upsampled to HD output. Bear in mind that render times will be fairly slow on longer projects. Upsampling from resolutions of 720 × 480 to 1920 × 1080 will more than double the resolution of DV.

11.40 This high-definition footage from Artbeats fills most of a standard monitor even at three-quarter size (Artbeats Family Lifestyles HD library).

4:2:2 MPEG Capability

Vegas is also capable of rendering broadcast streams for delivery to a media server in a broadcast facility such as a Telestream or Matrox Videoserver. This functionality is not for the typical Vegas user but designed exclusively for professional broadcast delivery formats. 4:2:2 broadcast streams have a delivery data rate of up to 80 Mbps, compared to a DVD delivery data rate of up to 15 Mbps. Most DVDs are at a substantially lower bitrate, but the spec allows for a higher than the currently used delivery bitrate.

The 4:2:2 format provides for greater luma and chroma information in the stream, allowing for higher quality video broadcast display instead of the standard 4:2:0 delivery of consumer-oriented DVD MPEG delivery.

Although it might be tempting to render to this format, there is nothing to be gained by the end user, unless it's as an archival format. No settop player can play back files at this data rate. If you intend to deliver an MPEG-encoded project for broadcast, check with the broadcast house in advance to learn what data rate they'd like to see the project come in at.

New Codecs

In Vegas, there is a new 4:2:2 YUV codec. This is of great benefit to those rendering files to archive or for multidelivery. Faster than rendering uncompressed, and enabling better image quality than 4:2:2 media, this is great for those doing SD-based (standard definition) projects as well.

11.41   Sony has created a 4:2:2 YTUV codec, found in Vegas Pro 8.

   Where this is of value to DV editors is when a project needs to be archived or delivered in multiple formats. Render the project to the 4:2:2 YUV codec, and then use the new .avi file to render MPEG, streaming media, and any other secondary format. Using this as an intermediary codec serves no value if delivering to a final MPEG format, for instance. Encoding MPEG from the Timeline is always the best proposition if MPEG is the only delivery format.

   When DV is dropped on the Vegas Timeline, the video is already compressed at 4:1:1. When color correction, transitions, and other changes to the media are applied, Vegas upsamples those changes to 4:4:4, or uncompressed media in these processes. The uncompressed sections then become compressed when the final file is rendered. Rendering to 4:2:2 keeps the new media at a higher quality than the 4:1:1 render. However, when media is rendered from the Timeline to MPEG, it's rendered at 4:2:0, creating yet a third transcode in the process of rendering. Therefore, if you are rendering any sort of project to a single-delivery format, it's always best to render to that format directly from the Timeline, saving transcodes and time. However, if there are multiple-delivery formats required, it's a good idea to render to either uncompressed or the higher-quality 4:2:2 format to input to a batch encoder, ensuring that the original source file is of the highest quality available depending on allotment of time in the final rendering process.

There is no benefit of rendering 4:1:1 DV project files to 4:2:2 and then rendering the 4:2:2 to MPEG, unless again, the final source files will be delivered in some format other than DV and in one or more other delivery formats. If you were to render to 4:2:2 and then convert that to 4:1:1 again for print to DV tape, information would actually be lost in the process due to transcoding.

Rendering to the 4:2:2 YUV codec is slower than rendering to the 4:1:1 Sony codec, as one might expect.

Scripting

Vegas has a feature that is terrific for users needing customized output and processing options. This feature uses JavaScript to define these behaviors. Vegas can literally be instructed to render several file types, to batch process, to match aspect ratios, even to build a video at random with random transitions from media in the Project Media! Scripts basically provide an open-ended function for Vegas users to implement code to instruct Vegas to provide unique behaviors.

To use scripting, you'll need to have the Microsoft .NET framework installed. The .NET framework can be downloaded at no cost from Microsoft.

Visit http://www.microsoft.com/net/ to order a CD or download the framework.

Many scripts are available on the Sony web site, as well as on the VASST web site, http://www.vasst.com. Writing scripts is a challenge for those not familiar with Visual Basic or JavaScript authoring. You can write scripts with any plain text editor, even Notepad. The Microsoft developer's web site (msdn.microsoft.com) probably has the most authoritative reference for the .NET scripting languages, but other tutorials are available on the web. In addition, several books on JScript .NET and Visual Basic .NET are available from Amazon.com and other bookstores.

11.42 Access the scripts by selecting TOOLS | SCRIPTING | RUN SCRIPT.

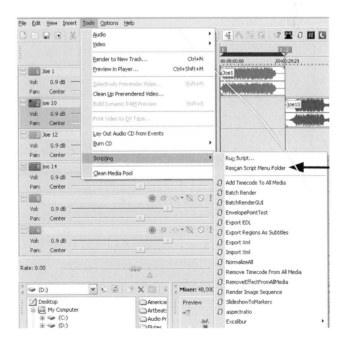

Here is a sample .js script that opens 3 tracks each of Audio and Video:

```
/**

 * Program: TrackSetup.js
 * Description: This script will create some initial tracks in Vegas for Video,
 *              Audio, Video Overlay, and Title. This is for people who don't
 *              like the fact that Vegas starts without labeled tracks.
 *
 * Author: Johnny (Roy) Rofrano
 *
 * Date: March 29, 2004
 **/

import Sony.Vegas;
import System.Windows.Forms;

try
{
    // Add three video tracks
    AddTrack(1, MediaType.Video, "Title");
    AddTrack(2, MediaType.Video, "Overlay");
    AddTrack(3, MediaType.Video, "Video");

    // Add threee Audio tracks
    AddTrack(4, MediaType.Audio, "Audio");
    AddTrack(5, MediaType.Audio, "Music");
    AddTrack(6, MediaType.Audio, "Effects");
}
catch (errorMsg)
{
    MessageBox.Show(errorMsg, "TrackSetup Error", MessageBoxButtons.OK,
        MessageBoxIcon.Error);
}

/*
 * Adds a track to the project with a name and index
 */
function AddTrack(index : int, mediaType : MediaType, name : String)
{
    var track;
    if (mediaType == MediaType.Audio)
    {
        track = new AudioTrack(index, name);    // create audio track
    }
    else
    {
        track = new VideoTrack(index, name);    // create video track
    }

    Vegas.Project.Tracks.Add(track);    // add the track
}
```

Running scripts can also appear to be intimidating, when in truth, running scripts is quite straightforward. After locating/downloading scripts, place them in a directory. The default location for scripts in Vegas Pro 8 is C:\Program Files\Sony\Vegas Pro 8.0\Script Menu. To run a script, select TOOLS | SCRIPTING | RUN SCRIPT, which will open a browse dialog box. Browse to where the .vb or .js scripts are stored. After adding scripts to the folder, go to TOOLS | SCRIPTIN G | RESCAN SCRIPT MENU FOLDER. This will place scripts in the TOOLS | SCRIPTING drop-down menu. This will save time in not needing to search out scripts in other folders.

Select the script you wish to run, which will start the script. Scripts are like trading cards that are available from many Vegas users, and a small cottage industry has sprung from this concept of having an open engine. VASST and others offer for-purchase tools that take advantage of scripting operations, potentially saving users inestimable time, depending on the sort of work-flow used. It's easy to become dependent on scripts, as they can perform many mundane tasks with one button. And with key mapping, you can map scripts to any button you'd like, making Vegas a totally personal system. At the time of this writing, well over 200 scripts were available and can be found online at www.vasst.com.

Scripts will continue to add to the power of Vegas and offer users a tremendous number of options.

One aspect of scripting that creates exceptional ease of use is to create a button on the toolbar for the script. This option allows rapid access to commonly run scripts. Up to 10 scripts may be associated with 10 buttons on the toolbar.

> If you have Vegas 4 and want to import scripts from Vegas 4 into Vegas Pro 8, you'll need to edit the line in the script text that calls for SonicFoundry.Vegas to Sony.Vegas. Otherwise the scripts will not function correctly.

To place a button/script on the toolbar, double-click the toolbar, which will open the Customize Toolbar dialog. Select a script button to add to the toolbar. In Figure 11.45, Script 3 is selected to be placed in the toolbar. This step places a button on the toolbar that can be associated with a script by pressing Ctrl+Shift+3 or by clicking the Script button. Vegas will open a browser window that allows you to select a specific script to be assigned to that button.

Another method of assigning a script to a toolbar button is to select TOOLS | SCRIPTING | SET SCRIPT and choose the script number to which you wish to assign

11.43 The script used in this instance locates in and out timecodes for all files on the Timeline, lists their running time/length, and saves them as an HTML file.

C:\Documents and Settings\DSE\Desktop\scripts\test.html - Videogeek's scans

File   Edit   View   Favorites   Tools   Help

Back   Search   Favorites   Media

Address   C:\Documents and Settings\DSE\Desktop\scripts\test.html

Name	Comment	TimecodeIn	TimecodeOut	Length
D:\Video\Alaska - Clip 002.avi	undefined	00:04:12:26	00:04:47:00	00:00:34:04
D:\Video\Alaska - Clip 003.avi	undefined	00:07:38:02	00:08:04:23	00:00:26:21
D:\Video\Alaska - Clip 004.avi	undefined	00:13:03:21	00:13:40:04	00:00:36:13
D:\Video\Alaska - Clip 005.avi	undefined	00:26:07:17	00:26:09:22	00:00:02:05
D:\Video\Alaska - Clip 006.avi	undefined	00:26:09:22	00:26:25:28	00:00:16:06
D:\Video\Alaska - Clip 007.avi	undefined	00:26:25:28	00:26:49:20	00:00:23:22
D:\Video\Alaska - Clip 008.avi	undefined	00:27:01:17	00:27:28:22	00:00:27:05

11.44 Assign a script to a button on the toolbar in Customize Toolbars. This button runs the RenderImageSequence script from the Vegas Pro 8 toolbar.

11.45 Select scripts for use in the Script browser.

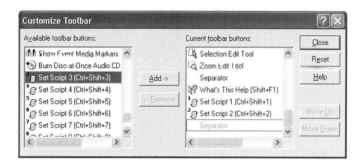

a script. This action will open the Browse Scripts window as well, from which a script can be assigned to a script number. This same script number can be associated with a button by following the steps outlined earlier.

Using Vegas with DVD Architect

To use Vegas with DVD Architect (DVDA), render the project as either an MPEG-2 or an AVI file. If the project is to be 5.1 at final output, render the file as an MPEG-2 file. Insert markers in the file for chapter points if desired. DVDA will recognize these markers as chapter points and will insert them as such if instructed to do so in DVDA.

Audio that is to be associated with the MPEG file, regardless of whether it is stereo or mono, should be rendered as an AC-3 file. DVDA will automatically convert stereo audio to an AC-3 file during the DVDA render/burn process. Audio in a 5.1 channel project file will not be embedded in the MPEG file in any form. (See the previous sections in this chapter on creating AC-3 audio for DVD Architect.)

Files that are rendered as 24p files will not be transcoded/recompressed in DVDA; they will stay in their native format. This feature allows 20 percent more video media to be placed on the DVD, which can be monitored/previewed in DVDA as well. Export of 24p NTSC MPEG-2 for DVD Architect is also supported as an output format in Vegas. Bear in mind that to view 24p media on an external monitor, the frames will have to have pulldown added, creating a 60i or 50i video stream that the external monitor can comprehend.

The best workflow I've found for rendering files for MPEG-2 and AC-3 files while leaving the system unattended is to use the Batch Render script found in Vegas Pro 8. Go to TOOLS | SCRIPTING | BATCH RENDER and run the script. An interface will open, looking like the one you see in Figure 11.46.

In this interface, expand the Main Concept MPEG option. In this subset, select the format of MPEG you wish to use. Do not simply check the MPEG tick box without expanding. During beta testing, I did this for a project containing 11 regions as I hadn't expanded the subset. It rendered all night, and the next morning, I had 209 files! Nineteen templates rendered for all 11 regions, and it created a mess. I've accidentally done this for AC-3 as well. If you check only the file format, Vegas will render a version of the file for each template setup in your preferences. Expanding the subsets allows you to select the specific format you'd like files rendered to.

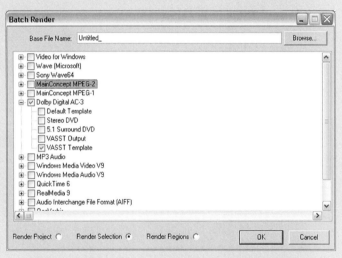

11.46   The Batching script renders multiple forms of Windows Media from one
         Timeline and one action.

For standard export to DVD Architect, choose the DVD Architect NTSC or PAL video stream and tick the box next to that subset option. Contract the MPEG set, and choose the AC-3 subset. Select either the "Stereo DVD" or the "5.1 Surround DVD" checkbox, depending on the project type. Let the project render, and when it's finished, you'll have both file types of the same name, stored in the same folder. DVD Architect will locate the audio with the video, and you'll be set. This batch script is great for rendering to .avi, .mpg, and streaming media while you're gone for the night or out to lunch. Long projects don't need as much babysitting.

Alternative Delivery

Creating High-Quality Portable Media

Just as the early days of television was to the established medium of radio, webstreaming video and portable media devices are to television today. The information presented in today's streaming content might be exceptional, but the quality of the view is compromised because of the delivery medium. But whereas television was a single technology with very limited content, webstreaming and personal media devices offer many opportunities to get your message across. Today, Flash files are commonplace, as will be the upcoming Silverlight from Microsoft. Additionally MP4, Windows Media Video (WMV), and even REAL Media are all streaming/downloadable media alternatives.

Vegas is one of the most powerful web-delivery authoring and editing tools available today. Preproduction, however, is equally as important as the editing and encoding ability when it comes to creating great streaming media. Although many resources are available for great streaming media authoring techniques, I've included some tips in this chapter for shooting and producing great media.

Shooting, Editing, and Delivering

Perhaps the most important part of streaming production is knowing more about video than simply how to turn on a camera. Understanding the basics of production is equally important to the flow of the production process and to the quality of the media itself.

People trained for working directly in broadcast are often the worst at generating quality streaming media shoots. Much of what is known about broadcast shooting is diametrically opposed to shooting good web video. Keep in mind that television is a lean-back experience, in which viewers are laid back, perhaps with a bowl of popcorn in hand, relaxing in some form.

12.1   The rule of thirds applies to broadcast images.

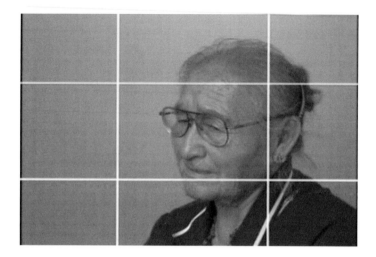

Streaming media, or media on a computer, is generally known as a lean-in experience, in which the viewer is close to the computer monitor, leaning in to view a fairly small image. This issue alone forces a completely different perspective for production of media. Of course, with the convergence of television and streaming media close at hand, this issue might well change in the near future. Both REAL and Windows Media support high-definition streams with surround-sound ability, and the quality of these streams is outstanding. A large percentage of the world is still on dial-up, so bandwidth will continue to be an issue in the near future.

Three processes are in the chain of web video production:

- Production

- Editing

- Encoding and delivering

12.2   Streaming media works best using more of the screen space or the rule of two-thirds.

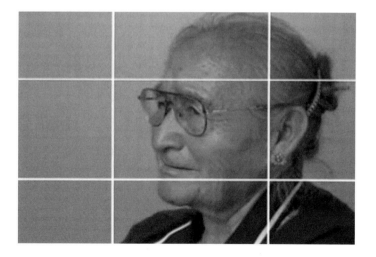

Production

Rule No. 1 for shooting good web video is to always shoot with a tripod. Handheld camera work, regardless of the ability of the cameraperson, simply has too much movement to be encoded well. Redundant information in the frame encodes well, whereas moving media, even if it's only slight movement, encodes poorly.

Shoot close in. Normally in broadcast-destined footage, shots are based around the rule of thirds. The rule of thirds is simple; divide the viewfinder into a grid that looks like a tic-tac-toe game. Any two points where lines intersect become the focal points of your subject matter, preventing the subject from being in the exact center. With streaming media, however, the message is more important than is the aesthetic of the picture. Clarity and a less informational background is the goal. Shooting for two-thirds imagery means bisecting three lines rather than only two in the framed image. Whether widescreen, standard 4:3, or odd sizes (always divisible by 8), shoot tight when possible.

Be as tight as practical. Limit any background movement. Never shoot in front of moving trees, roads, or other backgrounds where there is movement. In fact, shooting against a backdrop, greenscreen, or bland fixed set is generally best. Keep background information/imagery to its simplest form. This process makes it easier for the encoder to process information.

Don't forget audio. Audio is even more important in the streaming world than in the broadcast world, and it's pretty important in the broadcast world. Viewers of streaming media will forgive the poorer video quality of a stream. They generally will not forgive bad audio. Always use close-mic'ing techniques. Never use a microphone built onto the camera. The microphone is too far from the subject, and the sound will be muffled and full of reflections, noise, and ambience, which are difficult to remove. Use Sony Noise Reduction if necessary, and it often is necessary when an on-camera microphone is used. Unless the production is being delivered over the Internet or if it's absolutely live-or-die necessary, audio should be in mono rather than stereo. Aside from phasing issues, stereo audio is more difficult to encode than is mono audio, and the audience can rarely appreciate stereo audio on most computer systems. Of course, if the production is a music-oriented project, then stereo or even 5.1 surround may be preferable.

12.3 Well-lit face for streaming. High contrast and a tight shot make for a great stream at any speed. If the background is static, of one or two colors, and contrasted highly against the subject, Windows Media 9 is capable of delivering even a full-screen stream at 56 Kbps. This image is a 56 Kbps stream projected in a training session. (Photo by R. Grandia.)

12.4 Using a split screen allows camera angles to be less important and still keeps a two-part conversation visible and clean.

Limit or curtail reverb decay times, and cut off bottom- and top-end frequency information with an audio equalizer. This process leaves less information for the encoder to deal with. Normalize or maximize audio to ensure that it's as loud as possible. The encode process works best with highly compressed, loud media. Large dynamic ranges (quiet to very loud) do not encode well. Try to limit dynamic range to 12 dB or less.

Light well. Having great lighting is critical to any web video production. This issue is true more so than in the broadcast world because encoders have a difficult time distinguishing as many colors as broadcast equipment does. High contrast and low saturation always work best for web media. This is more of a challenge with HDV and AVCHD camcorders; these small-format camcorders have small sensors with a tremendous number of pixels on them, limiting their sensitivity to light.

Editing

Edit for clarity and content and with cropping in mind. Beautiful panoramic shots are wonderful for demonstrating high-definition TV or for displaying the great outdoors. Such shots are horrible for the web, however. Detail becomes so small as to be invisible. Is that detail really critical to the message that's being delivered? The message is the most critical consideration, and anything not directly related to the message should not be found in the stream. If the stream is to be viewed on YouTube or another low-bandwidth location, the detail will be entirely lost, so you're better off using a still frame vs a moving shot.

In the edit process, if two talking heads are needed, rather than showing the two heads in one frame, consider the CNN-style appearance in which each head has its own space, divided by a clean line down the middle. This setup accomplishes two tasks. First, it keeps the background frames redundant. Second, it requires less distance between the heads, so both heads may be cropped in more tightly.

Removing unnecessary information limits what the encoder has to look at. Encoding tools are not capable of separating a few pixels of a reflection on a window from the blowing hair of the subject. To the encoder, it's all just moving pixels, and nothing is prioritized over anything else. Cropping helps alleviate this concern because cropping allows for less information to be on the screen.

Less saturation is best in streaming media. Although the RGB color space allows for millions of colors, keeping colors to a minimum is best because it offers fewer color choices to the encoder. Reduce colors whenever possible. The hue, saturation, and luminance (HSL) filter in Vegas is excellent for this concern. Insert the Black Restore filter as well to ensure that black is really black. There is a preset in the Black Restore FX tool used for the web. Gradients of black are difficult for the encoder to compress and difficult for the eye to see in the production stage. This filter, used correctly, flattens out black in the stream.

When editing for streaming media, forget about long, beautiful dissolves and fades. These sorts of transitions do not encode well. Use linear wipes, hard cuts, or other straight-line transitions. Don't use titles with serifs, but do use clean-cut title fonts and keep them as large as possible. Sometimes no title is necessary if metadata is used to convey text information.

12.5   The broadcast shot allows for more background to set the stage and location of the shot.

12.6   Cropped for the web, this shot is more interesting when viewed from very close up, such as with a computer monitor.

12.7 Streaming media should not have as much background. This example shows a poorly cropped screen. Too much information is in the background, and the subject takes up too little of the viewing space.

Also, in the edit stage, be aware that extreme contrasts are harder to encode, so keep extreme variants in saturation limited. Remember that placing media on the web is about messaging, not brilliant colors and flashy editing.

To summarize:

- Use clear fonts for titles.

- Limit dissolves; use cuts or hard wipes instead.

- Avoid moving paths when possible. Use picture-in-picture or split screens.

- On headshots, crop to half, rather than thirds.

- When you want to deliver to low-band systems, keep audio in a mono setting. For both low- and high-bandwidth delivery, consider using both stereo and mono audio. Does stereo really add value?

- Don't limit yourself to the standard 4:3 aspect. If your video is about something involving heights, for instance, consider scaling the video to be tall and narrow. This process might also use less bandwidth and might allow for better audio or compression. It also might be that the stream quality will suffer, depending on the aspect selected. Either way, do not be afraid to experiment.

- Try a variety of codecs to see what allows for the best look. Perhaps put low-bitrate media in one codec and high-bitrate media in another codec.

- Try frame rates of 12 fps rather than 15 fps when bandwidth or file size is a concern. For slide and still-type presentations, use even slower rates, such as 5 fps.

- For headshots, try using color-key or chroma-key tools to create background masks. Then fill in with high-speed, blurred imagery. This process keeps the headshot clean, while causing the eye to focus on the headshot and not the black behind it. It also lends an MTV-type quality to the interview or presentation.

- Impress viewers by embedding metadata into the end or middle of the video files that directs their browser to open at the end, so that they are given other images to view following the video/audio presentation. If you are selling a product, the metadata could potentially send the viewer to a "purchase me" type of page.

Audio for Internet Delivery

Preproduction of audio for web streaming or Internet distribution is often overlooked in the streaming preparation processes. Oftentimes, videographers intent on placing media on the Internet or an intranet use tools built into the applications that are being used for editing media for the web. If these tools are the only ones available, little can be done to prepare the audio for the web without going through multiple renders and loss of video quality. The processing described in the next paragraphs applies equally to audio only and audio for video.

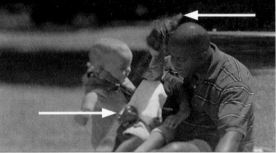

12.8 The image on the left shows a slow fade and letterboxing. The image on the right incorporates a hard wipe and no letterboxing. This image will encode/compress much better.

If third-party editing tools are available, use them to the best advantage possible. Most nonlinear editing packages come bundled with Sony's XP audio editing software. For this book, I've used Sound Forge 9.0, a full version. The tools used in this book, however, are all found in the XP version.

Audio takes a tremendous amount of unnecessary bandwidth in the streaming world. Most computer speakers can't reproduce sounds of any quality above 10,000 Hz (10 kHz) or below 125 Hz. If unnecessary audio is taken away, it leaves room for more efficient use of both video and audio bandwidth.

All video and audio compression tools use both high- and low-pass filters of some sort. The question is what is the quality of the filters and where are they cutting? Video tools simply aren't designed well for most audio processing chores.

How Is Audio Preprocessed for the Web?

First, start by fully rendering your file. You probably don't want to create too large a file, as large files are a bane in streaming media. If you want to save a step in the production process, render your file in an AVI format that is the view size for streaming media, such as 320 × 240 at 15 fps (using square pixels).

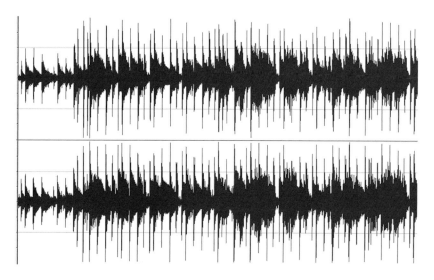

12.9   Notice the dynamic range of audio in the waveform.

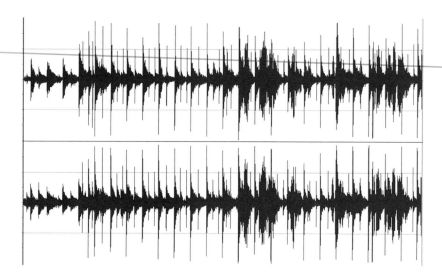

12.10   After EQ, the audio waveform contains less transient information because extreme low/bass frequencies and extreme high frequencies have been cut.

However, I rarely recommend doing so. In Vegas, you may open just the audio in Sound Forge (or any other audio editor) by right-clicking the audio and instructing the audio to open in the preferred audio editor.

Open the rendered file in your audio editor. Notice how the audio dynamic is fairly consistent across the spectrum. This audio has full dynamic range, containing both frequencies that multimedia speakers can't reproduce and frequencies that can't be heard. If it's a live recording, sounds such as microphone stand rumble use up to 100 times as much power to reproduce as the breath in a singer's voice. Those frequencies use bandwidth/streaming space that can better be used for video or audio enhancement/quality.

Using the graphic, paragraphic, or parametric equalizer in the audio editing tool, locate the high and low roll-off controls. Set the low-pass filter at 10 kHz and the high-pass filter at 100 Hz. These settings will cut off the extreme high-end and low-end audio right from the start. Just this preproduction task alone makes a tremendous difference in how the compression application accepts files for compression.

At this point, it might be advisable to do any final tweaks and enhancements with the audio. If you have any stereo-widening, reverb, or ambience-adding effects, now is the time to add them. Time delays and long reverbs do not compress well. Care and consideration, therefore, should be used at this point, so that streaming media will sound the best it possibly can on the receiving end. Multimedia speakers have a tendency to have a bump in the 5 kHz region, so if your media is music intensive, it might be advisable to reduce this frequency area by as much as −3 dB.

Notice the difference in the audio file's appearance in Figure 12.11 following the compression change. The waveform has less mass, and the transients become less apparent.

Be sure to have a preview listen to the file before moving on, making certain that the audio is the way you would like it to sound when it is received on the listening end of the stream.

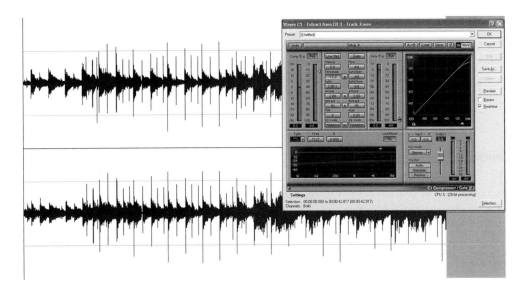

12.11 Use light compression to smooth out waveforms. In this illustration, a 2.1 compressor has been inserted, with compression starting at −12 dB.

Often in multimedia creation, particularly dealing with files generated directly in the computer environment, audio levels are not consistent across the project nor are the audio levels at optimum settings. These audio files may still be used and brought to maximum levels by normalizing them to an average level across the median plane. Two approaches to normalizing are used—normalize to peak values of XdB or normalize to an average RMS value. Use a normalization of an average RMS value if you wish to match the apparent overall loudness of a sound file. Normalize to Value selects the volume to which the sound file will be normalized. As an example, when using peaks, if the peak level is −10 dB and the Normalize to Value setting is −3 dB, a constant boost of 7 dB will be applied to the entire file.

When using RMS levels, normalizing to 0 dB means boosting the signal so that it has the same apparent loudness as a 0 dB square wave. This process usually creates a file that is very loud and often clipped or distorted. Normalizing to values between −12 and −6 dB is recommended.

Normalizing on a peak value allows for more dynamic interplay in the audio file. The file is scanned for its maximum peak value, which is then raised to −.03 dB. This process applies equally weighted amplitude across the audio file. Most normalizing functions allow for the introduction of dynamic compression at any stage in the normalization process. Using this tool is advisable as it prevents clipping at all stages, while allowing the normalize tool to bring audio up to maximum levels. This is especially desirable when the sampling frequency or bitrate of audio will be changing. Audio files should always be maximized before converting the format.

After the file has had the extreme low and high frequencies removed, has been equalized to the desired sound, and has been normalized, the file is ready for encoding/compression for streaming formats. If the file is an audio-only file, it is a simple matter to encode to REAL, Microsoft media, or QuickTime formats using the tools built directly into your audio application or using third-party tools. Be aware of the ability to insert command markers or instructional markers into the audio or video file. These command markers can display copyright information, authoring information, HTML redirections, and much more. If the processed audio file is part of a video file, it is an equally simple process to encode the video file for streaming. Reducing the audio content and maximizing the audio volume both make for more encoding bandwidth for the video portion of the file and provide a more efficient use of available bandwidth. These benefits are especially useful when dealing with low-speed connections, such as dial up service.

Until bandwidth and connections bring broadband to every home and business in the world, and even after that point for purposes of bandwidth and storage, content creators/providers need to learn every trick in the book and invent some new ones to keep media files appearing and sounding the best that they can. Audio is generally an afterthought in the video creation/editing world, although that is rapidly changing. Experiment a bit, listen closely, and you'll be surprised how great audio can really help out a less-than-great visual presentation. Don't forget metadata can be a great tool for audio-only delivery, as well as for video delivery over the web.

Delivery

Encoding is not much of a challenge if the techniques mentioned earlier are employed in production and editing stages. Vegas, however, offers a number of choices for the encoding/output side of media.

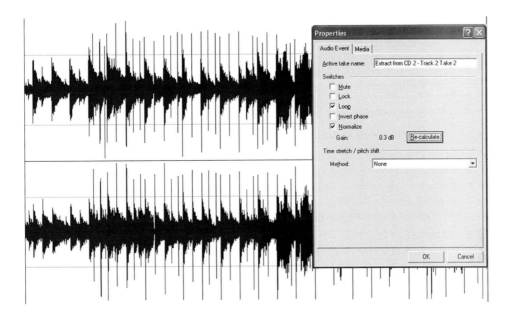

12.12   Normalizing a file to maximize volume.

An exceptionally valuable tool found in Vegas is the ability to encode portions of the Timeline for preview, rather than rendering out entire files, encoding and, if dissatisfied, repeating the entire process. Vegas is one of the only tools available today that can encode directly from the Timeline, complete with metadata insertions. This Preview from Timeline tool is valuable in that producers are able to see exactly what their media will look like when viewed from the web, directly in the media player of their choice.

Open the Streaming Project on the accompanying DVD.

The project file already has three sections of metadata embedded: two text instruction lines and one URL locater line. When viewed in the media player, the text data shows up at the bottom of the screen (in the Windows Media Player, select VIEW | NOW PLAYING TOOLS | CAPTIONS). Place the cursor on the Timeline at the first marker, labeled Insert Command Here. Press C, and a command dialog box will pop up. In the Command dialog box, use the menu and select Text. In the parameter box, type the words, *Then I go and spoil it all by saying something stupid.*

Select a small section of media on the Timeline over the top of the section containing at least one metadata flag. This section will be highlighted in gray [or blue if looping (Q) is enabled]. Open the TOOLS | PREVIEW IN PLAYER dialog (Ctrl+Shift+M). In the dialog, choose Windows-Media V9 (*.wmv) for the codec and select 256 Kbps for the streaming bandwidth. Click the Custom button, and in the audio attributes, choose the 48 Kbps, 44 kHz Mono (A/V) CBR setting. Click the Video tab, and in the Format window, choose Windows Media Video 9.

Now click the Summary tab and note the text boxes that may be filled out. This data is embedded with the file and shows up in the player on the client (viewer) side when the file is streaming. This dialog also provides a great means of data management for later use, as information about the file can be embedded in the file for database searches. Be aware that the last information entered in this dialog carries to the next time the tool is opened, so be certain to check this dialog with each stream.

Click OK in the Custom Template dialog and click OK in the Preview in Player dialog. Vegas will begin to render the file as a WMV file. After the file has rendered, Vegas will automatically call on the Windows Media Player to open and play the file. If the Captions option is enabled in Windows Media Player, you'll see the captions at the bottom of the Windows Media Player screen. This will show only the selected portions of the Timeline. In addition, only a temp file has been written for the streaming file. A full render will still need to be completed for a final output file.

What Is Metadata?

Metadata is what makes streaming reach out and touch someone. Metadata is embedded information in a streaming file that opens secondary browser windows, directs viewers to web pages, provides lyrics or text information to a song or informational media piece, and provides advertising opportunities, all from a streaming file. The author of the streaming file places the metadata markers on the Timeline, and viewers have a more in-depth experience as a result. Vegas has many metadata authoring tools found in the Command key (C).

12.13   Metadata may include song lyrics as displayed text.

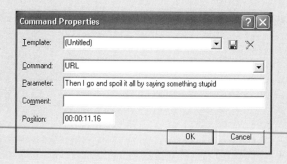

👆 **Tip**

Preview in Player is a powerful tool. Use it to identify trouble spots in the streaming media by previewing high-motion/intense-color areas. This process helps you determine how the video should be handled. Prerendering trouble spots at various frame rates before rendering a streaming file often helps make high-motion media look more polished. Tight cropping while following motion often helps as well, as it reduces background imagery.

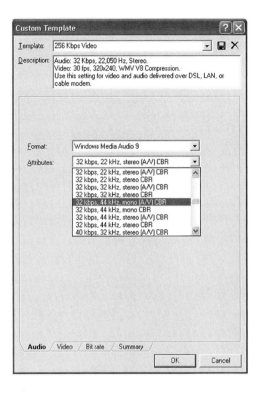

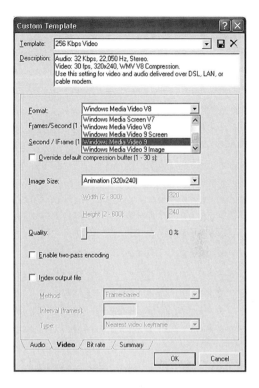

12.14 Streaming audio attributes may be set to user preferences.

12.15 Select the video codec and other attributes in this dialog.

Importing a Spreadsheet

Vegas has the ability to import a scripted spreadsheet. This asset is very important for the content creator who has concerns about complying with Rule 508 Assistive Technology laws. For any government-funded streaming endeavor, these laws almost always must be complied with. Colleges, training facilities, hospitals, corporate environments, and federally subsidized businesses, among others, must comply with these laws.

Vegas's streaming toolset enables closed-caption text to be embedded in the video or audio stream for hearing-impaired viewers. To do this, start by creating a four-column, tab-delimited spreadsheet in your spreadsheet application of choice and continue the process as follows:

1. In the first column of cells, type 00:00:00:00.

2. In each of the second column of cells, type the word *text* to specify the command format.

3. In the third column, type the text messages that you wish to be seen, for example, *When I was 17*.

4. In the fourth column, type marker information that you can use to identify the caption information. For example, they might be called *cap 1* or *line 1* in the cell.

5. In the last row of cells, leave the third column empty, which will clear the last caption text from the screen of the media player.

6. Select all information on the spreadsheet, or press Ctrl+A in Microsoft Excel. Copy all information.

7. In Vegas, select VIEW|EDIT DETAILS|SHOW|COMMANDS. Right-click in the gray box in the upper-left corner and choose Paste. Vegas will paste the spreadsheet information into the Edit Details window.

8. In the Edit Details window, click the first column, which will sort the captions by line number as named in step 4. Position the cursor where you wish the first caption to occur. Select the first row in the Edit Details window and play the video/audio file by pressing the spacebar. Press Ctrl+K to drop a marker for the first caption. Repeat for all subsequent captions. Caption markers can be dropped on the fly and moved on the Timeline by clicking and holding on the marker and then dragging to the desired position.

Tip

Be sure Captioning is enabled in Windows Media Player by selecting VIEW|NOW PLAYING|CAPTIONS. Otherwise captions will not be previewable nor can they be seen in the playback of a rendered file.

After all edits have been made, all metadata inserted, screen markers completed, and various points in the Timeline checked for quality, the file is ready to be rendered. Open the FILE|RENDER AS dialog and select the format of media you wish to stream, the bitrate at which to stream, and any summary information you wish to appear. If custom selections, such as variable bitrate (VBR) streaming or custom audio settings, are needed, click the Custom button. This action opens the same dialog shown during the Preview in Player exercise.

The Audio tab opens by default. As mentioned earlier, audio should be kept in mono to provide greater bandwidth for video. The Video tab is next on the menu tabs; settings can be adjusted according to need. Experiment with settings that best suit your requirements.

When you select various bitrates in the Bit rate tab, the file rendered by Vegas will be a multiple-bitrate (MBR) file. If only one bitrate is selected (the default), the file is rendered as a constant-bitrate (CBR) or VBR file. Viewers also generally receive a more stable stream with CBR than with MBR files.

The Summary tab allows for information, such as copyright information and author information, to be embedded with the file. This information shows up in the information bar of a REAL, Windows, or QuickTime media player and in most third-party media players as well. Other than rerendering the file, this information is difficult to remove and is a starting point in the concern for digital rights management.

After the custom selections/setups have been accomplished, you may wish to save the template settings for future use. A menu is available at the top of the Custom Templates dialog. Clicking the cursor in this menu allows you to rename the template, and clicking in the Description field allows you to create a new description of the template. After defining the name and description of the new template, click the icon that resembles a floppy disk, which saves the template for future use. After the template has been saved, the final render can take place.

Click OK in the Custom Templates dialog, which closes. Define where you want the final rendered file to be saved/rendered to and click the Save button. The render begins. After the render is complete, Vegas provides an option to open the folder in which the rendered file was stored. If you do not wish to see the Open Folder dialog in the future, you can use the checkbox that Vegas provides to disable this pop-up screen in the future.

The finished file is now ready to be uploaded to a web site and streamed. Bear in mind that with REAL and QuickTime media, unique streaming server software is required for streaming, as opposed to download-and-play files. REAL's Helix server is capable of serving all three stream formats, in addition to many other formats in the streaming world. A noncommercial free version with a very limited number of streams is available at www.real.com.

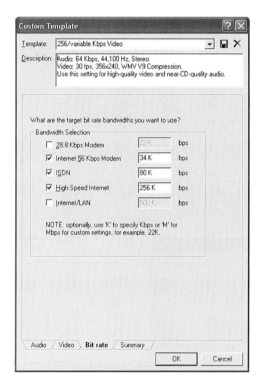

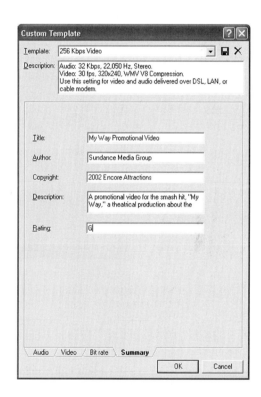

12.16 Checking multiple bitrates creates an MBR file.

12.17 Use the Summary tab to embed copyright, author, and other information that can be seen in the stream/media player.

Don't be afraid to use highly compressed media for more than streaming over the Internet. It's a great tool for delivering high-quality media on a CD to a potential client. With the ability to burn a high-definition file to a CD and to include a player installer on the CD for the client, this tool is very powerful in creating workflows between client and editor, while not taking inordinate amounts of time to show the client what the video project looks like.

Rendering for YouTube and Other UGC Sites

The YouTube, MySpace, GoogleVideo, and other user-generated content (UGC) site phenomenon is a rapidly growing monster. If you're not submitting video to these sorts of sites now, chances are you likely will be at some near point in time.

Most of these sites offer their own encoding system, which currently requires users to submit video to be encoded by their system. There are various methods of getting video onto these sorts of sites, but given constraints of time and/or size, it's most efficient to render longer Timelines to a compressed format prior to submitting files to a UGC site. Extensive testing from within the Vegas environment has shown that there are two excellent options for render/submissions to a UGC site.

Rendering the Timeline to either a high-bandwidth WMV file or an MPEG-4 stream will allow the UGC site the best opportunity to encode a high-quality Flash file. In Vegas, set up a template that allows for a 1 Mbps stream at a resolution of 640 × 480. The same settings apply when rendering to an MPEG-4 format. When rendering to MP4 for submission to UGC sites, use the Main Concept AVC encoder, and the iPod 640 × 480 template. The 320 × 240 video may be used for longer length projects; quality will suffer as a result.

Rendering for iPod/Podcasts

Vegas offers templates for the iPod; given the specific nature of the iPod units, it's best that the templates be left as they have been provided. If the video has a great deal of movement, the render may be improved by opening the Custom option in the render dialog and using the two-pass filter option. Checking the DeBlocking filter will also improve the video quality, but will increase render time.

12.18 iPod templates in Vegas Pro 8.

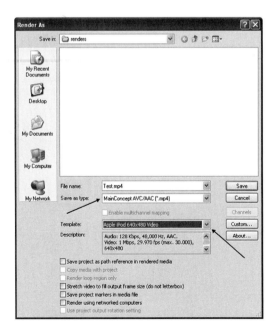

PSP Support

The Sony PlayStation Portable is a portable media player that is capable of playing extremely high-quality video in addition to video games, Internet browsing, and other sorts of entertainment. Be sure the PSP has the latest firmware available.

Old versions of the PSP firmware required convoluted paths to storing video. In the recent firmware changes, the \video folder is now directly accessible.

Access the renderer used for PSP export from the FILE | RENDER AS | SONY AVC dialog. In this dialog, templates are available in a variety of formats.

QVGA—512 Kbps
QVGA—896 Kbps
QVGA—1528 Kbps*
QVGA widescreen—512 Kbps
QVGA widescreen—896 Kbps
PSP full screen—896 Kbps
PSP full screen—1528 Kbps*

*These are two new templates added in Vegas Pro 8.

The PSP will show a thumbnail of your video. Place the cursor on the frame that should become the thumbnail representative of the video file. Export your video to a PSP device by browsing to TOOLS | EXPORT TO PSP DEVICE. The Export dialog will open, prompting for a name and template choice. Filenames may now be simple in the PSP device.

If the PSP is not connected to the computer, Vegas will prompt for the connection. Connect and power on the device, and select the Refresh button in the dialog.

24p HDCAM/DVCAM Workflow for the Independent Filmmaker

Dave Hill, Sony Pictures Digital

Overview

With the rapid and continued adoption of Sony HDCAM as the acquisition format of choice for the independent filmmaker, many people have asked how they could use Sony Vegas software as an editing tool for 24p HDCAM production.

Sony Vegas delivers many exciting new features, including cost-effective tools for 24p HDCAM editing using DVCAM proxies.

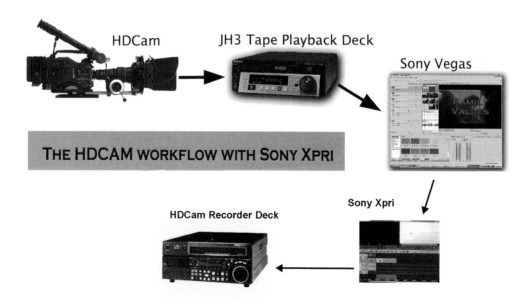

13.1   The 24p/XPRI workflow.

With Vegas Pro 8 you can:

1. Connect Vegas directly to a Sony J-H3 HDCAM deck and capture frame-accurate DVCAM down-converts over i-link. You can also have DV/DVCAM dubs made from your HDCAM masters and capture using your DV deck or camcorder.

2. Remove 2-3 pulldown from the down-converted 60i DV clips.

3. Retain original 24p HDCAM timecode in the DVCAM down-converted video files.

4. Cut your project in a 24p Vegas Timeline with perfect frame accuracy.

5. Create finished audio tracks in a 24p Vegas Timeline.

6. Create finished HD composites and video FX, and export as 24p uncompressed .avi.

7. Export a frame-accurate 24p EDL for final finishing in Sony XPRI or other 24p HD editing system. Finished audio and HD composites can be used natively in the finishing system, and HDCAM source clips will be recaptured as needed by the finishing system.

8. Even if you are not immediately delivering a 24p HDCAM master or doing a film-out, you can use this process to create extremely high-quality 24p DVDs and DVCAM or other SD masters, as well as 24fps web video.

24p HDCAM Acquisition

Sony offers an extensive line of HDCAM cameras and decks, many of which are also available for rental.

HDCAM information can be found at http://bssc.sel.sony.com/Professional/webapp/SubCategory?m=0&p=2&sp=19&sm=0&s=&cpos.

Setting Up a 24p Vegas Project

To ensure frame-accurate edits as well as a time-accurate soundtrack, you need to set your Vegas project up correctly prior to the start of editing.

Set the Trimmer time format to SMPTE Film Sync IVTC (23.976 fps, Video). This allows you to set in/out marks in the Trimmer using the original 24p source timecode. Timecode will still be properly tracked even if you do not set the Trimmer time format to SMPTE Film Sync IVTC (23.976 fps, Video).

Confirm that Quantize to Frames is on. Keep this on for all video editing. You can turn this off for fine-tuning the audio but remember to turn it back on when editing video.

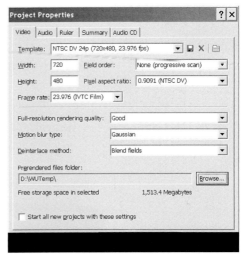

13.2 Set the project to NTSC DV 24p (or NTSC DV 24p Widescreen if the project is 16:9).

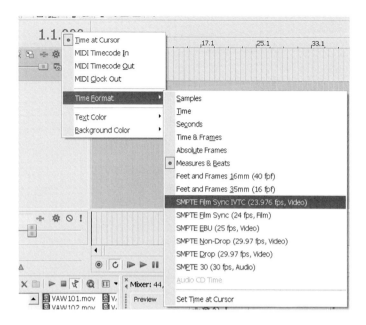

13.3   Set the project time format to SMPTE Film Sync IVTC (23.976 fps, Video).

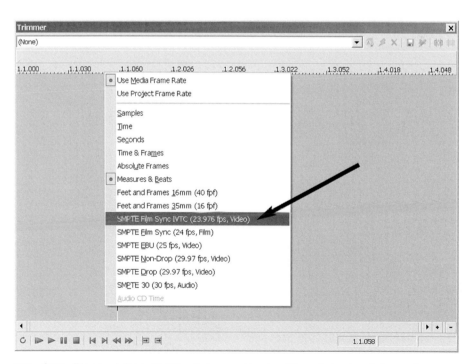

13.4   Set the Trimmer window to 23.976 so that you are trimming at the project and media frame rates.

Additional Capture Notes

You are now ready to capture your down-converted footage. It is recommended that you use the Sony Vegas Capture tool for capturing your down-converted DV footage directly from the J-H3 deck or from DV/DVCAM dubs. Other capture tools may or may not work correctly and have not been tested.

As always, proper tape naming and clip naming is essential during the logging/capturing stage—you will need a reference back to the original master tapes, and failure to name the tape correctly at capture time can result in time-consuming/expensive searching at the online facility.

It is not recommended that you capture across scene breaks in the original HDCAM tape. This may result in improper timecode or pulldown removal inside Vegas. For best results, log each scene in the Vegas capture tool, and then batch capture.

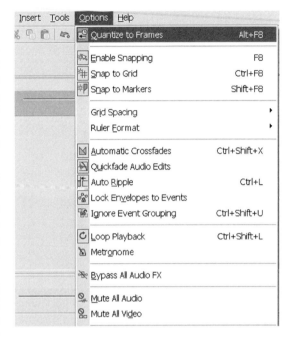

13.5   Enable Quantize to Frames from the Options menu.

13.6

Remove 2-3 Pulldown from the Downconverted 60i DV Clips

Once you have captured your down-converted DV clips in Vegas, you will need to remove the pulldown that is inserted by the HDCAM deck when creating 60i (29.97 interlaced) DV from 24p HDCAM original footage.

Load the captured clips into the Vegas Media Pool (this happens automatically when you launch the Capture application from within Vegas). In the Vegas Media Pool, select all of the down-converted clips, then right-click and choose File Format Properties. The dialog box shown in Figure 13.7 will appear. Check the "Enable 2-3 pulldown removal" option, and then choose OK.

If the original down-conversion was done correctly, the starting frame offset for all clips will be 0, pulldown removal will have occurred, and timecode will be tracked correctly.

The pulldown flag will be stamped into the DV file, so you can open these files in any Vegas project (version 5 or later) and it will be interpreted as a 24p DV clip. There is no need to close/reopen Vegas after setting the pulldown flag.

You can confirm that the footage has been flagged as 24p by checking the Media Properties for the DV clip. Format should be DV (removing 2-3 pulldown) as shown in Figure 13.8.

If you are working from a film transfer or multigeneration dub, you can still convert the DV clip to 24p DV, but you may have to set the starting frame value manually (starting frame offset value, 0–4). This may require some trial and error to find the correct starting frame.

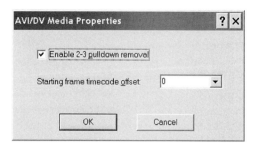

13.7   Enable 2-3 pulldown in the Media Pool.

13.8   Verify that pulldown is being removed.

Editing with 24p DV Video Files

As early as version 4, Vegas has included many 24p DV editing features, and they are described at http://mediasoftware.sonypictures.com/support/productinfo/24p.pdf. If you followed all the steps above and are not planning on an HDCAM online session, you can edit your project and make a great-looking 24p DVD or create SD masters or web video with no additional steps beyond the normal editing process.

24p Timecode

If you are planning on an HDCAM online session at some point (or need an EDL or XML project data export for any subsequent process), it is a good idea to confirm proper timecode handling before proceeding. The easiest way to do this is to add the Sony Timecode filter to one or more of your 24p DV files.

In the Vegas Pro 8 Media Pool, select a 24p DV file, choose Media FX, select Sony Timecode, and choose the SMPTE Film IVTC (23.976 fps) preset.

NOTE: This must be done at the media level, from the Media Pool and nowhere else.

If you choose to burn in timecode during the down-convert process, your video will look like Image 13.10.

After applying the Sony Timecode filter with the SMPTE Film IVTC (23.976 fps) preset, your video should look like Image 13.11. Importantly, note that the ORG timecode burned onto the frame matches the timecode displayed by the Sony Timecode filter.

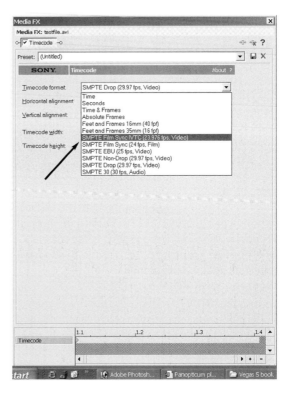

13.9 Insert the Sony Timecode filter to track time. Insert it in the Media Pool to reflect the timecode from the media rather than the Timeline.

13.10

13.11

A script could be used to apply (or remove) this filter, with the SMPTE Film IVTC (23.976 fps) preset, to all items in the Media Pool. Using Notepad, you can modify the scripts Add Timecode To All Media.cs and Remove Timecode From All Media.cs (scripts can be found in C:\Program Files\Sony\Vegas Pro 8\Script Menu).

In either script, change

```
var presetName = "SMPTE Drop (29.97 fps)";
to
var presetName = "SMPTE Film IVTC (23.976 fps)";
Save script to new name with a .cs extension.
```

Create Finished Audio Tracks in a 24p Vegas Timeline

If you are creating finished audio tracks for use in your final HD online session, you are strongly encouraged to check with the post facility for exact format requirements. Most facilities can accept 16/48 PCM .wav files for use in HDCAM sessions, which can be rendered from Vegas using the settings shown in Figure 13.12.

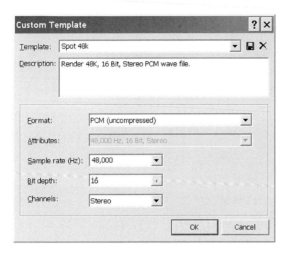

13.12   Render audio using a custom template like this one.

If you are cutting in a 24p Vegas Timeline and doing a 24p HDCAM online, you will not need to worry about time-stretching your audio during the online session if your render out WAV files as above from a 24p Vegas Timeline.

If you need to convert Vegas Pro 8 audio tracks to OMF, the following tool is recommended: http://www.cuibono-soft.com/Store/EDL_Convert_Pro_v3/edl_convert_pro_v3.html.

Create Finished Composites and Video FX, and Export as 24p HD Uncompressed .avi Files

If you are creating finished composites, graphics, etc., for use in your final HD online session, you are strongly encouraged to check with the post facility for exact format requirements. Most facilities can accept uncompressed 24p HD .avi files for use in HDCAM sessions, which can be rendered from Vegas using the settings shown in Figure 13.13.

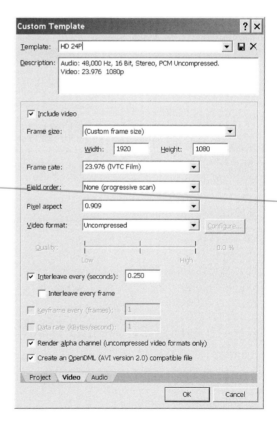

13.13   Use this render setting to output 24p HD .avi files.

Exporting a 24p EDL

You have picture lock, the soundtrack is complete, and you are now ready to export your EDL. Go to TOOLS | SCRIPTING | EXPORT EDL, and save the file with the .edl extension.

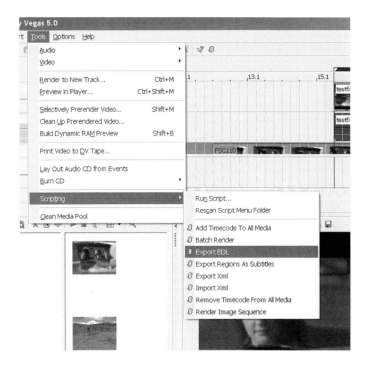

13.14   Use the EDL Export script to export a CMX 3600 list.

You are strongly advised to send the EDL to your post house prior to arriving at the online session. They can verify the EDL and note any errors, and adjustments can be made prior to the actual online session.

24p EDLs created in Vegas have been tested with Sony XPRI. Cuts and dissolves work correctly with one video track and two audio tracks in all tests. Speed changes, wipes, and other project data will not be exported with the EDL. Recommended practice for HDCAM online using Sony XPRI is the following:

1. Render mixed audio tracks from your Vegas project, for import into the finishing system (Sony XPRI).

2. Render HD uncompressed graphics and video FX from your Vegas project, for import into the finishing system (Sony XPRI).

3. Export one EDL per video track, for import into the finishing system (Sony XPRI).

24p DVDs

You can make 24p DVDs from a 24p Vegas Timeline. See the Vegas documentation for coverage of this process.

Exporting the Project to DV

You can render your 24p Timeline as NTSC or PAL DV. See Chapter 11 for additional information.

Index

10-bit color sampling, 374–377
32-bit float processing, 374–377
10-bit video, 372
4:2:2 MPEG, 469–471
4:2:2 YUV codecs, 470–471

A

AAF files. See Advanced Authoring Format
 (AAF) files
AC-3 files
 encoding to audio, 322
 outputting, 455
ACID loops, 269–270, 422
Add Folder icon, 425
Add Noise filter, 146
Advanced Authoring Format (AAF) files,
 exporting, 451–452
advanced video codec-high definition
 (AVCHD), 94–95
aspect ratio, 154–155
assembly track, 186–187
audio
 ACID loops, 269–270, 422
 advanced techniques, 240–259
 bus assignments, 245–246
 bus routing effects, 247–249
 cards, 436
 compression, 298–302
 De-Ess preset, 302–303
 dithering, 444–445
 editing (See audio editing)
 equalization (See equalization (EQ))
 extracting from CDs, 261–268
 FX-automated, 283–284
 FX packages, 250–254
 for Internet delivery, 479, 483–486
 levels, 437–438
 looping, 241, 244
 markers, 271–275
 mastering (See mastering)
 mixing (See mixing audio)
 multiple tracks, 239–240, 256–257
 music, 269–270
 muting, 65, 164, 292, 294–295
 noise reduction, 285–288
 plug-ins, 280–291
 punch-ins, 244–245
 recording (See recording)
 reverb, 305–306
 speed control, 276–277
 streaming media, 479, 483–486
 stretching, 275
 surround-sound, 307–319

takes, 32, 241–243
 thinning, 295–296
 volume, 306, 486
Audio Bus, 38
Audio CD tab, 27
audio editing
 extracting audio from CDs, 261–268
 markers and, 271–275
 with multicamera, 187–188
 placing on timeline, 260–261
 ripple editing, 279–280
 speed variation, 276
audio events. See also video events
 cutting, 262
 deleting, 279
 description, 235
 fading, 263–264
 grouping, 280
 looping, 267–268
 muting, 164
 normalizing, 165, 266–267
 pasting, 262
 ripple editing for, 279–280
 selecting, 263
 snapping, 277
 splitting, 263
 trimming, 277–279
Audio tab, 25–26, 446, 449
Audio Track, 37
audio tracks, 501–502
audio waveform, 484–486
Auto Ripple, 63–64
automation
 FX, 283–284
 mixes, 248, 323
 modes of, 293–294
 overview, 293
 plug-ins, 283–284
AV (audio/video) sync repair, 174–176
AVCHD. See advanced video codec-high
 definition (AVCHD)
AVI files, rendering of, 446–447
AVI format, 484

B

background
 color, 327, 344
 streaming media, 480–482
Backgrounds tag, 425, 429
bandwidth, 482, 483
Bezier curves, 193, 196–197, 331, 333, 358
Bezier mask, 359
Bezier tool, 359, 360
Black Restore filter, 481
Blackmagic Design, 104–106, 374
blue rays, 212–214
bluescreening. See chromakey tools
BMP format, 124
Boris FX, 206

Boris RED, 206
Broadcast Color filter, 232–233, 356
Broadcast Wave files (BWF), 320–321
Browse Folder window, 425
bump maps, 404–406
Bump Placement window, 404, 405
burning
 master CD, 441–442
 TAO CDs, 442
bus assignments, 245–246
buses
 assigning, 245–246
 mixes and, 247–248
 routing effects, 247–249
 viewing as tracks, 314

C

cameras. See also multicamera
 movement, 355
 output, 157
 PAL vs. NTSC, 152
 shooting modes, 156–157
 still images, 355–356
CD regions/track numbers, 41
CDs
 burning, 441–442
 master, 441–442
 Redbook-compliant, 442
 TAO, 442
child tracks, 373–374, 399, 402
Chromakey filter, 147
chromakey tools, 406–409
ChromaWarp plug-in, 149, 201
chrominance, 217
clips, 113–115
codecs, 470–471
color correction
 film like effects, 230–233
 filmlike effects, 152–153
 as FX, 229–230
 FX for, 375–376
 Histogram tool, 218
 illegal colors, 218–219, 221, 223, 232
 legal colors, 232–233
 parade display, 218, 221
 Primary Color Corrector tool, 221, 223,
  226, 227–228
 Secondary Color Corrector tool, 225–227,
  413, 414
 tools, 215–217
 vectorscope, 217, 221, 226
 viewing, 150
Color Corrector tool, 151, 220, 228, 413, 414
Color Curves tools, 226
color wheels, 223
colors
 background, 327, 344
 chromakey, 406–409
 compositing, 374–377

colors (Contd)
gradients, 228–229
illegal, 218–219, 221, 223, 232
legal, 232–233
masks, 388, 390
shadow, 329
titles, 327, 329
of web media, 480
command markers, 272, 275
compositing, 353
chromakey tools for, 406–409
color, 374–377
credit rolls, 383–386
3D Track Motion tools for, 369–372
envelopes, 160–162, 373–374, 397
garbage matte, 409–412
generated media, 380–383
holograph effect, 412–414
masks for, 359–361, 386–396
modes, 396–406
nested, 372–374
Pan/Crop tool for (See Pan/Crop Tool)
parent/child tracks, 372–373
Rotated Display tool for, 477–480
Track Motion tool for, 361–368
compression
audio, 298–302
for video, 442–444
Computer Name tab, 462
constant bitrate (CBR), 490
contrast, of web media, 480
controller devices, 291
Convolution Kernel filter, 147
Cookie Cutter FX plug-in, 382
copyright information, 490
CreativEase, 201
Credit Roll plug-in, 384
credit rolls, 383–386
crossfades, 63, 126–131, 264–265
selections, 184–186
CTI. See Current time indicator (CTI)
Cui-Bono Software, 450
Current time indicator (CTI), 331, 334
cursors, 67–68
curves, 196–197
Curves presets, 335–336
Curves tab, 335

D

3D LE plug-in, 209
3D-like imagery, 357
3D Track Motion tools, 357, 369–372
DAW. See digital audio workstation (DAW)
De-Ess preset, 302–303
DebugMode plug-ins, 149, 207–211
DeckLink cards, 104–106, 374
Defaults tab, 327
Deform tools, 348
deleting

audio events, 279
markers, 273–274
demoflash.swf files, 350
digital audio workstation (DAW), 435
digital rights management, 490
displacement maps, 399–402
Dither plug-in, 317
dithering, 318, 444–445
dockable windows, 10–19
Edit Details window, 13
Explorer window, 11
Media Generators window, 15
Mixer window, 12
Plug-In Manager window, 16
Project Media window, 13
Surround Panner window, 17
Transitions window, 14
Trimmer window, 12
Video FX window, 15
Video Preview window, 14
Video Scopes window, 16
DoubleTake, 189–190
Down-convert, 87, 496, 498, 499, 500
down-mixing, 319–320
downsampling, 449
Drop Shadow, 328, 329, 348
DV cameras. See cameras
DV (digital video). See also video capture
film like effects, 230–233
progressive scan, 230–231
rendering for, 460
DVCAM media, 495–504
DVD Architect (DVDA), 474–475
DVD drive, importing media from, 90–91
DVDA. See DVD Architect (DVDA)
dynamic link libraries (DLL), 255

E

Echo Audio Layla, 437
Edit Details window, 13
Edit Generated Media, 332
Edit menu, 28–33
Edit tab, 340, 341, 343
editing
Multicam, 179–181
multicamera, 179–191, 186–187
slip-editing, 126
streaming media, 480–483
timeline events, 124–134
trim-editing, 125–126
VEG files on nested timeline, 172–173
EDL Convert Pro, 450
EDLs, 449–451, 503
effects
bus routing effects, 247–249
filmlike effects, 152–153, 230–233
glow, 347–348, 367, 373–374
holograph, 412–414

Effects tab
Drop Shadow in, 348
for text, 347, 348
Empty events, 38
encoding, streaming media, 486
envelope points, 134
envelopes
compositing, 160–162, 373–374, 397
keyframe, 331, 334
motion blur, 415, 418
opacity, 157–162
position on path, 334
supersampling, 418
transitional, 134–135
EQ. See equalization (EQ)
equalization (EQ), 303–305
events, 439–440
graphic equalizers, 304
in mastering, 444
parametric equalizers, 305
event switches, 164–169
events. See audio events; video events
EXE files. See executable (EXE) files
executable (EXE) files, 457
Expand triangle, 329, 330, 333
Explorer toolbar, 107
Explorer window, 11
exporting
4:2:2 MPEG capabilities, 469–471
AAF files, 451–452
AC-3 files, 455
codecs, 470–471
dithering audio, 444–445
EDL support for, 449–451
and equalizers, 444
format, 435–436
high-definition video, 466–469
master CD, 429–430
mastering for audio for video, 442–444
mastering process (See mastering)
MPEG files, 453–455
24p EDL, 503
rendering process (See rendering)
scripting, 471–474
video events, 448–449
Eyedropper tool, 343–344, 408

F

faders, 296
fades
crossfades,   63,   126–131,   184–186,
264–265
events, 263–265
routing effects, 247
Fast Fourier Transform (FFT), 285
feathering, 359–360
Feathering tool, 359
file mapping, 464–465
File menu, 22–24

files
  AAF, exporting, 451–452
  AC-3, outputting of, 455
  AVI, rendering of, 446–447
  demoflash.swf, 350
  executable (EXE), 457
  Flash MX, 350
  MPEG, 453–455
  rings-opacity.veg, 374
  TGA, 449
  tvscreen.veg, 412
  XDCAM, 449
filmlike effects, 152–153, 230–233
filters. See also plug-ins
  Add Noise, 146
  adding to event, 143
  Broadcast Color, 356
  Broadcast Colors filter, 232–233
  Chromakey, 147
  Convolution Kernel, 147
  3D Pak, 149
  functionality, 146–153
  Gaussian Blur, 413
  HSL, 481
  Lens Flares, 148
  Levels, 376
  Mirror, 148
  PluginPac, 207–210
  velocity, 162–163
FLAC. See Free Lossless Audio Codec
    (FLAC)
Flash MX files, 350
FlowTexture plug-in, 201, 202
fonts, 326
frame rates, 467
Free Lossless Audio Codec (FLAC), 322–323
freeware application, 189
frequencies, 485
FX
  automation, 250–254, 283–284
  color correction as, 229–230
  properties, 143
  tempo-based, 253–254
  track, 252–253
FX Filter button, 440
FX packages, 250–254

G

gamma, 155, 220, 231
gamma curve, 231
garbage matte, 409–412. See also masks
Gaussian Blur filter, 413
Gaussian Blur parameters, 331–332
General Preferences tab, 421
generated media, 380–383
  icon, 332
  menus, 325
Generated Media tab, 326
GIF format, 124

Glow effects, 347
glow effects, 367, 373–374
gradient masks, 390, 403–404
Gradient Selector bar, 328, 329
gradients, color, 228–229
Gradients library, 329
graphic equalizers, 304
graphics
  importing static, 352
  placing on timeline, 123–124
greenscreening. See chromakey tools
Group menu, 32–33

H

handles, thinning, 295–296
Hard disk drive (HDD) recorders, importing
    media from, 92–94
hardware cards, for video capture, 103–106
  DeckLink cards, 104–106
  Xena cards, 103–104, 106
HD/SDI, 19, 20, 104–106
HDCAM media, 495–504
HDD. See Hard disk drive (HDD)
HDV, 19, 24, 155, 375–377
  camcorder, 103, 377
  capturing application, 86–90
  device selection, 105
  file format, 93–94
height maps, 404–406
Helix server, 491
Heroglyph, 212
high-definition video, 466–469
Histogram tool, 218
histograms, 218
holograph effects, 412–414
HSL filter. See hue, saturation, and
    luminance (HSL) filter
hue, saturation, and luminance (HSL) filter,
    481

I

60i video, 499
illegal colors, 218–219, 221, 223, 232
images
  cropping, 354–355
  flipping, 355, 357
  glow effects to, 367
  interlaced, 230–231
  picture-in-picture, 365–366
  progressive scan, 230–231
  scanned, 123–124
  still, 123–124, 355–356
importing
  AAF files, 451–452
  AVCHD, 94–95
  media from DVD drive, 90–91
  media from HDD recorders, 92–94
  media to timeline, 107–113

spreadsheets, 489–491
static graphics, 352
infinitiCAM, 188
Insert Assignable FX, 43
Insert menu, 36–41
  Audio Bus in, 38
  Audio Track in, 37
  Velocity Envelopes in, 37
  Video Bus Track in, 38
  Video Envelopes in, 36
  Video Track in, 37
Instant Boris FX, 206
interlacing, 230–231, 414
Internet delivery, of audio, 479, 483–486
Invert Mask feature, 230
iPod, 492
IRE scale, 218, 221

J

JPEG format, 124

K

Kerning, 347
Keyframe tool, 355
keyframes, 135–142, 331, 334
  setting, 334
  in SpiceMASTER plug-in, 193–198
  thinning, 295–296
  track-level, 402–403
Keyword search, 431. See also searching,
    with Media Manager

L

latency, 240, 256
Layout tab, 330, 333, 334
layouts, saving, 20–21
Legacy Titling tool
  Edit tab in, 340, 341, 343
  Placement tab in, 342
legal colors, 232–233
Lens Flares filter, 148
LensPro plug-in, 210
letterboxing, 154–155
Levels filter, 376
light rays, 212, 394–395
lighting, 404, 407
limiters, 298–300
Lock Aspect Ratio, 363–364, 365, 371
looping
  ACID loops, 269–270
  audio, 241, 244
  events, 267–268

M

M-Audio Oxygen, 291
Mackie Control devices, 288–291, 294

Macromedia's Flash format, 350
Magic Bullet plug-in, 211
markers
   and audio editing, 271–275
   command, 272, 275
   deleting, 273–274
   described, 272
   inserting, 40, 272–275
   naming, 273
   navigating, 273–274
   working with, 121, 122–123
Mask Generator modes, 393
Masking. See masks
masks, 359–361
   alpha channel, 386–387
   Bezier curves, 358
   chromakey, 406–409
   creating, 386–396
   creating garbage matte, 409–412
   feathering, 359–360
   garbage matte, 409–412
   gradient, 390, 403–404
   Mask Generator modes, 393
   opacity of, 359
   Pan/Crop tool for, 357–358
   shadows, 388–390
   split screens and, 391–393
   text reflection, 394–396
   titles, 387–388
   using, 386–396
Master Bus Mode, 25
mastering, 436–440
   audio for video broadcast, 442–444
   burning to master CD, 441–442
   compressors for, 443–444
   EQ in, 444
Match Output Aspect, 354, 355–356
mattes. See masks
media
   addition to Media Manager, 423–426
   generated, 380–383
   importing to timeline, 107–113
   importing from DVD drive, 90–91
   importing from HDD recorders, 92–94
   offline, 83
   organizing, 427–429
   placing on timeline, 115–123, 179–181
   producing rotated, 378–380
   recapturing, 83
   rotated display of, 377–378
Media Bins, 109–110, 111–112
Media Generators window, 15
Media Library, 422–423
Media Library Action button, 421
Media Library window, 424, 425
Media Manager, 17
   adding media to, 423–426
   creating library with, 422–423
   Media Library Action button in, 421
   options, 421–722

organizing media with tags in, 427–429
   searching with, 430–433
   setup for, 421
   user interface, 419–420
Media Manager toolbar, 420
Media Pool, 108–112
menus
   Edit, 28–33
   File, 22–24
   Group, 32–33
   Insert, 36–41
   Options, 61–67
   Tool, 42–61
   View, 33–35
metadata, 483, 407–408
metronomes, 65
MIDI clock, 66
MIDI control devices, 291
MIDI timecode (MTC), 65
Mirror filter, 148
Mixer Preview Fader, 33
Mixer window, 12
mixing audio, 296
   automation, 248, 323
   buses, 247–248
   compression, 298–302
   De-Ess preset, 302–303
   down-mixing, 319–320
   equalization, 303–305
   reverb for, 305–306
   submixes, 246, 249
   surround mix, 318–319
   surround-sound mixing, 307–319
   techniques for, 297–298
   volume, 306
Mixing Console, 17, 247, 296
monitors
   computer, 151
   external, 151
   HD/SDI, 19, 20
motion blur, 415–416
Motion Blur envelopes, 415, 416, 418
MPEG files, 453–455
.m2t, 93, 94, 167
MTC. See MIDI timecode (MTC)
Multicam. See also multicamera
   editing, 179–181
   naming tapes in, 178
   and Project Media, 179
   selections, 184
   tools, use of, 177
multicamera
   audio editing with, 187–188
   crossfades in, 184–185
   editing, 179–191, 186–187
   synchronization, 177
   time settings in, 177
   workflows, 182–183
multicamera track, creation of, 179
multiple bitrate (MBR), 490

multiple tracks, 5
   recording, 239–240, 256–257
   muting audio, 164, 292, 294–295

N

navigation keys, 338
nested tracks, 372–374
nesting, 170–172. See also VEG files
   composites, 372–373
network rendering, 459–466
NewBlueFX, 212–214
NewNoise plug-in, 201, 202
Noise-generated events, 404
noise reduction, 285–288, 479
NTSC camera, 152
NTSC standards, 218
NTSC video, 152–153

O

opacity envelopes, 157–162
OpenType tab, 337
Options menu, 61–67
outputting. See exporting
Ozone compressor, 442–443

P

24p DVDs, 504
24p HD .avi files, 502
24p media
   DVDA, 474
   HDCAM/DVCAM workflow, 495–504
   plug-ins, 152–153, 157
   timecode, 500–501
PAL cameras, 152
PAL video, 230–231
Pan/Crop icon, 357
Pan/Crop Preview window, 358, 391
Pan/Crop tool, 48–51
   to correct bad camera movement, 355
   for creating 3D-like imagery, 357
   for creating videos, 353–356
   default setting for, 358
   feathering tool in, 359
   keyframe tool in, 355
   masking tools in, 357–358 (See also masks)
   Match Output Aspect in, 354, 355–356
   Pen tool in, 358
Pan-Crop.veg project, 353, 357
Parabola preset, 335
parade display, 218, 221
parametric equalizers, 305
Parent/Child tool, 338–339. See also ProType Titling tool
parent/child tracks, 372–373
Parent Track Overlay, 398–399
Path Mode dialog, 359

pedestal, 221
Pen tool, 358. See also Pan/Crop tool
PhotoShop, 352
picture-in-picture (PIP), 189, 365–366
pixel aspect ratio, 24, 124, 154–155, 342, 352
Pixelan SpiceMASTER 2 plug-in. See SpiceMASTER plug-in
PixelStretch, 207
Placement tab, 342
playback, 184
PlayStation Portable (PSP), 493
Plug-In Chain button, 440
Plug-In Manager window, 16
plug-ins. See also filters
    adding to events, 143
    audio, 280–291
    ChromaWarp, 149, 201
    Cookie Cutter FX, 382
    credit roll, 384
    3D LE plug-in, 209
    Debug Mode, 149
    DebugMode, 207–211
    dithering, 444–445
    FlowTexture plug-in, 201, 202
    functionality, 146–153
    FX automation, 283–284
    LensPro plug-in, 210
    Magic Bullet plug-in, 211
    NewBlue FX, 212–214
    NewNoise plug-in, 201, 202
    Ozone, 443–445
    presets, 144
    ProDad, 212–214
    StepMotion plug-in, 203–204
    StepTime plug-in, 203
    Ultimate S 3, 188–189
    Ultrafunk, 440
    VelvetMatter, 212–214
    WAVES Ultramaximizer, 438
    Zenoté plug-in, 155, 211
PluginPac filters, 207–210
PNG codec, 448
PNG format, 124, 448–449
Position on Path envelope, 334
Position on Path slider, 333, 334, 335
postroll settings, 243
preamplifiers, 238, 256
preroll settings, 243
Presets toolbar, 335
Preview tab, 327
previews
    RAM, 150
    split screens, 145–146
    transitions, 131
Primary Color Corrector tool, 221, 223, 226, 227–228
print video to DV tape, 446
ProDad, 212–214
production, for streaming media, 479–480
progressive scan, 230–231

Project Media, 59, 107–115, 142, 154
    and Multicam, 179
Project Media window, 13
Project Properties window, 23–24
    Audio CD tab in, 27
    Audio tab in, 25–26
    Ruler tab in, 26
    Summary tab in, 26
    Video tab in, 25
projects, described, 235
ProType Titler. See ProType Titling tool
ProType Titling tool
    advanced titling tools in, 338–339
    basic tools in, 336–337
    curves presets, 335–336
    generated media, 325–326, 332
    Gradient Selector bar, 328, 329
    gradients library, 329
    Layout tab, 330, 333, 334
    lock aspect, 327
    opening, 326
    Position on Path slider in, 333, 334
    Transform tab in, 328
    workspace, 326
    Zoom tool in, 333
PSD format, 124
punch-ins, audio, 244–245

Q

Quantize to Frames, 61, 124–125, 179, 297, 298
Quick Text search, 431. See also searching, with Media Manager
QuickTime files, 108
QuickTime format, 124, 448–449
QuickTime media, 491

R

Radiance, 212–213
RAID, renedering, 468
RAM
    previews, 150, 396
    rendering, 468
raylight. See light rays
recompression, 19, 150, 446, 447, 463, 474
recording
    audio mixer in, 249–250
    basic setup, 236–239
    bus assignments in, 245–246
    bus routing, 247–249
    FX packaging, 250–252
    multiple tracks, 239–240, 256–259
    with takes, 241–243
    track FX for, 252–253
Redbook-compliant CD, 442
Redbook Master, 441
regions
    defining, 40, 121–122, 273

described, 272
uses for, 273
render farming, 459–466. See also rendering
render template, 462
Renderers tab, 461, 462
rendering, 445
    AC-3 files, 455
    AVI files, 446–447
    clients, 461–463
    distributed, 460, 462–463
    DVDA, 474–475
    exporting video to third-parties, 448–449
    file mapping, 464–465
    for iPod, 492
    loop regions, 458
    monitoring progress, 463–464
    MPEG files, 453–455
    network, 459–466
    non-distributed, 459–460, 463
    options, 466
    RAID, 468
    RAM, 468
    for UGC sites, 492
    VCDs/SVCDs, 456–457
    for YouTube, 492
resolution, of scanned images, 123
reverb, 305–306, 480
RGB parade display, 217, 218, 221
Rings-opacity.veg files, 374
ripple editing, 28–29, 279–280
RMS value, 486
Rotated Display tools, 377–380
Rotation slider, 330
Rubber Audio, 275
Ruler tab, 26

S

safe areas, 327
saturation
    streaming media, 481–482
    web media, 480
Scene Detection, 76–77
screenshots, 227
scripting, 471–474
SDI/HD, 19, 20, 104–106
Search Criteria Chooser, 432
searching, with Media Manager
    advance, 431–433
    keywords searching, 431
    match options in, 430
Secondary Color Corrector tool, 225–227
Selection bar, 334
selections, 67–68
setup, for Media Manager, 421
Shadow color, 329
shadows
    applied with Track Motion tool, 362–363
    credit rolls, 384

shadows (*Contd*)
  inserting, 366
  masks, 388–390
  text, 329–330, 348
Shatter3D, 207, 208–209
Show Bus Tracks, 33
Show Video Envelopes, 33
Shuffle feature, 167
sibilance, 302–303
slip-editing, 126
SMPTE color bars, 446
SMPTE colorbars, 219, 221
SMPTE video, 496–497
snapping, audio events, 277
Sony DR60, 90
Sony Sound Series Loops, 422
sound cards, 236–238, 239–240, 256
Sound Forge editing software, 483
SpiceMASTER plug-in, 191–200
  installation, 192
  keyframes in, 193–198
  overview, 191
split screens, 391–393
  previews, 145–146
Split tool, 31
spreadsheets, importing, 489–491
static graphics, 352
Static photo, 355
StepMotion plug-in, 203–204
StepTime plug-in, 203
Still images, 355–356. See also Camera
still images, 123–124, 355–356
stock footage, 427, 428
streaming audio, 479, 483–486
streaming media, 477–478
  audio for Internet delivery, 479,
    483–486
  delivery, 486–488
  editing, 480–483
  production, 479–480
  spreadsheet import, 489–491
subclips, 113–115
submixes, 246, 249
Summary tab, 26, 490
Sundance Media Group, 436
super video compact discs (SVCDs),
    456–457
supersampling, 416–418
  envelopes, 418
surround mix, 318–319
Surround Panner window, 17
surround-sound, 307–319
SVCDs. See super video compact discs
    (SVCDs)
sync cursor, 382

T

Tag Editor window, 428
Tagging
  media with Media Manager, 427–429

Tags, 427–429
takes, 178, 241–243
TAO CDs. See Track-at-Once (TAO) CDs
Targa files (TGA), 449
Television, 343
templates, saving, 20–21
tempo-based FX, 253–254
tempo maps, 240
tempos, 240
text. See also Titles
  credit rolls, 384–386
  editing, 332–333
  editing tools, 336
  effects to, 347–350
  gradient to, 329
  keframing of, 344, 349
  reflection, 394–396
  scale parameters, 330
  shadow, 329–330, 348
  shear parameters, 330
  size, 327–328
  style, 384–385
Text Block mode, 332
Text Edit mode, 326, 332, 336
TGA. See Targa files (TGA)
TGA format, 124
thinning, 295–296
Thumbnail
  view for video, 425, 426
TIFF format, 124
Time Display window, 10
timecode
  generating, 258
  synchronization, 257–259
Timeline
  editing VEG files on nested, 172–173
  importing media to, 107–113
  placing editing events on, 124–134
  placing images/graphics on, 123–124
  placing media on, 115–123
timeline
  deleting events from, 279
  keyframe, 431, 432
  placing audio on, 260–261
  placing media on, 179–181
  titler, 430–431
  trimming events on, 277–279
timeline view, 6–9
titles. See also text
  color, 327, 329
  compositing, 349
  effects to, 347–350
  Flash format, 350–351
  fonts, 327
  gradient, 328
  legacy titling tool for (See Legacy Titling
    tool)
  masks, 387–388
  opacity value, 332
  placing, 342–343
  properties, 343–347

ProType Titling tools for (See ProType
    Titling tool)
  text size, 327–328
  transferring, 339–340
Tools menu, 42–61
Track-at-Once (TAO) CDs, 442
Track Control pane, 4–6, 340
Track EQ plug in, 317
track flattening, 173–174
Track FX, 43
Track Motion tool, 52–54, 361–368
  glow effects with, 367
  Lock Aspect Ratio function in, 363–364,
    365
  shadows applied with, 362–363
  Zoom tool in, 363
Tracking parameters, 330–331
Tracking slider, 331
tracks
  described, 235
  glow, 373–374
  index marker, 441
  names, 4–6
  nested, 372–374
  opacity, 157–162
  parent/child, 372–373
  rendering, 55
  shadows, 373–374
  stereo, 266
  view, 6–9
Transform tab, 328
transitional envelopes, 134–135
transitions
  crossfades, 126–131
  options, 131–132
  previewing, 131
Transitions window, 14
triggers, 259
trim-editing, 125–126
Trim feature, 31
Trimmer tool, 113, 116–123, 260–261
Trimmer window, 12
trimming
  audio, 260–261
  audio events, 277–279
  24p projects, 496–497
tvscreen.veg files, 412

U

Ultimate S 3, 188–189, 214
Ultrafunk plug-in, 440
upsampling, 417, 449, 468
user-generated content (UGC) sites, 492
user interface, 419–420

V

variable bitrate. See VBR (variable bitrate)
variable bitrate (VBR), 490
VASST GearShift, 95

VBR (variable bitrate), 454, 490
VCDs. See video compact discs (VCDs)
vectorscope, 217, 221, 226
VEG files, 170–172
  editing on nested timeline, 172–173
Vegas
  basic tools in, 3–19
  installation, 1–2
  key features of, 70–72
  menus (See menus)
  saving templates/layouts, 20–21
  synchronizing to external devices, 257–259
  Track Control pane, 4–6
  windows, 9–19
  XP themes in, 69–70
Vegas Capture tool, 446
Vegas Preview window, 331
Vegas Project Media, 59, 107–115, 142, 154
Velocity Envelopes, 37
velocity filter, 162–163
VelvetMatter, 212–213, 212–214
Verdana variant, 327
video. See also DV
  10-bit, 372
  compression, 442–444
  events (See video events)
  film like effects, 230–233
  high-definition, 466–469
  interlacing, 230–231
  PAL, 230–231
  stretching, 458–459
Video Bus Track, 38

Video capture
  advanced tools, 80
  analog camera deck, 77
  animation-type, 79
  batch capture, 81–83
  drive specification, 75, 77
  future changes to, 85–86
  hardware cards, 103–106
  manually, 73–80
  methods for, 76
  options
  stills capturing, 83–84
  Verify Tape Name, 75–76
video capture
  24p HDCAM footage, 498–499
video clips, 113–115
video compact discs (VCDs), 456–457
Video Effects, 45–47
Video Envelopes, 36
video events. See also audio events
  aspect ratio, 166
  editing on timeline, 124–134
  exporting, 448–449
  groups, 166
  locking, 166
  masking on timeline, 357
Video FX window, 15
Video Preview window, 14
Video Scopes window, 16
Video tab, 446, 449
Video tab, in Project Properties window, 25
Video Track, 37
View menu, 33–35

virtual sound technology (VST), 254–256
voice-over (VO), 244
Volume Maximizer plug in, 317, 318
VST. See virtual sound technology (VST)

W

walla, 298
Wave Hammer plug-in, 316, 317–318
waveform monitor (WFM), 217, 221
WAVES Ultramaximizer plug-in, 438
web media, 480
widescreens, 327, 352, 479, 496
WMV file, 488

X

XDCAM, 95–98
  files, 449
  format, 449
XDCAM Explorer, 17
XDCAM HD, 95
Xena cards, 103–104, 106
XP themes, 69

Y

YUV, 77, 103, 375, 377, 470–471

Z

Zenoté plug-in, 155, 211
Zoom tools, 333

What's on the DVD

The DVD accompanying this book is packed with information, files, and samples to help you learn more about Vegas and make better media more efficiently.

Nearly 1000 ACID Loops
Raw HDV/m2t Files
Full Resolution XDCAM Footage
Over 50 Royalty-Free Photo Images
More than 50 Freeware and Trial Software Files
14 Motion Backgrounds for Use in DVD Architect
120 veg Project Files
28 Additional Bonus Chapters, Articles, and Forms
16 Themes for Vegas Pro 8
Test Tone Media for Calibrating Equipment
Video Training Files